August 27, 1971

FOR — SUE MILLER

Good Luck &
Successful Sailing!

Arthur Knopp Jr

P.S. YOU HAVE A
COLLECTOR'S ITEM
See Page 76. LINE 7 ☹ ☺

Race
Your Boat
Right

International One-Design *Bumble Bee,* illustrating four important points: 1. Spinnaker pole at right angles to masthead fly (Chapter VI). 2. Spinnaker pole more nearly at right angles to mast than on other boats shown, though not perfectly perpendicular as it should be (Chapter VII). 3. Leech of mainsail held down to an almost straight line by the boom-jack. Notice other leeches with more curve (Chapter VIII). 4. Five of crew on weather rail, rolling boat to windward, making steering easier (Chapters VII, X and XVI).

Race Your Boat Right

By Arthur Knapp, Jr.

Foreword by Thomas J. Watson, Jr.

Introduction by Harold S. Vanderbilt

Drawings by William H. Burroughs, Jr.

GROSSET & DUNLAP

Publishers   New York

Dedication

This Book is dedicated to those men who go out and serve on Race Committees everywhere and make the Sport of Yacht Racing possible.

During 58 years of yachting it has been my great pleasure to participate in many wonderful races organized and run by these men. It is with a desire to show in a measure my great appreciation for their efforts that I dedicate this Book to all Race Committees, EVERYWHERE.

Table of Contents

List of Illustrations

ix

Foreword for
Arthur Knapp's Book

Artie Knapp is a man intimately linked with racing sailboats for longer than he would care to admit. I could not have been more flattered, not only to have had him for a friend for the last 15 years but also to have had him as a shipmate on many long and short voyages.

It took me a long time to get up my nerve to ask Arthur Knapp to come sailing with me, although Olin and Rod Stephens assured me that his bark was worse than his bite. My own modest sailing prowess and the informal approach that my crew and I take to racing made one reluctant to ask him for the first sail.

Then we launched *Palawan* in 1966 and Olin and Arthur sailed to Bermuda with me. One man's voice is high and the other's is low, but deep down they are sensitive, understanding men with great leadership qualities. It was paradoxical that *Palawan* was removed from first in her class and second in fleet, even though we finished as second boat for boat overall and the damage was done by an IBM computer. I have been looking ever since to find out who operated it.

In any case, from that day to this I have admired the great depth of knowledge of Arthur Knapp and his ability to get a great deal out of a boat and a crew without being a martinet. He is the great practitioner of the velvet glove approach. Although he screams pretty loud across the water at friends and competitors, his operation in the cockpit and at the wheel is in such a low key that at times one wonders whether he really is paying attention; and yet even in the lightest possible breeze if one looks across the rail, one sees that the vessel is moving past the competition and being flawlessly handled by one of the greatest sailors on this earth.

You cannot sail with Arthur very long without becoming tremendously attracted to him as a friend. I have never seen him
lose his temper. He is the first to minister to a seasick shipmate or
an injured member of the crew, and yet his scientific knowledge
of everything from the bend of the mast to the tension of the
headstay and the functioning of the heads is superior to anyone I
have ever been shipmates with.

There were hair-raising moments, of course. In the 1970 Bermuda Race I had a feeling Arthur might be sailing his last
Bermuda Race because, like all of us, he was accumulating years,
and so I asked him to start the boat with his usual skill. He
pointed high on the wind for the bow of the destroyer while
four of us watched, trembling in the cockpit with stopwatches
and continued to reassure him that he was not "early." With
nine knots of speed we crossed the line first in the class about
one-half second after the gun, to the cheers of "Leggy" Knapp
Mertz and various members of Arthur's afterguard on the
destroyer. My enthusiasm temporarily waned when, in accepting
the trophy for third in class in my absence, Arthur made a great
safety speech about another boat who had circled a damaged
competitor and was granted 8 minutes by the committee thereby
beating us by two. Ever since then he has been our safety officer
and we rely on him heavily for morale lectures about how wonderful it is to have other people beat us.

Seriously speaking, one of the great pleasures of my life and
that of all hands who sail on *Palawan* has been the rich experience of Arthur Knapp's friendship, his fantastic ability to get the
most out of a sailboat and his charitable attitude in coping with
sailors who sail for fun as well as to win.

Tom Watson, Jr.

Preface

I wish to acknowledge the kindness of the late Commodore Harold S. (Mike) Vanderbilt, not only for the introduction he wrote for the first edition but for the care with which he read the original manuscript and the suggestions he made with regard to several details.

To "Cap'n" Thomas J. Watson, Jr., go my sincere thanks for writing the foreword to this edition, as well as the privilege and honor of having sailed many times in many races aboard his beautiful *Palawan* over a period of five years and now, again on his newer *Palawan*, a 68-foot S&S ocean cruiser, a perfectly lovely sturdy ketch.

May I say THANK YOU to Roderick Stephens, Jr., for reading my first manuscript and making constructive suggestions, and to his brother, Olin J. Stephens, II, for permission to print a diagram of the halyard hook of the 5.5-metre *Quest*, the yacht in which John B. Nichols, Gene Wallet and I won the United States Championship in 1959, four days after she was launched. May I add that I've sailed plenty of wonderful races with Rod and Olin aboard *Dorade, Mustang* and *Ranger*, as well as a number of 6-metres.

To the late Eugene V. Connett, III, go my greatest thanks and appreciation for his great help and patience with my "hunt and peck" system of typing and with my general lack of knowledge of bookwriting technique.

Clinton M. Bell has made many constructive criticisms and was one guy who really pushed me into writing the book in the first place—along with Gordon B. Duval and the late Oliver E. Miles.

To William H. Burroughs, Jr., go my thanks again for his drawings over a period of twenty years. He started with me as a teen-ager and is now a grownup with his own children and can still draw! Matter of fact, he and his parents and brother moved in across the street from us when he was a kid, and doggone if we didn't make sailors out of that whole family of four cotton-pickin' Southerners—and damned good sailors at that!

To the late John J. Lowitz, my thanks for his interest and suggestions, and to the late W. H. (Ham) deFontaine of *Yachting* for his kindness in letting me use his drawings of the several knots illustrated in the book.

To Pete Kraght, my thanks for permission to quote certain passages of his *Meteorology Workbook*. A complete study of *Meteorology Workbook* is heartily recommended.

To the late Commodore Morris Rosenfeld, and now to his son Stanley Z. Rosenfeld, as well as Fred E. Hahnel, Lawrence Marx, Jr., Jerry Taylor and Harvey Weber, my sincere thanks for their help and the use of their excellent pictures.

Captain John H. Illingworth, R.N. Rtd., is a GREAT GUY, a great sailor and I thank him for granting me permission to quote him and his marvelous book on 12-metres, *Where Seconds Count*.

To Bruce Banks of England, my sincere thanks for permission to quote him on the new Starcut spinnaker, as well as Jack Sutphen, Colin Ratsey, Ted Hood and Lowell North for their thoughts on the same matter.

I've sailed many races aboard *Palawan* with Chris Moore (Princeton '70) and professional Captain Paul Wolter, that gregarious, voluble, happy, always-cheerful and wonderful shipmate, as well as a great "Hamburger Yung." To both of them I am indebted, as well as to *Yachting*, for permission to quote in its entirety "De-wrapping the Spinnaker," a great article which Paul actually didn't want publicized until he'd quit racing and went to cruising 'cause he'd say, "Ah ha, there's another 'shpinnaacker' wrapped—we beat HIM!!!"

To Bill Robinson, Bob Bavier, Jr., and Dick Rose I say THANK YOU for their permission to use the above-mentioned article, as well as other quotes from *Yachting*. Bill Robinson is a cousin by marriage, so he couldn't say no. Bob Bavier, Jr., and his wonderful sea-goin' father, Bob senior, I've raced with and against for 40 years, so Bob couldn't say no. And I took Dick Rose in tow as a Frosh at Princeton—NOW, he knows more than I and is one helluva lot smarter.

To Philip L. Rhodes, original designer of *Weatherly*, go my thanks for permission to use drawings of her coffee-grinders. And to Bill Luders, Jr., who really made *Weatherly* the fast boat that Bus Mosbacher cleaned up with, go my thanks for his many favors.

To Henry D. Mercer, Arnold D. Frese and Cornelius Walsh, who made up the *Weatherly* Syndicate, go my thanks for inviting me to skipper *Weatherly* in the America's Cup Trials of 1958 and the ensuing three years. We tried hard and did our best, but our best was not good enough. For four years we had some great racing in 12-metres, won a lot of races and made *Weatherly* go very fast indeed. Had I not been stupid, I might have had the opportunity to race her in 1962, but a lot of what we learned about Twelves in those four years is to be found in this book. Furthermore, it is a matter of record, and a fact which has caused much favorable comment over the years, that our carefully hand-picked crew was a very happy, compatible and amiable group that got along with a minimum of friction and/or contretemps.

To Commodore Robert L. Hall go my heartfelt thanks for permission to quote his suggestions on swaged fittings.

May I add my thanks to "Jock" Bartlett of Grosset & Dunlap for his patience and forbearance with me over the past year, as well as for his help, planning and constructive suggestions.

Finally, to Norma F. W. Anderson, may I say *THANK YOU* for her splendid job of copy-reading this book.

May I add that several other titles have been suggested for this opus:

Race Your Boat Upright—'cause over the past 41 years I've dunked many times in *Sideboard Annie, Four Deuces* or *Agony*, my Frostbite dinghies.

Sink Your Boat Right—'cause at the Storm Trysail Race Week in '71, I managed to "submarine" a dinghy—not upset, just plain sail it under *by the bow*—in front of 500 sailors. Unfortunately (for me) several people had movie cameras.

The Gospel According to Knapp—believe me, it's heartwarming, refreshing and stimulating to have some young sailor walk up and say, "Gee, Mr. Knapp, your book helped me a lot—and my Dad, too!" I LIKE *THAT*, and rumor has it that this literary effort (which would have shocked my early English teachers) is known in some circles as just that. (I still wonder if the "gal" who wrote me from Tampa, Florida—against her husband's wishes—

ever got straightened out on the proper mathematics of the Vanderbilt Starting Formula.)

Well, there it is, boys, gals and fellow sailors, all written and *fini*, on my 66th birthday in Larchmont, New York (Zip Code 10538).

Arthur Knapp, Jr.

Larchmont, New York
January 5, 1973

P.S. And, oh yes—on January 31, 1972, I was "pushed" into mandatory retirements by Carlisle deCoppet & Co., after 44 years in the "Odd Lot" business on the New York Stock Exchange. As someone asked downtown: "How long were you with the 'Odd Lots'?" "44 years." "Well, shows-to-go-you, there is nothing permanent in Wall Street!!"

The next day, February 1, 1972, I moved over to Shields & Co., Inc., courtesy of Corny Shields, Mac Sykes and Ed Purcell. I'm a "two-dollar" broker for them, as well as for Prescott, Merrill, Turben & Co., Kidder Peabody & Co., Inc., Mitchel, Schreiber & Watts, and others. I'm having a ball, making an honest buck, running my fat fanny off and I'm down twenty pounds. Amen.

Addendum to the Preface for the Third Edition

You will notice, dear Reader, that in a number of cases, I have mentioned various products by name, their manufacturers or distributors. This may smack of commercialism. I promise you, "Scout's Honor Knickerbocker Grays" (as the saying goes) that this is not the case—it is NOT SO! I have mentioned these items only because I feel that they will be a help to you. I am not being paid in any way, shape or form for pushing or promoting or mentioning them. They are, in my opinion, items that will help you make your boat go faster. I have been shipmates with all of 'em and I KNOW they are GOOD! So, why not pass them along to you?

Arthur Knapp, Jr.

THE EYE-BANK FOR SIGHT RESTORATION, INC.

The day after the manuscript for my Second Edition was delivered to the publishers, on February 15, 1960, I entered the Manhattan Eye, Ear and Throat Hospital for a corneal transplant, a bit of wonderful modern eye surgery to replace scar tissue in the cornea, or front, of my right eye. (I spent 26 days there, while today they keep you only four or five days.) Now, thirteen years later, my eye is fine, thank YOU, and I do very well with it.

Needless to say, I am greatly indebted and forever grateful to my good Doctors (who wish to remain anonymous) and to THE EYE-BANK FOR SIGHT RESTORATION, INC., which provided the cornea. As a result of my enthusiasm for this operation and a bit of "hollering and screaming" about it on my part, I have been made a Director and the lay Vice-President. In order to "pay my way," so to speak, I have conducted an annual fund-raising campaign among my fellow Members of the New York Stock Exchange, where, from time to time during the years from 1939 until 1960, my right eye was covered with a patch. They have responded most generously and willingly, to the extent that over the past eleven years we have collected over Ninety Thousand Dollars.

Should anyone care to help this great cause and help give sight to others, either with money or as an Eye Donor, please write to THE EYE-BANK FOR SIGHT RESTORATION, INC., at 210 East 64th Street, New York, N. Y. 10021, or your local Eye-Bank, for further information.

Arthur Knapp, Jr.

January 5, 1973

Introduction

I first heard of Arthur Knapp in the early Nineteen Thirties when with ever increasing frequency his name appeared in the papers as the skipper or crew of a winning yacht. He first came into my life when in 1937 he consented to serve as a member of *Ranger's* afterguard. I learned a lot from him then about parachute spinnakers, and admired his unfailing thoroughness in executing any assignment. He has since become, in the opinion of many, the leading, and in the opinion of all, one of the leading, on soundings racing skippers of North America. But he needs no individual word of praise or introduction. His record speaks for itself. He stands alone, or almost alone.

And now he has written this book, and I think he has bitten off his own nose, for he has not only disclosed *all* of the secrets of how to win races, but he has done so in such a thorough and simple manner that anyone (boy, girl or grownup) who wishes to race or is racing can, by studying it and following *all* its dictates, become in not too long a time, a rival with whom the author will have to share his victories. I have read many books on sailing, but never one that covered as this one does every phase of how to win. Some are in many respects theoretical, this one is based on cold hard facts learned over the years in the usually pleasant but sometimes bitter school of practical experience.

"Verb. sap."—no racing yachtsman or would-be racing yachtsman can afford to be without a copy of Arthur's book.

HAROLD S. VANDERBILT

April 1952

CHAPTER I

The Variables

From time to time friends have asked me *What makes a boat win races?* Or they have asked *What makes one boat beat another regularly? Is it luck or skill?* The questions seem quite simple, direct and easy to answer, but in reality they require an involved and somewhat complex explanation. This book is an attempt to answer these questions.

There is no simple answer as to why one boat is faster than another, for there are many variables and factors to be considered. The variables can be listed, and I shall attempt to analyze them and explain them. Some experts have given these variables a percentage value in order to show the relative importance of each. I don't feel that I can place a percentage value on them which would be of any practical use to you, because I think that every factor is important and not one variable can be ignored. *Everything* counts in a boat race. This much I will say: if you can cut down on the number of variables, you will have quite an advantage over your competitors who fail to do so.

Let's list and consider these variables.

1. Your boat—the condition of the bottom and hull
2. The spars, running and standing rigging
3. The sails
4. The crew and their training
5. The equipment in and on the boat
6. Tide, weather and wind
7. Luck
8. The skipper himself (or herself)

These seem to be a fair analysis of the various factors which

1

can be said to go into the make-up of the modern racing boat. I
do not think you can give greater or smaller value to any of them,
because each has its own particular importance, whatever that
may be.

This much may be said, however: the first five variables can be
controlled within certain reasonable limits, barring unforeseen
breakage, undue strain, unpredictable mechanical failure, etc.
But proper diligence, due care and a certain amount of work will
greatly lessen the importance of, or even eliminate these first five
variables before the race starts. The last three—tide, wind and
weather, luck, and the skipper himself—are left to be considered.

Tide, wind and weather are always variables in every sense of
the word and present a problem of local knowledge to be studied
and coped with as they arise. A real knowledge of them is to be
gained only by practice or trial and error; and even then some
new situation will arise to confuse and confound you. They will
be considered in some detail in Chapter XII.

Luck, of course, enters all racing, all sports. If you have it
you're in; and if you don't, you're last. Luck does have these
peculiar characteristics, however: when *you* have luck it is *Good
Judgment*; but when the other fellow has it he's *just plain damn
lucky!* Luck cannot be discounted completely, but it is surprising
how often in racing a boat bad judgment is casually dismissed as
bad luck. And it is also surprising that the boats which are generally up front are the ones that have all the luck. I am just as
guilty as the next fellow in blaming *bad* luck, I am sure; but it's
an easy thing to do. Careful thinking back to the particular situation and a reconsideration of the various factors involved, will
generally reveal a flaw in judgment or a poor decision as to
proper tactics. Occasionally, but very seldom, pure luck will really be responsible.

The skipper is the really important variable. He's the one who
makes the decisions and takes the rap. I mean nothing disrespect-
ful to the Bilge Boy's Union (that powerful crews' organization
whose headquarters is in Bermuda) who claim that they and
only they are responsible for the victories of the respective boats.
They win the races, they say, and the skipper loses them! Maybe
so; but it's the skipper who must make the principal decisions, for
he is in command whether he is at the tiller or not. When it
comes to a quick, decisive maneuver, someone has to be head
man and make up his mind in a hurry. The skipper is the all-

important variable which makes the difference between winning
or losing a major share of the racing. Long practice, hard work,
due diligence, ample patience, constant application, a thick skin
and a strong back are a few of the phrases which might be listed
as requirements for the make-up of that last variable, The Skipper Himself. There are others, but these describe him fairly well.
He has to know all the answers if he wants to win with regularity.

The late Commodore "Harry" Maxwell, one of the smarter racing skippers of recent generations, had a very apt description of
the successful boat sailor. He maintained that the chap who wins
is not the one who makes the smartest moves or maneuvers, but
the one who makes the fewest mistakes. It seems to me that
"Papa Harry" hit the nail on the head with that remark. I am
indebted to him for another hint. Captain Richard "Cooch" Maxwell, U.S.A., prominent dinghy sailor, wit, and one of the Commodore's sons, one day passed on to me the information that his
father, watching our racing from a power boat, was of the opinion that I was taking too many chances and not sticking with the
fleet. A casual remark, lightly passed, it gave me considerable
food for thought, and resulted in a distinct improvement in my
series standings in later years.

Since a great deal of racing is done on a series basis, i.e., consists of a number of races whose total points on some basis determine the winner, I would say as a result of the foregoing
discussion that CONSISTENCY is one of the greatest single factors in racing your boat right. BE CONSISTENT AND DON'T
GET OUT ON A LIMB. The fellow who regularly gets second
and third places in a series will end up the winner in the end.
Spectacular skippers may get a first one day and a tenth the next,
but the steady, *consistent* lad will be content with his customary
second or third, and will take home the bacon. To be consistent
you must be conservative in your tactics, taking chances only
when absolutely imperative. Taking chances more often than not
results in making mistakes. If what Commodore Maxwell said is
true, and I believe it is, then mistakes are to be avoided.

As there are separate chapters in this book on the other variables I have mentioned, let us give further thought to that most
important one, the skipper. We speak of an outstanding skipper
as a good helmsman. What is a good helmsman? One who can
steer his boat with ability and dexterity? Yes, that and a lot more.

He uses all his senses: touch, balance, hearing, sight, and even his sense of smell! It is often possible to detect that first faint whiff of a new sea breeze coming in off the ocean; and who hasn't smelled the aroma of a bum cigar from a boat to windward telling him that he is probably being backwinded.

If I may be permitted a bit of poetic license, may I introduce one more sense: the sense of anticipation or looking ahead. The experienced skipper, using all these senses, thinks ahead, the "wheels go around" in his brain, and he sizes up the situation before him, figuring out how he stands, what his chances are, and anticipating maneuvers on the part of his neighboring competitors. He actually looks ahead and plans his strategy accordingly.

The competent helmsman can tell from all these senses what his boat is doing. His fingers on the tiller or a finely balanced wheel will tell him much. Quite unconsciously, the sound of the wind and waves will indicate some small but important detail to him. His sense of balance will call attention to that extra little puff of wind, as he feels his boat heel a bit more. He may be looking off in the distance for a mark or a competitor, not seeming to notice where his boat is heading, but all his senses combine to telegraph to his mind that a new draft of air calls for a slight change of course. No speedometer or wind indicator is required to tell him what his boat is doing, although I will agree that both can be of great help most if not all the time.

The good helmsman holds his tiller or wheel lightly between his fingers, so that he can "feel" his boat. The only time he grips it hard is when it is blowing great guns. In a slop of a sea his hand may "weave" or "roll" with the tiller as the waves exert their force and motion on the rudder. But he does not "saw" on the tiller, swinging it back and forth until he almost sets up a harmonic motion to the boat. Let the tiller swing gently as it wants to, but don't keep pushing and pulling against that barn door you have under your boat for a rudder, for you will only exert an equal and opposite force which will slow your boat down that much. Think of your rudder as something trailing after your boat to be used only, you might say, in an emergency. When the boat is "hung" right, with live ballast properly placed and sails trimmed just so, the boat will almost sail herself, with only an occasional nudge at the tiller.

Today's young skippers have an advantage which some of the older generations of sailors didn't have—the sailing class. They are being taught the whys and wherefores of good helmsmanship scientifically by competent instructors, whereas my generation for the most part came by their knowledge the hard way, by trial and error. Older beginners may have a more difficult time in acquiring that instinctive ability to become an expert helmsman. But as a shining example of a man who took up sailing and racing in middle age with great success, I would like to point the finger at the late Arthur Davis who didn't take up the sport until he was 41, and yet won the Sound Championship in the hot International One-Designs in *Patricia* when he was 47, in 1943.

A skipper can know, or think he knows, certain fundamental rules and basic facts and ideas, and still come in last, because the variables are always there to confound him. Part of the Credo of the Boy Scouts of America is *Be Alert, Be Observant, and Be Prepared*. Show me the skipper who is really alert, observant and prepared and I will show you a skipper who will win his share of races, for he will be better equipped to control the variables involved in winning races than his competitor who does not have these three characteristics. It might be fitting to add *Be Kind* and *Be Sporting*, especially to the lad who comes in last or nearly so. Give him a helping hand with his problems if you can. Don't forget that he who is last today may be first tomorrow, and, further, that if it weren't for those who get last, there could be no firsts either.

Be Alert, Be Observant, and Be Prepared! Say them quickly and they may seem silly. But if you are alert you'll be at the starting line and more than ready to go when the gun sounds, *with your boat properly tuned.* If you are observant, you'll be watching for that first faint breath of a new breeze striking in, or you'll notice by lobster pots or buoys that the tide has changed. And if you are prepared you'll have that can of oil handy to speed up the action of a snap shackle or block, or you'll have that little extra cotter pin which will hold the clevis pin in place which will hold up the mast which you will need to win the Championship.

Before getting into the problems involved in controlling the variables we have been discussing, may I interject a few words for parents of children from seven years of age and up who may have an opportunity to learn to sail and race. By all means let them do it, provided they are able to swim. If they are lazy or backward about swimming you have no idea what an incentive the very thought of sailing can be. Most yacht clubs, recognizing

the value of sailing classes, and realizing the necessity for bringing along the younger generation, have bought boats, organized
groups of would-be sailors and hired competent men to teach
them. The youngsters are given a good foundation in the rudi-
ments of sailing under competent supervision—something that
was sadly lacking in my day. And here is a point I wish to emphasize most strongly: with traffic conditions what they are
ashore, YOUR CHILDREN ARE A GREAT DEAL SAFER
SAILING A BOAT THAN THEY ARE DRIVING CARS OR
PLAYING ABOUT THE STREETS. That goes for good weather
or bad, thunderstorms or flat calms! During a regatta on Long
Island Sound on the Fourth of July fifteen or twenty years ago a
vicious thunderstorm broke just as the fleet was finishing. More
than a hundred racing boats were capsized or disabled and a few
sank, but NOT ONE single person racing, and many of them
were kids, was lost, although the papers were full of accounts of
fishermen, canoeists, and others who were drowned. Truly a
magnificent tribute to the ability of the youngsters to handle
their boats and themselves under adverse conditions.

You may worry, fond parents, when your offspring are out in a
nasty squall. You may fret and stew when they don't show up at
suppertime. They are probably becalmed a mile or so from home
and hungrier than bears at that, but believe me they are safe—
safe from one of the worst dangers of our age, the automobile. So
get your kids out on the water for it's not only a good form of life
insurance, but an investment in a lifelong form of sport and re-
laxation.

Now let's get on with how to race our boats right.

CHAPTER II

Preseason Conditioning

The successful campaigning of a racing yacht is not something that is done only during the summer. It is something that is done almost continuously, twelve months a year, if you want to win consistently.

Perhaps you are able to have the boat yard do all the work on the boat; you are then free to do the supervising and make sure that everything is done as ordered. You may be financially able to have the yard do all your work, but prefer doing some or all of it yourself. Or perhaps you are only able to own and race a boat if you do most or all of the work yourself. To my way of thinking, the man, woman or child who does the work on the boat starts the racing season with quite an advantage.

The boat he works on he must love and cherish; he is anxious to see her do well. He sands her lovingly and applies the paint with care. He takes more time and effort to do a given job than the yard carpenter, painter or rigger who is in most cases doing his job and no more. I mean no reflection on boat yards or the hard working men who labor under pressure from every boat owner in the yard, and often with little thanks from some critical skipper. I merely mean that the skipper who does his own work applies that T.L.C. (tender loving care) which puts "go-fast" into his boat. When I say he starts the season with quite an advantage, I mean he *knows* his boat better; he is more *at home* in her; he is better acquainted with all her gear, and can tell at a glance—almost without knowing why—whether everything is shipshape and ready to go.

From my first Perrine sneakbox, a 14-foot Butterfly class boat, aptly named *Flutterby*, through many Star boats, three Long Island Sound Inter-Club One-Designs, eight International One-

Designs, a couple of 6-metres, several 8-metres, five 12-metres, the America's Cup Defender *Ranger,* one 5.5, some International 14-footers and many ocean racing yachts, I have invariably found that when I had to work hard on the boat itself over a period of time, and therefore became more familiar with its special idiosyncrasies, I felt more at home on that particular boat and was more successful in racing in her.

You cannot step aboard a boat at the beginning of the season and expect to compete with some chap who has been fussing around his "crate" for several months. Other things being equal you won't beat him regularly over a period of time. You must *know* your boat to do her justice, and to know her you must have more than a nodding acquaintance with the boat, her sails, rigging and equipment. I think that the first sail in the spring, away from the dirt and grime of the boat yard, is the most wonderful sail of the year. You have worked hard, petted, pampered, sanded, painted, scraped, dusted and powdered your "love" and the joy of seeing her under sail and feeling that first surge of renewed life is something that only a real poet can describe. The lad who does some or all of his work is the lad who gets that thrill—and he stands a pretty fair chance of winning a few races.

But before that first sail there is much work that probably began the previous fall. Hauling out calls for cleaning off the hull and a possible coat of paint on the bottom. The hull should be scrubbed off with fresh water and cleaned out before the winter cover is put on. (Inside ballast in centerboarders should be removed to prevent straining the hull as it dries out.) Many boats are stored in a shed. I feel that outside storage is equally good, and usually less expensive. Inside storage makes it easier to work on the boat during the winter months, and since the floors are generally dirt, there is a certain amount of dampness which retards the drying out of the boat. By the same token, it is somewhat less comfortable to work inside and can be not too satisfactory for painting. Outside storage allows you to throw the cover back on good days and work in the warm sunlight, to the benefit of the boat and yourself.

As the boat is being put to bed for the winter, sails should be washed in fresh water, dried fully, folded and put away in a dry place. On *Bumble Bee,* since we had seven suits of sails whose total value would not be covered by insurance were they all lost in a fire, we divided the suits up as evenly as possible according to racing value, and stored them in separate places. If one group should be destroyed we would not lose our complete inventory, and yet we would have insurance coverage. Rigging should be checked, tied up and stored in a dry place, and *properly* tagged, lest it get mixed up with gear from another boat. All rigging should be checked for wear and deterioration and plans made to replace it if necessary. Plans should be made in the fall, *not* in the spring, for time consuming replacements or changes in gear and equipment. Turnbuckles should be freed up and greased in the fall.

Swaged fittings on shrouds, halyards, life rails, etc., should be examined periodically for cracks and defects. Unfortunately these swaged fittings sometimes corrode and crack for various reasons. Careful examination with a magnifying glass or a microscope will reveal defects not visible to the naked eye. If you find such cracks replace the shroud, or the swaged fitting itself immediately, whichever suits your purposes better. DO NOT, UNDER ANY CIRCUMSTANCES, TRUST A SWAGED FITTING WITH ANY CRACKS LARGE OR SMALL, LONG OR SHORT.

In order to help prevent corrosion which may eventually lead to cracked fittings, my friend Bob Hall has gone very thoroughly into the problem and I quote his advice.

PROTECTIVE SYSTEM FOR STAINLESS STEEL SWAGED CABLE

By Robert L. Hall

The development and introduction of a special paint system, known commercially as RUST-OLEUM, has raised the possibility of its use for the protection of both bare and rusted areas in stainless steel exposed to corrosive environments. Theoretically, the chemistry of RUST-OLEUM appears to make it an ideal protective coating for any metal surface.

The vehicle is fish oil; and this specially processed vehicle has the property of being able to penetrate through the rust to the bare metal. By this mechanism, further corrosion is inhibited. Experiments with a radioactive tracer have confirmed this means of penetration. Moreover, organic compounds in this paint act to seal further attack and provide a decorative finish at the same time. Any tightly adherent scale or rust (loose rust particles should be wire-brushed off) is an acceptable surface for receiving RUST-OLEUM 769 DAMP PROOF RED PRIMER. After the primer is permitted to dry from 24 hours to three days, a finish coat of any of several RUST-OLEUM colors may be used.

The following procedure was used to inhibit corrosive attack and add protection to several stainless steel swaged cables and fittings that had been subjected to marine air atmosphere:

1. Brush off adherent salt deposits at the junction of the cable and the fitting.
2. Thin RUST-OLEUM 769 to the proportion of one part of RUST-OLEUM thinner and three parts of 769 RED PRIMER.
3. Stand fitting on end with cable at the top. This is to permit the thinned primer to enter the spaces between the cable and the inside of the fitting by gravity.
4. Apply thinned primer with a small brush, applying the paint from about a half-inch length of the cable from the fitting. Repeat this application at least four times with a fifteen minute wait between applications.
5. Permit the primer to dry for a period of 3 days.
6. Paint with a cover coat of 634 RUST-OLEUM QUICK-DRYING BLACK. No. 412 FLAT BLACK may also be used. Dry for 24 hours. Then repeat the application again.
7. Thinning the first cover coat one to one will improve the penetration of the cover coat.

To polish out stains of rust on the fitting, make a paste of chromium oxide, C.P. Grade, and apply it with a hand buffer. The chromium oxide is compatible with the chemistry of the stainless steel.

I find that after a long hard season of campaigning a racing boat, a vacation from racing her and also from thinking about it is most welcome. But that vacation comes only after she is safely and thoroughly put away for the winter. The proper lay-up job cannot be neglected if you wish to win races the next year. (I find that dinghy racing in the winter provides a pleasant change from hard formal racing to the informal fun of "tooling" an 11½-foot cockleshell through the ice floes.)

February sees the job of refitting begin again, and since a smooth bottom is one of the greatest single factors in winning a boat race, the greatest emphasis should be given to getting it in top condition. In the case of smaller boats like Snipes, Lightnings and 110s (with the keel removed), it is quite a simple matter to turn them bottom-side-up and do a good job with a minimum of backache. Star boats which are equipped with trailers whose supports can be removed, so that the boats can be tipped sideways at any angle in either direction, are a bit more backbreaking. My own experience with Stars was before the days of trailers and I found it most convenient to remove the keel, turn the boat upside-down and rig the winter cover as a sort of tent to keep both the rain and sun off. My daughter's 110 was trailed each fall to the lot next door and turned upside-down. A framework and tarpaulin protected it from the elements. The bigger boats like Atlantics, International One-Designs, Luders 16s and 6-metres present a tougher problem and there is only one answer: get down under the bottom and go to work.

Long experience has taught me that the only way to get a really good bottom on a boat is to use wet sandpaper—known in the trade as "Wet or Dry," though it is really garnet or aluminum-oxide paper and not sandpaper at all. It can be used either with water or dry, but works much better when wet. It is made with shellac rather than glue, and experts tell me that good craftsmen let it soak overnight to get the best results. The wet sandpaper job gives a cleaner finish in the end, completely free from dust. While you may get a bit wet, you won't be covered from head to foot, inside and out, with a complete layer of paint dust.

In the early spring I took to Johnny Nichols' boat yard a large thermos jug of hot water to temper the ice water in my pail. This also serves to make the paper more pliable. A tablespoon of Spic and Span, Oakite, or detergent will also simplify the first sandpapering job. When a hose is not available a sponge can be used to wet the surface. Fresh water should *always* be used, for a deposit of salt is no good to paint over.

There are several electric sanders which can be used with water, such as the high speed Black & Decker hand drill used with the "Du-Fast" sanding attachment, the "Guild" and the "Speedway," but care must be taken to keep the machines and your hands dry. An old towel attached to your belt will serve to dry your hands and save you from being electrocuted. Some experts feel that ordinary wet-sanding with a block of wood, cork or rubber is superior to an electric sander. Being congenitally lazy, I feel that the electric sanders are a great time and labor saver, and I have used one for several years without mishap.

I cannot emphasize too strongly the importance of doing a thorough wet-sanding job, as it is equal to one or more coats of paint. It also keeps paint from getting too thick and, as a consequence, cracking. Since sandpaper is inexpensive, use it freely and. not too long. Your labor and time are more valuable, so let the paper do the work. Do the sanding a panel at a time, and clean the sanded area as you go along, to prevent any wet paint dust from drying on the surface. It will fill the cracks and holes and is difficult to remove when dried. Don't apply paint until the surface is *clean and thoroughly dry*—overnight or at least several hours on a good drying day.

While most sailors are familiar with the proper method of preparing or using a sheet of sandpaper or garnet paper (wet or dry, it makes no difference) it might be well to explain how you can get more mileage out of your paper. Beginners will just take a sheet of paper, fold it over and go to work. This is not correct and wastes half the paper, for you have two abrasive surfaces rubbing together. The proper way is to fold the paper in half, *carefully*, both ways and then tear the paper in half across the narrow side—standard sheets are rectangular not square. Then fold one torn-half in and the other torn-half over on top of it as in the diagram below. You are now ready to go to work with a neat pad of paper which is reasonably thick and substantial. Each rubbing surface lies against a smooth back surface and there is no waste. When you have used up both the outside surfaces, merely refold the paper so that they are inside and you have two other brand new areas to utilize.

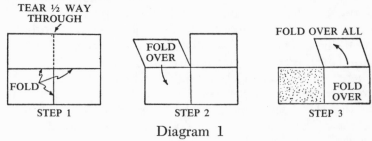

Diagram 1

When working on a large area of work, use the whole piece of paper, but for doing small jobs or narrow sections of coaming or molding tear your paper into four sections and fold each small section as outlined. The job will be easier and you won't waste paper.

When using the "Du-Fast" electric sander on curved surfaces, with the rubber pad, the rubber pad can be made to sit more securely if you place a strip of sandpaper on the machine under the pad before you clamp on the outer piece.

On boats which are to be left in the water a good anti-fouling bottom paint should be used. Boats that are "dry-sailed" (hauled out on a trailer after each weekend of racing) are generally painted with a hard enamel; but, except in fresh water, an anti-fouling paint is indicated for all other racing boats but, in many cases with Stars, Lightnings, Solings, Etchells, Cal-40s and Ericsons (of all sizes) NO BOTTOM PAINT IS APPLIED—only the smooth, slippery Gel-Coat is used. The newer plastic anti-fouling paints developed during the last war are excellent and can be smoothed and polished to the Queen's taste. There are many expert skippers who feel that the smoothness of a boat's bottom can be over-emphasized, but my own feeling is that if you KNOW in your own mind that the bottom of your boat is smoother than—or at least as smooth as—the next fellow's, you will have a *psychological advantage,* and, believe me or not, your boat will go faster. If you *know* your bottom is in tip-top condition, you will be able to dismiss that possibility as a reason for a competitor gaining on you; you won't have to worry on that score.

The first coat of bottom paint should be applied quite thin. (Two thin coats are always better than one thick coat.) Having allowed ample time for the first coat to dry—at least 24 hours, and more if possible—a second sanding with a finer paper is done. The first spring sanding can be done with #4/0 Wet/Dry paper. The second, third and fourth are done with #6/0, and the final, before launching, with #8/0, or even finer Carborundum paper; but #8/0 is too fine to be used between coats as it does not leave a proper "tooth" for the next coat.

After the first coat is applied and sanded, digs and cracks can be filled with some type of filler that sets up hard. Seams should be filled with a seam compound that will remain more or less elastic and can squeeze out as the seams swell in the water. Most seams which dry out during the winter and spring will close up without filling, and care should be exercised *not* to fill them unnecessarily, for excessive seam compound will cause planking to warp and buckle. Experience indicates that before the final bottom painting is done, it is advisable to put the boat overboard to swell up for a couple of weeks. Then the boat is hauled out again, and the final coat or two of paint (thinned out a bit, of course) is applied. This system cannot always be followed, but it is a great help in getting a superior bottom and is strongly urged in cases where boats tend to dry out and open up.

If seams have opened up excessively in extremely dry weather, tallow or soap applied to them will slow down the leaking until they take up. Masking tape over the seams also works well and, surprisingly enough, will stay on when the boat is left in the water to swell. Care must be taken in removing the tape not to remove patches of paint with it.

Most yards make a practice of "cutting in" the water line with a sharpedged tool, which makes it easier to paint the water line; but it seems to me that the rough surface resulting should be avoided by using masking tape for a guide. Here again, care must be taken in removing the tape, which should be taken off IMMEDIATELY after painting—not left on to harden to the paint.

On *Bumble Bee,* two types of bottom paints were used, the upper half being a white anti-fouling hard racing paint, and the the lower half a more anti-fouling plastic red bottom paint, since the white, though less anti-fouling, looks better against the dark blue topsides. It was easier to keep the upper section clean, hence the more anti-fouling paint was used below. Since the fish are the only ones to see the line between these two bottom paints, no exact line was drawn between them.

As the weather warms up, the winter cover can be removed and work commenced on the topsides and the interior. As it is advisable to keep the interior and bilge dry, the regular cockpit cover can be used for this purpose; this is easier to rig over a ridge pole than the regular winter cover over its frame. If there is no protection against the sun beating down into the boat, it will have a tendency to blister the newly applied bottom paint, and if water is permitted to lie in the bilge it will tend to soak through the wood and blister the new paint. The bilge should be sanded and vacuumed before painting, but not washed unless absolutely necessary. The decks and brightwork should be washed before sanding, then sanded well and painted or varnished, as the case may be. Usually a touch-up coat and a final coat of enamel or semi-gloss will take care of the deck, with a good sanding before the first coat and a light one between coats.

The varnished brightwork presents a different problem. If it is kept well varnished and is washed off with fresh water each weekend during the summer, it should last several seasons without a complete scraping, a tedious, long job which requires care and hard work. Should it have to be done it should only be commenced when the whole job can be done in one day, i.e., scraping, sanding, staining and one coat of thin varnish. A sharp scraper and a good cream paint remover, carefully applied so as not to ruin surrounding paint, and left on long enough to fully loosen the old varnish, are of paramount importance. Scraping— and sandpapering—should be done *only with the grain of the wood;* otherwise, marks and scratches will show through the new varnish. Excess varnish remover must be washed away with turpentine before sanding, which should be done with a sanding block and garnet paper—coarse paper at first, followed by lighter paper and finally aluminum-oxide paper.

Mahogany comes in various shades and tones and in most cases is colored slightly darker with an oil stain and filler which tends to close up the grain of the wood. This is applied, allowed to dry for a time and then rubbed off before the first coat of thinned varnish is applied. Most manufacturers advocate waiting from eight to 24 hours for the filler to dry, but as time is generally of the essence, I have often applied the first coat of varnish immediately, with no apparent bad results. Five or six coats of varnish are essential for a good job, the first coat being the only one thinned out. Sanding between each coat is a *must,* again always with the grain of the wood.

Modern synthetics have produced wonders in paint, and one of these developments has been "epoxy" based paints and varnish. A. E. (Bill) Luders, Jr., working with the Marin paint people came up with very fine epoxy paint and varnish which were used on the Mercer Syndicate's 12-metre *Weatherly.* The varnish and/or paint comes in two separate cans—equal amounts in each. The two when mixed cause a chemical reaction and they are good for about 16 hours—the moral being: mix just enough of equal parts to do the job at hand, for after that it is no good. The varnish and paint jobs on *Weatherly* were amazing, superb and better than any I've ever seen. The varnish stood up very well all summer without a touch of new varnish applied. The topsides, a light "baby" or sea blue, looked almost good enough to

launch her the second season without a paint job (and then only
a light coat was applied). The bottom of *Weatherly* was a skipper's dream—slick, hard and smoother than the proverbial baby's
spanked behind. Mr. Luders, Sr., said that what is needed in a
shipyard these days are plasterers not painters, for the epoxy
bottom on *Weatherly* was applied with a trowel NOT A PAINT
BRUSH. (Note—*Columbia* also had an epoxy bottom, but this
was applied in the conventional manner with a brush.) Our
epoxy was even applied over a fairly rough surface—in other
words, the mahogany was NOT rubbed down and smoothed off
the way a boat is normally prepared for painting. The epoxy
surface was allowed to harden, then scraped with cabinet scrap-
ers and finally sanded. It is somewhat anti-fouling, though it is
my opinion that the anti-fouling properties gradually disappear.
However, at the end of two seasons, *Weatherly* still had one of
the slickest bottoms I had ever seen—and the maintenance was
practically nil. A very, very light sanding or even washing was
sufficient to put 99 percent of the bottom in A-1 shape. The late
Commodore DeCoursey Fales, that wonderful veteran of many
ocean races, put a similar bottom on that *grand dame, Niña,* and
he told me that he was more than satisfied with it. Note of caution: if you use epoxy, be careful to mix only as much as you
need even if you must mix more later—for it goes "to pot" after
14 to 16 hours and is useless.

The mast, boom and spinnaker pole are given the wet-sanding
treatment with soap added and a good rinsing afterwards. Today
many spars are either metal or painted wood. I think painted
wooden spars look better and keep their appearance and are easier to put into condition than spars with a varnished finish. If
your spars are painted, bear in mind that a good wet-sanding is
as good as a coat of paint and prevents the spars from becoming
loaded up with excess paint. If the spars are grooved, be careful
not to fill the groove with paint. If there is a metal sail track,
keep that clear of paint. In either case, the groove or track should
be cleaned off with sandpaper before the mast is stepped or the
boom set on the boat. One touch-up coat and one full coat of
enamel or semi-gloss will suffice to do a good job on the spars.
Don't overpaint!

Aluminum masts, booms, spinnaker poles and reaching struts
(which are used to hold spinnaker guys off the shrouds and re-

lieve some of the strain on the guys) are increasingly popular these days on all types of boats. Anodized, or polished, these spars are almost impervious to salt-water corrosion—with a bit of care and attention they'll last forever.

The rudder, rudder head and tiller should be checked for wear and tear before launching. Frequently the rudder head or tiller will work loose and play will develop. This should be corrected before launching because there is nothing as annoying as a loose tiller to the skipper who wants to "feel" his boat. Check all bolts, keys and keyways for slack and play. A touch of oil or grease will help keep things shipshape and mechanically perfect for a long season of racing.

Mechanical and cam cleats, which should have been examined the previous fall, should be checked again, as should all winches, blocks and sheaves. How awful a squeaky jib halyard block or mainsheet block sounds as you sail around the course! And how they give away your every move and maneuver to your competitors.

Last but not least, let your boat soak up for several days or a week before you take your first sail. Don't strain her and loosen her fastenings by sailing her hard the day she is launched. Let her "ring" back into shape by swelling up and you will have less cause to pump the rest of the summer.

Iron Keels

It seems to me that ever since I can remember there has been a rusty iron keel to contend with each spring. First it was on old No. 62, *Southern Cross*, my first Star boat. Later on there were other Stars including *Peggy Wee*, No. 455, and *Corliss*, No. 1538. Then my daughter Corliss had a 110, also with an iron keel, and each spring it was: "Daddy, when are you going to do the keel on my boat?" Daddy, after 45 long years, was still at it. Fortunately, science has supplied an answer to the rust problem—galvanizing or cadmium plating. (Unfortunately the keel on Corliss' 110 was not plated!)

There is only one way to prepare a really chipped or rusty keel, and that's with an old chisel and lots of elbow grease. The job is made easier if the keel is off the boat, and a thick cream paint remover, liberally applied and allowed ample time to soak in and loosen the paint, helps somewhat. After all the old paint and gurry are removed, a rotary wire brush on a high-speed drill can be used to more or less shine up the iron (though it is impossible to get a real shine).

After the keel is cleaned off, give it several coats of red lead, allowing a week, if possible, between coats. NEVER sand the red lead between coats, so be careful to apply it as smoothly as possible. The reason for not sanding is to make sure the metal is thoroughly covered and protected. If you sand it there are bound to be high spots which will become uncovered with the obvious result that they will eventually rust. There are other rust preventatives, such as zinc chromate, but I have found nothing which does a better job than a good grade of red lead. R. Snowden Andrews has had success with aluminum paint on iron keels.

Epoxy red lead is another fine rust preventative and can be used very successfully, especially with synthetic paints and fillers. The procedure is the same, but be sure, as with other rust preventatives, that the surface is very clean and free of old paint. And, mind you again, mix only as much as you need.

Refinishing a keel is a job which, if properly done, can take a couple of months; so plan ahead and do it during the winter. If you are able to remove the keel and get it into your cellar or garage you will make the operation a lot easier for yourself. I prefer to paint first one side and then turn it over after it's *completely* dry and then put a coat on the other side. Make sure there is a thick layer of padding smoothly laid out under the keel, for uneven or lumpy padding will lift spots off the underside. In the case of 110 keels it is possible to stand them upright on their top flange and do the painting all at one time. Several 110 skippers I know have had experience with this procedure, but for my part I have been afraid that being overbalanced the keel might topple over.

When the red lead is thoroughly dry, the next step is to fill and cover the holes and indentations with some type of cement or filler. Kuhl's "Trowelast" and "Krakno" put out by R. F. Johnston Paint Co., are excellent, and Woolsey has a cement which is also very good. We used Krakno on *Bumble Bee* as a hole filler on both bottom and topsides. It is easy to apply, sticks wonderfully and is easy to smooth off. When doing a keel with any of these, it is advisable to thin them to the consistency of a very thick cream, thicker for example than a heavy paint, and apply them with a brush. If there are any very deep or large holes they can be filled later with the thick cement by means of a putty knife. After drying completely the cement is rubbed with sandpaper, either wet or dry. (Please note that when I use the words "sand" or "sanding" I refer not only to sandpaper, but to garnet or aluminum oxide paper. "Sanding" is a general term which covers all rubbing with abrasives. Garnet paper works better than ordinary sandpaper and is generally used around boat yards, aluminum oxide coming in the finest weights.)

In sanding the cement, be careful not to rub through the priming coat of rust preventative. A good rule to follow is not to rub any more on a spot where the primer starts to show through. Several coats of filler or cement are necessary, with careful sanding between, using finer grades of paper between each succeeding coat. There are excellent synthetic fillers and cements now on the market, and if you plan to use synthetic paints these are far better to use.

When using a putty knife to fill holes with cement *always over-fill* the hole, letting a bit of cement rise above the surface, for it shrinks as it dries and will not give a smooth job if this is not done. When you are satisfied that the cementing job has made the keel as smooth as necessary, apply the final coats of bottom paint or enamel, being sure to thin the first coat well. I repeat that three or four thin coats are much better than two thick ones. And be sure to wet-sand between coats of paint. Great care must be exercised in sanding on all corners and edges where it is extremely easy to rub off too much paint.

Hot-dipped galvanizing on a keel does wonders in eliminating rust as well as the annual job of refurbishing. Cadmium plating proved very satisfactory on the keel of Star boat *Peggy Wee,* but Star Class experts tell me that the hot-dipped galvanizing is about as good. After galvanizing, it is advisable to cure the keel by "pickling," a chemical curing and cleaning process; or by letting the keel stand in the weather for six months or so. Galvanizing seems to slowly exude certain gases that may cause blisters in the paint if they are not eliminated. If you have time, let the keel weather; if not, pickle it. Galvanizing is not expensive when you look at it from the long-term, labor-saving point of view. Moreover, rust will considerably reduce the weight of a keel, resulting in a tender boat. As a case in point, in the early nineteen thirties Star No. 61, *Little Bear,* owned by John R. Robinson, who won the World's Championship in 1924, had a keel so reduced in

weight from rust that frequently the boat would lay over in a
breeze and the crew would have to step out onto the keel to right
her. This is a true story.

It is not necessary to do a full scraping job on an iron keel
every year. Minor rust spots can be chipped down, cleaned, red-
leaded and cemented without going over the whole keel. But
here again it is advisable to give the red lead considerable time to
dry. If you cannot afford the time, there are other primers which
require less time to completely harden. DuPont, for example,
puts out a zinc powder with a separate can of liquid vehicle and
you can mix the amount you need, and don't forget epoxy red
lead.

Metal centerboards are a tougher proposition to cope with, for
they will rub off most any paint on the sides of the trunk. My
only suggestion is to proceed as with keels, but don't apply too
much primer, cement or final coats of paint. If the covering on a
metal board is thin, it will have less tendency to chip or rub off,
but I am afraid there isn't anything you can do to an iron board
that will prove too practical or long-lasting. Bronze boards can
be polished and left unpainted, for the bronze is a good anti-
fouling agent in itself.

Most class rules prohibit any changes in the leading or trailing
edges of keels, centerboards and rudders. If there are such rules
in your class, there is nothing to be done, for any changes would
not only be illegal but unsportsmanlike. However, if changes are
permitted, it is a good idea to examine the edges of keel, centerboard and rudder. A round leading edge seems, from all experiments not only with boats but airplanes, to be the best, while the
trailing edge should be knife-sharp if possible. Square edges are
a terrific drag and should be eliminated. I am often surprised to
see supposedly competent boat designers overlook this rather
simple problem of leading and trailing edges. A boat complete in
almost every other detail and right up to scratch in all its gear
and equipment, will come out of the yard with great square trailing edges on its rudder. There is hardly anything that will slow a
boat more—except maybe a bucket tied on the bottom somewhere. Some years ago experiments were made with various types
and shapes of centerboards and rudders in Frostbite dinghies.
Wooden boards and rudders with a certain amount of thickness
and an elongated teardrop shape proved superior to those with

thin metal and knife edges. It would seem reasonable to assume that the thin sharp metal plates would be faster, but such is not the case. The shaped wooden board and rudder turn in the better performance, so look to yours and see if you can improve them— but make sure first that you are breaking no rules.

And here is another little gem of conditioning—not really preseason, but all-season—which could be of great interest especially to those who "dry-sail" their boats. By a rather devious route in January '58, it came to my ears that *Sceptre* was planning to use a liquid detergent, Lux, on her bottom. In fact, the word I received was she even planned to have little holes in the bow which would exude Lux to make the bottom "wetter" and to make the water slip by with less resistance. Of course, I assume that her bottom was to be coated with Lux beforehand too.

To make a long story short, I phoned Olin Stephens—since I myself was without a boat (or 12-metre) at that point and wanted to do what I could for the defense of the America's Cup. We agreed that I would try the idea on my dinghy, *Agony,* racing in the Frostbite Fleet at Larchmont, and that Olin would check up in the towing tank and see what he could see. The first time I "luxed" *Agony's* bottom it was light air and I had a very definite feeling that I was going faster than the other boats. The towing tank said that Lux made a boat one to one and one-half percent faster. In other words, in a one hour windward leg for a 12-metre, it could be good for something like 15 to 20 lengths— and, as they say, "That ain't hay!" So I continued during that winter to Lux the bottom of *Agony* and I *still* do it!

When, on April 1, 1958, I was invited by the Mercer Syndicate to steer *Weatherly,* I naturally told them all about it and we tested the Lux in the towing tank with the same results that Olin Stephens got—namely one to one and one-half percent faster. To my knowledge, it was never actually used on *Sceptre,* but maybe in the dark of night they *did* apply it when she was out on the railway. Nor did we use it on *Weatherly*—though *Vim* did apply some sort of silicone spray (which presumably did not wash off so easily). My feeling on the matter was that when you tow a 12-metre at six knots ten miles out to the America's Cup starting line there will be very little Lux left on the bottom as most of it will have "sluffed" off. If it could be incorporated into some paint so that it would "sluff" off gradually, then you might have a great thing; but in its normal state, I am reasonably sure it won't last too long. On a dinghy or some such small boat it's another matter, but I doubt its efficiency on a Twelve.

In the summer of '59, at Newport, just for the fun of it, I did, personally—and with the help of Gay Smith, who is tall and could reach up to the waterline, and of Mark Cluett, who is short and could reach under the keel, when *Weatherly* was hauled out at "Sam Spade's" Newport Shipyard (Samuel C. Spencer, President at that time of Newport Shipyard was known as "Sam Spade" because of the porkpie hats he wore perpetually. John J. Flynn—a "foine" Irishman, one of the very best, and a GREAT GUY to boot—was Manager during these years. At the present time, John Flynn is Manager of the Goat Island Marina in Newport, Rhode Island, and if there is anything you ever want or need for your yacht—or for anything else, for that matter—John Flynn is the man who can get it for you, and Goat Island Marina is a very fine Marina to dock at) put Lux on the whole bottom just before she was launched on a Wednesday morning. Since we didn't race 'til Friday, I am quite certain that all the Lux was "long gone." But it was an IDEA, and—what the heck—you can't win boat races unless you have ideas!

As a case in point on ideas, in a 1960 issue of *The Wall Street Journal* there was an article regarding a "rubber skin," similar to a porpoise skin, developed by the United States Rubber Co. The idea is that the "skin," about an eighth of an inch thick and supported on or from the bottom of a boat by many tiny little "pillars," flows or undulates with the water as it rushes by, and therefore reduces the skin friction, and gives greatly increased speeds to the boat. A study of fish and porpoises indicated to the research men at United States Rubber that their great speed comes not so much from slickness, but from the fact that their skin undulates, or gives with the waves of water, and thereby stops turbulence which causes friction, which, in turn, reduces speed. A letter from me to the Research Center of U.S. Rubber brought a very cordial phone call from their Dr. Lorin Schoene and, while the thing is not fully developed yet, maybe I'll come up with an even faster bottom on *Agony* than Lux! Since 1962 I haven't heard nor seen anything more on this idea, so I can only presume it has been scrapped.

This chapter should help you control and eliminate a good part of variable number one.

CHAPTER III

Tuning the Racing Yacht

Tuning your boat is a problem that takes time, effort and patience. It is not something which can be done in an hour or so on a sunny afternoon when there is no race. I have seen skippers jump into a launch with a cheery *So long boys, see you in a couple of hours. Going out to tune her up.* Tuning just isn't accomplished that quickly. It goes on all through the season, although much of it must be accomplished as early as possible.

Checking the running rigging and sheets, seeing that blocks are properly oiled, checking your compass, keeping an eye on fittings, cotter pins and clevis pins, an occasional trip up the mast to inspect the rigging aloft, a look at the mast itself to be sure it hasn't changed shape or position—these and many other little things are what really constitute the tuning of your boat. To win, show or place with regularity, you must constantly watch and check the little details, and there is only one person who can do the job—*the skipper.*

Check the running rigging before you leave the yard, if possible, and certainly before the first race. All running and standing rigging should have been given a complete going over during the winter. Before your first race make sure that the lines fit their blocks or that the blocks fit their lines. This may sound elementary, but it is one of those many little things which will help you win races. *You just can't disregard any little detail.* A spinnaker sheet which does not run through a block properly may be responsible for the collapse of the spinnaker at a crucial moment, causing you to lose the few feet that may make the difference between winning or losing a championship. A rope may look fine on the outside, but take a second look. Open up the lay and find out whether it looks black, tired and queer on the inside. If it does, throw it away and get some new line.

23

Adjusting and Tuning the Mast

The position of the mast and the tuning of the standing rigging are trial-and-error problems that have harassed the experts for years. Should the mast have a rake or should it be plumb? Should the rigging be so tight you can play a tune on it, or so slack that you can tie knots in it? I confess that I don't know the correct answers to these always perplexing questions, although I do prefer more or less slack rigging. Some boats go well with a raked mast while others seem to go well with the mast plumb, or even over the bow. I have seen boats with rigging set up so tight that it sang which would sail equally well with those whose rigging seemed to hang in bights. There doesn't seem to be any proven scientific reasoning to back up either school of thought. However, it is always essential to have the mast straight athwartships. In other words, set up the shrouds so that the mast does not bend too much to leeward—or to windward. Rake your mast or set it plumb, but don't let it hang over the side. No doubt the mast was removed the previous fall without recording the position of the stays or turnbuckles, but you may recall where you had it; or there may be marks left on the threads of the turnbuckles which will provide a starting point for this phase of tuning.

The first step is to determine whether or not the mast is in the middle of the boat athwartships. This is done either with a steel tape hauled to the masthead or by stretching the main halyard itself first to a point on one side of the boat, say a chainplate, and then to a corresponding point on the other side. This should be done to at least two corresponding points on either side of the boat to insure a more definite check. A steel tape, though it is the best way to do the job, is not always available, but by carefully stretching the main halyard with the same tension on either side a completely satisfactory job can be done. It should be noted that any adjustments in the lower shrouds for the purpose of straightening any local bends or curves in the mast may throw the masthead a bit to one side, and this centering of the masthead must be given a final check after making the other adjustments to be sure there has been no major change. It is hardly necessary to point out that if the boat is to be equally balanced on either tack, the mast should follow, as nearly as possible, from deck to masthead, the upward projection of the center line of your boat.

The turnbuckles on the shrouds should have been loosened up

and oiled during the winter, and although they may have marks on them indicating where they were set the previous summer, under the tension of the rigging the boat may change shape somewhat, and the rigging may ring down after a few sails; so further adjustments will no doubt be necessary. Adjustments to remove local bends can be made at the mooring by pulling on the shrouds on one side together, and also separately, while sighting up the groove or sailtrack. The tension will show to a certain degree which shrouds need tightening and which loosening. Of course, final adjustments cannot be made until the boat is under sail, but steps in the right direction can be taken at the mooring which will make the whole job easier.

When you get the boat under sail (preferably in a moderate breeze and smooth water), sight up the groove or track and see whether the mast is straight or has a fair curve, or local bends between spreaders. A slight luff will take enough strain off the rigging to permit the turnbuckles to be adjusted easily. Then sail her full again and check the groove or track. Are the lee shrouds slack or taut? If one is taut, it may have some influence on the straightness of the mast. Make sure, and then put her on the other tack and repeat the process. On getting back to your anchorage, check again to see if the adjustment of the turnbuckles has altered the original centering of the mast.

Never leave the boat with the cotter pins out of the turnbuckle barrels, or the locknuts loose if no cotters are used. Turnbuckles have a nasty habit of working themselves loose when pins are not replaced. Locknuts are *not* as positive as cotters and should be avoided if possible. They are sometimes easier to adjust than cotter pins, but are not to be trusted.

Ranger's MAST

As a splendid example you may recall that *Ranger*, in 1937, before she was even under sail, lost her brand-new duralumin stick. Her shrouds were made of steel rods, heat-treated for additional strength. As the ovens could only take rods 17 feet long, the panels were made up of two rods joined with turnbuckles. There were three sets of spreaders with rods between each set and a diagonal rod running from the end of a lower spreader to the butt of the next above. To preserve the maximum strength it was rightly decided that no holes should be drilled in the rods for cotter pins through the turnbuckles. Locknuts were used instead.

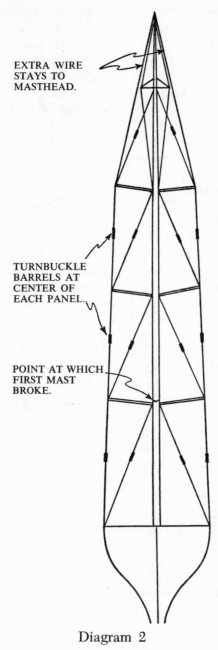

EXTRA WIRE
STAYS TO
MASTHEAD.

TURNBUCKLE
BARRELS AT
CENTER OF
EACH PANEL.

POINT AT WHICH
FIRST MAST
BROKE.

Diagram 2

In order to have everything work well mechanically, plenty of oil was applied to the turnbuckle barrels, rod ends and locknuts. Oiling was the right and proper thing to do.

Tragedy struck when *Ranger* had been under tow of Commodore Mike Vanderbilt's *Vara* for a number of hours off the Maine Coast en route from Bath to Newport, Rhode Island. With the constant rolling back and forth, in spite of steadying sails carried, one or more locknuts, which had very carefully and thoroughly been set up at the shipyard, loosened up and the turnbuckle barrel vibrated itself off. With one panel loose the rest of the shrouds progressively loosened and it wasn't long before the 165-foot mast was waving back and forth like a fishing rod, finally breaking off above the lower spreaders and falling overboard into about 300 feet of water.

Quick action by the brave crew in loosening the clevis pins of the jib stays and backstays, at the risk of their lives, saved the hull from serious damage, and *Ranger*'s beautiful, new, shiny mast slipped into the depths of the Atlantic. The lower section remained in place, since it was supported by the only set of independent diagonal rods. This lower section was returned to the Bath Iron Works in Maine and 21 days later a new mast, built up from the lower section, was stepped in *Ranger!* The moral of this story: if you use locknuts instead of cotter pins check your turnbuckles frequently, and never leave your boat either under way or at your mooring without cotters in the turnbuckles.

TAPE

Tape—industrial, Scotch, or dry-back adhesive—can be very useful aboard a boat. In addition to these, my old friend, Ted Kenyon, the designer and builder also—through the Kenyon Instrument Co.—of the well-known and efficient Kenyon Speedometer, some years ago brought out another popular and most successful item, namely Kenyon Tape. I doubt if there are any cruising or racing boats of any size who haven't at one time or another used Kenyon Tape. It is almost an indispensable detail aboard ship, but try to keep it dry; it isn't much good after a wetting.

To this list you must also add the colored plastic tape—it comes in all colors now—which can be used in place of friction tape or Kenyon. It is very elastic, very sticky and very long wearing, as well as neat in appearance.

Locknuts can be taped which will help prevent their working loose and they *should* be. All cotters or sharp edges should be taped to prevent the tearing of sails or cutting of hands.

JUMPERS AND DIAMONDS

Jumper stays and diamond stays on boats so equipped, can generally be set up before the mast is stepped, but occasionally they require minor adjustments before the final tuning is complete. Jumpers, the two forward stays which run from the masthead over a V-shaped set of spreaders and then back to the mast at a point more or less equidistant from the masthead, are set up, before stepping the mast, so that they bend the mast forward a bit at the top. When the sail is bent on, the mast will pull back at the top to a straight position or even with a bit of bend aft. Since most, though not all, masts with jumpers are also equipped with permanent backstays, increased tension on the backstay will correct this forward hook. More about this later in connection with the relationship between jibstay, jumpers and the permanent.

Diamonds are likewise set up before stepping, and quite taut at that. Sighting along the track will readily determine whether the tension is correct on either side. It has been my experience that, once these are set up in the yard, no further adjustment is usually required during the summer. This may not be true with new rigging, as even with the modern stainless-steel wire and Trulock fittings there is a certain amount of stretch.

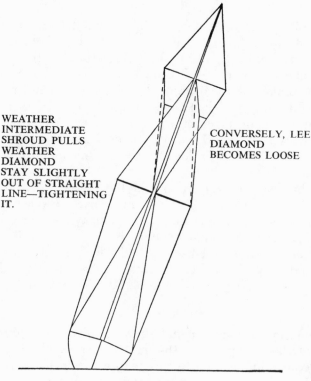

WEATHER INTERMEDIATE SHROUD PULLS WEATHER DIAMOND STAY SLIGHTLY OUT OF STRAIGHT LINE—TIGHTENING IT.

CONVERSELY, LEE DIAMOND BECOMES LOOSE

Diagram 3

Rod Stephens, prominent yacht designer, ocean racer and ex-Commodore of the Cruising Club of America, is responsible for a device that holds the diamond section of a mast straighter and relieves some of the compression strain on it, since the diamonds need not be set up quite as tight as in the conventional rig. In the accompanying diagram you will see a short stainless steel wire strap, securely fastened to both the diamond and the upper stay so that it will not slip. This is rigged in such a way that it tends to pull the upper stay and the diamond out of their normal straight line positions. The result is that the windward diamond is tighter than the leeward one, for the weather upper stay pulls it slightly out of line and therefore tightens it, while the upper leeward stay, being slack and more or less free, hangs without much strain on the leeward diamond which then assumes a straight line.

FORE-AND-AFT TUNING

It is always a surprise to me that so many skippers do not seem to grasp the problems of *fore-and-aft tuning*, as it might be termed. For some reason they can't figure the relationships between the jibstay, jumpers and permanent backstay. The fact is that these are vitally inter-related. Each of the three controls another and they all control each other. In other words, the jibstay, jumpers and permanent backstay are in a state of equilibrium where the tension of any one of them is dependent on the tension on the other two. Tighten the permanent and you tighten the other two, and vice versa. This is an important thing to bear in mind, and on it depends the whole tuning or curve of your mast.

A secondary but important factor in controlling the fore-and-aft shape of the mast is the relationship between the positioning at the partners and at the heel. (Obviously this does not apply to boats with masts stepped on deck.) In other words, wedges at the deck must be fitted with due regard to the position of the mast at the heel, or conversely the heel must be adjusted so that it is in proper adjustment with the mast as it is wedged at the partners. If either is out of alignment, the result will be an improper shape to the mast part way up, say in the vicinity of the lower spreaders. If the wedges at the partners are too thick on the after side the mast will tend to be bowed forward at the lower spreaders. If they are too thick on the forward side at the partners, the mast will tend to bow aft at the lower spreaders, a most unnatural situation which is dangerous in that it may cause the lower spreaders to collapse.

Whether you have runners or backstays is not of paramount importance. The backstays or runners merely help the permanent and jumpers; they do not supersede them. The backstays or runners will make the whole job easier and, by proper adjusting, can be used to help in the reshaping of the curve of the mast. If you have the older type jibstay-backstay and separate headstay, but

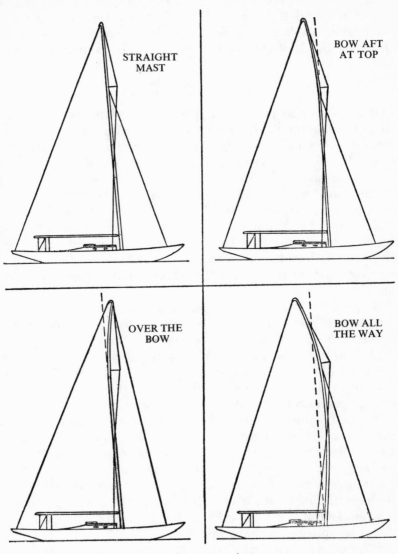

Diagram 4

no permanent, you can do the same job of changing the fore-and-aft curve of your mast, but it is not quite as easily controlled.

Why change the fore-and-aft shape or curve of the mast? Why not a straight mast? Every sailor knows that different weather conditions demand differently shaped sails—a full sail for light air, a flat one for heavy air and a medium one for in-between air. But how can you carry enough mainsails to cover every situation? The answer is you can't, but you can change the shape of your mainsails by changing the shape of your mast, i.e., by bending the mast or straightening it up.

Sails are made with certain definite curves in the luff, foot and leech. The curve in the leech, known as the roach, stays there indefinitely. It is that big, beautiful rounded curve of the leech of the sail which adds unmeasured area to your sail. The curves in the luff and the foot, by the time the sail is roped, are never seen. They are the curves which give draft and shape to your sail. The formulae for these curves are the closely guarded secrets of the individual sailmaker. The curving or shaping of the luff and foot are the factors which determine whether a sail is a winner or a loser, a good sail or a bad sail. I am told that for a Frostbite dinghy sail of 72 square feet, measurements of the curve in the luff get down to thirty-seconds of an inch!

Now what does all this mean? Some years ago Walter von Hutschler brought his Star Boat *Pimm* to this country, with a very light set of bending spars and won the World Championship. By means of a slack headstay and movable wedges at the deck, Walter was able to bend his mast so that most of the draft was removed from his mainsail for going to windward. The boom, rigged with a mainsheet block near the middle, also bent downward in such a way as to remove draft from the sail. The net result was a full sail for reaching and running, but a very flat sail for going to windward. While the light rig helped the stability of the boat, I think the principal gain came from the flattened sail for windward work. The success of *Pimm* was followed by a rash of light and extra-light rigs in the Star Class, which in turn was followed by a rash of broken spars in the class all over the world. But von Hutschler made his point: unwanted draft in a mainsail could be temporarily removed by bending the mast and/or boom.

If you slack off the headstay of a Frostbite dinghy and don't have the shrouds too tight, the mast will look at times like a dog's

hind leg, but the draft will be gone from the sail. The mast step
and thwart will hold the mast at the lower end and the upper
part will take a curve aft which will, to a degree, be influenced
by the draft of the sail. In a Star, which has a more complicated
set of rigging, the curve can be more or less controlled by the
headstay and wedges at the deck (in some cases, instead of using
the deck wedges, the heel of the mast is moved by an adjustable
crank or "mast-raker" which I think is a cumbersome rig and has
been discarded by most Star boat men).

Lightnings, Luders 16s, Atlantics, 210s and International One-
Designs, equipped with jumper stay and permanent backstay
rigs, are easy to control. Unfortunately in the case of Lightnings,
210s and Atlantics, class rules do not permit the permanent backstay to be adjusted after the start of a race. The International
One-Designs, on the other hand, have no restrictions on this very
valuable tuning device, and we used it to the nth degree. The
permanent backstay crank on *Bumble Bee* got such a workout
each race that it fairly sizzled!

If you have the conventional headstay or jumper stay and
backstay (running or permanent) rig, you can control and adjust
the shape of your sails as you please and in such a manner as to
get the most out of them. With the headstay rig, the shape and
curve of the mast can be controlled by adjustments of the headstay. If you want a flat mainsail for going to windward in a
breeze, slack off the headstay as much as necessary. With the
jumper stay and permanent backstay rig, the permanent does the
job. Crank up the permanent backstay turnbuckle as much as
required. Where there are jumper stays, but no permanent, the
jumpers themselves must be slacked to allow the mast to take a
curved shape. With the latter rig it would be awkward to go aloft
to the lower spreaders to adjust the jumpers; hence some boats
have their jumpers extended to a point on the mast where the
turnbuckle cranks can be reached from the deck. Many International One-Designs are so rigged, by running the jumper stays
over properly shaped fairleads at the lower spreaders and thence
to two crank turnbuckles on the fore side of the mast about six
feet above the deck. There is no harm in this type of rigging, for
it is close to the mast, offering little wind resistance, and it does
what it should by reason of its extra length, having more stretch
and give in a hard breeze.

Our backstay turnbuckle on *Bumble Bee* could be, and fre-

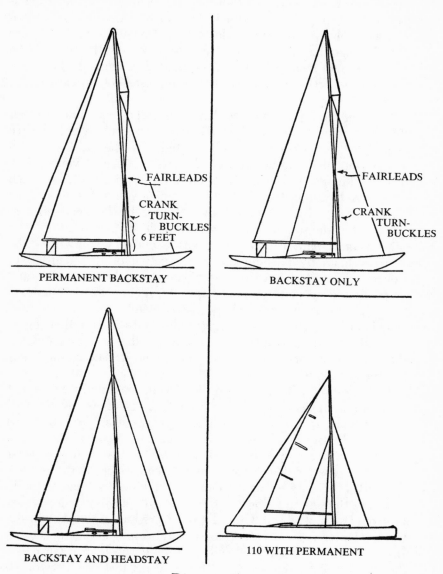

Diagram 5

quently was, adjusted a distance of ten inches. When up tight it
pulled the top of our mast back three or four diameters, or from
nine to twelve inches. When slack the permanent was quite loose
and the mast had a slight tendency to look over the bow at the
top. (You will recall that when the mast was stepped, the jumpers were set up in such a way that the mast bent forward somewhat at the top.)

Bending the top of the mast back has certain advantages other
than flattening the mainsail. It also frees the leech, which in turn
makes steering easier, as well as tightens the jibstay which
makes your jib stand better and, therefore, improves your ability
to point higher. These are both important and should be given
due consideration. If you flatten your mainsail for windward
work and at the same time "free" the leech, the dead air will
move out of the sail quicker. Tighten the leech and you bottle up
this air and create a force which has a tendency to increase the
weather helm by pushing the after section of the mainsail to
leeward. You must have a taut jibstay to make your jib stand
properly and keep its proper shape. A sagging jibstay creates a
baggy jib whose designed shape is completely gone. Every time
your boat hits a sea the whole rig jumps and the jib either jumps
to windward or sags farther to leeward. Either one destroys the
shape of the jib and the air currents around it. The result? Your
boat just won't go as fast as she should.

The question of how much to bend your mast and under what
wind conditions is a tough one to answer, and there are no hard
and fast rules to go by. I like to bend my mast aft for windward
work in all strengths of wind. Naturally, we bend it more in a
breeze than in a very light air. The whole sail seems to set better
and have a better flow, as well as a "freer" leech, if the mast is
bent aft. (It is interesting to note that bending the mast actually
increases the sail area, for it flattens the sail and thus increases its
projected area. The sail being flatter, it presents more area to the
wind.) I prefer the greatest bend in the top section, to get the
"freer" leech which automatically results. If you have a fair curve
the whole sail becomes flatter, but it seems to have little or no
effect on the leech.

On *Weatherly*, since we had running backstays as well as a
permanent backstay, we could do quite a lot with the fore-and-
aft shape of the mast. (Actually, we also had a lower runner
joining the running backstay early in the season, but we found

that the mast was so stiff fore and aft that we didn't need the runners—even in a rough bouncy sea—so we promptly took 'em off.)

With my many years of steering an International One-Design, where I had the permanent backstay turnbuckle handle at my finger tips, I saw a wonderful opportunity to get *Weatherly's* permanent under my own thumb too, and had a tackle rigged to a #3 winch with one of my nice wooden jam cleats right close behind me. (See page 189.) Most of the time somebody in my crew yelled bloody murder whenever I turned 'round to ease it off, but it was fun doing it and it worked great—and we had a nice Revlon "Shocking Pink" nail-polish mark on the Dacron tail so we could tell where to trim it to get maximum bend aft in the mast. We also used this Revlon nail-polish, as well as marlin (but never tape, for it can slip and slide on the wire) to mark our backstays after previously determining, by Vic Romagna's musical ear and the acoustical strain gauge, what the proper tension was.

Reaching and running present a different problem. Your boat will probably go faster with more draft and it will certainly go faster if there is a bit of spring in the rig. A rigid rig seems to bounce the sails about more and consequently disturb the air currents. It may even be, as some suggest, that a boat will go faster if her mast is plumb on a reach or run. My own thought is that the spring in the rig, or the looseness of the rig, is the important factor. But whatever it is, you'll make your boat go faster off the wind if you'll ease up quite a bit on your backstays and/or the permanent. This goes for small boats as well as big ones.

On *Ranger* we never set up fully on backstays on leeward legs. There were marks on the wire backstay pennants to which they were winched for windward work (a strain gauge was used at a previous time to determine where the marks should be); but off the wind a certain amount of slack was given to allow the rig to spring a bit. It would be impossible to say that this actually helped *Ranger's* speed, but since we knew that it helped on smaller boats it was worth doing, and Skipper Vanderbilt was not one to let any little trick slip through his fingers. And twenty-one years later, if it was worth doing on *Ranger* in '37, it was most certainly worth doing on *Weatherly* in '58; so we followed the same procedure ALWAYS on a reach or a run. In fact, in one trial race against *Vim* when we both jibed 17 times on the last leg, it was quite a moderate breeze, so we just left the backstays forward and relied completely on the extremely light permanent backstay to keep the mast in the boat.

HELM

While emphasizing the importance of bending the mast, the position of the mast fore and aft must not be overlooked. Sail your boat around for a time on the wind and on a close reach. Does she have a tendency to run up into the wind quickly if you release the tiller, or does she gradually work up? Assuming that everything is as it should be (by other things I mean jib leads and crew placement which will be discussed next) your boat should have a slight weather helm—a tendency to work into the wind when close-hauled, particularly when a puff hits her. In going to windward you want her to help you get there. If you have a lee helm (i.e., your boat tends to veer to leeward rather than windward when you release the tiller) your boat will be more or less fighting you all the way up the windward leg, a most regrettable state of affairs. Assuming that you have a properly designed boat to begin with, such a situation means that the mast is too far over the bow. The matter of weather or lee helm is governed by the relation of the center of lateral resistance of the hull to the center of effort of the sails.

The theoretical center of lateral resistance is that point on the side of the boat at which if you pushed, she would move sideways, without, so to speak, altering her course. The center of effort of the sails is found by measuring the area of each sail on the sail plan, finding the centers, and then combining the relative centers. It is obvious that different sized sails will produce different centers of effort, a large mainsail moving the center farther aft than a small one. The center of effort of the sails should be a little abaft the center of lateral resistance of the hull when sailing. In other words, the center of effort of the sails should act as a lever, with the center of lateral resistance as the fulcrum to push the boat up into the wind. If the center of effort is forward of the center of lateral resistance, the boat will have a lee helm, and if one center is exactly over the other, there will be no helm at all and the boat will sail in a straight line. (Author's Note. A year or so after my book was published in 1952, my very good friend and almost severest critic, the late Prescott Wilson, expert sailmaker, pointed out to me one day that the above paragraph is not strictly correct, that there are certain technical errors in it that aren't quite true. I had planned possibly to rewrite or rephrase the thing. However, a later consultation with another good friend and shipmate, Olin J. Stephens II, indicates that, while it is *not* technically accurate, the whole explanation is simple, clear, concise and, under the circumstances it gives a reasonably fair analysis of a highly complicated situation that most readers wouldn't understand anyhow. Ergo, let's leave it the way it is. If you don't agree, sue me! But in its own little way, it will help you to tune your boat properly, I hope!)

One might think that the latter situation would be the ideal, but such is not the case, as a boat which has a slight weather helm will work out to windward. The good skipper can feel his boat working out, trying to get to windward, while the tiller of a boat with no helm has about as much feeling and life as an equal length of bologna. You may have heard some expert skipper speak of the "feel" of his boat. "She felt right today," or "there was no feel to that tub no matter what I did." He was referring to the liveliness, the zip, and the slight tendency of the boat to claw out to windward. The "feel" of a boat may vary with different suits of sails or with various positions of the mast and/or crew, or with the speed at which you drive her.

Up to a certain point you should have no trouble balancing your boat with almost any good suit of racing sails, but if one suit doesn't seem to do it, try another. Usually the mainsail is the most important balancing sail. The principal thing to keep in mind is that your boat should have a slight weather helm. Try her out, adjust the mast, move it forward at the top a bit and see if there is any improvement in the helm if her tendency was to eat out too much to windward. If the boat doesn't want to work out to windward at all, the chances are that the masthead is too far forward. Move it back at the top by slacking off on the jibstay and headstay (if you have one), or move the whole mast aft by slacking the jibstay and moving the heel back by shifting wedges. Somewhere along the line you will find the right combination, but it may take time. You might even try another jib.

Don't try to do it in one afternoon or by taking a short sail with some friendly competitor. To my way of thinking, an actual race is the only thorough way to tune a boat. Your competitors are doing their best to beat you and they will provide a yardstick with which to measure the performance of your boat. Analyze the reasons for your good or bad performance, but be sure to analyze them honestly. In other words, don't blame the sails or the boat for something *you yourself* are responsible for. If a decision is wrong you made it; if a sail tears or rigging breaks, you should have checked it; if a member of the crew lets go a line at the wrong moment you are to blame—you should have given better instruction. The skipper is the fellow who, with the help of his crew, must tune up the boat and he must do it in actual races to do it right, and he must do it with an open, analytical mind.

As a case in point, and by way of explaining one of the reasons why *Ranger* was such a successful racing yacht: every afternoon that we sailed or raced, after we had picked up our mooring the afterguard, consisting of Skipper Mike, Mrs. Vanderbilt, Rod and Olin Stephens, Zenas Bliss and myself went below and held a discussion in the cabin. We talked about anything and everything that had occurred during that particular sail from all angles, but with constructive criticism. We talked over problems of teamwork, tactics and standard practice, making all kinds of suggestions, some of which were later proven good and some bad. If there was something the skipper didn't like in the way we handled certain maneuvers, he told us so. By the same token, if he did something we didn't think exactly right, we told *him*, too. The very fact that our skipper could take criticism pleasantly shows why he was so successful in organizing and sailing a yacht in defense of the America's Cup. He recognized the importance of tuning, organization, and the final responsibility of the skipper for the success or defeat of his boat.

On *Weatherly* in the 1958 Cup Trials we made an effort to follow the same procedure and held conferences in the main cabin with all hands present, including our one professional sailor, Tom Hatteberg, a very fine Norwegian lad. Things were considerably different from '37, when there were 26 professionals and five amateurs—plus Mrs. Vanderbilt—as against ten amateurs and one professional on *Weatherly* in '58. We talked out various thoughts and ideas and made copious lists which were posted on the main cabin bulkhead and checked off when finished. We were, if I do say so myself, a reasonably happy ship and I personally think we had less internal problems than other boats and, because the crew was more or less "hand-picked," we had fewer prima donnas. Even I, myself, made every effort to keep my temper at all times, for one of the best ways to lose a boat race—or anything else for that matter—is to get mad and let your temper flare. One major point I learned from Rod Stephens many years ago: Never bawl out a crew member in front of the rest of the gang. There are times when this is difficult, I admit, but it is much better to get the man aside later and explain the problem quietly and sensibly. You'll find your crew will stick with you and be happy sailing with you and, what is more important, you'll get better teamwork and win more races.

By way of illustration, albeit a funny one, I recall some years ago when I was breaking in a new dinghy crew on *Agony*, my godson, Robert Stewart Walden, then aged about nine. I took him aside and said:—

"Bobbie, if I get excited and yell and holler at you, it means nothing. Don't pay any attention to me!"

"I know," he answered, "Mommie told me!"

"Secondly," I went on, "don't talk and gab about non-essential things. We just don't talk when racing."

"I know. Mommie told me."

"Third," I finished up, "be sure and ALWAYS go to the bathroom JUST before we go out to race."

"I know," came back Bobbie for the third time, "Mommie told me!"

CREW

An all-important factor in the tuning and racing of your boat is the crew. Whether you have a crew of one, five or ten, you owe it to them as well as yourself to give them a chance to get tuned up before the season opens. If you can keep the same crew every day all season you are extremely lucky. If you can keep them from one season to the next you are luckier still. It hardly seems necessary to point out that properly organized teamwork (the skipper's responsibility) will gain you an unpredictable number of places in each race.

Teamwork is noticeably lacking in the early races of the season. Assign each man or woman a particular job and have them stick to it. Most women are not physically able to do the same job that some ex-tackle can do, but there are others with which they can cope and in which they can give an excellent account of themselves. (Incidentally, they have a certain restraining effect on the tempers and manners of the male members of the crew.) Yacht racing is a sport in which women can compete on an equal basis with men. Lorna Whittelsey, now Mrs. Frederick H. Hibberd, beat the tar out of the men for the Championship of the hot Interclub One-Design Class. Mary Etchells, wife of E. W. (Skip) Etchells, a World Champion of the Star Class, did a great job as crew for her husband, and was the first woman crew on a World Champion. My sister, Allegra Mertz, has given an excellent account of herself in races against men and women as skipper and crew. Aileen Shields Bryan, daughter of the redoubtable Corny, has won several Championships against men, while Wilma Bell, "Pop" Stanley's daughter, has proven herself an agile and able crew, the equal of any man, on *Bumble Bee* over the years. "Sis" Hovey Morss has raced many, many years with her father, brothers and husband Sherman Morss. She was aboard *Weetamoe*, *Rainbow*, the famed *Robin* and helped steer *Easterner* in the '58 Cup Trials.

But whether male or female, or mixed, give the crew the opportunity to learn your boat and your way of doing things on it. Anyone can learn to do a bang-up job as crew if the skipper will take the time to explain WHY things should be done in a certain way and then provide the opportunity for plenty of practice at it. If you have a small crew of only one or two, pick a couple of congenial, agile people, for there is hardly any point in racing with uncongenial people on board. If you have a larger crew of four or five, the various jobs can be allocated according to strength, ability and agility. Every member doesn't have to be a Tarzan, for often quick wits and intelligence will more than compensate for lack of strength. William H. "Pop" Stanley, who owned *Bumble Bee* and took part in practically every race, was 73 years old when he finally, regretfully, retired after ten years of intensive racing with us. He enjoyed a taste of racing in 1943 and bought *Bumble Bee* the next year. I don't think he had ever been on a sailboat before that, yet he developed into a first-class, dependable, hard-working and most efficient crew member. He was one who needed NO watching to see how his job was going. Naturally a man of his age couldn't haul on a mainsheet or spinnaker guy, but he was excellent on the jib halyard, spinnaker lift and foreguy, and overhauling the weather jib sheet when tacking. Because of his efforts and practice there was never any worry about whether his jobs would be done correctly and on time. Nor do I say this because he owned the boat; he was a working member of the crew, pulling his weight and more, along with the rest of us.

PLACEMENT OF WEIGHT

Placement of weight is an all-important factor in winning boat races. It would be ideal if the crew could be placed amidships fore and aft, and to windward or leeward in a light air. It is a terrific advantage to have all movable ballast, crew and gear, centered amidships; but in actual practice it can't be done, for there obviously isn't room in the middle of the boat for everything. If weight is distributed in the ends of the boat she will "hobby horse" or "see-saw" a lot more than if the weight is concentrated in the middle. Balance it athwartships, too, so that the boat does not have a tendency to list one way or the other. It is so easy to throw things into the bow or stern to get rid of them, but it will reduce the speed of your boat to some degree.

In a breeze, you can't pile your live ballast one on top of another on the weather rail. You can try it, but the chances are you will be looking for a new crew next season. Personal comfort, wind resistance and mobility for maneuvers must be taken into consideration. It would be wonderful to have all five members of the crew of an International One-Design lying on the weather rail in a hard breeze, and it can be done when a long hitch on one tack is contemplated; but when you are maneuvering in close quarters and tacking frequently it just isn't feasible to have five people scrambling in from the high side. In a Star or a Snipe yes, but it just won't work on anything bigger than 30 feet overall.

There are two schools of thought on this live ballast business. One school thinks that in a day racer, with or without cabin, the live ballast is more effective if kept low and as far to windward as possible in a breeze, off the deck and in the cockpit or cabin. This view is held particularly by the Bermudians in their International One-Designs. The other school, of which I am a member, feels that the weight is more effective and will give more leverage in a hard breeze if put on the weather rail. If the weight of the crew, preferably the rear end, is put over the side of the boat, it exerts a more effective force because it is farther out from the center of the boat than it will be if sitting down inside the hull. Besides, it seems to me that the crew on deck will get a lot more enjoyment from the race if they can see what is going on.

On *Weatherly* in the early trial races, we put practically all our crew "over the rail," so to speak, and had them hanging out over the side. We had discussed this idea and felt it would be extremely helpful, for it meant moving roughly 2000 pounds out approximately three feet; in other words a gain of 6000 foot-pounds tending to overcome the heeling moment of the boat. Unfortunately, *Weatherly*, because of her slack bilges, has a tendency to be somewhat tender and to appear to heel more than the other Twelves, and the crew hanging over the side gave somewhat the impression that we were afraid she'd maybe go all the way over. Since all the contenders were very, very allergic to giving any untoward impression to the all powerful America's Cup Committee, we held a council of war after a couple of races and decided to give up this idea of hanging over the rail. I am told on reliable authority that *Vim* also wanted to put their crew over the side (for the same reason we did) but refrained for fear of giving said Committee a poor impression. I will say, however, right here and now, that I can't see anything wrong with the idea, and I will furthermore go on record as saying that I am positive such a maneuver will add stability to the boat. (Later the Aussies did do it, and successfully!)

In a regatta in September 1972, I was "guest" skipper aboard Marty Lyons' *Alice* when a quick nasty squall came up. We were beating up toward "42nd Street"—red bell 42 off Scotch Caps—and it was blowing maybe 20–25 knots with a smooth sea. We were laying over so far that water was pouring into the cockpit over the lee rail with three young men on the weather rail and me steering from the weather side. I finally climbed up on the rail, too, and was lying across the boat "Star-boat fashion" when the boys discovered me and started to laugh—me at 65 and with arthritis yet. But I managed it, the boat straightened up a bit and we sailed on with the lee rail out and the boat balancing very nicely. I'd like to say we won, but a poor third was all we got, and yet my 200 pounds on the weather rail really did help.

The fore-and-aft placement of weight is a matter of balancing the helm as well as the boat's pitching motion, and of convenience or maneuverability. If you wish to place your live ballast in a certain spot, the dead ballast may be relocated accordingly without doing irreparable ˙harm. The fellow who lies on the weather rail should be given as much comfort as practical, so don't make him lie on top of a winch; let him move forward or

aft, within reasonable limits, of course, and then shift some gear
to compensate if necessary. In placing the crew keep in mind
convenience and maneuverability. In an International One-
Design, for instance, it is a fairly simple matter when tacking in a
breeze, for one member of the crew to clamber from one side to
the other around the fore side of the mast. And yet I have seen a
boat on which all the crew work aft into the cockpit and out the
other side, causing no end of confusion. Why not go right across
the cabin house you may ask? The boom-jack is in the way, and
the crosser-over invariably gets fouled up in the jib sheets. Stars,
Lightnings and Comets present no such problem, but the boat
equipped with a genoa presents a pretty problem for the lad
trying to shift over forward of the mast.

Beating to windward in a sloppy sea, there will be less "sousing" of the bow if the crew (be it one or five) is moved slightly
aft. At the same time the center of lateral resistance will be
moved aft, thus somewhat relieving the weather helm. In every
case, however, it has been my experience that a boat will go
better if the ballast, live and dead, is concentrated as much as
possible. This has been proven time and time again to my satisfaction in the dinghies—and I presume to the satisfaction of
other dinghy sailors, for most of them do it. The skipper and
crew in a dink play cozy and sit on the rail or in the bottom very
close together. The motion of the ends is easier and quicker. The
same thing follows in larger boats, so adopt this rule as closely as
you are able, and concentrate your weights amidships, with
slight variations for balance under various weather conditions.

Mike Vanderbilt in his splendid book on America's Cup
Yachts, ON THE WIND'S HIGHWAY calls attention to this detail on
page 135, in a NYYC Race from Mattapoisett to Edgartown. As
we neared the weather turning mark, Vineyard Sound Lightship,
Mike ordered the big ballooner put forward in the "chute" (a
very light semicircular aluminum trough some 3 feet wide by 25
feet long, that ran from the sail bins up the bow stem to a small
hatch just under the jibstay. Stopped jibs were put into this
chute when required.), whence it was to be hauled up through
the forward hatch to be hooked onto the jibstay. Four or five men
were detailed by Rod Stephens to do the job. The difference in
Ranger's motion was so apparent that Mike immediately ordered
the men aft.

The thwartships balancing is a matter I would think well

known to all, but for the benefit of those not familiar with it, I will go over the general principles. In a hard breeze it is advisable to keep your boat as upright as possible, to keep her "on her feet," so to speak. Of course, it's impossible to keep a boat perfectly upright when it's blowing, but do the best you can by getting as much live ballast as possible to windward. An agile crew can help materially by lying out on the topsides, but be sure he's agile enough to hold on and get back on board quickly. His weight will count heavily, if I may use the phrase, but you are a dead duck if he loses his grip and falls overboard.

In Frostbite dinghies, with a smooth sea and steady breeze, it is possible not only to keep them upright, but even heel them to windward. Believe me, when you can do that, they will eat out to windward at a terrific rate, and still keep footing. In dinghies the skipper and crew must hook their feet under the centerboard cap or seat and lean back to do their balancing act. Strong stomach muscles are a definite advantage. As a case in point, Bob and Gladys DeCoppet, though outweighed by 20 pounds, won the Frostbite Championship two years in a row, blow high, blow low, making up for their lack of weight by being able to bend back like pretzels, thus getting their weight farther out than their less agile competitors (which included your then 210-pound author!).

In light air, particularly with chine-built boats, it is advisable to heel them to leeward on a windward leg. In all boats the sails will assume their proper shape easier and set better when there is little or no air, if the boat is heeled. Since speed is not great, ideal hull form is not of paramount importance under such conditions, and chine boats will therefore knife through the water better, with less tendency to slap their bottoms into a wave, if heeled. The same is also true of reaching in light air in any type of boat; roll her over somewhat and she'll move faster.

Running, in light or heavy air, is a difficult matter which will be discussed at length in the chapter on Spinnakers. It is sufficient to say now that, at all times, the boat should be on her feet and even heeled slightly to windward on a run.

JIB LEADS ON 10-DEGREE LINE

Where to set the jib sheet leads is a question that has been bothering skippers for lo these many years. I have had them way in and way out, experimenting and trying one position and then

another. I am indebted to my sailmaker friend Prescott Wilson
for suggesting a standard position which he felt was about ideal
—the "10-degree" line. The jib is trimmed at some point on a line
that runs at a 10-degree angle to the center line of the boat, from
the jib tack aft. I have varied the position slightly from this 10-
degree line depending on the strength of the wind, moving leads
inboard slightly in a hard breeze, or out an inch in light air.

Plotting this 10-degree angle and
line on your deck is not difficult.
The real problem is to make certain
that you measure the actual center
line. It is essential that you make
several measurements at various
checkpoints to be positive that you
have found the true center line of
your boat. If you don't, you may
find your boat faster (or slower)
on one tack than the other.

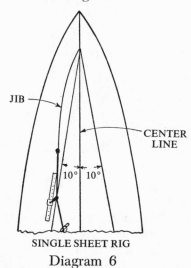

SINGLE SHEET RIG
Diagram 6

Having satisfied yourself that you
actually have the center line, measure back five feet on it from the
tack of the jib along the deck.
Then measure out on either side,
perpendicular to the center line,
10½ inches, and mark the two
points. (On larger boats you can measure back ten feet and out
21 inches for the same angle.)

When you run a line forward from these two marks to the tack
of the jib you will have two lines each of which is at a 10-degree
angle with the center line of your boat. Then fasten the jib track
down so that the jib sheet, when trimmed through the lead block
or fairlead, would theoretically touch this line. There is one more
step when double-lead jib sheets are used. The angle of the double sheets must be bisected and the thwartships lead must be
moved in or out to such a position that the bisector of the angle
touches the 10-degree line. To accomplish this, tie a light piece of
string or marline to the block on the jib through which the double sheet runs. (The jib, of course, must be hoisted, and while
jibs of entirely different cuts might cause slight variations, that
possibility is remote.) Hold the string or marline in the plane
made by the two parts of the jib sheet and bisect the angle made

by the two. The string should then touch somewhere along your
10-degree line. If it doesn't, the thwartships lead must be adjusted.

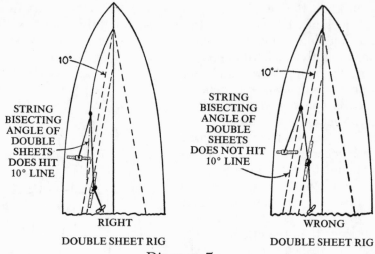

Diagram 7

Having settled somewhere along the 10-degree line as the
proper thwartships position, the fore-and-aft lead must then be
taken care of. This lead will naturally vary with each individual
jib, especially with those from different sailmakers. For the purposes of the fore-and-aft adjustment we can now ignore the
thwartships adjustment, which has been taken care of by the 10-
degree line. Assuming that the fore-and-aft track (no matter
whether it's a double or single lead) has been fastened down in
position, all that is now necessary is to move the fore-and-aft lead
to such a position that the jib draws properly, that is to say, it
breaks or luffs first in the right spot and the leech looks right.

For the sake of simplification, let us confine the discussion to
loose-footed working jibs. (Club-footed jibs are in a class by
themselves and once you have installed the jib traveller the problem is solved, unless you wish to experiment with a shorter traveller, which is a matter of personal opinion or preference.)

It is my opinion that, in general, no two skippers will agree
absolutely on the proper sheeting of a jib. This is understandable,
for no two jibs will look alike in all details, even though made by
the same sailmaker, for the reason that different usage will cause
certain variations, either temporary or permanent, to take place.

Let us assume that the jib has a good shape and a good leech. Where should the jib break or luff first and what should the leech look like and what should it do? I believe that the normally shaped jib should break (or luff or lift) a little above the intersection of the mitre and the luff wire, which is not quite halfway up the luff. The leech should be not quite a straight line, curving slightly to leeward and falling off a bit as it reaches the neighborhood of the head of the sail. As the sail is eased, I like to see this falling off at the top become more pronounced. If the fore-and-aft leads are not too far forward the head of the jib will do just this. In other words, I like the flow and leech of the jib to "look" past the lee side of the mainsail and not into it. This allows the dead used-up air to get out of the jib and make room for more. If the jib breaks too high up the sail and the leech seems too free, then the fore-and-aft leads must be moved forward, and vice versa.

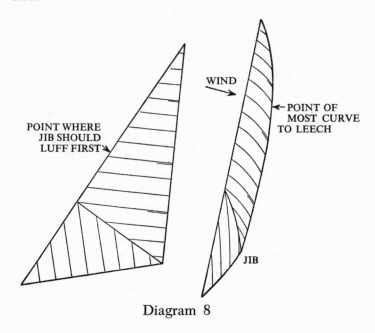

Diagram 8

One skipper will tell you that the jib sheet should be a continuation of the mitre line; another will say that the jib sheet should be sheeted forward or aft of the point where the mitre line, if extended, would hit the deck. I feel that the mitre line has nothing to do with the proper sheeting of the sail. It should be sheeted at an angle which looks best to the individual skipper. Let us assume that the jib has a good shape and a good leech— not tight or floppy, for if it is tight or floppy nothing you can do with the leads will help very much. The leech either needs a minor adjustment, or the whole sail needs a bath, probably the latter. If after a good bath and drying out, the leech is still tight, try stretching it by hand, pulling the tabling. On the other hand, if the leech is still loose and floppy, it may be a job for your sailmaker to take up a bit in a few of the seams, or put in a leech line.

During the last couple of years, Stars and Solings have developed and (hopefully) perfected a self-tacking jib. This has been accomplish by using a semicircular track or slide just forward of the mast. The sheet, a wire one, comes off the jib from an aluminum plate on the clew of the jib that has a number of holes in it to adjust the up-and-down pull on the leech. The sheet runs through a block on the track slide forward to a sheave right under the jibstay. From there it goes under the deck and aft to a five- or six-part rope tackle with a gate cleat on the forward side of the coaming. By means of a "barberhaul," the in-and-out position of the block on the slide may be controlled. I am quite frank and sincere in stating here that the jib with this contraption on a Soling looked horrible—the leech "looked in" at the bottom and sagged off at the top, quite contrary to what I've been brought up to like. However, the experts on this particular Soling assured me that this is the way to do it nowadays, and since they had just done well in a Soling Series, I subsided and kept my mouth shut. Nevertheless, I STILL don't like it.

In discussing this same deal with some top-notch Star skippers, I find that they don't like it either—mainly because, they say, there is not enough room forward of the mast on a Star to set up the semicircular track FAR ENOUGH aft. The track interferes with the adjustment of the mast on a downwind leg, preventing the mast from being pushed forward at the deck to angle the mast forward on a run.

Now these same Star boat experts,—there are quite a number I've talked to recently who are practically unanimous on the subject—say that their jibs are no longer trimmed on the 10– degree line, that they trim them in a lot closer, almost on the 5–degree line, letting the jib fall off a bit at the top. So, "wha hopens?" All that I've explained to you about 10-degree lines above goes out the window, or does it? I haven't, I'll admit, raced a Star in many years, and things do change, and yet there are certain established ways and methods of trimming jibs and mains that have proven successful over a long period of years. I think I'll stick with 'em—you go try the others. Maybe they'll work, maybe they won't, but you'll have the satisfaction of proving to yourself what's right and what's wrong.

I will state that on many, many of the newer large ocean racers, the genoa sheet tracks are set inside the life rails—NOT outside, on the railcap, as in the past. The effect is to make the slot between the mainsail and jib narrower and, theoretically, more efficient. Eventually, we had this sort of rig on *Palawan* and it seemed to work very well indeed. The general effect was to have the whole of the deck-sweeping #1 jennies trimmed inside the life rails. Their shape was good and seemed to make the boat go better. Being inside the railcap and life rails, when there is any kind of a sea or slop, this rig also prevented the foot from scooping up any water. It is interesting to note how popular these deck-sweeping genoas have become in late years. I won't say we were the first, but we DID have a very large Ratsey jenny on *Weatherly* which was deliberately designed with a very very full skirt on the foot to sweep the deck and close the opening between the foot of the sail and the deck, thus preventing wind or air currents from escaping under the jib and forcing this air back through the slot of the main and jib. It struck me as a great idea at that time and now, 15 years later, I haven't changed my mind.

Main Sheet Leads

Skippers have experimented' with forms and locations of main sheet leads for years in attempting to improve them aerodynamically and to make them easier to trim. I can't see any very great advantages to or differences between any of them. On *Bumble Bee*, for example, we had three offset blocks on deck, one aft on the starboard side, one on the king plank and one forward on the port side. Two single blocks on the boom, spaced about 14 inches apart, provided a four-part main sheet. There are those who suggest that this type of arrangement has the effect of trimming the main slightly differently on one tack or the other. I can't see that there is any measurable difference. Several International One-

Designs have their three deck blocks on the center line or king plank, on the theory that it will trim the boom more amidships, but I fail to see any particular superiority and the race results certainly don't show any.

Ranger was equipped with a six-part main sheet, four parts of which lead to a double block on a traveller. By means of two geared winches this double block could be cranked to windward or leeward. Mrs. Vanderbilt cranked long and valiantly on these gadgets to get the lead to windward every time *Ranger* tacked. *Ranger* was so fast that it is really difficult to say whether this did any good; but in the back of our minds was the theoretical idea that it helped. Since it was our purpose to leave no winch unturned to make *Ranger* a success, the job was delegated to Mrs. Vanderbilt and she struggled mightily with it, though it is my recollection she roundly "cussed" the gadget every time.

Star boats are somewhat similarly rigged, so that the length of the traveller can be controlled, though not pushed to windward. In a strong breeze the traveller is kept amidships, while in light air it is permitted a certain amount of scope on either side. Frostbite dinghies are usually equipped with a wire traveller running from either corner of the broad stern. I have experimented with various lengths for this traveller and always come to the same conclusion—the boom should be permitted to swing as far as it wants to across the whole length of the traveller. Limiting the swing altogether or to a smaller amount does not seem to be of any particular benefit and if anything, I think is detrimental. If I were asked to ascribe a reason for this apparent difference, if any, between a Class J boat and a dinghy, I would say it had something to do with the fact that a J boat is proportionately narrower and closer-winded than a dinghy.

Weatherly had a traveller which went almost all the way across the deck. We had two tackles with which we could pull the mainsheet slide across the boat and also limit the amount it moved across. It was our custom to keep the block fairly well centered in light air and move it several feet in a strong breeze. I will admit that this particular piece of equipment did not seem to work as well as the one on *Columbia* and I think that in another such Series I would like to have a slide which is equipped with eight rollers—four in each plane—similar to the gooseneck slide which Carleton Mitchell had on the roller-reef gear on his very famous and beautiful *Finisterre*.

I have mentioned above that *Ranger* had a traveller which we cranked to windward—and that was way back in 1937. It is interesting to note that practically every boat nowadays has a full-length (or, possibly, it's better called a full-width) traveller. Star boats, IODs, ocean racers and even Frostbite dinghies are now so equipped. On *Ranger*, we cranked the traveller to windward to ease the leech. Nowadays, in light air, yes, you crank it a bit to windward, but in any kind of a strong breeze you let the traveller slide off to leeward with the idea of changing the angle of incidence of the apparent wind to the mainsail. The most noteworthy effect of this is to ease the helm, reduce any weather helm and hence make your boat go faster. There is, of course, with a genoa jib, the added effect of narrowing that "slot" between main and jib.

I stated above that on Frostbite dinghies it was best to let the boom slide as far as it wanted across the *wire* traveller. That was in 1960. Now—since about 1967—I've "reversed my field," because my nephew, Jamie Brickell, a really gung-ho expert sailor who raced *Agony* for three years, installed a full-length piece of sail track which allowed the block on the traveller to slide *alll* the way across the stern or transom. Some of the other younger experts started doing this some years back too and they beat me— soo, it's that simple: If you can't lick 'em, join 'em! And the strange or funny part of all this seems to be that no matter what the strength of wind, you let the traveller run all the way out in light air or a heavy breeze. It doesn't seem to make sense, but it works. Ergo, *DO IT!*

My experience over recent years in larger cruising racers seems to bear this out, too. For example, on *Wainscott Wind*, a 41-foot centerboard yawl, in a good 15- to 18-knot sail breeze on Buzzard's Bay, we "vanged" the boom out (i.e., rigged a tackle to the end of the boom and pulled the end of the boom out toward the rail in lieu of a traveller). As we pulled the boom out—and down —we eased the main sheet, say six or eight inches. The net result was that we defeated a sister ship by a mile or more in an eight-mile beat. That was really an eye-opener to me and I've never forgotten it. Again, the general effect—lacking the conventional traveller—was to sheet the boom further out, changing the angle of incidence of the apparent wind.

On the other side of the coin, I was aboard *Kate* a PJ-48, S&S design, owned and skippered by Bob Hubner, as a Watch Officer in the 1972 Vineyard Race. This brand-new fiber glass cutter steers like a dream, balances beautifully, goes upwind and down like a scared rabbit and is a lovely boat to sail on and race. She has a very wide traveller, and it is the practice of the experts aboard to pull the traveller slide about eight to twelve inches to windward on a beat. This, of course, has the general effect of bringing the end of the boom (in fact, the whole boom) more or less amidships and widens the "slot" between the main and the jib. My point here is that this is contrary to my preconceived notions of how you use a traveller. Sure, in light air, I agree that it eases the upper leech and makes the main a bit "softer" if you pull the traveller a bit to windward. (See Diagram 10 on page 59.) But when it breezes on and your lee rail begins to submerge, my school of thought says that you should EASE the traveller to leeward (a) to ease the helm and (b) to tighten the upper leech, thus flattening the mainsail somewhat. Sailing, as I do, on many different yachts, both large and small, I find various crews have entirely different ideas as to how you solve a given problem. But I have also learned, with advancing age and experience, to put my "two cents" in and then to subside and let 'em do it whatever way they wish. It does little good to be argumentative on little things, and the results are generally the same anyhow. All of which brings to mind a delightful line from *The Caine Mutiny:* "There's a right way, a wrong way, a Navy way and MY WAY, and while you're on MY ship you'll do it MY WAY!!!"

It is not my intention here to be overly critical or in complete disagreement, and it may be that *Kate's* shorter boom and bigger foretriangle call for such moving to windward of the traveller. And, likewise, it may be that *Palawan* (with her comparatively longer boom) goes better with the traveller eased to leeward. However, I'll go back to my 11½-foot dinghy *Agony* and state categorically that she goes faster with the traveller way out, as I've already written above. So, "you pays your money and takes your chances!" To my way of thinking, One-Design racing provides the *Real* Test!

TRIM OF SAILS

If you want to get the jump on the rest of your class at the start, you must have your sails properly trimmed immediately after gunfire, or better still, a little before. Here is another variable, and an extremely important one. You must have a flying start with your boat "rarin'" to go and your sails must be adjusted to their optimum positions so that you keep up your maximum speed. Remember it's not the start, it's the fellow who's ahead a quarter mile from the start which really counts. Where a whole racing fleet is overlapped as it crosses the line, differences of feet and almost inches will often determine whether you're going to have free enough air to pull out on some sluggish competitor. You can't wait for five minutes to get your main sheet down or your jib adjusted to the last inch. You must do it now, right away, to get away and stay away out in front. But how far to trim them? I would say that your sails should be trimmed until they look pretty, efficient, aerodynamically perfect and right. That's a rather broad statement in extremely general terms, but to me it covers the situation quite well.

JIB AND MAIN TRIM

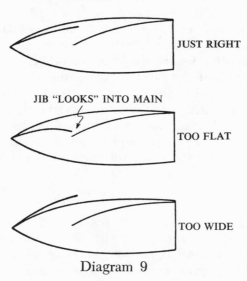

JUST RIGHT

JIB "LOOKS" INTO MAIN

TOO FLAT

TOO WIDE

Diagram 9

Diagram No. 9 illustrates almost better than words my thoughts on proper trim of jib and main. There is no point in repeating here the problems involved in jib trim, except to add the obvious fact that jibs require harder trimming in a strong breeze than in a light air. A heavy wind puts more tension on both material and sheets, resulting in more stretch in both; consequently the amount of linear trim for a light breeze would prove inadequate when the wind is blowing hard. Actual experience in many different types of boats leads me to believe that, my suggestion and diagrams to the contrary, it is almost impossible to get a jib too flat in a very hard breeze. Under such conditions, even though the jib "looks" into the main (i.e., the leech takes such a shape and curve that the dead air gives the appearance of blowing into and backwinding the mainsail) keep the jib extremely flat, for its value as a balancing medium more than offsets its aerodynamic disadvantages. The mainsail at such a time should be eased somewhat, thus freeing its leech, reducing the tendency toward weather helm and further enhancing the balancing aspect of the flat jib.

Genoa jibs or overlapping jibs are a slightly different breed of cat. It is my firm belief that it's almost impossible to trim a genoa too flat in anything but a drift. However, the leads of a genoa are quite critical and they must be adjusted with extreme care. The break in the luff should appear, as on a working jib, somewhere above the mitre line, and in the natural order of things the leech should follow the apparent curve of the mainsail in that neighborhood. In other words, the leads should be such that the leech of the genoa and the belly of the mainsail form a slot whose width is more or less the same throughout its length. On larger boats with spreaders, don't be afraid to trim the genoa right into the spreaders. If chafe and wear take place, have the sailmaker add little patches to take care of it, just as you sew larger patches in the area where the jenny rubs against the shrouds and turnbuckles.

Stretchy-Luff Jibs

Since the Second Edition was published thirteen years ago, the character and construction of jibs—both working and genoa—has changed somewhat. What has come to be known as the stretchy-luff jib has become very popular and is used with great success on a vast majority of the "hot" racing boats, large and small.

The stretchy-luff jib is just what it sounds like—a jib with a luff that can be pulled and elongated in accordance with the strength of the wind. As the wind increases, you crank up on the halyard, or, in some cases, down on a Cunningham hole (see

Page 88). This has the general effect of pulling the draft in the sail forward as the wind picks up.

The luff wire in these sails (or at least as the construction is done at Ratsey & Lapthorn, according to my good friend George Colin Ratsey), is replaced by a twisted Dacron line of suitable diameter—say a three-eighths-inch line for boats about 40-feet overall, maybe a half-inch for larger boats. The jib is hoisted and the "scallops" cranked out of it. Sail it a bit and see how it looks —if the draft is too far aft, crank a bit more, and *more* as the breeze picks up. ONE WORD OF CAUTION: Make sure that there is a "DANGER MARK" (i.e., a red nail-polish mark or a marline seizing OR BOTH—where the splice of the halyard starts going into the masthead sheave.) DON'T, FOR THE LOVE O' PETE, LET SOME EAGER-BEAVER CRANK ABOVE THIS DANGER MARK—or you may end up with no halyard. As a corollary to this "danger mark," René Coudert, one of *Palawan's* several foredeck impressarios, always put a second mark on the jib halyards with corresponding marks (in different colored marking pencils and/or tape) that indicated how far you hoisted the halyard for winds of various strengths. No guesswork here; it was cut-and-dried.

In other cases, jibs are fitted with a Cunningham hole some-where near the tack, depending on the size of the jib. Generally, in this case, the jib is fitted with a wire luff and extra reinforcing material along the luff. The luff wire is set up according to your own taste, and by means of a tackle or a wire lead from the Cunningham hole to the deck (or even through the deck) and is then hauled or slacked to get the most efficient draft.

May I point out that this stretchy-luff system is used on only the largest genoas, the #1 jennies which come in two weights, in normal practice. The #2, 3 and 4, being somewhat smaller, are obviously designed for heavier weather and their draft is so de-signed or cut into the sail in the very beginning.

Leech Strings

Leech strings, in my humble opinion, are absolutely essential on all Dacron headsails and mainsails, and on jibs a foot-string is advisable at least on genoas, though not on heavier "double-head-rig" sails. Most sailmakers put 'em in, but if they don't, I strongly urge you to specify them. Leech strings have to be adjusted ac-

cording to the strength of the wind. In light air you slack 'em off
a bit to prevent a "cupping" of the leech, or a tight leech. You'll
find that as it breezes on, you must take up a bit, an inch or two,
maybe more. There's nothing that drives me up the wall like a
flapping and vibrating leech. May I point out in this connection
that to tie off your leech string, a rolling hitch (see Page 369—
Knots) is far and away the best and most efficient knot. I wish I
had a nickel for every time I have explained and shown this knot
to really able sailors—I'd be *rich*, believe me, and not sitting
down here in the cellar rewriting *The Gospel According to
Knapp*. The rolling hitch won't jam, nor will it slip, but it *CAN*
be worked up *OR* down without being untied.

This might be an appropriate place to mention the worsted or
silk ribbon telltales which are used on jibs (and even on mainsails) in increasing numbers these days. These wool or silk ribbon telltales—roughly a foot or more long, depending on the size
of your boat—are sewn or stuck with tape onto the luff of your
jib approximately eight to eighteen inches in from the luff rope
and spaced strategically up and down the luff of your jib and/or
mainsail. Of course, they must be on both sides of the sails. In
operation they are simplicity itself. If the windward telltales and
the leeward telltales (which are quite easy to see right through
most sails) fly aft in a straight line, you are RIGHT IN THE
GROOVE (and you should be *FLYING*). If the windward ribbons tend to curl up, you are tooooo high, and if the lee flies curl,
you are tooooo low. Sooo, straighten up and fly right!!! Believe
me, dear Reader, they *DO* work—and they are one helluva lot
cheaper to install than a Brookes and Gatehouse set of instruments, about which more later. There was a square window in the
jib (some feet up) of one yacht I recently raced on, so you could
see the red worsted easier through the sail. That's a great idea, but
you've got to be very, very careful of that flexible window in
putting the jib away—too frequent bending will wreck it.

When tacking, never slack a genoa sheet—nor a working jib
sheet for that matter—until the boat is head-to-wind and the sail
goes aback. In the first place, you reduce slatting. In the second
place, the genoa will practically "wipe" itself across the mast and
shrouds, thus really giving you much needed assistance in the
tacking maneuver. In the third place, with both genoas and
working jibs, by holding on to the sheet until the last second, as
you swing the bow of your boat up toward the axis of the wind,

you will gain additional drive from the headsail which will help keep your speed up. If you have been in the habit of slacking off your jib sheet—before you swing your bow to tack, try sometime holding the sheet until you are actually head-to-wind, and notice how the jib doesn't even begin to break, much less luff, until you are almost in the eyes of the wind. You are bound to gain additional momentum from this method of tacking, regardless of the type of jib you have.

Teamwork counts in racing with a genoa. Maybe you can muddle through with a haphazard crew when using a smaller working jib, but when it comes to jennys, your gang must know their stuff. The "slacker-offer" should, very carefully, work one or two turns off the winch so that the jib doesn't go out any, and so that he doesn't lose any fingers. He must be sure that the rest of his sheet is neatly laid out, and that no heavy-footed crew members are standing on it. On small boats the genoa will, as a rule, swing itself across the mast, but bigger boats require a "tacking line" of some sort. This is generally a Dacron line tied or snap-shackled into a grommet in a reinforced patch somewhere in the neighborhood of the shrouds. This reinforced patch also helps eliminate chafe against the shrouds, and I might add that similar patches should be applied to the jib in the area where the leech touches the spreaders—also, obviously, to reduce chafe. I'm repeating myself (again) for emphasis. The Dacron line—a reasonably heavy one so that you can get a good grip on it—is led to a snatch block fastened on deck near the jib stay and then aft of the mast ON THE WINDWARD side. At the signal to tack, and as the lee jib sheet is slacked, one or two men pull hard on this tacking line, thereby pulling a large amount of the foot forward, away from the mast. As the boat swings and the jib clears the mast and swings over, they let go the tacking line and—if at all possible—help heave in the new lee sheet. At the first possible opportunity the tacking line should then be passed over to the new windward side to be set for another eventual tack. This operation on *Weatherly* was accomplished by having a husky man down the fore hatch, from where he could pull the tacking line (which led over a special roller on the lip of the hatch) without running the risk of being beheaded by the flailing five-sixteenths-inch wire genoa sheet.

The trimmer with only one turn on his winch trims hand-over-hand as the sail swings over, throwing additional turns on the

winch from time to time as the sail comes in. When he can't pull
hand-over-hand any more, the man on the winch handle takes
over and cranks or pumps as the case may be. If the jib doesn't
come in smartly, the helmsman has to put his tiller over hard to
keep his boat from running up into the wind again, resulting in a
terrific force exerted by the rudder in a direction to slow the
speed of the boat—and on top of that any drive from the jib to
push the boat ahead is completely lacking. How often have you
seen some big cruising boat tack without getting her headsail
sheeted in quickly and watched her wallow and almost stop,
taking what seemed like hours to get moving again. Purely the
result of no teamwork or an improperly trained crew, the fault
for which, of course, lies with the skipper for not giving proper
attention to his variables.

It might be of interest to point out here that the helmsman can
assist the winch-winders immeasurably during a tack by a bit of
attention and some thought. During my four years (1958 through
1961) as Skipper of *Weatherly*, we experimented with our tacking operation. We found that if, after the jib wiped across the
mast and shrouds, *if*, *if* I held the bow steady and didn't fill away
completely, the coffee-grinders were able to get the jib trimmed
and home with dispatch and speed—and, surprisingly, without
any great loss in speed. Just by keeping an eye on the bow and
the jib I was able to make their job quicker and easier. There is,
believe me, a knack to getting a Twelve around and off and running. We must have done some things right, for during those four
years, *Weatherly* won the Hovey Bowl (emblematic of the
Twelve-metre Season's Championship) three times, the Queen's
Cup three times, The Astor Cup, the Clucas Trophy (for the
longest run on the New York Yacht Club Cruise) twice and, in
1961, the Cygnet Cup. (And I quote the NYYC Race Committee:
"For the first time in several years there was one outstanding
performance by a yacht on the Cruise. As a result, the Race
Committee is very pleased to award the Cygnet Cup to the 12-
metre *Weatherly*—a deserving yacht—ably sailed and manned.")

Why I was so stupid as to write "a memorandum," hurt the
feelings of that fine yachtsman, Henry D. Mercer, and, in the last
analysis, *lose* the Captaincy of *Weatherly*, I'll never know—a
perfect DUMBKOFF. And yet, Bus Mosbacher later proved that
Weatherly was a GREAT 12-metre, successfully defending the
America's Cup in 1962. To Bus—and his crew—again go my

heartfelt congratulations. It has taken me many years to get over that BONER, but I am over it now, thank YOU!

To trim mainsails so that they look right, two points which I think many skippers overlook, ignore or are not acquainted with, should be emphasized. The first is the behavior of or course taken by the boom as it is sheeted in the last little bit; and the second is the resulting effect of such final trim on the leech of the sail. It makes no difference what form of main sheet leads you use, the general effect is the same. To illustrate the first point see Diagram 10.

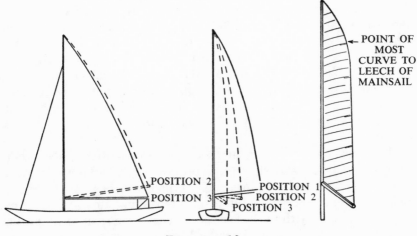

Diagram 10

As the boom is trimmed, say from a reaching position to that for a beat, it swings in on a plane which is more or less parallel to the deck of the boat. But when it reaches a certain point which is rather hard to describe in so many words, it changes its plane of direction and dips down. (See Positions 1, 2 and 3.) While somewhat exaggerated in order to make the point clear, in Position 3 the boom has dipped at quite a sharp angle, almost a right angle. Try it some time and see that as you trim, your boom comes in and then suddenly seems to change direction and drop toward the deck. The effect of this dip is my second point, i.e., the boom drops and tightens the leech. If the drop is too great, the result is a very tight leech, and possibly even more weather helm. Aerodynamically it is bad, for it traps dead air in the mainsail and retards the new air with a resultant reduction in the speed of your boat. The reason for this effect is that the main sheet can no longer pull the boom *in*, and any further hauling on the sheet tends only to pull the boom *down*. My suggestions for efficiently trimming a mainsail are these: Watch the boom and the leech of the mainsail as the sail comes in and stop trimming when the boom starts to drop and the leech starts to become too straight a line.

The leech should not be pulled too tight. It should, as in the case of the jib, have a bit of curve in it. In tall narrow mainsails the greatest depth of this curve (which is quite easy to see if you will look up from the end of the boom or even from where you are sitting at the tiller) should come somewhere in the area of the top and second battens—say the upper third of the sail. Variations in the strength of wind, just as with the jib, will alter the tension on both sheets and material and will require corrective adjustments on the main sheet. Trial and error will tell you how great this curve should be, some boats demanding more than others, and different wind velocities calling for tighter or looser leeches.

It might be interesting at this point to mention three other items or gadgets and show how proper trim is attained by and interrelated to them. Cam cleats, vernier winches and the bent mast all contribute their bit to accomplishing this job of trimming your sails with nicely curved leeches. The bent mast on the wind, of course, helps to free the leech of your mainsail, and at the same time gives you the flatter sail more suitable to windward work. The cam cleats and vernier or worm-gear winches permit quick and accurate trimming of sails, absolutely no lost motion or wasted time. For example, cam cleats and winches on both ends of *Bumble Bee*'s jib and main sheets insured fast, positive action. The jib leads were so critical that the head of the jib reacted immediately to changes in the wind's intensity. Since I steered on the leeside with one eye on the luff and leech of the jib, one hand on the handle of the lee jib winch and the other on the tiller, the jib always got its required constant attention.

TELLTALES

Telltales on the shrouds are an extremely important and absolutely necessary supplement to the masthead fly. Their tremendous value in racing is in direct opposite proportion to their size. How you can race a boat successfully without telltales I do not know. The masthead fly is so useful and beneficial that Chapter VI is devoted entirely to it. Telltales are equally helpful and should be rigged almost before the first Spring sail is undertaken. Many varied types are to be had, ribbon, worsted, thread, and even balanced feathers or metal flys. My own choice is worsted, any kind or color of knitting wool yarn, for it is readily available, easy to see, steadier than most other materials, and long lasting. Even when wet, it is so light that the slightest zephyr will waft it out. A nylon knitting yarn might prove superior, for nylon absorbs very little moisture and dries quickly. George D. Emmons of Kennebunkport, Maine, advisor to *Weatherly* in '58 and her navigator in '59, devised an excellent type of telltale from "gals'" nylon stockings by cutting the stocking in a strip about 14 inches long and tapering from a couple of inches wide to a very narrow end. These make most excellent and helpful telltales, so tell your lovely playmates not to toss out their worn-out hose. Save 'em for a very useful purpose! They—the telltales—are fastened to the shroud with a small piece of the afore-mentioned Kenyon tape.

Two telltales should be rigged on each outer shroud at whatever desired height. Fasten them on the rigging far enough apart so that they won't wrap together, and have them just long enough to be seen easily. Tie a couple on the permanent backstay or regular backstays, where they'll be useful running downwind. Glance at your telltales frequently and get used to them. They'll show you, within reasonable limits, what the wind variations are and once you are familiar with their vagaries and fluctuations you'll have a wonderful indication of the flaws in the wind. You'll know when to luff and when to bear away, almost before the luff of your sails tells you.

There are, to be sure, some limitations to the value of telltales on the shrouds. They are not, for example, as true an indication of the apparent wind as the masthead fly, but in their sphere can be used to greater advantage. The masthead fly, being in clearer air, will be less subject to surface influences or deflections caused by rigging and sails. But you are apt to pick up a crick in your neck if you bob your head up and down between the masthead fly and the luff of your sail when beating to windward. Telltales are generally rigged in the same general plane as the area of your mainsail which luffs first or the most frequently. Furthermore they are in the general plane of your view ahead. You can take a quick look at them or see them out of the corner of your eye.

In actual practice they should make certain definite angles with the mainsail, depending on your course and the wind. I can't describe to you what these angles are or should be, but I will promise you that once you have become accustomed to tell-tales in the rigging you will find that they are a tremendous help. To my way of thinking, a racing boat is no more complete without telltales than it would be without its rudder. That goes for anything from a dink to a J boat, too.

Kenny Watts, expert sailmaker of Torrance, California, together with his electrically inclined associate, Wally Broce, some years ago came out with a gadget he calls a WIND GUIDE. It is an electrically operated "gismo" with a very light wind vane at the masthead which operates, by means of selsyns (Do YOU know what selsyns are? I don't!) and six wires coming down the mast to a "slave" needle on a dial in the cockpit. The slave needle repeats the wind heading of the vane at the mast truck and gives you a reasonably accurate, though bouncy, reading of your apparent wind at the masthead. Guest Products followed soon after with a similar gadget and several other outfits are producing them today—many of them having also been transistorized in the interest of saving "juice" aboard ship. They are a fine thing, I feel, and we had two dials on *Weatherly*, one for the helmsman (as if, God help him, he didn't have enough to watch already) and one for the spinnaker trimmer, the second one being installed just inside the forepeak hatch where he could see it.

Tom Watson's *Palawan* was equipped with all the Brookes & Gatehouse, Inc., equipment available and necessary—namely: an anenometer; a Wind Guide (360 degrees around); an expanded Scale Wind Guide (45 degrees only on either side), which gives you a wider and more accurate needle for use on the wind; an electric device with a needle which can be set on your desired compass course—and any deviation or variance from this desired compass course registers "left" or "right"; a speedomoter in knots; plus another dial (the sixth and last), which had an adjustable needle that could be set straight upright—at twelve o'clock—by means of a knob, and which showed you, from then on, whether your speed increased or decreased. All these were set in a housing just forward of the companionway hatch, within readable distance of the helmsman—truly a helmsman's dream!!! And then some guy up in the bow would yell: "Hey, Knapp, you're high!" or words to that effect. All you had to do was to get used to this panel and then steer quick.

A Bendix Fathometer—with a repeater over the Navigator's Table—plus a Konel Radio Telephone, a Bendix self-steerer (these last two were, of course, never used when racing) and a large Constellation Compass, with a red compass light and rheostat, completed *Palawan*'s navigational equipment. With a skeg and large rudder aft, she steered with no trouble at all and is a beautifully balanced yacht under all conditions.

There are a number of other manufacturers of these navigational racing instruments, such as Kenyon, Omni, Cygnet, and E.M.I. of Buffalo. And, lest we overlook it, let me remind you of what is known as "The Poor Man's Wind Guide," a simple yet effective gadget for the truck of your mast, consisting of two wires sticking out at an angle of about 45 degrees, with a balanced wind vane above to show the apparent wind. The two wires poking out at (roughly) 45 degrees aft, may be bent or adjusted to whatever angle the individual skipper desires. Then, when on the wind, he can look up and adjust his course accordingly. For my part, I find this gadget, though simple and dirt cheap, rather tough on my neck. Looking up to the top of the mast is not only neck-breaking but also distracting as far as other factors are concerned. Later on, I will reverse my field on this deal, 'cause you ABSOLUTELY MUST HAVE A MASTHEAD FLY—electronic or otherwise—to trim your spinnaker pole efficiently (see Chapter VII on SPINNAKERS). Soooo, like a woman, I can and will change my mind, for as they say, that's a woman's prerogative.

CHAPTER IV

Paraffin, Lubriplate, Oil and Grease

Oh! Knappy with his oil can, put in many hours of toil.
There's not a spot on Ranger *he hasn't tried to oil.*
But now he's exercising, it's himself that needs the oil,
As Ranger *sails along.*

The above doggerel, composed by Gertrude Vanderbilt, charming and energetic wife of the skipper of *Ranger*, and the only member of the opposite sex ever to race on an America's Cup Defender, was one of several verses composed about the afterguard of that fast yacht and sung to the tune of "The Battle Hymn of the Republic." It just about covers a self-appointed task aboard *Ranger* which I felt extremely important. (The exercising was brought on by the habit of Skipper Mike arising full of vim and vigor about 0800 every morning, and collaring Rod Stephens and me to do setting-up exercises with him. Olin Stephens and Zenas Bliss were too smart for that, they slept late. Rod and I finally *got smart*, rose earlier, ate breakfast, and left the mothership *Vara* to go aboard *Ranger* before Mike caught us.)

The oiling job, however, I did with a will. Nothing escaped me, and many were the moans which went up from the crew when a drop or two of oil inadvertently landed on the Port Orford cedar deck. There were no squeaks or groans in the hull itself, or I think I would have attempted to oil them, too. Nevertheless, nothing squeaked, winches clicked contentedly, sheaves turned smoothly and noiselessly, snap shackles opened without being cursed at, and the spinnaker pole slides on the foresides of the mast could be cranked up and down without undue strain and effort even with the 18,000-square-foot spinnaker pulling great guns. (This was the world's largest sail.) There were, to be sure, occasional black spots of oil on the big DuPont Cordura quadrilateral jib and on the genoa jib where they wiped across the mast, but no one could say that the mechanical gear on *Ranger* did not work easily, quietly and properly for lack of oil.

Early in my youth on my Star boat, *Southern Cross*, I discovered to my chagrin and dismay that jib hanks or jib snap hooks should *NOT* be oiled or greased. The jib hanks worked fine, but the jib was a mess the next time I took it out of the bag. Moral: NEVER, NEVER OIL JIB HANKS OR JIB SNAP HOOKS. They can be polished, if all the polish is removed, or buffed or rubbed with a bit of emery cloth, but never oiled. They and all tracks are about the only things on a boat, however, which should not be oiled. I can even remember using Vaseline years ago on the bottom of a boat, an idea something akin I guess to the old pot-blacking of many years ago. It seemed to make the boat go faster then, but I am not so sure now.

Rod Stephens and I do not agree at all on this question of oiling jib hanks. In fact he even feels that metal sail tracks should be given a touch of Vaseline in order to make a mainsail slide up or down easier in a hard blow. He says that he always oils the hanks on his jibs, being very careful, of course, to wipe off ALL excess oil, so that he'll have no trouble and waste no time in changing headsails when required. He says further that the mainsail on his N.Y.Y.C.-32 *Mustang* will always come down on the run when he lets go the main halyard, no matter how hard it's blowing.

Personally I feel it is much better to clean and/or polish the sail track before stepping the mast as outlined in the chapter on Tuning and I would never put Vaseline on a track except on a very large boat where the sail slides can be easily removed from the mainsail. I sadly fear that the grease would get on my sails, just as they would with oiled jib hanks. Rod has showed me pictures to prove that there are no grease marks or stains on *Mustang*'s sails, either jib or main, as a result. However, he cannot sway me from my original position. But since I hold Rod Stephens and his opinions about boats in the greatest esteem, I pass his views on the subject along to you and will let you make up your own minds on the question.

However, now all of you HEAR THIS—nine years afterward, in 1960, I assumed the well-known "woman's prerogative" and changed my mind, namely: *I now agree with Rod that ALL* *hanks and slides SHOULD be oiled and/or greased.** Experience over the years now makes me believe that Rod is right and I was wrong, absolutely wrong. Sails do go up and down or on and off much easier and quicker when things are well oiled. JUST BE SURE TO WIPE OFF THE EXCESS, HOWEVER.

A block of paraffin, a can of heavy body oil (also known as electric motor oil, SAE-20), a tube of LUBRIPLATE—No. 105-white—the stuff they use in outboard motors in the underwater gears, plus a can of waterproof grease are the NUMBER ONE items on my list of required and necessary equipment on "ye compleat racing boat." They are so important that I feel they are deserving of separate sections devoted to an explanation of their uses and high priority.

PARAFFIN

A half block of paraffin, the kind your mother used to use to seal jelly glasses in the summer, is almost indispensable with the modern grooved spars. Rub a bit on the bolt rope and tabling near the headboard and clew of your mainsail. Do it often and notice how easily the sail will run up the groove. Rub a bit into the groove itself and notice the difference in the way the sail runs freely up the mast or out on the boom. Chafe and wear on the tabling will be reduced to a minimum, thus prolonging the life and shape of your favorite main. Suppose you are in a hurry to change a mainsail before the start of a race when a sudden shift of wind or a change in intensity indicates such action necessary. Isn't it better and more efficient to have a sail that runs freely in the groove? Can't you save valuable time in the sail-changing maneuver? Use a bit of paraffin. Suppose you get caught in a bad squall and want to get your sails down, and down in a hurry. Paraffin will prevent the bolt rope from jamming, the sails will come down easier and your boat will ride it out to race another day.

OIL

A thirty-five cent can of oil, heavy body or electric motor oil (SAE-20), possibly the least expensive item on your boat, may make the difference between winning and losing a Champion-

---

* In 1973 I still agree—oil 'em and grease 'em, but wipe off the excess CAREFULLY!

ship. There are very few mechanical things which will not work better with a drop or two of oil. They will work better, work easier and work quicker. A jammed spinnaker pole end fitting may spell disaster on a jibe. A spinnaker sheet snap shackle which won't open may delay the taking-in of your spinnaker at the end of a leeward leg. Many places can be lost, and are lost, in every race this way. Who gets blamed? The crew—for being awkward and clumsy. But who is actually to blame? The skipper —for not having a can of oil to ease up that snap shackle.

Sheets will run through blocks easier if the sheaves are well oiled, and kept well oiled. A squeaky block will tell your competitor every time you trim your sheet, besides being annoying to those on your own boat. I can't think of anything more nervewracking on a quiet, calm and peaceful day than the squeak and squeal of a dry sheave. Nothing can be more upsetting to the nerves or more distracting to the concentration of the skipper than the moan and groan of a dry block.

Cam cleats—or gate cleats if you prefer that name—are of a simple and positive design and they'll work beautifully if properly cared for. Proper care is very simple, just a drop of oil once in a while and take them off in the Fall for a check on the condition of the springs. Winches will work easier and more regularly with the same treatment—a drop of oil occasionally; and take them apart in the Fall for a look-see at the springs.

The masthead sheave should be given a careful treatment before the mast is stepped with a touch of heavy oil and a spot of waterproof grease besides. And it won't hurt to work a few drops into the spinnaker and jib halyard sheaves.

Ordinary light oil will wash off rather quickly and require more frequent use. Frank Bissell, able skipper of the Bermuda Racer, beautiful clipper-bowed yawl *Burma*, suggested to me some years ago that a *heavy body* oil available at most stores would prove more durable and lasting. Experience has proven him correct and we've used it ever since. Occasionally it has been hard to find, since not all stores do carry it, but diligence will be rewarded, for the heavier oil will last longer around salt water. It is also known as Electric Motor Oil (SAE-20).

There are several other silicone-based sprays available, but one of the best, either afloat or at home is called "IT"—and I heartily recommend it. A couple of years ago, I sprayed the drawers and runners of a very heavy sideboard in our dining room with "IT."

Nary a problem since. For sheaves, snatch blocks and other hard-to-get-at places, "IT" comes with a little tube about four inches long which can be inserted in the "squeeze-cap" and, by golly, *IT*'ll get into any nook or cranny—no pun intended!

Grease or Lubriplate

A can of waterproof grease, also known as waterpump grease, will be found useful too. Lubriplate, which can be bought gray or white in color, is the stuff they use in outboards, and it is indeed a great boon to yachtsmen—easy to use, very effective and highly waterproof, it has almost replaced the ordinary pump grease as far as we are concerned. Your bilge pump, winches, and stuffing box (if any) will all work better and give longer and more efficient service with a touch of this all-important item. Turnbuckles will remain free-turning and unfrozen with an application of waterproof grease, but the surplus on the outside should be carefully wiped off after the rigging is finally adjusted. And the fine easy adjustment necessary for a nice-looking luff on your mainsail can be accomplished by dabbing a bit of grease inside the gooseneck slide. The rudder can be made to swing more easily, sensitively and quietly by working a touch of grease into the rudder post. On 110s, 210s and Stars, waterproof grease can be used in place of white lead—and with less mess—to insure a tight fit of the keel bolts.

Weatherly and *Columbia* were both outfitted with new aluminum drum #6 winches by Guest Products Corp. They were very light, very strong and also very quiet winches (because of rollers pawls being used instead of ratchets). Having rather intricate works inside, they required constant attention—so on *Weatherly* Pete duPont IV was delegated to take charge and Lubriplate them regularly—one each day—and there were six aboard. It wasn't long before Pete had his cute blonde wife, Elise, helping him, and they developed quite an ingenious yet simple system to insure the pawls and bearings—two dozen long stainless-steel rods in each winch—from going overboard. They cut a round hole, just the size of the base of the winches in a cardboard beer box, put it over the winch and went to work. Nothing could fall out or overboard! Elise usually ended up with a spot of the aforementioned Lubriplate on her cute little nose, but they did a thorough job and we never had one single bit of trouble with our fancy winches.

So get yourself some paraffin, a can of heavy body oil, Lubriplate, silicone spray and a can of waterproof grease. Use them freely and use them often and let's not hear any more boats squealing and squeaking their way round the course. Naturally, where unpainted decks, such as teak or clear pine and cedar are concerned, care must be used in applying oil and any surplus should be wiped off before it drips on deck. Just remember that there isn't anything mechanical on a racing boat that won't work better and give better service if oiled or greased, including a stopwatch. The stopwatches are hardly a thing for the average skipper to monkey with, but they should be given a yearly check-up by your jeweler. Infinitesimal details, silly little things, you may think or say to yourself. Yes, they are; but they are part and parcel of the thousand and one little details which when taken together will help you, will make you win boat races.

CHAPTER V

Sails

Sails—their selection, their care, and their use—are problems which confuse even the experts. How can you blame the novice if he is befuddled by the riddle of sails, when even two experienced skippers cannot always agree on what is a good sail, or when it should be used? Experience over the years will help you to select what you think is an excellent sail, only to find that after a series of races some other sail which doesn't *look* as fast, is actually the better sail, the sail which wins races consistently. What is a good sail? What makes a sail fast? I am quick to admit that at times I don't know. Furthermore, I am willing to bet my bottom dollar that many other skippers don't know either.

Starting with Manfred Curry and his YACHT RACING—THE AERO-DYNAMICS OF SAILS AND RACING TACTICS (my bible as a youth), I have read many authors of yachting and racing books who have given their opinions as to the optimum shape, size and appearance of the perfect sail. "Bird's wing," "airplane wing," "airfoil," "vacuum," "drive," "flow" and "camber" are all phrases used to define or explain their ideas on sails. Theoretically, among other things, the draft should be close to the mast, and the roach (curve of the leech) should be ample to give proper shape and large area. All very well and good—but can you tell me why it is that an old sail with the draft way aft and no roach will win races consistently? I confess that I don't know, but I have seen it happen with regularity in many one-design classes (which I think is the ultimate test of a sail).

Time and time again, some skipper will come up with some old "rag" barely suitable for a winter cover and clean up consistently. Mind you, I don't say *I'd* rather have an old sail to win races with, for like everyone else I like and hope to be able to buy new sails. But I do say that very frequently you may find in your inventory an older sail which will help you win many races. Maybe you don't even need that new suit of sails, though I am sure I may run the risk of having the sailmakers heap coals of fire upon my head for so suggesting.

We all need new sails from time to time, just as a woman needs a complete new Easter outfit just to feel right and look right. A boat feels better, goes better, and looks better with a new suit of sails. But look through your sails, try them out (preferably in a preseason race which doesn't count) and see if perhaps you aren't able to discover a good one. For example, when *Kenboy*, Sound Inter-Club One-Design, owned by the late M. O. Griffiths, won the Class Championship in 1933, our latest suit of sails was dated 1929. We just didn't have any sails which weren't at least four years old. *Bumble Bee*, which won her Class Championship as well as the All Season Trophy in 1944, had Prescott Wilson sails all dated 1941 or earlier—though I will admit the 1941 sails had seen very little use—and we still used that 1941 mainsail frequently as a heavy weather sail in 1953!

Ranger, successful Defender of the America's Cup in 1937, winner of 32 races out of 34 completed that season, used Ratsey mainsails which were hand-me-downs from *Enterprise* in 1930, and had been used also on *Rainbow* in 1934 and 1936. *Ranger's* No. 1 mainsail, her best all-weather mainsail, used in three of the four 1937 Cup Races, was sailed 87 different times in four seasons. Another 1930 mainsail, an excellent heavy-weather mainsail, flatter than the No. 1, was pieced out and made larger by adding several cloths at the tack. These cloths, which can be seen in some pictures of *Ranger* because of their different color, were so deftly added that they altered the shape and cut of the sail not one bit: truly a wonderful example of what well-cut and well-cared-for sails can do.

In 1952 I had the good fortune to "rediscover" a 1947 Prescott Wilson mainsail on my Frostbite dinghy, *Agony*. It worked such wonders in comparison with four newer sails, also by Wilson, that I used it regularly to turn the trick. Corny Shields had a 1937 Wilson mainsail on his International One-Design, *Aileen*, which he used with great success in every strong easterly on Long Island Sound for fourteen years, winning many races with it and always placing well up. Unhappily it finally gave up the ghost.

My point is that while it is nice to have new sails, don't give up hope because you don't have them or can't buy them. If you have given your sails good care, if they had an inherent good shape to begin with, you can pull them here or haul them there and they can be made to do a good job. In other words you yourself can alter the shape of your mainsail by pulling a bit more or less on the luff or the foot, by stretching the tabling of the leech, by bending the top of the mast more or less, or by using battens of various thicknesses. Cunningham holes in the foot and luff can also be of great help in improving the shape of your sails, both jib and main—assuming, naturally, that they are legal and permitted in *your* particular class (see Page 88).

Jibs cannot so easily be pulled here and there into a different shape, but hand stretching of the foot or leech may help, and you will be amazed what a good bath in fresh water—*cold*, not hot or warm—will do for the shape of any sail, jib, mainsail or spinnaker.

Salt water is the one thing which will do more to destroy the shape and remove the "drive" than any other cause I know. Have you ever noticed how awful a jib looks when it is rehoisted after lying on deck during a spinnaker leg in a heavy breeze with seas breaking over it? It looks as though it wouldn't even make a decent sack for potatoes; but a thorough washing in fresh water and a careful, complete drying will bring back its shape. The same goes for the foot of a mainsail soaked by salt spray. The water will harden and stiffen the area of the foot which has been wet, while the rest of the sail remains dry and unchanged. The results should be obvious. Furthermore, if the salt is not removed, even though the sail is thoroughly dried, the salt will pick up water on the next damp day, and the sail will again change shape.

I wish to emphasize this point about the disastrous effect of salt water very strongly. (It hardly seems necessary to mention that salt left in a sail will eventually rot it and hasten the end of its usefulness.) It is amazing to me that so many sailors don't seem to realize the many benefits which they will derive from frequently washing, hosing, or tubbing their sails, cotton or synthetics. Time and again I have seen jibs and mainsails which were hard, stiff and completely out of shape. A thorough washing out restored their shape and apparently their elasticity and "life" as well. By washing, I do not mean soap and water either, just plain water. Sailmakers will do the soap and water job for you if you feel it necessary, but my experience has been that plain fresh water and lots of it will do a bang-up, even better job for you. If the sail is small, put it in a tub and rinse it several times. A big sail should be spread on a clean thick lawn and hosed on both sides. Finished? OK, do it again, or until you think the salt is completely out. Hang the sail over a line carefully, or hoist it on your boat if it's not blowing hard. Slatting about in a hard breeze will not do a sail, wet or dry, any good, merely causing undue chafe and wear to both the material and stitching, so pick your weather carefully. This is especially true of synthetic sails—probably more so. The stitching in a cotton sail melds or sinks into the material, or at least part of it does, so there is some protection against chafe and wear. However, synthetics are hard and smooth. The stitiching is also hard and smooth. IT DOES NOT SINK INTO or meld into the synthetic material; it just lies on the surface and does not, you might say, become part of the material. Therefore, synthetics are much more subject to chafe and general wear and tear because the stitching, lying on the surface, has almost no protection from chafe, and it even has a tendency to slide back and forth which obviously causes even more chafe. On this score it is more important to examine the stitching on your synthetic sails quite regularly to see if it has worn. If it has, "middle-stitching" will help solve the problem and prolong the life of the sail. By middle-stitching I mean have the sailmaker run another line of stitching down between the double line of stitches.

Racing sails should never be hoisted without battens, for the leech will not stand properly nor take its normal position, thus causing the material to be pulled out of shape.

Whatever happens, don't let anyone tell you a synthetic sail does NOT need washing in fresh water. They most emphatically do. They'll pick up salt, become harsh and brittle and even somewhat out of shape, just as cotton will. The one advantage is that washing will NOT shrink a synthetic sail. Nor does rain or wetness seem to hurt them. In fact, they thrive on wetness.

On *Peggywee*, a Star boat, in 1930, Newell P. Weed and I had a suit of sails made of an extremely light Egyptian duck, much lighter than the usual Star sail. In a year and a half we used those sails exactly three times, winning each time. We used them only when we were certain it wasn't going to rain and there was very

little chance of a strong breeze. On one occasion we did get
caught in a smoky sou'wester and did that jib and main look
awful! Fortunately, no permanent damage was done. And that
sail *must* have been a tough one, for in 1954, twenty-four years
later, I was at the Rochester Yacht Club giving a lecture and I
met the young man who then owned *Peggywee*. He took me out
and showed me the boat—a most welcome sight to my senti-
mental eyes—and a bag of sails marked "Burrows-1930," Burrows
being the name Pres Wilson was operating under at that time.
We took the sails out of the bag and, right there, in my own
awful printing (no mistaking *that*) were the words "very very
light 1930" in all three corners of the sail. In line with the flexible
Star rig adopted after these sails were made, the luff had had a
tapered piece of material added to make it bigger and draftier,
but there was no question but what it was the very suit of sails
we'd used in 1930. In 1958, the owner gave me this 1930 jib and
main. I show them off proudly at any lecture I give—even NOW!

On another occasion we were caught by a late afternoon
thunderstorm in *Bumble Bee* with a brand new suit of sails and
no extra suit aboard to substitute. We dropped out rather than
risk getting the new sails wet, with the result that we lost sixteen
points for that race and lost the series by half a point. Since that
day, *Bumble Bee* never started out for a race without two complete suits of sails aboard, a practice which I strongly recommend if you are not too weight-minded. We frequently have
changed jibs on a leeward leg when one jib became wet or
seemed less suitable for the next leg. As a result of this policy of
using new sails sparingly and having two complete suits of sails
aboard, we have in several cases raced our newest sails for almost
two full seasons before they received their first real wetting.

When and How to Use New Sails
Year: 1951

New cotton sails invariably tantalize and fascinate the average
skipper, leading him down the road to Temptation. He just can't
bear to think of those beautiful new "duds" just sitting there in
their sail bags, unused. The Song of the Sirens rings in his ears,
he tumbles, says to himself, "It isn't going to rain or blow today
(I hope)" and bends on his brand new finery. What happens? It
pours. Temptation has lured him, not exactly to his doom, but far
enough so that he has lost a certain amount of area from shrink-

age (shrinkage which will never come back) and an infinitesimal amount of zip from his newest equipment. To many skippers new sails are like a coin burning a hole in the pocket of a small boy. Neither can wait to use the sails or spend the money.

How many times novices have come to me with the question: "I've sailed my new main and jib about seven hours just reaching back and forth; do you think it's OK to race them today?" The weather? Oh! it's blowing maybe twenty-five. I try and explain to them that they won't really do any better with the new sails, that old ones will be just as satisfactory, and that they'll be better off in the long run to save their new gear for a later drier less windy day.

Perhaps late in the season when the points are close and a Championship is at stake, it is wise to be bolder. Then you are justified in trying to get everything you can out of any of your gear. You actually won't hurt your new sails very much, but you will do some small harm to them. And it's those small, those little things, all added up, which go toward making your boat a winner. They don't seem important in themselves, but taken together they spell Victory. In point of fact, I can't prove to you that a rain or a very strong wind will do any permanent harm to new (cotton) sails, but experience over a period of years leads me to believe that I am correct.

The above three paragraphs were written in 1951 before the general use of synthetics. By and large, I feel that the new synthetics, too, should be treated with a certain amount of respect and given a fair shake in breaking in. However, I will repeat that rain and dampness do NOT seem to hurt synthetics—they seem at times even to be better because of a spot of rain. I will also repeat, and probably will do so later in the book too, that ANY sail will be better for having a good fresh-water bath and removing the salt from it.

To this is should be added that while cotton will have a tendency to shrink a bit from a bath, the opposite is true of synthetics—THEY TEND TO GET BIGGER AND STRETCH WITH A FRESH-WATER BATH. George Moffat, expert skipper of the International 14-footer, *Dorade*, and the IC dink, *Satyr*, (Bob Coulson wants to know how you can get a "gal" to crew in a boat named *Satyr*?) is the authority for the thought that the ideal way to shrink a synthetic sail is to spread it over a (clean) black car in the bright sunlight, or, in the case of a large syn-

thetic sail, on the lawn in the bright sunlight. So just in case you
have a sail which is an inch or two oversize, (as in the case of a
Lightning or Star sail) keep this little gem of incidental intelligence in mind.

On the other hand there are those who feel that continuous
exposure to bright sunlight—or ANY sunlight, for that matter—
can damage synthetic materials. My good friend Jack Potter—
that gregarious and energetic Owner and Skipper of the 68-foot
ketch, *Equation*, the oversize dinghy of the ocean-racing Fleet—
takes ALL his sails off the spars every night. No sail covers for
Jack—he stows 'em all below in the dark regions of his fast
"bucket." He reasons that the ultraviolet rays from the sun can
penetrate even through sail covers and harm his Dacron sails. A
minor point, to be sure, but well worth thinking about. I had the
honor and pleasure of racing with Jack aboard *Equation* in the
Lipton Races off Miami, Florida, in 1971, 1972 and 1973. She is a
lovely steering yacht, fast upwind or downwind and we did quite
well in Class—but not in Fleet—all three years.

"Breaking In"

Stretch new sails enough to produce a good shape, so that they
are smooth and so that you get out most of the wrinkles. Even
though you race with them—untried, so to speak—if you do it in
light air, the stitching and the material have ample opportunity
to adjust themselves without undue strain or pull. On the face of
it, it would seem obvious that you would be foolish to dash out to
your boat for a race with a new suit of sails that you haven't even
looked at or tried out. But having satisfied yourself that you don't
have a "clunker" with hard spots through it, I see no reason not
to race your new sails when the wind and weather are propitious.

Hard spots are bumps, lumps or waves which show up when a
sail is bent on and sailed. They don't often show up in the loft
and they will sometimes work themselves out. They may appear
all the way across a sail or only part way and are caused by a
variety of reasons. Crooked spars, bent track, sloppy, careless, or
inept workmanship, and poor design are mainly responsible.
Hard spots very often develop when a sail is wet or full of salt,
but these will vanish when the sail is washed and dried. Time
and stretching will often eliminate a minor fault, but generally
speaking reroping will be required.

An unroped sail lying on the floor of the loft is curved on all three edges, the maximum curvature being in the leech—(i.e., the roach). To rope the sail, it is stretched flat on the floor and spiked at the corners and at intervals all along the luff and foot. The rope is then stretched tight around the outside of the spikes, after which both sail and rope are marked with a red pencil at intervals of, say, six inches. Both sail and rope are lifted off the floor and turned over to a sailmaker who, sitting on a time-honored sailmaker's bench, begins the roping process.

Here is where the possibility of error creeps in and here is where a hard spot may find its beginning, for the two marks in each six inch interval must coincide exactly or the sail when hoisted will not be smooth. The tension on the bolt rope having been released, the rope has shrunk somewhat and gone back to its original length. In effect what the sailmaker does is to sew six inches of sail to approximately five inches of rope. For the needle of the really experienced sailmaker this is no problem and his marks meet on schedule, but careless workmanship can cause variations. Maybe the bolt rope itself is of poor quality and will stretch unevenly, throwing askew the best sailmaker's efforts.

Poor design and too much roach (which some over-eager skipper demanded and the too-anxious-to-please sailmaker attempted to supply) are often contributing factors when hard spots are found. Sometimes they'll disappear, but more often recutting is necessary. Experience seems to show that it is best to attempt to work a hard spot out before going through a recutting job. It is my confirmed belief that the less monkeying you do with sewing, roping and shape of a sail the better off you will be in the long run. There are naturally times when such work is unavoidable, but be deliberate and careful about it if possible. As I have already suggested, a lot can be done with a sail by stretching or slacking it on the foot or hoist, or by stretching the leech, or by different battens (later in chapter).

Lest there be some confusion, let me make it quite clear that the above paragraphs on breaking in sails are equally good for cottons or synthetics. In point of fact, I feel that you can do more in shaping a synthetic (than a cotton) by pulling and hauling here or easing a bit there. There is not as much actual stretch to a synthetic, but you sure can do lots with the shape of a synthetic mainsail by maybe pulling a little more (or less) on the luff and/or the foot.

One modern improvement of this mechanical age that I think

is perfectly wonderful is the zipper. Ted Hood of Marblehead, who made us some marvelous sails for *Weatherly*, put a large zipper along the foot of the mainsail for the 5.5 *Quest*, owned by the Sewickley Syndicate and skippered by your author. The zipper, starting at nothing at the clew and tack, had a fair curve in the middle with an arc of about six or seven inches. Zipped up it flattened the foot of the main, and eased out it made a nice, full, light-weather sail. Ratsey & Lapthorn have done the same thing with many of their mainsails. It is quite a gadget and it works. But one word of caution, DO *NOT* TRY TO "ZIP" UP THE ZIPPER WHEN YOU ARE CLOSEHAULED ON THE WIND. YOU'LL TEAR THE ZIPPER OFF THE SAIL. It can be readily unzipped, but you *must luff or ease the main* to relieve the strain before zipping up.

Stencil Sail Bags

All sail bags and sails should be stenciled with the name of the boat, racing insignia, racing number, and number of the sail itself. For the latter, the best and easiest system seems to be to number them chronologically as you buy them. Inexpensive but adequate stenciling equipment can be bought at most any stationery store, but be sure to buy the kind with large letters (at least 1½ inches). Put the lettering on both sides of the bag and down low, so that it can be easily seen when the drawstring is pulled and tied around the neck of the bag. The actual job of doing a stencil is easy. Be neat about it, however, and don't get too much ink on your brush or stipple. The few minutes it takes to properly mark all your sails and bags (and even other equipment, especially slickers) will be repaid a thousand times over. For example, bags will be easily identifiable, so short tempers resulting from lost bags or trying to find some unnumbered sail will be eliminated. The right sails will be aboard when you want them, and should any be mislaid or misplaced they will find their way home quicker and easier. A neat wrinkle on the market is a pencil called a MAGIC MARKER which comes in a variety of colors. Shaped like a fat firecracker, about three inches long and an inch in diameter, it is simple to use, doesn't run or stain and dries quickly. It costs under a dollar, and has a number of other practical uses about a boat. Its fiber or material wick is angled at about 45 degrees, so that you can mark a bag or anything with narrow or wide lettering, just as you choose. Mighty handy to have around the home or office, too.

Some skippers number their sails by marking them and their bags with the year purchased. This system is fine in that it tells you the age of the sail, and the year may be of particular significance to you as skipper of that boat. However, it also tells your competitors what year's sail you are using or have used if he sees it lying around the launch, dock or porch. In addition, if two sails are purchased in one year (a rather rare occurrence in these days of high taxes) some sort of extra numbering or lettering is required. It may be considered by some as unsportsmanlike or selfish to attempt to hide the vintage of your sail from the other competitors, but I do not agree with this argument at all. Your sails and equipment are entirely your own business and I see no valid reason for advertising what you plan to use if you don't care to. Therefore, the system of numbering bags 1, 2, 3 in chronological order makes the most sense to my way of thinking.

The number should also appear somewhere on the sail, so that there can be no confusion in bagging loose sails. As a matter of fact, on *Bumble Bee*, though we used this system of numbering, the actual year of purchase was familiar to most of the crew, and was therefore in the back of everyone's mind, though we might call a certain sail by its number in the chronological sequence system. But whatever system you may decide to use, get your bags marked with the name and number of your boat and some sort of identification for each sail, and make the markings large enough so that they can be easily seen. I can't think of anything more embarrassing or annoying then discovering you've left your best suit of sails in a club launch or that someone else has your sails because the bags looked alike. A minor point to be sure, assuming that you are able to get your hands on your own sails before the race starts, but nevertheless one of the many minor points the sum total of which will help you win boat races.

The BO and IC Frostbite dinghy classes have worked out a simple but effective system for identifying sails. The Class Measurer upon approval of each sail stamps it with a stencil with a string of three or four numbers in it. The first two numbers indicate the number of the boat and last one (or two) the chronological number of the sail. Under these numbers appear two other stenciled numbers indicating the year purchased. For example, the stencil $\frac{201}{48}$ appearing on the tack of a sail would indicate it was racing number 20, the first sail purchased for the boat, and that it was purchased in 1948. Using the stenciling system I suggest above the sail bag would be marked with the name of the boat, the numbers 201, and the class insignia—if possible.

Color Coding of Sail Bags

Commodore Arthur J. Wullschleger, of the Larchmont Yacht Club, Skipper of that beautiful 48-foot S&S yawl, *Elske*, on which I raced to Bermuda in 1972, has developed a color-coding system for his various sail bags that is so good, and yet so simple, that I feel compelled to explain it to you. Various colored bands are sewn on each bag, using one color but a different number of bands to identify each type of sail and each individual sail. For example, the lightest spinnaker bag has one red band around it, the next heavier has two red bands, etc. Blue is for genoas—one blue band for the lightest and largest genoa, two blue bands for the next heavier genoa, etc. For his large double-head rig, Arthur uses two yellow bands for the #1 Yankee jib topsail and one yellow band for the big staysail, while the small double-head rig has two black bands for the smaller #2 Yankee jib topsail and one black for the small staysail. The #3 (smallest) jib topsail has three black bands. Such sails as the spinnaker staysail, tallboy (a very tall, narrow staysail, just coming into everyday use, which when properly trimmed—and it *IS* a problem to trim it properly —draws very well), mizzen staysail and so forth are so small and easily identified that their names are printed on the bags in large letters. All these sails have their own proper stowage space underneath the cockpit seats (or below decks) and are readily available. To my way of thinking, it's a fine system, saves time and effort and works very well.

On other boats I've raced on, the same sort of color coding is done for genoa sheets, spinnaker guys and halyards, each being painted or colored with its particular "brand," that correspond to cleats.

Numbers and Insignia

The question of numbers and insignia, I suppose, resolves itself into a question of point of view. On the basis of the old saw "Does Macy tell Gimbel," I have for a number of years attempted to get my sailmaker to put the numbers and insignia in the same general area on my sails using material of the same color, dark blue. (*Bumble Bee*, having a dark blue hull, the blue seemed to be indicated.) Though my friend Stan Ogilvy, in his book SUC-CESSFUL YACHT RACING, takes minor exception to this practice, for the life of me, I can see nothing unethical or unsportsmanlike in it. When competition is as keen as it is in the International One-Designs or the Inter-Club Dinghies (*Agony* has red letters and numbers on all her sails, in case you are interested), I see no earthly reason for advertising to my arch enemies (all of whom I think and hope are my very good friends ashore) which sail I "think" will be the most suitable. I say "think" for you could never tell before—or at least up to ten minutes before the start what the capricious and fickle skipper of *Bumble Bee* would de-cide regarding sails. The vacillations of the skipper and the un-certainty of the wind have been responsible for as many as three sail changes before one start that I can think of. On this question of having similarly shaped numbers and letters in the same ap-proximate area in various mainsails, when *Weatherly* was being built in '58, we had Ratsey make up extra numbers and letters to be used on the mains we ordered from Ted Hood, and had Ratsey measure the placement of them as well. One afternoon young Colin Ratsey (who was racing aboard *Columbia*) came with us on *Weatherly* to check some Ratsey sails. He wasn't sure whose main we had on that day and looked at the shaping of the charac-ters so he could tell. And EVEN Colie didn't know what main we had set. By golly, if you can fool the sailmaker you've made the grade! Incidentally, it was Colie Ratsey who suggested to us dur-ing that summer's campaigning of the Twelves, that it was a smart move to take off the mainsail each night rather than furl it on the boom, the thought being that you approach the next day's sailing with an open mind as to which main to use, and probably more important, you then do not "telegraph" the message to your nearby competitors as to which main you obviously used the previous day.

If I were desirous of knowing which sail any particular skipper had on, I wouldn't hesitate to ask him. I am quite sure that any or all of my particular competitors would answer me, too, and truthfully. By the same token, if any asked me, and they have, I would tell and have told them. Further it has been my custom over the years to offer help and advice gratuitously to those who

have obviously had less or little sailing experience. In most cases
it has been gratefully received and accepted in the sportsmanlike
spirit in which it was offered. On the other hand, it would be
presumptuous of me to offer suggestions or unsolicited advice to
someone like Mike Vanderbilt, Corny Shields, Rod Stephens, Bus
Mosbacher, Bill Luders or countless other experts who have
beaten me regularly, though I've had the pleasure of getting my
licks in against several of them. I think you will find all of them
and most other sailors willing to answer any and all questions put
to them on any particular feature of their boats, gear or ideas on
racing. Certainly in writing a book of this sort, one must lay bare
one's soul, philosophy of sailing and knowledge of racing, or he
won't find many buyers for the fruit of his labors. Believe me,
everything I know is being written here. If you don't find it, I just
don't know it. But let's get back to the subject.

NECKING SAIL BAGS

While it is a matter of small importance, it might be worthwhile to pass along what I feel is good practice in tying up or
closing a sail bag. Many people grab the drawstring, pull it tight,
and throw in an overhand slip knot. Standard practive aboard
Bumble Bee was to grab the drawstring at any point *except the
knot,* pull it tight, and then wrap it as many times as possible
round the neck of the bag as low on the bag as possible, throwing
in a couple of hitches round the neck as you get toward the end
of the line. Doing it in this fashion makes it easier to throw in the
hitches and to untie them. Truly a very simple detail and yet, if
you watch ten sailors neck a sail bag, nine of them will take
hold of the drawstring at the knot. Incidentally, tying up the
neck of the bag this way keeps dirt or dampness completely out
and makes the bag itself easier to grip and carry.

BATTENS

Battens may appear on the surface to be inconsequential items
worthy of little consideration except to be sure you are amply
supplied with them. You should have battens of different weights
or thicknesses. Proper battens can greatly improve a sail. As supplied by all the various sailmakers I know of, they come in one
standard weight, heavy. I suppose that battens, like other more
or less mass-produced items, must be designed and cut to con-
form to certain over-all standards. In other words, battens are

manufactured to stand up well under all conditions. Ergo, make them heavy so they won't break.

Standard battens as supplied are fine for heavy weather. In fact, in extremely heavy weather it's even a good idea to put two battens in one pocket for additional strength. However, for light and medium weather I have found that your mainsail will set better if you plane down the inboard or forward ends almost to wafer thinness. They'll break quicker, a lot quicker, but you'll do better in your racing, so it's worth replacing a few battens, isn't it? If ash, the wood most commonly used for battens, is not available at your local lumberyard, they'll probably be able to supply you with oak which seems to work as well, and they'll probably be able to cut the battens out roughly for you, even plane one end if necessary. Finish them up yourself with various grades of sandpaper and elbow grease. Just a little tip in drilling the holes for the batten ties: drill them carefully and from both sides to prevent splitting the ends; or better still drill them in a short distance from the end of the batten and then saw off the required amount. Most of our battens on *Bumble Bee* had three holes across the end, for some of our mainsails have single ties and some double.

The jib battens need not have the same limberness desirable in mainsail battens, so this discussion does not apply to them. However, save your broken mainsail battens to cut down for jib battens, for you may need extra ones. It has been my unfortunate experience to lose or break many a jib batten. The ties, no matter how carefully or completely you knot them, come loose and the batten flies overboard. If you sew them in, some careless soul steps or sits on the jib bag, and pop, another breaks, requiring the services of the sewing kit. Broken mainsail battens can be an almost unending source for jib batten replacements.

You will notice that I have mentioned ties, as well as holes in the batten ends. The trick closure in the leech of a mainsail dispensing with the tie is *verboten* as far as I am concerned. The offset opening makes it a very quick and easy operation to insert a batten, but it also makes it very quick and easy for the batten to put a "knee" or crease in the sail at the forward end of the batten pocket. The battens in all sails, cruising or racing, jib or mainsail, should not touch the forward end of the pocket. They should clear the ends of the pockets by an inch in small and medium boats and by two inches in larger boats. If the batten is tied to the tabling in the leech of the sail and is shorter than the pocket, there is no chance of putting a "knee," such as you will get in an unpressed pair of trousers, at the inner end of the pocket. If your sail shows signs of "knees," examine the battens and shorten them the required amount.

Automobile-top snaps for batten pockets fit in the same category as the trick closure as far as boats with permanent backstays are concerned. Some time ago a number of International One-Design sails were fitted with these snaps. All but the lower one had to come off, for they caught on the permanent every time you tacked. A cinch to open or snap shut, they sure were a nuisance in tacking. In 1973, 22 years later, I still feel the same way about "slip-in" battens and trick closures. They are still no good for my money and "strictly for the birds," though widely used by many expert sailors. I still like the "tie-in" batten and S.O.P. aboard the various yachts I skipper is the very simple but positive "shoelace" knot, a single bowknot with the other long or standing end of the tie tucked through the single bow and snugged up tight. No problem of flipping out a batten with this knot!

In many classes the Rules limit not the length of the pocket but the length of the batten; hence the pockets can be of sufficient length to prevent "knees." It has been my experience in *Bumble Bee* that a short, limber batten in the top pocket of the mainsail, makes for a better curve in the upper section of the sail, and in my opinion enhances the shape of this part of the sail. The full-length batten causes a sharp break in the shape of the sail, while the short batten holds the roach and yet gives a fairer curve. The thin inner end of the batten, of course, improves the whole situation.

It must be borne in mind that the thin-ended battens can be used only in light to moderate air. Jibing or luffing in a hard breeze will definitely increase the rate of mortality of these tender sticks. Yet they are more than worth the risk, and they pay their way by improving the mainsail. Our inventory included several different grades of thickness of the inner end, so that we are able to select the desired weight for the prevailing strength of wind. Care must be exercised in hoisting and lowering the sail not to catch the backstays in the battens or to have some heavy-footed crew member walk on them.

Fiberglass and plastic battens have come into use in recent

years and those who have tried them tell me that they have proven very satisfactory. The only thought which comes to mind is that if the forward ends were thinned as much as wooden battens can be, they might be brittle and therefore break too easily. Battens on Twelves came in two types. Ratsey used double battens in each pocket tied together at the outer end, i.e. there were two medium-weight battens for each pocket with a lashing holding them together in holes near the leech end. Hood, on the other hand, used a single batten, but much thicker through. Since either set were of virtually the same length, in normal weather we used a single Ratsey batten in the short top pocket, a double Ratsey in the next pocket and a single Hood batten in the bottom pockets. This gave a certain amount of extra curve and spring to the battens in the upper area and kept them stiff and straight in the two lower pockets. On top of this John Nichols of Nichols Yacht Yard in Rye and Mamaroneck, New York, who was a regular on *Weatherly* in '58 and '59, fiberglassed several battens of each group to give us some really tough and sturdy battens, for use in heavy weather.

Size and Shape of Sails

It has always been my aim to get sails just as big as the law or rules will allow and with ample draft. My feeling has been that a sail which just fits the spars is the right size. I don't want it to stretch to the spar limits in a year or so. I want it there right away or after an hour or two of sailing. All the size and area in a sail is there when it leaves the sailmaker's loft. No amount of pulling or hauling will ever make it any bigger. The shape of the sail will change but once you put it on your boat it won't get any larger in area (unless, of course, you add cloth to it).

In point of fact, a cotton sail gets smaller with use. The material shrinks to a certain extent, expecially when it gets wet (an important reason for keeping your newest sails dry as long as possible) and it never stretches back again the full amount. Though you may think the sail is getting bigger as you haul it out on the spars and it eventually gets too long for the spars, necessitating recutting or shortening, this is merely the sail changing shape. It is a gradual and natural shifting of the material itself. As the luff and foot get longer, the roach gets smaller, eventually disappearing altogether, leaving a hollow leech. The weave of the material as it is continually pulled in one direction gives in the other direction and gets smaller in the latter direction. Try it with a handkerchief and you will see what I mean. Pull the handkerchief from two opposite corners and see the other two corners contract toward each other. More or less the same thing happens to your sails and probably quicker, for they are pulled in two different directions.

In the synthetic group, I feel that there is much less tendency for Dacron and Orlon to change their shape very much. Nylon is springier and has more stretch and probably will pull out of shape on the luff and foot if you yank too hard, but it is not too difficult to see when you are pulling Dacron and Orlon too vigorously. (See Diagram 11.)

In order to get a sail as large as possible, it should have as large a roach as possible. Roach, the outward curve of the leech, is generally limited by rules in most classes, but if it isn't limited by rules its maximum girth is limited by the length of battens. In other words, you can't put too much roach into a sail because the

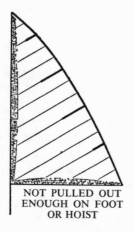

NOT PULLED OUT
ENOUGH ON FOOT
OR HOIST

PULLED TOO FAR
ON BOTH FOOT
AND HOIST

Diagram 11

battens won't be able to support it and the leech just won't stand up, falling off to leeward or breaking to windward. Over the years, enterprising skippers, realizing the importance of ample roach in giving them maximum sail area, have piled so much roach into their sails that most classes have added so-called girth limitations to their sail measurement rules. This is a rather sensible idea, too, for there were some monstrous sails to be seen in some classes and it was well nigh impossible to make the leeches stand under all conditions. While legislation has curbed this excessive roach, nevertheless it is wise to put as much roach into your sail as the law will allow. Since sails are what make your boat move through the water, it is only plain common sense to get the biggest sail you are allowed under your rules. I don't mean to suggest that you cheat by getting an oversize sail, but I do very definitely feel that you are entitled to and should get the largest possible sails permissible. To do that get them with maximum roach and maximum length on the foot and hoist, both jibs and mainsails.

For maximum mainsail area, it is important to have the sail designed so that the boom is at right angles to the mast. In other words the greatest area in a triangle of fixed dimensions is to be found in a right angle triangle. For years, until Pres Wilson finally straightened me out, I felt that a drooping boom, i.e., a boom that sagged down as close to the deck as possible at the clew, was the most desirable because more roach could be cut into the longer leech. He was able at the same time to convince me that the roach in a *right angle triangle* mainsail would actually add more area and add it higher up in the sail where it would do more good. This same idea does not follow for working jibs, except a club-footed jib, because of the construction of the fore triangle which would make it impossible to trim a jib on most boats with a right angle clew. Genoa jibs, being a different breed of cat, do not enter into this question of maximum area.

It is obvious that if you order a suit of sails of maximum dimensions for your racing boat you may eventually run into a certain amount of trouble if they stretch beyond the linear measurements of the spars. Don't worry about the roach, for as I have mentioned above it automatically gets smaller. Don't worry either about jibs, unless there are rules in your class which require remeasuring from time to time. If so, you'll just have to have your jib cut down in size if it has grown too large.

In the case of mainsails, it is entirely possible that before the end of the first season you may be obliged to do some shortening. On the other hand, with due care, it is also possible that your sail will not become oversize. If you will follow the simple rules outlined below there is a fair chance that you won't have to resort to recutting. If you have to shorten the hoist, a "smitch" can be easily nipped off the head of the sail without upsetting its shape.

The tendency of sailmakers of my acquaintance is to cut off too much, so tell them exactly how much you want removed. It is more expensive to do the job twice, to be sure, but be sure also that you keep every square inch of your nice fat maximum sail area. But why not use your Cunningham hole, instead?

For light air, a ring sewn to the tabling of the foot of the mainsail or a grommet in the tabling, about 12 or 18 inches from the tack, can be pulled in toward the tack a certain amount (to be determined by trial and error) and tied with a piece of reef line, stretching the sail from the ring to the clew by means of the outhaul. This serves to throw more draft into the mainsail at the mast. It can almost turn a flat sail into a light-air sail and will most certainly improve it. I have used this idea quite often and successfully on Stars, Sound Inter-Clubs, International One-Designs and even ocean racers. It does work.

Ratsey & Lapthorn work a reinforced hole into the bolt rope (which they call a "Cunningham hole"—after Briggs Cunningham of six-metre and *Columbia* fame) on the luff as well as the foot of many larger cruising mainsails to obtain the same result. This idea is also very helpful where sails have become too long for the spars or have over-stretched on a very dry day. There is a bunching at the tack which is relatively unimportant, but the rest of the sail is given a much better shape than would be the case if the luff and foot could not be properly pulled out.

The above paragraph on Cunningham holes was written in 1951 and I see no reason to alter it or change it in any way— except to emphasize that the Cunningham hole in mainsails and jibs is even more important now than it was twenty-two years ago. With synthetic sails, it is vital to change the shape of your sails as the wind increases or drops. Every sailmaker in the world is using them today and every sailor worth his salt knows how valuable they are. Just as the boom-jack or boom-vang has become a most necessary, helpful and useful gadget, so has the Cunningham hole. The moral?? Don't be without them.

In shortening the foot of a sail many sailmakers prefer to cut the tack back rather than take any off the clew or outer end. Unless you wish to put additional draft in the luff of your sail, it would seem to me better to cut a small slice off the clew, as we have done quite successfully on one or two mainsails on *Bumble Bee*. Shortening at the head or clew of your sail rather than the tack reduces your total area much less and I feel is the better way to do it.

The suggested rules to avoid shortening sails then are as follows, and they apply in part to old sails as well as new sails. Since most jibs have wire luffs, these rules apply primarily to mainsails —however, I repeat, don't let some "Jerque" (French spelling) winch up a jib halyard so far that the mast is hanging on the jib halyard rather than the jibstay. You may say: "But on my boat you are SUPPOSED to hang the mast on the jib luff and jibstay. What about that?" *OK*, in that case the halyard and jib luff are DESIGNED to take the load, but on a vast majority, this is NOT so. Ergo, don't do it!

Now for the rules:

1. Don't feel that it is necessary to pull the bolt ropes an extra half-inch each time you use your sail. Get to KNOW your sails and pull each sail accordingly.
2. WASH your sails frequently, as outlined above.
3. Slack off on everything as soon as you cross the finish line before sailing home—jib halyard, main halyard, outhaul and the permanent backstay. I may overestimate the importance of all of this last rule, but it was standard practice on *Bumble Bee*, *Weatherly* and *Palawan* and, I feel, very helpful in avoiding the recutting of sails.
4. Don't forget or neglect the Cunningham holes. They are of absolutely paramount importance.

RECUTTING

How often you hear some skipper say: "I just sent my sails back to my sailmaker to be recut"? My own feeling is that in nine cases out of ten he is wasting his time and money as well as the sailmaker's time. There are rare occasions when recutting (whatever that means) will improve a sail. Perhaps the sailmaker can remove a hard spot which came from inept or careless sewing in the first place. Other than that, it is my firm opinion that a sailmaker can do little to improve a sail without reducing the area. He can remove the rope from the sail, reshape it, rerope it and return it to the owner (meanwhile hoping and praying it is an improved sail), but at the same time he has removed a certain amount of material that can never be replaced. And here again, in this revised edition, 22 years later, I "ain't" changed my mind! Mess around with recutting a reasonably good sail, brother, and you are inviting trouble with a capital "T."

Area is one of the things which helps make your boat go, so hold on to it. It will make your boat go faster, only a little bit faster maybe, but just enough faster to beat the other fellow across the finish line by inches. That's all you need, a few inches here and a few inches there, to win more races.

REEFING

Just by way of proving that most skippers in smaller racing boats want maximum sail area at all times, have you ever noticed how few recently made sails in the so-called hot classes have any provisions for reefing. Why? They have found them unnecessary and a handicap in their desire to have and to use the greatest possible spread of canvas. To go one step further, it can be said that reef points and grommets would disturb the smooth flow of a mainsail as well as permitting a "leakage" of air. Cruising boats or ocean racers present a different problem because of their powerful hulls and proportionately greater displacement. Smaller racing boats, operating in more or less protected waters, can afford to ease sheets and "lug" sail to windward and then take advantage of the full sail area reaching and running.

In a 1952 overnight race aboard *Mustang*, N.Y.Y.C.-32-footer, owned and skippered by Rod Stephens, it was an eye-opener to see the actual job of tying in a reef done in less than three minutes, while going to windward at that. Early in the morning in a quickly freshening breeze, it was decided that a reef was in order, with the thought in mind that it would ease the motion of the boat without reducing her speed. A *suitably labeled* bag of gear was brought up from below consisting of linen lines of proper length for the tack and clew, and cotton reef line for lacing through grommets. Rod organized the whole deal in such a way that the actual tying in of the reef was accomplished in very short order and with a minimum loss of time and speed. The lanyard at the tack was rove off in such a manner as to allow a quick and proper lashing job there, and with his usual agility Rod climbed out on the end of the boom and rove off the outhaul rig. At that point the topping lift was snugged, the mainsheet eased a bit, the main halyard slacked the required amount. The tack was then securely lashed down and the outhaul lanyard hauled out, snugged and lashed 'round the boom. Following this, other members of the crew quickly tied in the reef points. The whole job from the time we slacked the main halyard until it was winched up again (with an accompanying luff) and the mainsail sheeted in, was less than three minutes! Truly a smartly executed reefing maneuver. I am sure that most of us who have spent our lives racing around triangular courses would have a tough time trying to tie down a reef in twice the time.

It would be helpful here to point out that for any offshore racing, Rod always carries loops of nylon fish line (messenger lines) through the leech cringles of the two reefs in his mainsail. When a reef is called for, the outhaul rig, a five-eighths Dacron line, which is "pointed"—i.e., has a point and loop at one end through which the nylon fish line is secured—and then the outhaul line is run up through the reef cringle, down to the boom through a pre-measured and pre-fitted cheek block, forward to a winch on the side of the boom near the mast. After the other end of this line is fastened around the boom by means of a CLOVE HITCH, topped off with a single half hitch to prevent slippage. The outhaul is then winched down to its proper position and the "round-the-boom" short line is lashed around the boom and/or through the clew cringle to secure the whole deal. Truly a seamanlike and fast maneuver—and it is used by many ocean racers who prefer reef points to roller reefing or the new "pre-installed" or prefabricated reefing systems.

Bob Bavier, in his "From the Cockpit" column in the October 1972 *Yachting*, came up with an article on "Jiffy Reefing," that I think bears some discussion. With the permission of *Yachting* and Bob, I'd like to point out a few of the essential details, for in many ways, it is practically the same as Rod's method, but Bob has added a few refinements—which you may or may not agree with, but they sound good to me.

First, Bob has added stainless-steel hooks, two of 'em, welded on either side of the gooseneck, onto which you fasten the cringle of the first (and on the other side, the second) reef. Cheek blocks and pad-eyes on the boom, appropriately placed, pull the clew cringle down to where it should be, by means of a reefing line taken to a good-sized winch on the mast. This leaves you with a bit of a mess of loose sail, which you lash down in due course with three-eighths-inch Dacron line through oversized reef points, the thought being that the larger line is easier to handle.

According to Bob, the end results are far better and faster than any roller-reefing gear—and on these two points I'm inclined to agree. It's difficult to get a really *good* reef with roller-reefing gear, and it always seems to me that rolling a reef in takes an interminable length of time.

Lowell North of San Diego has another type of reef, which he terms a "wire reef," and uses on boats up to 40 feet. A wire cable, about three-sixteenths of an inch, is put into a sleeve which follows a circular arc (up) into the sail, of about an 8-inch curve. When the tack and clew are fastened down, this wire cable is tightened by means of a winch and it supports the sail in between—without any reef points.

Medium and Heavy Weather Sails

I have never felt that it was worthwhile to purchase a heavy weather sail deliberately. On one occasion, with the new Frostbite Inter-Club dinghy *Agony,* I did get two different sails—one a big full sail, and the other flat and slightly small. I won't say that the flat, small sail was a complete failure, but it never has been what I would term a really successful racing sail. Perhaps it was because when it is blowing hard enough to make a small sail go fast, dinghy racing is generally cancelled as a safety measure. On the other hand, even in racing larger one-design craft, I can't recall any small sail that was exceptionally outstanding. There have been many times, of course, when a small sail has done well in a continuously hard breeze, but frequently a drop in wind velocity will leave the fellow carrying cut-down or small sails somewhere out in left field.

The answer would seem to be that the small boat racer, who is generally whipping about a triangular course with runs and reaches as well as a beat, figures that he can lug his large sail area on the windward leg and then use it to advantage on the run and reach. That certainly is my point of view—the result, if I may be permitted to hazard a guess, of early unhappy experiences with small or reefed sails. I will go on record, anyhow, as feeling that way; and state that I always prefer my sails to be up to size for triangular racing. Beating to Bermuda through the Gulf Stream with a whistling wind from south-southwest will alter my view-point quickly, I will admit, but that is a horse of another color and a horse of a different size, too.

As to the shape of sails for a medium or hard breeze, it follows

that the harder the breeze the flatter should be the curve or draft
of the sails. With the modern tall rig and its intricate panels of
stays, the problem of eliminating unwanted draft is not insurmountable. Even the simply stayed rig in a dinghy (headstay and
two shrouds) can be utilized to produce a curved spar and a
flatter sail as has been explained in the chapter on Tuning. In
other words, excess draft in a mainsail can be limited to a degree
if desired. The boom-jack, too, can be used to flatten your mainsail, for if it is properly set up and hardened down, it will have
the general effect of bending your boom down in the middle—
with a resultant decrease of draft in the foot of the main (see
Chapter VIII).

Jibs, in my opinion, do not cause any particular worry, for as
you trim your jib more in a harder breeze, the draft tends to go
out of it. The problem here is that if you continually use a jib in
hard breezes, it will eventually lose all its draft and become flat.
As a precaution, then, it is advisable to keep one (or more, if you
have ample) for light air. It is not easy to change to a second
mainsail in a race, but it can be done and has been done. It
should be available in case you want it, or in case you rip the one
you are using.

For many years I have been a great believer in material as
light as possible for light-weather sails: for example, the extra-
light material in one suit of *Peggywee*'s sails mentioned earlier in
this chapter. Sails made of such light material can only be used
on rare occasions and tend to run up the cost of boat racing
frightfully. Though I think they are great for special occasions
and purposes, I feel that extremely light-weight material for sails
in one-design classes should be frowned upon. They give a definite advantage to the chap with the fattest wallet, for they are
not practical as all-purpose sails. For international or rule-class
racing, where winning is the only goal and expense is no object, I
say get all the super light-weight mainsails and jibs necessary;
but for local or intersectional one-design friendly competition,
there should be a minimum limit on the weight of material allow-
able. However, it is fair and reasonable to say that, in general,
synthetic materials can be a bit lighter in weight than the corresponding weight of cotton. Your sailmaker is the best authority
on this. Be guided by what he thinks.

May I point out that in 1958 *Weatherly*'s mainsails were made
of 12-ounce Dacron—one was even 14-ounce and two of 10-

ounce. The heaviest mainsail *Intrepid* had in the America's Cup
in 1970 was of 7-ounce Dacron, material woven by Ted Hood and
his Father on their antique but excellent machines at their Marblehead, Massachusetts, sail loft. The weaving and heat-applica-
tion process has been improved, "natch," but it just "shows-to-go-
you" how synthetic materials have been improved, and also how
tough, rough and rugged they are. As previously stated, modern
Dacron sailcloth is so strong and powerful that it can tear the rig
out of your yacht if the rig isn't properly designed to *take* the
additional stress and strain.

ONE-DESIGN SAILS

One-design sails are an even more sensible idea for purely one-
design class racing, if I may be permitted to wander even farther
afield for a moment. There are, I admit, disadvantages and insurmountable ones in large, widely scattered one-design classes as
far as this one-design sail idea is concerned, but in certain compact groups the principle is a good one. If you have one-design
boats why not go a step further and have one-design sails? Corny
Shields worked very hard and did a splendid job in putting over
this one-design principle in the Class B One-Design Dinghies in
1937 and the International One-Design Class (Long Island
Sound Fleet) in 1939. Four or five (I can't recall the exact number) groups of sails were bought by each of the classes over a
period of years (not necessarily consecutive years) and allocated
by drawing lots. In each particular group so ordered, there was
very little difference in the sails. As between groups of sails, there
also were very few great differences, though it is my opinion that
the 1937 Ratsey dinghy sails were outstanding, a few of them still
being used 20 years later on B One-Design and Inter-Club One-
Design Dinks. On *Bumble Bee* we used our four one-design
mainsails and two of our one-design jibs in our regular racing
inventory.

The War, of course, disrupted the buying of new sails. Faulty
material in the first batch after the War turned a number of the
International One-Design Class skippers against the one-design
sail principle and it was voted out much against the wishes of
Corny and myself. During the period of the one-design sails,
probably 70 or 80 suits of sails were delivered in the four or more
groups. It is my opinion that, with the exception of three or four
suits delivered after the war which were not quite right, all the

sails were reasonably similar. Since all sails were assigned by lot, each skipper took his chances on what he received. Many skippers in the Class were of the opinion that they could improve their sails and their standings for the season by going to different sailmakers. It might be interesting to note that the results later were not dissimilar from the results of the racing under the one-design sail system. Corny and I stuck with the one-design sailmaker, and many of the dissidents came back to the fold, too. It is my firm conviction that one-design sails have a definite place in really one-design class racing. Restrictions on sails, hull and rig must be tight—extremely tight—in order to get truly one-design racing. That's why the Etchells-22 and the Shields Classes have prospered so well. There are rumors flying around to the effect that the Etchells-22 may eventually become an Olympic Class, primarily due to its tight Rules, as well as racing ability.

Many of our currently popular one-design classes have been ruined by loose regulations and loopholes in the rules which allow early boats to be outbuilt and outmoded. For example, in some classes there are either no regulations, or insufficient ones, dealing with spars or standing rigging, while other classes permit fancy and expensive construction with extremely light-weight planking. To me this completely ruins a one-design class, for it means that the fellows with the most money can outbuild the rest of the class. This sort of thing is fine in a "rule class," but it has no place in one-design classes. This is merely my opinion, of course, and I am sure that there are many who will argue the point with me, yet it is my feeling about one-design racing. On the other hand, since there are loopholes in any regulations, technically speaking, a smart skipper cannot be greatly criticized for being alert and taking advantage of them. Such is the general pattern of Life itself, is it not? Such, too, I suppose, is the idea behind this book, to suggest to you ways to make your boat go faster, though I hope and pray in a truly sportsmanlike manner.

The problem at hand is the choice of sails, other than new ones, for medium and hard breezes. I have already said that I do not believe in frequent recutting of sails, except in cases where they are too long for the spars, which is not recutting at all, but shortening, or except in cases where hard spots develop. It has been my experience that sails as they are used tend to flatten out, therefore if you use a chronological system for numbering your sails and use all your sails more or less regularly, you should,

after a period of time, end up with a series of graduated sails for
different weather conditions where your newest sails are for light
weather and your oldest sails are for heavy weather. Someone
will bring up the very sensible question "Why use your oldest
sails for the heaviest weather? Won't they have a greater tendency to blow out or rip?" They will have a greater tendency to
blow out, of course, and the individual skipper will have to decide for himself when his sails have reached the retirement age. I
wouldn't care to help a man decide whether his old sail would
last another race, but I will tell him that if he has cared for it
properly, washed it in fresh water frequently, and maybe had it
"middle-stitched," it will last a lot longer than one which has not
had these things done. Obviously there are exceptions to every
rule, and it is impossible to lay down a formula which will cover
everyone's sails; but by and large it seems to me that a simple,
reasonable way to select a given sail for certain weather conditions is on an age basis. If your equipment is of standard size and
weight, as ours was on *Bumble Bee*, this system works very well.
In actual practice, weather conditions being what they are on
Long Island Sound, we often could not decide among three
mainsails and two jibs which ones we would eventually want
(and even then we often changed our alleged minds), so we took
them all, eventually dumping the third mainsail off on some ac-
commodating power boat. Where equipment is of different
weights or sizes, a different formula for selection must be worked
out.

Synthetic Materials

There is not much question but that synthetic sails are here to
stay. When this book was first written 22 years ago, synthetics
were just beginning to be experimented with and to be used. No
one quite knew which material, nylon, Dacron or Orlon, was the
best. And since nylon was, shall we say, the "oldest," it was used
most often. Nylon was good, no question about it, and it seemed
to do better and be better in many respects than cotton. For
example, wet weather did not bother it. It didn't shrink like cotton; on the contrary, it stretched a bit. However, by very nature,
nylon is elastic and stretchy. And in a mainsail or jib this did
have disadvantages. For spinnakers and other very light sails,
this did not make any particular difference, and in many ways
was helpful. The net result is that practically every spinnaker

today is made of nylon, a very tightly woven, light—yet strong
—material which, if you hold a patch to your mouth, you cannot
even blow through.

Dacron, and to a lesser extent Orlon, have taken the place of
cotton and nylon in mainsails and jibs. Dacron, very strong,
smooth and slippery makes a beautiful sail and will take lots of
abuse. It is used, I would guess, almost 100 percent for mainsails
and jibs in medium to large boats and has proven itself eminently
satisfactory. It holds its shape well, and if its weight is correct to
begin with—in other words, not too light for the job—it will not
distort even in the hardest breezes. The luff and foot, as stated
earlier, can be pulled and hauled or eased to make a beautifully
shaped sail for the prevailing strength of wind. And here the
Cunningham holes can be used *most* effectively.

Orlon has been my great love over the past few years in the
smaller boats and for the life of me I cannot figure out why, in
general, it has become more or less unavailable. For some unac-
countable reason, you just can't seem to get it; the manufacturers
just aren't making it. You tell me why, I can't find out. To me it is
a fine, strong and extremely fast material for sails. It has a slip-
pier finish than Dacron, more like an oilcloth finish; and I think
that (laugh at me if you will) the breezes slide over it easier—
less resistance because of the glossy shiny finish. My first Orlon
was made by Ratsey in 1953 for my one-design Inter-Club Class
dinghy *Agony,* and it was an instant success (i.e., Ratsey received a rush of orders for similar sails). My 1954 Ratsey Orlon
was, in 1970, my best light-weather sail, even after 16 years. My
1956 and 1957 Orlons are still good in moderate to strong breezes.
All of these were of so-called 3½-ounce material. In 1958, no
more Orlon was to be had, except in 5-ounce weight, so most of
us ordered a Ratsey dinghy sail in Dacron. Glen Foster in his
Ordeal had good success with his Dacron that winter, but, although the sails theoretically were the same, and indeed looked
the same, I couldn't make my boat go "for sour apples" whenever
I used it. The answer was simple: DON'T USE IT! And I haven't
used it very often. In '59 I ordered a 5-ounce Orlon, obviously
heavier than my first four, but it goes well in a hard breeze and
holds its shape very well. Ergo, I use it for hard breezes and go
back to the '54 3½-ounce Orlon in light air. Just to remind you,
too, these sails get dunked regularly in fresh water, as mentioned
heretofore, and take my word for it, you can see and feel the

difference in the sails and the race results. DON'T NEGLECT
TO WASH 'EM OUT!

In 1960 Ted Hood made up some 3.2 Orlon and several of us at
Larchmont bought sails from him. Mine, although I didn't care
for it at first, principally because I don't think I gave the sail a
fair chance, has turned out very well and won me quite a few
races in medium, moderate and heavy air.

In 1970 I was able to "glom" onto the last piece of 3½-ounce
Orlon in this world. I had the good fortune to acquire it from my
good friend and shipmate Kenny Watts, of Torrance, California.
Jack Sutphen, of Ratsey & Lapthorn, was anxious to try a new
design they'd developed on my Inter-Club dinghy, *Agony*. It is a
great sail and goes fast. In fact, it has replaced that ancient 1954
Ratsey Orlon mentioned above. But think about it—that Orlon
sail was 16 years old and still won its share of races.

To me, therefore, Orlon is ideal for small boats, say, up to a
Star boat or a 210, but beyond these I think that, with its
"chintzy" or oilcloth finish it is undoubtedly too hard to flake, furl
or stow. This chintzy finish will crack and fracture if you furl it
too often in the same manner, or just stuff it in a bag. It must be
flaked down carefully and rolled up lightly and NEVER, NEVER
sat upon or crushed down in the bag. Matter of fact, I feel that
both of these two fabrics, Dacron or Orlon, should be treated
with a fair amount of care, discretion and good common sense.
They are not like cotton or nylon which can be beaten, crushed,
twisted or even flogged, with no apparent damage. So treat them
gently. And one word of caution: BE MOST CAREFUL OF
SMOKING AROUND A SYNTHETIC SAIL! YOU SURE CAN
BURN ONE HELLUVA HOLE IN 'EM WITH VERY LITTLE
EFFORT. I KNOW! I'VE DONE IT! One very simple, easy and
lazy way to whip the end of a Dacron line or sheet is to *carefully*
hold it over a flame until the ends soften up and melt together.
But again, BE CAREFUL—'cause it can burn beautifully!

Conclusions on Sails

In concluding this discussion about sails, cotton or synthetic, I
should like to offer several suggestions which will help and improve your equipment.

1. Stretch cotton sails according to strength of breeze, and
   dampness or dryness. Do not pull them too hard on a damp

day or a light day. Dampness, however, does *not* hurt synthetics.

2. Always slack off foot and luff when cotton sails get wet.
3. Never stretch the luff and foot hard when you go out to race. Wait until just before your start. Always slack off luff and foot immediately on finishing.
4. Remember that you can alter the shape of your mainsail by pulling more or less on the hoist and/or luff, and by stretching the tabling on the leech, as well as by heavy or light battens, and finally by bending the mast more or less. This is equally true of cottons *or* synthetics.
5. Don't neglect the Cunningham holes. If you "ain't" got 'em, put 'em in. And USE THEM!

CHAPTER VI

The Masthead Fly

The masthead fly, wind sock, or nighthawk, to my way of thinking, is one of the most indispensable items related to successful yacht racing, and in most cases the most neglected. Take a look at your competitors the next time you are racing and check those who have some sort of wind-direction indicator at the masthead. You may be surprised to see how few are in use in most classes. Larger racing boats and cruising boats generally carry a sock or club flag at the masthead, but an unusually small number of racing boats are to be found which avail themselves of this important detail. Why? I can think of no reason unless it is sheer laziness or lack of knowledge of its great importance and assistance.

The masthead fly is indispensable as an indicator of the apparent wind (telltales on the shrouds will also show the apparent wind, but they are apt to be influenced, to a degree, by mast and sails and hence are not always accurate). What is a definition of apparent wind? True wind? The true wind is the wind as it blows across the water—or land—at your boat. Theoretically, it is a steady wind, blowing from the same direction at the same speed. Actually, as we know full well, this is not so, for both the direction and strength vary all the time; but for the purposes of this definition let us assume it is steady. The apparent wind is the deflected wind caused by the motion of your boat against or across the true wind. Its strength and direction may be found by laying out a parallelogram of forces, one of whose sides is the strength and direction of the true wind, and the other of whose sides is the speed and direction of your boat, as in the diagram below. The true wind of seven knots is indicated by the line AB, while the speed of three knots and direction of the boat is indicated by the line BC. The resultant, the vector, BD shows the direction of the apparent wind and its speed, about 9 knots.

After a 1952 talk before the Junior Racing Class of a prominent Long Island Sound yacht club, I was told by a friend that I had been nicknamed "The Man with the Masthead Fly." I had spent considerable time in emphasizing to the kids the reasons I felt the masthead fly was so valuable and absolutely essential. I am sure that a rash of metal or plastic pennants quickly appeared on boats belonging to those youngsters!

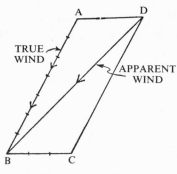

Diagram 12

There are many types of masthead fly available. On larger yachts and cruising boats, the flying of club flags and private signals is not proper etiquette during a race (in fact, it is now strictly forbidden by the rules of the North American Yacht Racing Union, except on a 2-masted yacht), so a nighthawk or windsock is generally flown from the mainmast. All are flown on a staff and are fastened to the staff by means of a light wire gadget so that they will revolve freely about the staff. On *Ranger*, America's Cup Defender, it was found, after Rod Stephens was hoisted several times to the top of the foretriangle in a bos'un's chair and then shinnied the last 30 feet up to clear the fouled nighthawk, that a light stiffening wire in the nighthawk itself would make it stand out better and prevent it from fouling on itself or the staff. In recent years these socks have been made of nylon and therefore are lighter and more durable. Many recent cruising boats have been fitted with a masthead light which makes it possible to see the masthead fly at night, to my way of thinking one of the greatest boons to the overnight racer ever dreamed up.

On smaller racing boats, etiquette or not, the masthead fly can be, and generally is, permanently fixed at the top of the mast. It should be small and it should be light, to avoid excessive weight and windage aloft. It should be small so that your competitor cannot see it too well and thereby derive any comfort, joy or satisfaction from it. Yet it should be big enough so that it can be easily seen from the cockpit or foredeck. It can be made of metal or plastic on a light bronze or aluminum rod or staff, and *must be*

painted a solid color. Since these flies are generally balanced on
the foreside with an adjustable weight, care should be taken
each spring, if the fly is repainted, to see that it is in proper
balance. At the same time a drop or two of oil will do no harm.

Columbia in '58 had a rather *large* rectangular blue nylon pennant with a stiffening wire in it for a masthead fly and it was
permanently mounted up there. She flew it all summer until after
the Final Trials, when *Vim* pointed out to them that it had been
more of a help to *Vim* than it had to *Columbia* because of its size.
Down it came in a hurry.

On *Weatherly*, we tried to avoid a masthead fly or sock and
used only the little vane of the Kenny Watts Wind Guide. This
vane was painted red, and, though small, was reasonably easy to
see from on deck, or read from the repeating dials in the cockpit
or in the forepeak hatch. The hoisting of the usual wind sock was
literally and really "murder" to the Wind Guide's weather vane,
for, though the vane was located way aft on the "crane" at the
masthead, the motion of the boat invariably knocked the aluminum staff of the wind sock into the vane before the halyard was
properly secured and, that, of course, bent the very dickens out
of the very light and tender vane. Our thought behind all this
minute wind vane was to be able to see it ourselves but for our
competitors not to see it too.

Now, in 1973, with all the complicated "spinach" at the truck
of the mainmast of large yachts—namely anemometers, wind
guides and/or permanent masthead flies—it is virtually impossible to fly a club burgee without wrecking any or all of that gear.
The suggestion was recently made that the Rules of Etiquette be
altered to permit the flying of the burgee from the starboard
spreader.

For small boats, Owen P. (Jim) Merrill, sailor and sailmaker,
of Merrill Sails, 423 Burlington Avenue, Delanco, New Jersey,
08075—a new address from my last Edition—developed a very
fine light masthead fly of two $\frac{3}{16}$-inch-wooden rods, the cross-
piece of which has a feather in the after end; it is balanced on the
first (upright) rod by means of a pin. It doesn't weigh much and
I've used one from time to time on my dinghy—very successfully,
I might add.

It is interesting to note here that Dick Rose, Princeton '60, who
writes for the "Racing Clinic" in *Yachting*, had an article on Page
34 of the November 1972 issue, in which he described this fly and

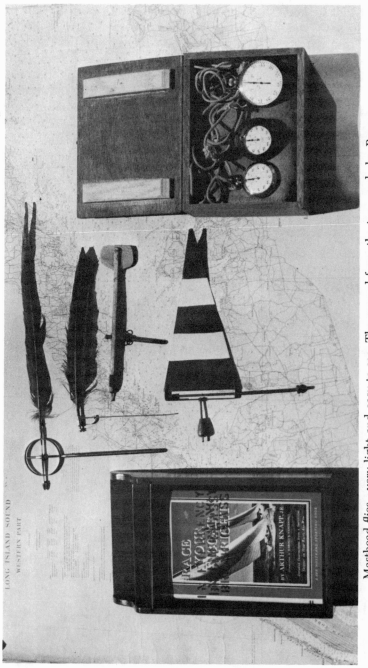

Masthead flies—very light and easy to see. The second from the top, made by Burrows Morley of Saginaw, Michigan, weighs 1¼ ounces. The one of balsa wood was made by Dan Strohmeier for a dinghy. Masthead flies must be of a solid color—no private signals or club burgees. Three types of yachting timers, with reversed figures to provide time left to gun, are shown in the box in which they live. Vic Romagna secretly installed the box with book aboard *Weatherly*. The unbreakable Lucite reads: IN EMERGENCY BREAK GLASS.

the fact that he had "shortened the wooden staff by about half its length to save weight." With Dick's permission, as well as the Editors' of *Yachting*, I have quoted him above; but I'm frank to say that I wrote and told him I thought he was going a bit overboard in shortening a little piece of wood which could only weigh half an ounce—and besides, I myself feel that it is better and wiser to have the longer staff to get away from wind currents about the truck of the mast. Dick is a perfectionist, and a very fine sailor, and a nice guy, and a lot smarter than I am, but I cannot agree with him that weight-saving of this amount is worthwhile—even if you add up the sum total of all of 'em. His column in *Yachting*, however, is very worthwhile reading and most instructive.

Buzz Morley of 1 Center Woods, Saginaw, Michigan, made the best light fly I've ever seen. It weighs ¼ of an ounce, yes, that's correct, ¼ of an ounce. It's made of a pheasant feather stuck into a light fitting of metal that can be balanced by means of two little lock nuts, and this combo swings by means of another very light piece of metal on a steel rod no bigger than a pencil lead—and not a fat pencil lead either. Really a terrifically light gadget, effective, simple and easily readjusted when a new feather is required. You certainly don't add any weight aloft when you use this, and I've been very happy with one on my dinghy *Agony* for some years.

Dan Strohmeier, ocean and dinghy racer par-excellence, has made several highly efficient masthead flies out of comparatively bulky pieces of balsa wood—and by bulky I mean somewhere between ¼ and ⅜ of an inch thick—strong enough and yet extremely light and easily balanced.

There is only one other principal disadvantage to the masthead fly. It makes it a bit simpler for your competitor to tell— either from his fly or yours, or both—whether he is cutting your wind. However, what is sauce for the goose is sauce for the gander, and the fly will help you to avoid this situation.

The real advantages of the masthead fly are so numerous that I cannot understand why more racing boats are not equipped with them. As far as I am concerned, it is indispensable for the proper trim of a spinnaker and spinnaker pole. And it is equally helpful to a boat which does not carry a spinnaker. Being higher than anything else it will generally indicate, before 'most anything else, the first zephyr of a new breeze. I say here "will generally indicate before 'most anything else" since a new breeze usually, though not always, is seen at a distance on the water before it strikes in. It occasionally indicates a wind which is a few feet up off the water and which may not hit the lower areas of the sails at all, giving to the lower areas an appearance of luffing.

In 1952 at Marblehead, in International One-Designs, we were fortunate enough to ghost by the leading boat and win a race ONLY BECAUSE WE HAD A MASTHEAD FLY. An exasperating southerly kept coming in very lightly and then backing off. Our masthead fly indicated an apparent beam wind. The telltales on the shrouds and a luff in the lower part of the sails indicated a head wind. As the southerly backed off, the leading boat, thinking it was headed, bore off. Our fly was still across the boat and we held our course, gradually and very, very slowly pulling up on the leader and finally (after about fifteen minutes of concentrated sailing at a snail's pace) passing him. Not once did our competitor look up at our masthead. The lower part of our sails was all aback, but the small upper section did the trick, and all because of the masthead fly.

For the proper trim of sails on a reach, particularly on bigger boats, the fly is extremely helpful. With a bit of practice the proper angle of incidence of the fly to the sails can be quickly and efficiently determined and the sails adjusted accordingly. *On the wind* in a normal breeze, I find it easier and more convenient, though just as efficient, to use the telltales on the shrouds, and the luff of the jib, to determine the most advantageous course to steer. Even here I frequently glance aloft to check any variation. And don't forget the "Poor Man's Wind Guide" mentioned earlier. On a run, as will be explained later in the chapter on Spinnakers, the masthead fly is absolutely essential to the proper and most efficient angle of trim of the spinnaker pole. The pole must be adjusted so that it is at right angles to the masthead fly. It should be hauled aft until it is just square to the masthead fly and no more, and it should be adjusted frequently as the wind changes. If there is to be any allowance or error in this angle of trim it should be on the forward side. In other words, the pole should be trimmed too far forward rather than too far aft. This rule of thumb for the angle of trim of the pole gets the spinnaker further away from the main (in a fore-and-aft direction) and yet provides the greatest unblanketed area of the spinnaker to be presented to the wind. The latter part of this statement can be more readily understood if you'll picture the spinnaker pole at right angles to the apparent wind as being the greatest possible distance that you can get the tack of the spinnaker (and therefore all the available area of spinnaker) away from the blanketing effect of the mainsail.

The masthead fly, as stated earlier in this chapter, can be used to your advantage to determine whether you are on a competitor's wind—just as he can use it to your disadvantage in determining if he is on your wind. A glance at a weather competitor's fly will tell you if you are in his wind shadow. Or it will tell you if you are cutting your competitor to leeward as you are struggling hard to get by him. Suppose you are racing small boats in a harbor where there are larger yachts anchored. This is often true, for example, in dinghy racing, or junior racing. A quick look round the harbor at various masthead flys or flags will tell you what the wind is doing at the moment in each spot and will determine for you the optimum tack to take. In larger boats a quick check with binoculars may often tell you what boats behind you or ahead of you on a run have in the way of wind direction. On a reach or beat this is not as satifactory, but on a run it is often quite helpful. Often the masthead flag on a Committee Boat or a club burgee on a flagpole ashore will indicate what tack will gain the most places on the finish line. A luff on the starting line and a quick look at the masthead fly or sails will indicate which is the favored end of the starting line—if any.

CHAPTER VII

The Spinnaker

The development of the double or "parachute" spinnaker has increased the importance of the leeward legs from a tactical point of view and has made racing much more interesting from the point of view of the crew. It has been my experience in recent years that we have passed more boats going to leeward than to windward, and I find that the crew, having more to do, keeps on the alert and gets much more enjoyment from the racing. Since the single spinnaker is becoming, like the whooping crane, more or less extinct, this discussion will be confined with a few exceptions to the so-called parachute, double or balloon spinnaker, an isosceles triangle whose base is the foot of the sail. Any use of the words "parachute" or "spinnaker," unless otherwise noted, will refer to the parachute spinnaker. Personally, I do not like the use of the phrase "balloon spinnaker," since there is apt to be a chance of confusing it with a balloon jib.

The setting, handling, and trimming of a spinnaker is virtually the same on any boat, whether it be an America's Cup Defender, a Bermuda ocean racer; or a Lightning. The gear is of the same general type, though obviously varying in size and strength, and more time must be allowed on a larger boat; but the basic principles are the same. It was my privilege to be Spinnaker Trimmer on the Cup boat *Ranger*, and while its 18,000 square feet was somewhat terrifying at first, demanding proper respect at all times, after a bit of practice we treated that spinnaker as one would on an International One-Design.

While the 18,000-square-foot parachute was the spinnaker aboard *Ranger* which saw the most use, there were also several smaller ones available, including one old type single-luff sail. Just to show that the old single spinnaker is not without its particular

Ranger running with her 18,000-square-foot parachute spinnaker. Notice the tack and clew the same height above the water. The "bowsprit" is to keep the big kite from dragging under the bow should it collapse. Shown in her wake are *Rainbow, Endeavour II* and *Yankee*, racing on the New York Yacht Club Cruise after the 1937 Cup Races.

virtues I will digress for a moment to give you a splendid example of one of its very practical uses. In a race after the Cup Races of 1937, on the New York Yacht Club Cruise, in which five America's Cup boats participated, the course was from Mattapoisett 'round Vineyard Sound Lightship, a beat of perhaps 20 nautical miles, thence a run of 20 miles to West Chop and a reach of eight miles to the finish line off Cape Poge, Martha's Vineyard. It was a beautiful summer day with a freshening sou'wester for which Buzzards Bay is famous. By the time *Ranger* rounded the Lightship with a terrific lead, the breeze was really piping and it was decided that the big balloon jib and single spinnaker would suffice, for *Ranger* was romping along at practically top speed anyhow and it was difficult to figure any way she could be caught.

A little trick with a single spinnaker which had been taught me by my father, who used to race rather successfully in the Gardiner-designed Bird Class at the Bayside Yacht Club in 1911–1913, served almost to make a double spinnaker out of the balloon jib and single flat small spinnaker. (Further, it brought many complimentary remarks from Skipper Mike who apparently hadn't seen it used that way before.) By sheeting down hard on the clew of the small spinnaker, and making the clew fast near the tack of the jib, the wind from the spinnaker was made to flow into the ballooner, with the result that the ballooner was full almost the whole run, though partially blanketed by the huge mainsail. Older yachtsmen may say, "Pooh! We've done that many times," which is no doubt true, but very few of the younger generation of racing men have ever raced with anything but the more interesting and more exciting parachute spinnaker.

OK!! So what else is new? There isn't anything new under the Sun!! Now, almost 60 years after my father taught me how to set a single spinnaker so that it flows into the jib, along comes Ted Hood with his "HOOD SHOOTER" that does exactly the same job, set alongside a parachute spinnaker. And up goes the cost of racing your yacht again, because if you "ain't got" the SHOOTER, you just "ain't gonna" be with it.

The SHOOTER is a light-weight headsail (three-quarters or one-and-a-half-ounce nylon—trade name "Marnack"), designed with a concave or hollow luff, so that it will flow out from the spinnaker and not into it. It is used on a dead downwind leg, or even a very broad reach, and you lower your mainsail to get the most efficient flow of air into this headsail combination. With the

New Hood "Shooter" downwind sail. The new sail is designed to be flown opposite a spinnaker with apparent wind from downwind to broad reaching. The "Shooter" gives a yacht as much as 25 percent additional effective sail area with no penalty or change in rating under IOR Mk III.

high aspect ratio and short booms of the modern rig, the mainsail doesn't really do you much good on a dead run anyhow, and this SHOOTER of light, tough material, in any color combination, really does its stuff. Apparently the IYRU, at its November 1972 meeting, gave official sanction to the use of the SHOOTER and the lowering of the mainsail—which in itself isn't all that important—but you must have the mainboom stuck out there to leeward to sheet the SHOOTER properly and most effectively. My father's *Loon*, of the aforementioned Bird Class at the Bayside Yacht Club, would look almost like a modern ocean racer, except that this SHOOTER is right up there in area, *BIG*, just as big as your largest genoa, and it would make his club-footed jib look very small indeed.

NYLON Is the Material

Cotton is long gone as a material for spinnakers. If you see a cotton spinnaker you can bet your last dime that it is an old, old spinnaker. Dacron and Orlon never caught on, and while experiments were no doubt made with these materials (I do not know of any myself), their lack of elasticity would, I am positive, preclude their use for spinnakers.

Nylon, with its inherent strength, great flexibility and resiliency, is the ideal material for the big "kites." Ted Hood, Kenny Watts and Bainbridge are the principal makers of spinnaker material—as well as other sail cloth of course—the lightest grade being about .5-ounce material. Most spinnakers, be they Blue Jay or 12-metre, use 1.5-ounce. There is also a material known as "ripstop," 1.5 ounce, which is woven with heavier cross threads spaced approximately ¾₁₆ of an inch apart. This has the general effect of stopping a rip, shall we say, before it gets started—but unfortunately this doesn't always hold true. Ted Hood, in Marblehead, in many cases weaves his own material under the able direction of his father, "the Perfessor," who is about as quiet and taciturn as *his* very laconic son, but one helluva nice guy withal. A couple of years ago, maybe three, Hood came out with a spinnaker called a "FLOATER," and believe you me, folks, it was LIGHT, *so* light, in fact, that printed right on the bag were the maximum winds considered "safe," namely: "DON'T USE IN WINDS OVER SIX KNOTS ON A REACH OR EIGHT KNOTS ON A RUN." Take my word for it, if you don't own one, those "Shpinnaackers" are gossamery. You trim 'em with a length of

Dacron reef line, ⅛-inch stuff, and they "sit" up there, pulling nicely, in practically a zephyr, a catspaw, and you walk away, slowly but surely, from your competition. Ted won't say what the weight is of these FLOATERS, but the "weisenheimers" have arrived at an educated guess of half an ounce or maybe less. Anyhoo, it's a GREAT sail, but pay strict attention to the rules on the bag, or the FLOATER may take off for Hood's Loft via air- mail.

Dyed nylon is very color-fast, and never "runs," and its effi- ciency is unimpaired. By this, I mean that dyed or colored nylon is every bit as good and effective as plain white nylon. Hence any day of a race you are apt to see myriad colored and patterned spinnakers flying across the water, designs and shapes of all sizes and all hues of the rainbow.

You may have noticed the red-topped spinnakers on that most famous ocean racer, *Finisterre*. They are red on top by definite design. It was suggested to Carleton Mitchell that red (or black —but who wants a *black* spinnaker?) absorbs heat. Therefore, a spinnaker made of red nylon would pick up the heat of the sun, develop a thermal draft UPWARDS and have a reasonably effec- tive tendency to lift higher and stay full easier or longer. On the other hand, looking at a completely red spinnaker for any length of time would be rather hard on the eyes, so "Mitch" compro- mised and had the upper part red and lower white. I can't prove to you that it was 100% effective, but *Finisterre* was a hard boat to beat on a spinnaker leg, and the theory does sound sensible, doesn't it?

With this in mind, and partly because *Weatherly* was a very light pastel blue, we had all our spinnakers from Hood and Rat- sey made with a blue top and white bottom. Kenny Watts, of Torrance, California, made us a storm spinnaker out of "ripstop," but it was all white because blue was unavailable on the West Coast at that time. We went to Kenny for a storm spinnaker because of his long years of experience with the Honolulu Race —truly a slide downhill with spinnakers most of the way. To this may I add that we tried—in line with my policy of trying "to confuse the enemy"—to have all the spinnakers look alike in spite of differences in size, so that the competition wouldn't know which spinnaker we had on. We had big spinnakers, small spin- nakers, full ones and flat ones, but we wanted to keep to our- selves the effectiveness of each nylon spinnaker—and it worked!

Rosenfeld

Twelve-metres on 1958 New York Yacht Club Cruise—*Weatherly* at left. Note her crew all on weather rail which was effective even on a boat of this size. Note also boom-jack with "Go-Fast" which is attached at the same point leading down and forward to the rail. Masthead fly on *Weatherly* much smaller than on mahogany-hulled *Easterner*.

As a case in point—somewhere along the line in the late 1950s or early 1960s, Colie Ratsey came up with a new, very light spinnaker cloth and we ordered a chute made of it for *Weatherly*, as usual, with a blue top and white bottom. But we didn't want our competitors to know we had a *new* spinnaker, so it was ordered with two fairly large square patches in the middle, with the thought that when our "arch enemies" first saw it they would say to themselves, "Oh pooh! that's an old sail—*look at the patches!*" Pretty sneaky, what? Well, when we got it some weeks later, I looked at this gorgeous new sail—totally forgetting that we ourselves had asked for the patches—and exclaimed, "What the hell are those patches doing there?" I fooled myself, too, but it was one superb spinnaker nevertheless.

Something new ALWAYS turns up in yachting circles and yachts—someone always comes up with some new, bright idea. This time it's the STARCUT SPINNAKER (admittedly first brought out by Bruce Banks of England, a couple of years ago), a spinnaker that can be used most successfully with the apparent wind maybe 15 to 20 degrees forward of the beam—sometimes, under the right conditions of smooth sea and moderate air, with the apparent wind even further forward.

I reprint here, word for word, the instructions provided with each and every STARCUT delivered by Bruce. I "stole" this copy from Warren Brown's PJ-48 *War Baby* and I do it with Bruce's explicit permission.

Furthermore, I include here, too, Ratsey & Lapthorn's version of the Starcut, known as the CHUTING STAR, in a photo of *Lightnin'*—that most successful One-Tonner—together with "V.P." Jack Sutphen's written instructions for the proper use and trim of their Starcut CHUTING STAR.

I've talked with Ted Hood in Marblehead, and his firm is coming out with what they term a FLANKER, made from a really lightweight but very strong Dacron, non-stretch, which has taken him some time to develop. On Page 110, you'll find a picture of another Hood sail, the SHOOTER, a lightweight nylon sail for almost dead downwind sailing (in conjunction with a parachute spinnaker) which, in my opinion, is going to cause a revolution in downwind racing tactics. It's one helluva sail, believe you me and it's bound to cause some furor and repercussions, and yet it has great merit.

In the last Lipton Cup Race in February 1973, I was happy and pleased to be invited by Jack Potter (that veteran Frostbite dinghy sailor) to go along as advisor on his "big" dinghy, the 68-footer, *Equation*, with the 11-foot, 10,000-pound centerboard. She's a great boat to sail on and steer and she goes like the hammers of hell, upwind or downwind. The 18-mile leg home from Fort Lauderdale was supposed to be a run, but turned into a reach and we put up a Hard version of the Starcut with a beautifully trimmed tallboy under it. Although I've raced on a number of boats with Starcuts, this was actually the first time I'd seen one in action. Wally Ross's design seems to me to be a fine one—we passed several of the other big babies and almost caught *Blackfin*, a slippery boat six feet bigger than ourselves. I was duly impressed with the Starcut and with its ability to be carried, even when the apparent wind got as far forward as 40 degrees on the bow. The breeze was light to moderate—only about 6 to 8 knots, slightly on our quarter—and we "pulled" it around, therefore, almost 65 degrees. But the seas were fairly smooth, not too bouncy, and our Starcut pulled us along at maybe 8 to 9 knots.

THE STARCUT SPINNAKER

by Bruce Banks

If the Starcut Spinnaker we are sending to you is the first one you have had, we would like to draw your attention to certain points which will help you to get the best advantages from it.

Because it is designed for very close reaching, it can be sheeted in much closer than normal spinnakers. This means that the sheeting position becomes almost as critical as that of a windward sail. The greatest power and the best control of shape of a Starcut spinnaker are obtained when the spinnaker is sheeted through a block on the toe-rail located at a distance aft of the mast equal to the length of the spinnaker pole. Best of all is a short length of track extending forward and aft of this point. This will allow the sail to be sheeted a little further forward in very light winds when the more downward pull of the sheet will increase the curvature of the head and gain more power. It will also allow it to be sheeted a little further aft in strong winds when it is preferable to allow the head to slacken off to reduce heeling moment.

The great merit of the Starcut spinnaker as a reaching sail is associated with configuration of the panels, designed in such a way as to match the weave of the cloth with the radiating lines of stress from each of the corners. This mechanically perfect design enables the sail to remain almost totally free from distortion, quite irrespective of the strength of the wind. Thus the Starcut spinnaker, while benefiting greatly from this mechanical rigidity, is much more susceptible to shock loadings which in normal spinnakers are absorbed by vast distortion in the cloth. While many years of experience have gone into the design and workmanship of the reinforcing at the corners, we strongly recommend that the Starcut spinnaker, when used for reaching in very strong winds, is set on a rope halyard which will be capable of absorbing a very large amount of the shock which can occur as a result of a broach.

Techniques of trimming are learned quickly with experience. The stronger the wind and the closer the reach, the lower the pole should be carried. Under limiting conditions the pole should be pulled right down into the pulpit. Set like this and sheeted to the correct position, the Starcut spinnaker should give more power than any genoa with the wind 50 degrees off the ship's head in light winds and calm water. Because this sail sets so much closer to the boat than the high-flying type of spinnaker, a large headsail set on the outer forestay will cause interference and may render the spinnaker ineffective. It will also make it impossible to fill the spinnaker once it has collapsed. Either a tallboy tacked well aft of the stem, or a very low-cut spinnaker staysail tacked well forward, or both, can be used under certain circumstances, but long-luff genoas should be avoided.

THE STARCUT SPINNAKER

by Jack Sutphen, Vice-President

of Ratsey and Lapthorn, Inc.

It has been a long, long time since any sail made such an impression on the sailboat racing fraternity as the Starcut spinnaker. Nobody questions where it started and most American sailmakers are quick to credit Bruce Banks of England for his revolutionary design, simple as the reasoning behind it is. A mainsail is supported on two of three sides, a genoa (and reacher) on one side, but a spinnaker only from three corners, and herein lies the problem that the starcut design overcomes. When a sail of lightweight material can be made to hold its shape under load, its potential—over a wide range of wind conditions— is easy to assess, when this sail can be 75% greater in area without a penalty than a 150% reacher then it is certainly a "must" sail in any racing inventory.

Given these assets it's not hard to see why other sailmakers have come up with variations of the Starcut that appear, in some cases, to improve on the original. Which is the best will only be proven on the race course, but enough experience has been gained by those using the sail in many races to arrive at some conclusions as to its use and where it fits into the racing boat's inventory.

One question usually asked is: "Does the Starcut replace the reacher?" Like most any question about racing sails there are some "ifs" and "buts"; however, in most cases the answer is YES. Except for the big boat (over 50 feet with room to carry as many sails as the owner can afford and do so without disturbing the designer's floatation figures), the Starcut can, and does successfully, take the place of two sails—the reacher and storm spinnaker.

In the case of the storm spinnaker, it does the job more by coincidence than intent because it is made of 1.5-ounce nylon, or heavier, is designed and constructed to withstand heavy loads without distorting, and has somewhere between 8 and 10% less area, with most of this out of the upper section.

The real worth of the Starcut is, of course, seen on a close reach with the wind anywhere from 90 degrees off the bow to as little as 45 degrees. We have been told of many cases where our Chuting Star has been carried productively with the wind 45 degrees off the bow, but experience has shown that the breeze must be moderate and the sea quite flat for this close carry.

The range of this sail is really quite wide. Even though it is heavier than the standard spinnaker, it is usually half the weight of a reacher, so its usefulness can begin in light air on close reaches. As mentioned above, it is at its best in moderate air on reaches with the wind anywhere from 45 degrees to 90 degrees off the bow. In heavy air its flat surface, derived from the radial clews and head and narrow shoulders, reduces heeling and the resultant broaching or oversteering.

There is still one more big advantage gained with the Starcut. The great majority of IOR-rated boats have #1 genoas and reachers of 150% overlap. The Starcut is allowed the 180% overlap of a spinnaker and is designed to have at least 75% more area than the 150% headsail without any rating increase. A modest staysail, such as is carried with a reacher, can be carried to equal advantage with the Starcut, and in some conditions a large staysail works well and gives even more area.

The Starcut is set out of a turtle, or in stops, in the standard manner, but the pole set and sheet trim are quite different. We have found with our Chuting Star that the pole is carried considerably lower than with a regular spinnaker, usually only a couple feet above the pulpit. The best height is a matter of trial and error, because it will vary with the wind velocity and sea conditions. The sheet will lead to the rail at a position approximately 25% forward of the counter. In light to light-moderate air the sheet may be moved even further forward to tighten the leech and shape the head. In heavier winds the sheet lead can be moved aft which opens up the sail and reduces heeling.

It must be remembered that the Starcut is a much flatter sail than a running spinnaker and the leading edge must be watched closely at all times as to trim. Under most conditions a staysail, with a modest foot length set back a third of the way from the bow to the mast, will work much better than a regular genoa on the stay.

When used as a storm or heavy weather downwind sail it should be treated as a regular spinnaker. The pole and the clew should be kept low to eliminate oscillating. An important "DON'T" with respect to the Starcut: Don't keep it on if the wind comes aft as far as abeam in anything up to fresh conditions. Your regular chute has more area, and unless the boat is difficult to control will move it faster.

The design of our Chuting Star spinnaker, with its many narrow panels radiating from the head and both clews requires considerably more time in cutting and sewing it together. For this reason they are somewhat more expensive than a standard spinnaker. But there is little doubt that, because of their superior reaching ability and their added use as a fine heavy weather chute, they are well worth the extra cost.

Proper Stopping

Obviously, proper stopping or preparation of a spinnaker is a paramount factor in the speedy and successful setting of the sail. Speed is essential—but if the sail is not properly prepared the speed is wasted. To begin with, the spinnaker should be treated in the same manner as any other sail (see chapter on Sails) and washed out occasionally in fresh water. No matter how expert the crew, it is impossible to get a spinnaker up *or* down without once in a while dipping part of it in the drink—and if it's salt water, the salt must be removed.

There are several different but equally adequate methods of preparing a spinnaker, and I use the word "prepare" rather than "stop," since all of them do not involve actually stopping the sail with thread or rotten twine. Except on larger boats (over 40 feet) spinnakers can best be prepared ashore, and it has been my experience that, except in an emergency, they should be stopped, stuffed, or folded ashore where there is generally more room and (very seldom) more time. In this connection, it is advisable to delegate to the most reliable member of your crew the responsibility for seeing to it that the spinnaker (in its own properly marked bag) gets back on board. I recall an instance on another boat several years ago where this duly appointed member of the crew unhappily left his yacht's spinnaker ashore. It is said that his head, properly shrunken, now sits on the mantelpiece of his skipper's home, alongside the also shrunken head of another crew member who in an earlier race had fallen overboard.

Should the stopping method be used, it can be done in the ordinary manner or with legs—with or without a breaking line. Experience over the years has proven to me that the simplest and easiest way is to hang the spinnaker up—between two poles for example—tying the head to one pole and stretching the leeches out straight and tying them to the other pole. The sail can be held up by the head and foot by crew members, but since they generally tire easily or get talking with some blond and forget their job, the method least upsetting to the nerves of the skipper seems to be to tie the sail up somehow. The leeches MUST be taut so that when the sail is hoisted the stops are not subject to undue cross strains which would tend to pop them at the wrong time. For boats under 40 feet, such as 6-metres, IODs, Shields, Solings, Etchells and Lightnings, #60 cotton seems to be about the right thread to use. Some skippers prefer worsted and some even use rubber bands. We use #60 and drop the spool inside the stopper's shirt, leaving the end out.

Starting at the head the sail is bunched, the leeches checked to be sure they are clear and not twisted, and the six or eight inches of material on one leech is rolled and tucked round the sail to make a neat cylindrical or tube-like effect. When the professionals do this they use the term "Skin me out." Some skippers prefer merely to bunch the sail; however, in my opinion this allows the wind a chance to get in the sail and blow out the stops prematurely. Others roll the whole sail up tight, but this makes the sail hard to break out and is as equally unsatisfactory as the plain bunching. While this whole operation can be done by one person, it is far better to have two or even three people working: one bunching, the second "skinning out," and the third tying stops.

The first stop is tied two or three feet from the top or head of the spinnaker, the "skinner-outer" grasping the sail with two hands and twisting slightly so that the stopper gets a tight stop. The "skinner-outer" can help by holding a finger on the first tuck of the square knot—again, so that the stop is a good tight one. If the stopper wishes to do the job alone, he can insure a tight stop by taking two tucks in the first turn of the square knot and then twisting the two parts before completing the knot. As for me, to be doubly sure that my "square" knots are on the "square" and don't slip, I always tie a third knot.

Actual practice will determine how far apart to put your stops, but two or three feet on a small boat seems adequate, depending on the strength of breeze. Halfway down the sail double stops are indicated, especially in a strong breeze, but here again actual practice will determine where and when to double up. Certainly the bottom stop in a plain stopping job should be quite a bit heavier, for the sheet can always be yanked hard enough to break it out when necessary. On boats that have especially large spinnakers, stopping with "legs" is extremely helpful. I have found that on an International One-Design, legs make the breaking out much quicker and there is less chance of a twist aloft. On cruising boats, especially with masthead spinnakers, legs help the breaking out job in that they allow the pole to be trimmed well off the jibstay before the sail is broken. (Working a spinnaker pole off a jibstay on a large boat is no quick and easy feat.)

The tying of the legs is not difficult. On a 35-foot boat, at a point three feet (more or less) from the bottom, tie a fairly heavy stop, say four or five thicknesses of thread, and have one person hold the sail at this point while another person takes one clew of the sail and holds it somewhat away from the other clew. The center of the foot of the sail is carefully folded and rolled up and held at the heavy stop, and thread is wrapped continuously round this bundle of skirt and tied. One or two tight stops are put below this bundle on each leg and then, for safe handling, a light stop is tied to hold the clews together. The sail is then folded back and forth to form a bundle two or three feet long, and one or two stops of several thicknesses are put around the whole thing so as to give the spinnaker setter a neat tight bundle to handle on the foredeck. The whole bundle is then carefully tucked in the spinnaker bag, and the thread put back in its own little pocket sewn on the outside of the bag. This method of folding and doing up the stopped sail is used with either the plain stopping job or with legs.

When stopping a spinnaker for a larger boat, say 60 feet or more, a breaking cord, ¼-inch or ⁵⁄₁₆-inch in diameter, may be used. The stops in a sail of this size will be of rotten twine and a loop is taken round the breaking line with each stop, thus facilitating the breaking out of the spinnaker. In my opinion, legs and a breaking line make a very happy and successful combination for a larger spinnaker. More work and effort are required but the results are worth it.

THE TURTLE

For boats whose jibstays are set back from the bow a very splendid spinnaker setting device made its appearance in 1950, first at Marblehead and later on Long Island Sound. This simple gadget, nicknamed a "Turtle," was thought up by Phil Benson of Marblehead and his design for it appeared in the August 1950 *Yachting*. A piece of plywood and an old inner tube are all the parts required, fastened together with screws and a couple of light strips of wood. In shape, it is a triangle cut to fit the bow, the forward quarter being cut off to form a quadrilateral. Variations of design have been developed, but the basic idea is the same, the covering material being left loose and baggy at the forward, closed end and tight at the after, open end. Other coverings, such as nylon and plastic materials have been used, but an old inner tube seems to be about as good as anything since it is waterproof and will stretch a certain amount.

The spinnaker can be stuffed in the turtle foot first, care being taken to keep each leech on its own side of the turtle—with no twists—to prevent turns and twists when the spinnaker is pulled out. On our boat we stuff the turtle ashore, since a better, more compact job can be done if the spinnaker is folded and powdered first, before stuffing. However, with a bit of practice the turtle can be successfully stuffed on board.

Our method ashore is to lay the spinnaker down on a lawn or a floor and fold one leech over the other so that the top leech overlaps the under one by about the width of the turtle. The rest of the sail is then folded in two or more folds, just to the edge of the UNDER leech, in such a manner as to make the whole length of the spinnaker about the width of the turtle. The top leech, lying off to the side, is then flipped over the top of everything, giving you the folded spinnaker with a leech on either side. Starting at the foot, the spinnaker is flaked down with folds the length of the turtle and the leeches are held carefully on either side as the flaking is done.

At this point a "secret weapon" enters the picture, a can of powder—any kind, dusting, baby, or what have you. As the spinnaker is folded and flaked, a few shakes of the powder assure a slippery sail when it is hoisted. The turtle itself is also profusely doused inside, before the folded sail is pushed into it. (And what a sweet-smelling spinnaker we have as it emerges from its turtle in an apparent cloud of smoke!) Care must be taken in pushing the folded spinnaker into the turtle not to disturb the folds too much, and to have a leech at each side with the head in the middle. These three are left hanging out of the open end of the turtle, so that halyard and guys may be quickly and easily hooked on at the proper time.

As a further development of the turtle, many of the Long Island Sound IODs have installed a permanent turtle forward of the jibstay. In itself, it is quite simple to make and involves installing a quadrilateral hatch with a strong hinge at the forward end.

Fred E. Hahnel

In preparing the spinnaker for the turtle it is laid out so that the TOP leech, held in left hand, is approximately 18 inches away from the UNDER leech, held in right hand. The center of the sail is then folded TWICE to the UNDER leech so that it forms a tube of uniform width.

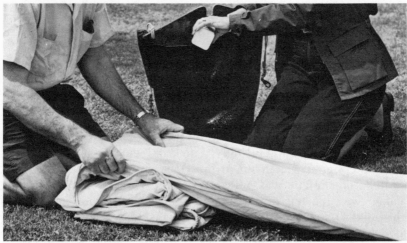

Fred E. Hahnel

The spinnaker is then flaked down and powdered before being stuffed in the powdered turtle.

The Three-Pocket Turtle

Probably one of the fanciest and most rewarding gadgets of
the '58 America's Cup Defense was the so-called Three-Pocket
Turtle, designed by Frank MacLear, in charge of *Weatherly's*
foredeck (until he later became navigator), and made up by Ed
Raymond with the able assistance of "Mat" MacShane. It was a
development of turtles used on smaller boats with the added
feature of two separate pockets on the ends to hold the stopped
"legs" of the spinnaker. It was about three and a half feet long,
two feet wide and stood up about 12 to 14 inches when stuffed
with various spinnakers. (See Diagram on Page 125.) The Dacron
covering was sewn to a one-inch tubular aluminum rectangular
frame, the forward end (for convenience and identification only)
red, and the after end green. The spinnaker was stopped with
legs of roughly 15 to 20 feet and, starting at the bottom of the
spinnaker, it was stuffed in the main bag of the turtle, with the
legs being stuffed into the end pockets. Care was taken to keep
each leech free and next or near its own end of the turtle so that
there would be no twists. A flap covering the opening was lashed
down with light stopping thread for easy breaking.

When the spinnaker was needed, the turtle was lashed on deck
forward, the stops on the flap broken and the legs pulled carefully out of their pockets for the required length, sheet and guy
hooked into them and the haylard hooked into the head of the
spinnaker. With one method of setting and/or jibing the spinnaker, the tack of the spinnaker was shackled directly into the
pole itself. In the other method, where four guys were used in the
setting and/or jibing, two were wire and two Dacron, the spinnaker was shackled in the double wire-Dacron guys and the wire
itself was slipped into the pole end and the spinnaker was pulled
forward and out to the pole end by hauling on the wire guy via a
coffee-grinder, or more fittingly, a pedestal winch.

As the signal was given to hoist the spinnaker the sheet was
pulled and the guy was pulled, all at the same time. As the spinnaker was hoisted approximately halfway up, the genoa was
dropped ON THE RUN (unless it was blowing very hard, in
which case the genoa was not dropped until the halyard was all
the way up—but then the genoa came down on the run) and
every effort made to get the spinnaker drawing as quickly as
possible. To say the three-pocket turtle speeded up spinnaker

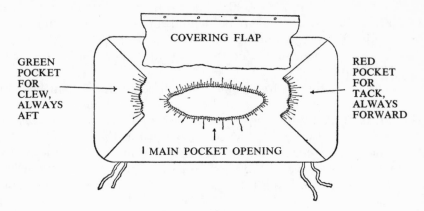

GREEN
POCKET
FOR
CLEW,
ALWAYS
AFT

COVERING FLAP

RED
POCKET
FOR
TACK,
ALWAYS
FORWARD

I MAIN POCKET OPENING

Weatherly's turtle

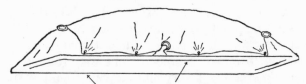

RECTANGULAR ALUMINUM TUBING FORMS
FRAME OF TURTLE

Quest's turtle

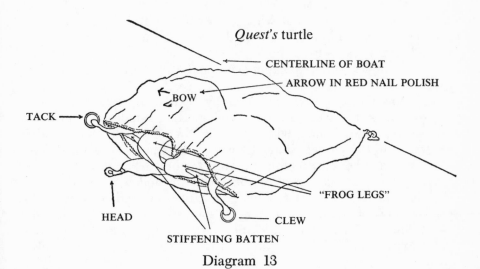

CENTERLINE OF BOAT

ARROW IN RED NAIL POLISH

BOW

TACK

"FROG LEGS"

HEAD

CLEW

STIFFENING BATTEN

Diagram 13

setting on *Weatherly* is the understatement of the year. Using Frank MacLear's great brainchild in a race rounding Point "Jude" Whistler one day, the America's Cup Committee clocked us at six seconds in getting that "rag" up after rounding the mark! Not bad!

If I may digress for a minute to tell you a story about how Vic Romagna got on *Columbia*. When we were eliminated from the Final Trials by the Cup Committee we offered to *Columbia* our sails, turtles, whatever they wanted—just as they were offered to *Vim*. Rod Stephens called me next morning to say they'd like three turtles—we had SIX, one for each spinnaker—and our best spinnaker man. Well, they got the turtles, and Vic was the spinnaker man. He and our turtles made good on *Columbia* and he got into the Cup Races. But how did Vic get on *Weatherly* in the first place? Down on the Floor of the New York Stock Exchange where I am a member, then associated with Carlisle & Jacquelin, odd-lot dealers, practically everyone was "in" on all the details of the boat, selection of crew, etc. When it finally came to the point where I had to make a choice of one of three men for the last berth on *Weatherly,* a very fine Italian friend of mine, Frank Gallo, said "Knapp, you'd better pick the Guinea or that boat will never go!" I'm a great fellow for following hunches and I "picked the Guinea." So Vic got into the Cup Races and I didn't—poetic justice of one sort or another, but he IS a good man and a GOOD spinnaker man—*except* when he argues with me about whether the pole should be forward of the perpendicular to the apparent wind or cocked up in the air. I STILL say the pole should be at right angles to the apparent wind and also to the mast. THAT'S THAT, *CHIDRULE!**

On the 5.5 *Quest,* designed by Sparkman & Stephens and owned by that very generous and sporting syndicate from Sewickley, Pennsylvania, which John B. Nichols, Gene Walet and I raced to the United States Championships in 1959, we had four days from her christening and launching on a Monday to get her ready for the first race of the series the following Friday. All three of us were new to Five-Point-Fives and rather green as to methods of setting spinnakers. We'd been told some passed the spinnaker forward in a plastic waste-paper basket which they hooked onto the jibstay and hoisted from there. Someone else

---

* *CHIDRULE*—an Italian slang expression for a large cucumber.

Quest, a 5.5-metre running with her crew sitting well to windward to heel boat well to windward. Note jib tied up with a stop, a time-saving maneuver used by most 5.5s.

went forward and just tossed the spinnaker in a big mess right up in the air—and IT WORKED, for we later on saw it done in the Five Race Series!

But on *Quest,* we figured that going out on the bow of a 5.5 was strictly "NG" for big lugs like us three—we each weighed over 200 pounds—so we had Ratsey make us up a flat Dacron envelope turtle with two smaller envelopes to tuck the legs into. (Diagram 13.) This envelope was about two feet long and 18 inches wide. It had a batten in one side of the mouth and shock cord in the other—adjustable, too. The forward end had a red tab sewn on it and in the forward pocket we put the longest leg, stopped, of course. The two spinnaker guys—and we had several pairs of different weights—were hooked together and rigged on deck at all times, reaching all the way back to quarter-blocks on the very corners of the reverse stern. Just forward of the jibstay there was a "bullnose" or rounded lip, around which could be pulled the two connected snap-shackles, depending on which jibe we wished to be. Now this gets complicated, so pay close attention: even the spinnaker halyard could be hooked into these snap-shackles on the spinnaker guys and hauled around the jibstay, depending on which side you wished to have the halyard. Don't scoff! It worked and worked well, as long as you gave the halyard itself lots of slack. The pole was hooked into what was to be the guy BEFORE the pole was pushed forward and hooked onto the mast, and the fore-guy could be snapped into the middle of the pole as it was being passed forward. Hoist the halyard, pull the guy and pull the sheet—all at once! Believe me, children, this *whole* operation was done from the cockpit! Nobody had to get on deck. And most of the other 5.5s didn't even bother to lower their jibs when the spinnakers were up. Some lashed them snug to the jibstay with a stop, but some still left them up and used them as a spinnaker staysail or "cheater." We generally lowered our jib part way and tucked the leech under a piece of shock cord which Gene Walet had cleverly rigged on the foredeck.

PANDORA'S BOX

A young lady from Southport, Connecticut, named Pat Skinner, is responsible for a device for spinnaker setting known as Pandora's Box. It is simply a square corrugated box with two corners slit slightly. The spinnaker, starting with the foot and each clew in a slit corner is flaked down, keeping the leeches clear. When needed, the boxed spinnaker is taken on deck, guys and halyard attached, and the sail hoisted. The box generally goes overboard, but can be replaced with little effort and no expense. Nowadays, with plastic pails or wastebaskets so comparatively cheap, they are frequently used to stuff a spinnaker. Even the spinnaker bag itself can be easily converted for use as a form of turtle. Suitable hooks, attached by shock cord or reef line, are used to fasten either one in the lee shrouds to be ready for another day.

PAPER BAG

A variation of the turtle and Pandora's Box has been seen in the form of a large, heavy paper bag with two holes cut in the bottom, big enough for the clews to be stuck through. Here, again, the guys and halyard are attached, the sail hoisted, and the bag tears apart and goes overboard.

Of the various methods here described, it is my opinion that the turtle is the easiest in the long run, and also the most efficient. It takes less time to prepare than the stopping method and the sail itself is hoisted and drawing quicker, and the turtle itself is there to use again if required. I saw one boat in the International Class which stopped the spinnaker before stuffing it into the turtle. This seems to me to be gilding the lily—or turtle—and completely unnecessary, since the greatest advantage of the turtle is the great speed with which the spinnaker is hoisted and immediately drawing. Experience over the past years proves to my satisfaction that this hoisting or setting method works equally well on a close reach, a broad reach, or a run. I do not think that more than three times in 200 or 300 settings has the spinnaker twisted or fouled up in any way.

SPINNAKER SET FLYING

There are occasions when it is desirable to set a spinnaker in a hurry, and there isn't time to stop it or even stuff it in a turtle. Perhaps the air is light and the spinnaker has only been taken in a few minutes before. (Good practice dictates that the spinnaker be restopped or restuffed in a turtle the moment the opportunity presents itself.) Let us assume that the spinnaker is needed in a hurry, and it may be one of those moments when much distance or many positions can be saved if the spinnaker is hoisted immediately. It can be flaked down starting at the foot in very short order and then placed carefully on the lee bow deck under the jib, due caution being exercised to make sure it doesn't fall overboard. The guys and halyard are attached so that it can be hoisted underneath and to LEEWARD of the jib and made to draw in very short order. I do not advocate this maneuver except under very desperate conditions; but it *can* be done.

Guys

Spinnaker guys for all degrees of wind should be standard equipment. On a 35-footer ⅜-inch line is adequate for heavy weather, with ¼-inch for light weather, and reef line or fish line for very light air. Guys should be twice the overall length of the boat and should be changed when a variation in the strength of wind indicates such action is necessary. By using light Dacron reef line as a spinnaker sheet, when other boats were using ⅜-inch, we have kept our spinnaker full and drawing while the others' were drooping and impossible to fill.

I cannot emphasize too strongly the need for lighter sheets in light air. The after-guy is less important than the sheet in this respect, but you can never tell when you will have to jibe and then the heavy after-guy, becoming the sheet, will drag down the clew of the spinnaker and valuable speed and position may be lost. There are conditions on a close reach, however, when the pole will be steadier and jump around less with a heavy guy—for there is obviously less stretch in a heavier line. But you must be ready to change the guy to a lighter one when a jibe is being contemplated. And the change should be made *before* the jibe and not afterwards. Obviously, there may be conditions and circumstances which do not allow this change beforehand, but if possible it should be done.

Guys can be made of linen, Italian hemp, manila, cotton, Dacron, or even sisal, but my experience shows that nylon does not make a satisfactory spinnaker guy. Nylon, while it is soft, pliable, easy on the hands and a pleasure to work with, stretches when a strain is put on it, and it keeps stretching as the strain increases. It probably won't break, but it invariably stretches at the wrong time. Manila is strong and inexpensive, when compared with linen or Italian hemp. Dacron has all the good features of nylon, but doesn't have the one bad one—stretch, indefinite elasticity— and therefore is a great boon to the yachtsman. And, since it doesn't rot, my vote is for Dacron and damn the expense. Its qualities of strength, pliability, and softness make it ideal, but it *is* more expensive. Sisal and cotton have gone the way of the dodo bird, at least in my book—they are EXTINCT, KAPUT, FINISHED! So, again, my vote is for Dacron; it is far and away the best line for sheets and halyards, costs a lot, but lasts a long time. Please note, also, that Dacron does not shrink or bind up when you put a half hitch on a cleat. In fact, it is somewhat on the slippery side and a half hitch is, to my way of thinking, mandatory. I've seen sailors brought up with manila and linen sheets or halyards who abhor the thought of putting a half hitch on a cleated sheet. With Dacron it's a MUST!

SAMSON AND PIMM SHEETS

Walter Von Hutschler introduced in this country a type of line which he tells me is more or less common on boats abroad. Named "Pimm" sheets after his famous Star boat, the line comes in cotton and also Dacron, and in appearance is quite similar to clothes line. However, Walter's lines are plaited, i.e., are woven over a core, while clothes line which is braided has no center core. It is quite soft and yet easy to grip, will not kink or foul itself up and does not get hard when wet like ordinary cotton. Because it is of a relatively smooth form it runs through blocks very easily, and comparatively larger sizes (which are easier to grip) can be used successfully. Johnny Nichols and I both used Pimm sheets on our Frostbites in 1952 and found them very satisfactory. In fact, Johnny liked the line so much that he has laid in a supply in all sizes available in his yards in Rye and Mamaroneck, New York.

The Samson Cordage Co., of Boston, through fellow sailor "Tiggie" Woodland, offered to make us some sheets for *Weatherly* in 1958, particularly a main sheet. They had a special method of making a Dacron-plaited sheet with a nylon core (somewhat akin to the aforementioned "Pimm sheet"). They felt that their sheet would be strong, stable and non-stretch. So we ordered 200 feet of ¾-inch diameter line with 200 feet of ¼-inch line "tapered" into or onto it. This tapered section—roughly four feet in length—went from ¾ of an inch gradually down to ¼ of an inch, and, believe me, it was a beautiful job, done somehow on their ropemaking machines. Since our main sheet rig was "double-ended," i.e., we could trim it from #6 winches on either side of the cockpit, this tapered sheet worked out to the Queen's taste.

We rove off enough off the heavy sheet to have it come to both winches—when we were on the wind, and to make things simpler we marked the proper spot on the far side of the heavy line with our Revlon nail polish. (You have no idea how useful a half-used little bottle of nail polish can be aboard ship.) When we went from a beat onto a run we slacked out the light sheet, and when we were well organized and straightened out with our spinnaker, etc., we hauled out the rather short bit of heavy sheet and had a nice light flexible sheet on our main which, in very light air, required no vang or forward-guy to keep it from dragging in the water. If, on the other hand, it was blowing very hard, or if we were going from a beat to a close reach we could ease out from the heavy side of the main sheet, and just forget the light side of the sheet.

At the end of the 1958 season, Samson Cordage "borrowed" back their sheet, washed it and exhibited it in various Motor Boat Shows, and, washed, it looked almost like new. We used it again very happily and successfully in the 1959 season, as well as in 1960 and 1961. Just so that the other rope companies cannot say that I am playing favorites, may I mention that Columbia as well as Plymouth supplied us with all kinds of very wonderful Dacron lines of various sizes for sheets, halyards etc., just as they did the successful Defender of the America's Cup, *Columbia*. Plymouth's very excellent "Goldline" made up several sets of absolutely superior docklines for *Weatherly* and her comfortable tender, *Skipper*, a Huckins 52-footer. Being in the nylon family they had just the proper amount of stretch and strength.

Nowadays, almost every yacht up to roughly 60 feet uses one make or another of braided or plaited Dacron sheets. A few have nylon cores, but most have Dacron cores covered with the aforementioned braided or plaited Dacron. They run through blocks easily, very seldom kink, are easy to handle and are as strong as the Devil himself. Most rope halyards and wire-halyard tails are made of three-stranded, twisted Dacron. Here again, strength and long life are the paramount features, while the stretch factor is very, very low (almost non-existent), which is why it is so popular for sheets and halyards on yachts, both large and small— IODs Shields, Etchells, Stars, One-Tonners and even sixty-odd-foot ocean racers. In the 70-foot range, wire sheets are generally used in heavy weather—no question about it—but here again, even the big yachts have sets of braided line for light to moderate air, because they are so much easier to handle.

May I mention in passing that in most boats today, bowlines (rather than snapshackles) are used to fasten sheets to jibs and/or genoas. They are easier and just as quick to fasten, flog less, beat up the mast less and, quite frankly, hurt your thick head much less if you are unfortunate enough not to duck or keep clear of 'em.

However, do make sure you tie a really *short* bowline in any genoa. It can be embarrassing, annoying and get your Skipper in a complete tizzy if the genoa can't be sheeted all the way in because some careless "Jerque" tied a long bowline.

On another score, if your genoa sheets—or even your main sheet—wear overly much, just turn 'em end-for-end and lo! you've got practically new sheets.

What is true of nylon, as far as spinnaker guys are concerned, is also true for sheets and rope halyards. It stretches at the wrong time. Many people prefer nylon because it is so strong, soft and long lasting. It, like Dacron, will outwear most other line three times over, but I still don't like it on any cleated sheet, guy, or rope halyard. As a mooring line or a sheet on a dinghy or Lightning (where good sense demands that you hold the sheet in your hand, and hence stretch is unimportant) it is completely satisfactory from all angles. As a tail, spliced to a wire halyard or wire sheet, Dacron is better and will prolong the life of the halyard considerably, for in a rope-wire splice the rope tail is the part which generally gives up the ghost first, and Dacron with its long-wearing qualities just fills the bill.

Spinnaker guys, sheets, and even rope tails on wire halyards, like sails, should occasionally be washed out in fresh water, not only to make them soft, but to prolong their life. A line full of salt will not run through a block or sheave as easily as a freshly washed and dried line. While this may seem inconsequential and slightly ridiculous, it is one of the many small things which, added up, win a great many boat races.

Proper Sheets Leads, Reaching, Running

I mentioned above that all guys should be twice the overall length of the boat. This is so that the spinnaker trimmer may sit forward and trim his sail on a reach with the sheet led all the

way aft—or to the end of the boom, if class rules allow it—to a
block on the extreme stern of the boat. A sheet less than twice the
length of the boat will not permit this, and it is most desirable
from several viewpoints.

First, the trimmer should be on the forward deck in order to
see his spinnaker completely. Secondly, if the sheet is led all the
way aft, the clew will be free to lift when it wants to and will
have less tendency to back-wind the mainsail, since the longer
lead permits it to blow farther to leeward. Some one-design
classes permit the spinnaker to be trimmed from the end of the
boom, as do the cruising and ocean racing boats. I feel that in a
one-design class this is not sensible, not seamanlike, and is even
dangerous. It demands additional and, usually, complicated gear
to do the job properly and puts a premium on a specially adept
crew. If no one can have it in a one-design racing class, everyone
is on an equal footing and there is no advantage to any one boat.
On the other hand, on cruising and ocean racers, especially with
masthead foretriangles, there is some merit in trimming to the
boom. The gear is heavier but more easily handled (because of
additional winches, etc.) and two sheets can be used without
materially affecting the trim of the sail, but allowing a quick
change from boom-end to stern trim when indicated. Here's another tip on sheeting a spinnaker—if you are on a fairly close
reach with the main trimmed in fairly close, it is quite a simple
matter to haul in all four parts of the main sheet by hand and lift
the spinnaker sheet *over* the boom. This has the general effect of
letting the clew of the spinnaker lift up a bit more and, consequently, frees up the leech. This operation is not too difficult, even
when it's blowing fresh, and it does improve the spinnaker. If
you're using two sheets, the deal is simplified, but one word of
caution—BE SURE TO GET THAT SHEET *UNDER* THE
BOOM AGAIN BEFORE YOU TAKE THE SPINNAKER IN, or
you're in for deep, deep trouble. Right? RIGHT!!! On the other
hand, this idea is absolutely no good at all if you are broad-off
(well off the wind), for it widens the spinnaker too much, makes
it much too flat and increases the amount of spinnaker behind the
wind-shadow of the mainsail. *Soo*, dead before the wind, DON'T
DO IT!

When running, it is unimportant where the sheet is trimmed,
forward or aft, since it generally binds on the underside of the
boom anyhow, even on a 6-metre with its high boom. However,

there are times when, in a light air with a slop of a sea, the spinnaker trimmer can stand on the forward deck and trim by holding the clew of the sail in his hand. This not only has a tendency to steady the sail, but also permits him to govern the amount of "lift" of the clew and, therefore, also the tack. (See later discussion of this point in this chapter.)

AFTER-GUY

The after-guy may be trimmed from its standard position from the pole, to the stern lead block, and thence to a winch or cleat (which I do not like since its long length permits too much give and take in the puffs); or it can be led from the pole to a block, fairlead, pad-eye, or snatch block on deck, somewhere in the middle section of the boat, and thence to a cleat or winch; or it can be led directly from the pole to a winch canted aft, a method which we have found to be very fast and fairly efficient. In both of these latter methods the balance of the sheet is left alone and ignored, still left in its original position through the after-lead block on the stern (hence, ready to be used as a sheet after a jibe). The winch, being canted or tilted aft enough to allow for a proper lead, thus preventing riding turns when the winch is cranked, eliminates the necessity for a lead-block or fairlead and therefore saves valuable time in setting, jibing, or taking in the spinnaker. Obviously, on some boats the winch cannot be canted and the only remedy is a snatch block (which is greatly preferred to a closed pad-eye or fairlead) which can be quickly opened and the sheet inserted or removed. Anything to simplify or speed up the handling of the spinnaker—or any other sail for that matter— is of the greatest value and should not be ignored nor neglected.

Speed is essential, as I have said before, to save the few seconds which may, and generally do mean the winning or losing of a boat race. For example, for a jibe with the above described method, it is a fairly simple matter—and quickly accomplished— for one crew member to hold the after-guy while another removes the turns from the winch, takes up the slack that leads aft to the block on the stern, and throws that part of the guy round the winch. You are now ready for the guy to become the sheet and the lead is where it ought to be—way aft. This is, of course, done just before the jibe is executed. The aforementioned stretch or give and take on the guy occurs, but at this stage, and for such a short time, it is comparatively unimportant.

Swivel Shackles and Brummel Hooks

Many types of hooks are used on spinnaker guys, but the most efficient and trustworthy seem to be pull-pin swivel shackles or else Brummel swivel hooks. Both are made with long bails so that there is room for both the splice of the guy and the pole fitting, thus allowing a twisted sail to swivel and clear itself. Ordinary galvanized snap hooks are sometimes used on guys and they are considerably cheaper in price, but they are very apt to foul up on rigging and stays, thus causing no end of confusion.

I am somewhat embarrassed to admit that we used these snap hooks on our light sheets with much cursing and swearing every time they catch on something. My only excuse is that they are in some ways quicker and easier to operate, lighter, and as I have said, considerably cheaper. Since our spinnakers in the International One-Design Class are, almost without exception, equipped with 1½-inch diameter metal rings seized with wire to the grommets in the clews, it is a comparatively simple matter to change sheets for lighter or heavier ones in almost no time.

Brummel Hooks, a patented type of interlocking hook, have proven very quick and efficient. They are light and strong and well designed. Their only disadvantage is that in changing sheets, one hook must be removed before the other is hooked in. This, with a clumsy crew—or even with an agile crew—can be a very dangerous maneuver. The consequences are obvious and disastrous. For my part, I will stick to the pull-pin swivel shackles, well oiled, of course. Barlow, Barient, Merriman Holbrook and South Coast make very good swivel snap shackles with monel pins.

Pole and Fittings

Since the spinnaker pole on a parachute spinnaker is generally supported by a lift, its weight (within reasonable limits, obviously) is comparatively unimportant. The pole, therefore, should be designed to take a good load and should not be so light as to whip round like a fishing rod. On cruising boats, or racing boats of the larger types, weight and ease of handling are important factors, and light, hollow, but strong and stiff, spinnaker poles are indicated. But on boats under 35 feet, weight is not the important factor, while strength is, so don't try to use a toothpick for your spinnaker pole. Rod Stephens, on his NYYC–32, *Mustang*, ex-

perimented with a square spinnaker pole. He reasoned that a
square pole is stronger and it lies against the jibstay on a close
reach with less strain or chafe. Of course, even so, adequate
chafing strips, in the way of the jibstay, are necessary on both
ends of the double-ended pole.

Weatherly started her career with conventional round wooden
poles, then ordered round aluminum tubular poles (which didn't
arrive 'til the Cup Races were over); but finally ended up with
two beautiful aluminum "sandwich" poles made by Grumman

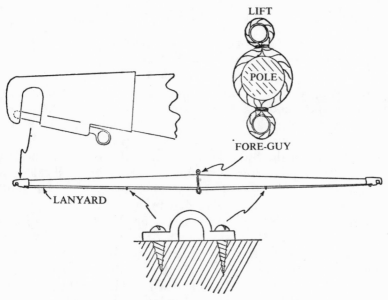

Diagram 14 Spinnaker Pole and Fittings.

Aircraft under the direction of that very pleasant and expert
sailor, Bob Hall of Huntington. These poles were more or less
square, but with rounded corners, rather bulky in size, very, very
strong and unusually light for their size. Annodized, they have
stood up very well and the aluminum end-fittings, surprisingly
enough, have likewise stood up extremely well under the chafe
and wear of the new "double-sheet" jibing method now in vogue.

Likewise, the cast-bronze fittings on the ends of the pole
should be strong and substantial. Most types of these fittings
seem to have been designed with too little metal (and therefore

insufficient strength) at crucial points of strain. There are good fittings to be found, however, if one hunts far enough, fittings which are strong enough and work easily and efficiently when speed is essential. In general, these castings are either conical or cylindrical in shape, with a hook or open eye fashioned on the end, into which slides (to close the eye) a bronze or stainless steel pin with a spring in back of it to hold it shut. (See Diagrams.) Kretzer Boat Works on City Island have the best type of this fitting which I have run across for boats 35 feet and under. The fitting itself is substantial and the sliding pin is stainless steel with an eye in the back end to which a lanyard may be fastened for pulling the pin open. On our pole we had run a lanyard the length of the pole from one sliding pin to the other, so that the fitting might be opened at any time from any point on the pole.

In the larger yacht fittings, the ends are cone-shaped and can be easily slipped into a cone-shaped cup on a slide on the foreside of the mast and locked in position with a pin. On smaller boats the fitting is hooked into an eye on the slide on the foreside of the mast. It is interesting to note, in this connection, that with the eye fitting on the foreside of the mast the pole may be put into the eye from the top or bottom, and the swivel shackle on the guy may also be hooked in from above or below. One spinnaker man on our boat prefers one method and another man prefers the other. Arguments wax heavy on the relative merits of both methods. It is also interesting to note that in most fittings the pin pulls from the end and not from the bottom or side (by means of a knob). The knobs generally get bent or knocked off and are most inefficient and hard to work. These fittings should be kept well-oiled and packed with a bit of grease or Lubriplate from time to time for proper action.

SETTING THE SPINNAKER

In the actual setting of the spinnaker a major part of the job is done beforehand. By that I mean the spinnaker is stopped and bundled or stuffed in a turtle or cardboard box, the guys are rigged and the pole is—at least in the smaller one-design classes —placed on deck, all before the start of the race. It is generally a simple matter to determine before the start when the spinnaker is going to be used and on what tack or jibe. Knowing this, the afterguy and the fore-guy can be rigged to the pole. It is also important to try to determine, if possible (and it is not *always* possible), on which tack you will approach the weather mark, and thus to determine on which side of the jibstay the spinnaker halyard shall be led or rigged.

In every modern boat which I have seen the spinnaker halyard leads from a point on the mast above the jibstay and jib halyard. This means that unless the spinnaker halyard is carried at all times forward of the jibstay and fastened on deck at some point forward of the jibstay (a practice which I deplore because of excessive windage and interference with the luff of the jib), on one tack or the other, there may arise a problem in getting the halyard forward to the jibstay from the mast. Now, in 1973, I still deplore this practice of carrying the spinnaker halyard on the bow. Whenever I see it—and I DO see it much too often, *much too frequently*—it gives me THE COLD SHUDDERS! DON'T DO IT!! As stated earlier in this book, it disturbs and upsets the windflow going into the luff of your jib. DON'T!! PLEASE!!

As explained earlier, it's a simple matter to haul your spinnaker halyard around to the preferred side by hooking it into the guys, giving it lots of slack and just plain hauling it around. If you're on a large yacht, just send some able fellow forward to take it around, but be sure to do it when the halyard is to go from the weather side to the lee side—it's a lot easier that way. But, of course, there are times when you're on the wrong tack and you have to stay on the wrong tack, and then there's nothing to do about it but "wrastle" it 'round by brute strength and sheer stupidity to the desired weather side.

Let's assume that you have decided that you will attempt to approach the weather mark on the starboard tack—a tactical maneuver which is an excellent idea IF you can manage it—and so, before the race starts you rig your spinnaker halyard so that it leads from the starboard side of the jibstay. On the windward leg you are pushed off on the wrong tack and you find yourself approaching your weather mark on the port tack. The problem is to get the halyard forward on the lee side of the jib without wasting too much time and without having a man spend the whole afternoon on the bow (or so it will undoubtedly seem to the skipper). Someone reading this will ask: Why not a double-ended spinnaker halyard? A very good question indeed, to which the answer is that a double-ended spinnaker halyard means that the spinnaker man forward must hoist his own spinnaker as well as set it, a practice which I feel is outmoded and inefficient on anything under 40 feet overall. It is far better to have the spinnaker hoisted from the cockpit and let the poor spinnaker man struggle only with the actual setting of the sail and the pole. On larger boats there is room for two men to work forward without sinking the bow, but on smaller craft this can't be done.

With the advent of the turtle, many skippers set their spinnakers on the bow with guys attached before the start of the race. While I am a great advocate of the turtle, and we use it all the time, it is my opinion that there is too much weight too far forward for too long a time in doing this. In addition there is considerable windage and interference with the flow of wind on the tack of the jib. We pass our turtle forward as we near the weather mark, hook it on with its three snap hooks and attach the guy and sheet and, as we get quite close to the mark, attach the halyard. If turning the mark involves only easing sheets rather than a tack or jibe, the lift is also attached (to the center of the pole at which point the fore-guy is already fastened). It is easy to determine beforehand whether the next leg will be a dead run or a reach and so determine and explain to the crew approximately how far aft the pole must be pulled with the after-guy when the spinnaker is hoisted.

There is a problem that occasionally arises as you approach the weather mark. Can the spinnaker be carried at all? Is the next leg so close a reach that you would do better without a spinnaker? A check of the compass direction of the next leg and a check of the true wind will generally settle the question; but once in a while even this won't answer it. The practical solution, particularly when a turtle is being used, is to get everything rigged and then decide *after* you have rounded. Setting a spinnaker from a turtle takes so little time that you will have lost very little to your competitors if you hesitate for a few seconds before you decide to hoist or try a vector diagram. (See pages 301–302.)

If the spinnaker is definitely indicated, as you ease sheets or complete a tack or jibe in the rounding of the mark, a crew member aft starts to hoist the spinnaker from the turtle. When the halyard is about halfway up, it is time to start pulling, fairly slowly, on the sheet; the spinnaker man forward raises the inboard end of the pole to fasten it to the mast, the lift is taken up and the after-guy hauled back. There should be a mark of colored yarn on the spinnaker halyard so the crew hoisting can tell when he has reached the proper degree of hoist, without wasting the time to look at the sail itself. The halyard is cleated securely and the jib is lowered on the run, the spinnaker trimmer forward bunching the jib on deck and making sure it does not hang or fall overboard. In the meantime, the guy and lift are adjusted, as outlined later in this chapter, and the crew in the cockpit trims the sheet as necessary and passes the end of the sheet forward to the spinnaker trimmer on the forward deck, who by this time should be finished getting the jib down and organized. The halyard, if the boat is rigged with jumper stays, may need minor adjusting to prevent the sail from being cut by the jumper stays.

If the conventional stopping method is used, rather than the turtle, the method to be followed is more or less the same as outlined above, except that the spinnaker man does not go forward as soon with the stopped and bundled spinnaker. His job is further complicated by the bulk of the spinnaker in his arms. He cannot put it down and leave it; he must watch the sail and try to keep it dry. (With the turtle there is no worry about the spinnaker getting wet, since it is protected by the rubber cover until hoisted.) He must keep a more careful watch on the sail as it is hoisted to see that it doesn't go overboard, catch or break out before it is supposed to. All in all the job is tremendously simplified by the turtle and in my opinion valuable time is saved in setting the spinnaker.

Fore-Guy and Lift

The design and layout of the fore-guy and lift are important in the proper and efficient handling of the spinnaker. The fore-guy, also known as a martingale and downhaul, should be substantial in strength with a minimum of stretch (hence nylon is out). The lift need not be as heavy, and it is a good idea to use a different type of line from that used for the fore-guy: for example, Dacron, Italian hemp or linen for the lift and manila for the fore-guy. For speed in handling the two should be cleated near, even next to each other. On bigger boats this is not always possible, but where possible it makes for faster handling. On smaller boats one person can handle both lift and fore-guy, and making the two of different types of line will cause less confusion. After a bit of practice anyone on the boat will grab the heavier manila line for the fore-guy without hesitating to think which makes the pole go up and which down. It is also important (on smaller boats) that these two lines be quickly and positively handled. (On big boats all

things take more time and more beef, and the element of speed is
not so desperately important.) In other words, cam cleats (see
illustration in chapter on Cam Cleats) are definitely indicated if
it is at all possible to use them. Cam cleats are quick, easy, positive and make the fast handling of lines a "lead-pipe cinch." Time
consumed in wrapping or unwrapping a line about a cleat is
absolutely wasted when it comes to the fore-guy and lift. Speed
counts in this operation and anything which can be done to speed
it up helps win the boat race!

Angle of Pole and Height of Lift

The fore-guy, lift, and mast-slide fitting should always be adjusted in such a manner as to have the spinnaker pole always
PERPENDICULAR to the mast and in PROPER RELATION-
SHIP to the height of the clew above the water. In geometry it
can be proven that the shortest distance from a point to a line is
a perpendicular to that line. It can likewise be proven that, in
spinnaker setting, with the pole of a definite fixed length, the
greatest distance from the mast to the spinnaker (which is
greatly to be desired) is a perpendicular to the mast. To draw
properly and most efficiently (either running or reaching—it
makes no difference) the spinnaker should be as far from the
mast as possible. The pole perpendicular to the mast will do just
this. A pole cocked any appreciable amount up in the air is NOT
right. Please note that I use the words "appreciable amount." A
slight variation from the perpendicular will do little damage for a
few minutes, compared to the damage which could be caused by
some 200-pound crew member jumping up and down on deck
every few seconds to adjust the inboard end of the pole. On the
other hand, a pole which droops down at the outer end drives me
completely "nuts" and I, for one, can't stand it.

May I back-track for a moment and reverse my field in the
interest of safety at sea? Rod Stephens, in the many Bermuda
Races I've sailed with him (and in other distance races, too,) has
always taken the position that in a very strong breeze, the spinnaker pole should be *cocked up* so that it is more or less in the
plane of, or in the line of the after-guy. More accurately stated,
the inboard end of the pole should be somewhat lowered, so that
the end result is the cocking up of the pole in the plane of the
after-guy. The reason for this, he has pointed out, is to put equal
strains on the lift and fore-guy and put the pole itself in "direct

Rosenfeld

Mike Vanderbilt's *Vim* has a good safe leeward position on the other two Twelves. Her spinnaker pole is cocked up too high, but the inboard end of the pole was soon hoisted.

Rod Stephens' NYYC-32 *Mustang* close reaching with a beautifully set spinnaker, pole perpendicular to the mast, at right angles to the wind (against the jibstay), clew and tack the same height above the water and the sheet led to the stern. The ballon forestaysail fills in the lower area and does not interfere with the spinnaker.

compression." In other words, with the pole more or less in line with the lead of the after-guy there is compression on the pole, but no tendency to bend the pole (by reason of the pole and after-guy being out of line with each other). Try it sometime, and you will find that with the pole sticking out forward at right angles to the mast, and the after-guy leading down at an angle to the stern, there is a lot more strain on the lift than on the fore-guy. Pull the inboard end of the pole down a bit, adjust the lift (down) to compensate, and I'm sure you'll find that the lift and fore-guy are equalized as to strain and that there is practically no bending moment on the pole itself. I repeat, a small matter of "safety at sea," but please remember it at the proper time, because it may mean that you'll still have a spinnaker pole and spinnaker at the Finish Line.

George Moffat suggests that instead of making a pole, say, four inches square, it could be made eight inches deep and three inches wide, thus making it stronger in an up-and-down direction and even, says George, adding possible unmeasured sail area.

The lift, fore-guy, and mast-slide provide the *modus operandi* for keeping the pole perpendicular. They also provide the method by which the tack of the spinnaker is kept in PROPER RELATIONSHIP to the height of the clew above the water. The spinnaker is an isosceles triangle whose base is the foot of the sail and whose equal sides are the two leeches. THIS BASE OR FOOT MUST BE KEPT PARALLEL TO THE WATER (OR HORIZON) AT ALL TIMES. The clew or sheet (side) will lift as the wind picks up and will drop as the wind decreases. The lift, fore-guy and mast-slide must be adjusted as often as appreciable changes in the wind lift or lower the clew, in order to keep the tack of the sail (or pole end) an equal distance above the water, or in other words, the foot parallel with the horizon. The angle of heel of the boat itself makes no difference. The foot of the spinnaker must always be parallel to the horizon.

I cannot emphasize too strongly the importance of this particular point in proper and efficient spinnaker handling, The wind, in the open and away from headlands, blows along the surface of the water in layers (one might say) parallel to the water. It does not, except in other rare instances, blow up or down. Therefore, to get the greatest efficiency out of a spinnaker it should be trimmed and adjusted in such a manner as to present its fairest and greatest plane surface to the wind, i.e., an isosceles triangle whose base is parallel to the water or horizon.

I have seen many, many boats with the clew of the spinnaker almost dragging in the water, the pole high on the mast and "cocked" up besides. Their spinnakers were not drawing properly and it was difficult to keep them full, yet their crews and skippers could not figure out why other boats went by them. You cannot make a spinnaker lift and draw by "cocking" the pole up in the air and hoping a vagrant puff will lift the rest of it. THE SPIN-NAKER POLE MUST BE PERPENDICULAR TO THE MAST AND ADJUSTED TO THE HEIGHT OF THE CLEW. To make the clew lift and flow in a very light air, a light sheet (reef line or marline) will materially help (see paragraph on "Guys").

It is most interesting to note that Captain J. H. Illingworth, R.N. Rtd., in his most excellent book, WHERE SECONDS COUNT, published in England in 1959 by Adlard Coles, Ltd., (and I heartily urge you to read this thorough and complete story and diagnosis of the 1958 Cup Trials and Final Races) agreed with me almost completely in outlining his ideas on proper spinnaker trimming. His thoughts coincide very, very closely with mine as stated on these pages. He agreed with me that at times some of the boats seemed to carry their spinnakers (and poles) too high to get the most out of them. At times, Vic Romagna, our spin-naker trimmer par excellence, and I had words on the subject of proper spinnaker handling and/or trimming. (I've already told you how Vic happened to get aboard *Weatherly*, but he was an eager-beaver, willing, helpful, alert, cheerful, and enthusiastic as all get-out, and he well deserved his eventual berth on *Columbia*. Right now, he can't argue back, because I have the typewriter and he "ain't" here, so I can speak freely, can't I?) Vic, at times, wanted the pole higher, or more forward than I did. I suppose it was because of my many years of steering a smaller boat, where I had to watch the spinnaker as well as steer, but I simply wanted to "put my two cents in" on the trim—and the boys up forward insisted that was *their* job and I should keep out of it. Anyhow, we talked it out, quietly, *of course,* most of the time, but rather loudly at other times. The net result was that "Captain John" agreed, in principle, in his book with my thoughts, and even stated, on page 56: "and boats like *Weatherly*, whose spinnaker trimming was very good, were often doing better with an almost horizontal, or only slightly cocked-up boom." Actually, the spinnakers on the Twelves were a different breed of cat from most spinnakers in use on smaller boats. And, keep in mind, this is supposed to be a treatise on racing normal, everyday medium and small boats—not necessarily Cup Defenders, so let's not get too far afield. But the "shoulders" on many of the 12-metre spinnakers were very large and I think that on a close reach with a spinnaker, it probably paid off to lift the pole abnormally so that these shoulders would R-E-A-C-H as far out in front of the jibstay as possible. In the last analysis, however, I still stick by my guns: namely, the pole perpendicular to the mast, at the height determined by the height of the clew, and the pole perpendicular to the apparent wind as indicated by the masthead fly.

TRIM OF GUY

The trim of the after-guy has caused many sailors no end of trouble, but a very simple device mentioned in the previous chapter, The Masthead Fly,* makes the proper trim of the after-guy a simple matter. THE SPINNAKER POLE SHOULD BE TRIMMED SQUARE TO THE MASTHEAD FLY, but never more than square. In other words, the pole should be trimmed aft until it is perpendicular to the apparent wind. The masthead fly gives the truest and most reliable picture of the apparent wind. Telltales on the shrouds will not. If there is to be any allowance at all on the 90-degree angle of the pole to the wind, make the allowance on the forward side. DO NOT TRIM THE POLE BEYOND 90 DEGREES, for this brings the whole spinnaker (when properly trimmed and full) too close to the mainsail and has a tendency to backwind the mainsail as well as to trap dead air (which it is very desirable to get rid of) in the spinnaker itself. Conversely, if the pole is trimmed very far forward of the 90-degree angle a greater part of the spinnaker will be blanketed by the mainsail, with an obvious resultant loss in speed.

And it doesn't make any difference whether the boat is on a dead run or a close reach, the same rule holds true. It is a matter

---

* By "Masthead Fly," as used here, I mean any type of wind indicator at the truck of the mast, mechanical or electronic. If you are lucky enough to have an electronic fly up there, you, the Skipper, can sit there at the wheel or tiller and "second-guess" your crew on the proper angle of the pole. On the other hand, sometimes these electronic marvels konk out, so it's kinda nice to have a mechanical fly up there, as well.

of only a second or two to check the trim of the pole with the masthead fly and make the necessary adjustment.

On *Bumble Bee,* our after-guy led from the pole directly to a winch, which was canted aft so as to prevent "riding" turns on the winch (see paragraph above on "After-Guy"). Generally speaking, a single turn on the winch and a turn on a wooden jam cleat (see chapter on Cleats) will suffice to permit a quick and easy adjustment of the guy when a wind shift occurs or a change in course demands an adjustment. In a strong wind, several turns on the winch are necessary, together with a few pumps on the handle which was underneath the deck.

On the America's Cup Defender *Ranger* in 1937, it was my job as spinnaker trimmer to stand just in the lee of the mast* where I could watch the trim of the spinnaker and also see the "nighthawk" at the masthead. Here, things being bigger, any adjustment took more time, but the principles were the same. A change in the angle of the "nighthawk" brought a bellow from your author to the men way aft on the stern and prompt cranking or easing on the coffee-grinder winch. The principles are the same, big boat or small boat, and how anyone can get the most out of a parachute spinnaker without the frequent use of a masthead fly, I am frank to say I do not know. As previously pointed out, the masthead fly gives the only true indication of the apparent wind, and any change in the apparent wind calls for the immediate adjustment of the trim of all sails. Such immediate adjustments, minor though they be, are the things which, together with all the sum total of other minor, minute details, help win boat races.

EASING, TRIMMING, JERKING AND TWITCHING THE SHEET

The spinnaker trimmer is one of the most important members of the crew, and should be treated with due and proper respect. He must be diligent, alert, quick and on his toes at all times. He is in much the same position as the relief pitcher in baseball. It is frequently his ball game to win or lose. A good spinnaker man or trimmer can very often pull his skipper out of a bad hole. I am frank to admit that many, many races I have lost to windward

---

* Way back in 1937 it is obvious that we were not aware that all excess "lard" should be sitting or standing way out to windward on a leeward leg (to try to heel your boat to windward), as pointed out by Jack Wood—and mentioned later on in this book. I repeat it here, for emphasis, 'cause it sure eases your steering.

have been won again—or at least greatly improved—by the diligent efforts of a wide-awake spinnaker man; with, of course, adequate assistance from the rest of the crew.

The advent of the parachute spinnaker has changed the leeward legs of a race from dull, uninteresting things into generally exciting tests of sail handling and teamwork. As pointed out above, the spinnaker must be properly and promptly hoisted. The guy, lift, fore-guy and sheet must be trimmed and adjusted—and with some teamwork it goes more efficiently. They must all be adjusted frequently to get the most out of the sail. But the one who does the most work on the leeward legs is the spinnaker trimmer. He must watch the luff of the sail constantly.

Spinnakers are perverse critters, and the moment the spinnaker man lets his eyes stray from its luff the spinnaker collapses—just as if it were secretly and slyly watching the fellow for a momentary lapse. The spinnaker sheet must be constantly eased and trimmed. To get the utmost from a spinnaker, the spinnaker trimmer must ease his sheet as he can, taking care to be ready instantly to jerk it in should the luff show any sign of "breaking," folding or collapsing. A quick jerk or twitch on the sheet will generally serve to "fold out" or open the collapsing luff. This jerk or twitch must be sharp and quick, bringing in, say, a foot or so of sheet. While simple in a light to moderate breeze on a small boat, a turn on a winch will make the job easier in a hard breeze.

On larger boats, two men tailing on a sheet round a winch are required, or, if available, a few quick turns on a coffee-grinder winch will do the trick. *Ranger's* 18,000-square-foot cotton spinnaker required prompt action by two men cranking and one man tailing on the sheet, and at times even this did not prove adequate, so a light "jerking" sheet was attached to the clew and handled by a man forward by the shrouds. Should the luff tend to collapse, he would pull down hard on the "jerking" sheet and generally the luff would open out again. However, he had to be ready to release the "jerking" sheet quickly, since the great surging spinnaker would have yanked him overboard in a hurry. If pulling down the clew temporarily did not solve the problem, a few turns would be taken in on the sheet itself by means of the winch. However, as on smaller boats, this trimmed-in sheet would be eased out again as soon as the sail would take it.

This might be a good spot to point out to you that with the newer spinnaker designs, especially Ratsey & Hood, you need not be afraid to let the luff of your spinnaker "fold in" a bit. You and your spinnaker trimmer will have to decide just how much,—depending on the size of your boat and your particular spinnaker. However, they can be allowed to "fold" just a bit without immediately trimming.

As a corollary, it is my opinion, and has been my experience that IF, IF your spinnaker wants to fold a LITTLE, and IF, IF you KNOW in your own mind how much it can fold, let it do it, because (again, in my opinion) you'll get a bit more speed out of your boat. But be sure to keep an eagle eye on the luff, so that if it does go much further, you can trim it quickly before it collapses entirely. And when THAT happens, you'll hear from your skipper or the helmsman in no uncertain terms.

My line of reasoning on this is quite simple: A boat will go faster if you get her in the groove and let her go. Sure, it's great to have eager-beavers in the crew who are on their toes all the time, alert, enthusiastic and on the qui vive. But the Good Lord deliver me from some JERQUE (French spelling) who, just when you get things all set and going for you, wants to ease the jib or—"let's trim the main a touch." Over the years, I've raced with a number of these guys—they have a little bit of knowledge, but they are definitely NOT all that GUNG HO! Who was the philosopher who said: "A little bit of knowledge is a dangerous thing"? He was SO right, for some overly enthusiastic IDIOT can upset the whole balance of the boat by jumping about to CHANGE SOMETHING just for the sake of CHANGING SOMETHING, when the boat's goin' like Hell anyhoo!! I don't mean that all hands except the helmsman should go to sleep—stay awake and look about. You might discover a new breeze or a shift even—but why change everything when you've just gotten the boat *alll* HOOKED UP?

The spinnaker man must work his sheet in and out constantly to compensate for wind shifts and the vagaries of the skipper's steering. Since the sail must come in instantly when he jerks, it is obvious, as stated above, that a sheet that stretches (nylon) is unsuitable for the job. The sheet must be adequate for the strength of breeze, but if it's a zephyr, get out the reef line or marline sheet. Let the clew of the sail lift and flow by means of a light sheet. Don't drag it down with a heavy one. Just watch the difference in the lift, flow and shape of a spinnaker with a light piece of marline for a sheet and one with the usual heavy-

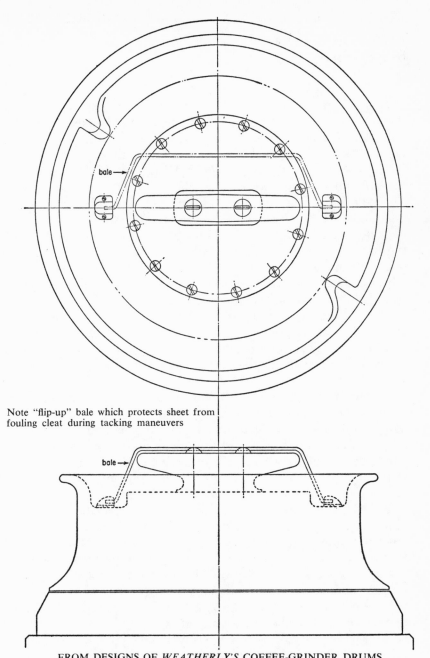

Note "flip-up" bale which protects sheet from
fouling cleat during tacking maneuvers

FROM DESIGNS OF *WEATHERLY'S* COFFEE-GRINDER DRUMS
REPRODUCED BY COURTESY OF PHILIP L. RHODES

Diagram 15—see page 197

weather sheet. And watch how the boat with the light sheet runs
by the others.

There are three methods of jibing a parachute spinnaker: (1)
the standard method, in which the pole is unhooked from the
mast, fastened to the clew, and pushed out over the former leeward side as the main boom is jibed; (2) the "free-wheeling"
method, as we call it, where the pole is completely detached from
the sail and the sail jibes itself as the main boom is swung over.
The pole is ducked under the jibstay and then rehooked on the
sail; and (3) the "free-wheeling" method with modern refinements in the form of two extra guys, i.e. two guys on *each* clew of
the spinnaker which, in essence, make it much quicker and easier
to re-attach the spinnaker to the pole. The first method is good
when you are going from one jibe on a dead run to the other jibe
on a dead run. The second method is better on a jibe from a dead
run to a reach, or on a jibe from one reach to another reach, and
the third is far superior on any large cruising boats, ocean racers
or 12-metres. There are, I might add, slight variations in this last
method, but essentially they are similar and the end results the
same.

On any jibe teamwork is absolutely essential. One slip or false
step on the part of any member of the crew can result in the
damnedest snafu you can imagine. Practice, and a complete
understanding by all hands of what is going to be done, are the
only things which will solve the problem. Everyone concerned
should have advance word as to what is contemplated in a jibe,
or when one is contemplated. Occasionally it is advisable or necessary to execute a quick jibe when close by an adversary. A few
judicious whispers can pass the word to all hands on your own
boat. Any motion or movement on your boat might advertise the
forthcoming jibe to your competitor and prompt action with
proper teamwork may and probably will make the jibe not only a
surprise to the competitor but a successful jibe, too.

In jibing on a dead run the first move, after alerting the crew
to the fact that a jibe is contemplated, is to lower the lift to a
point where the pole may be easily handled by the spinnaker
trimmer. The sheet is taken from the spinnaker trimmer by another member aft or in the cockpit. If the old sheet (which will
become the after-guy upon jibing) is led aft to a lead block on

the stern, the man in the cockpit takes the sheet at any convenient point between the clew of the spinnaker and this after lead block, ignoring the rest of the sheet which leads 'round the lead block forward to the cockpit. In other words, he takes the bite of the sheet and, if it is blowing hard, takes a quick turn round a winch or a cleat.

In this jibe it is best to have the pole more or less square to the hull in order to simplify the jibing operation for the man forward. Frequently it is not possible to do this immediately, since such a trim might collapse the sail; but sometime during the operation the sail must be square to the boat, or, to put it another way, the trim on each sheet must be equal. It is a splendid idea during a practice jibe to mark the sheets at this particular point with a whipping or serving of colored yarn, so that the crew may tell at a glance when the spinnaker is trimmed to the point which will make it easiest for the man forward to jibe the pole.

This equalized position of the spinnaker obviously may occur only momentarily, but it is at this instant that the pole can be jibed with the least effort and trouble. The fore-guy, though cleated to prevent the pole from lifting too high, is given a foot or so of slack. Practice will prove what is the best amount of slack to allow. The old after-guy, led directly from the pole to a winch or cleat, is temporarily held while the turns are taken from the winch, and the unused section of sheet, led aft to the stern lead block, is brought into play again.

The spinnaker trimmer unhooks the pole from the mast and hooks it into the former sheet fitting (or clew) as the main boom is swung over. In many cases, the boom is swung over and held amidships by a crew member. I find in boats such as IODs, it is just as easy for the skipper to perform the job, as this leaves the crew all free to handle the spinnaker. The spinnaker trimmer, as he hooks the pole into the former clew, MUST PUSH THE POLE OUT IMMEDIATELY TO WHAT IS NOW THE WINDWARD SIDE. This MUST be done as soon as possible to prevent the spinnaker from collapsing. It takes speed, strength and agility, but it must be done quickly. At the same time, the sheet and guy must be eased or trimmed, one trimmed and the other eased, depending on the next course to be steered. The fore-guy and lift are adjusted as soon as possible to the proper position, depending, of course, as explained before, on the position of the new clew or sheet. If necessary the pole is raised or lowered on the mast to keep the pole perpendicular to the mast, which maneuver may call for a further adjustment of the lift and fore-guy.

In using the "free-wheeling" jibe the guys are reorganized as outlined above, the guy (which will become the sheet) being led all the way aft, and the sheet (which will become the guy) being taken at a convenient spot in the bight and led to a winch. However, in this case, the lift, having been lowered to a point where the spinnaker man forward can reach the end of the pole, is the line that will be eventually slacked away instead of the fore-guy. Just a second or so before the main boom is jibed over, the spinnaker pole is unhooked from the tack of the sail (though, of

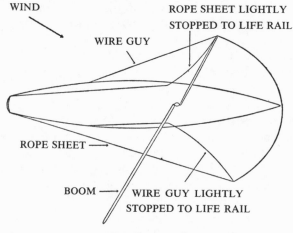

Diagram 16

course, the guy is still hooked on). The pole is ducked down under the jibstay as the lift is slacked away and the main boom jibed. The crew on the sheet and guy jockey the sail around the jibstay, the former sheet being slacked off and the new sheet (or old guy) being trimmed quickly as the course of the boat is changed.

The crew must be careful to ease and trim with considerable teamwork, but the job can be easily accomplished and in many ways is easier and a lot quicker than the conventional method. Having ducked the pole under the jibstay, the spinnaker man lifts the pole up to the sail (and the lift itself is taken up at the same time) and hooks the sail to the pole. A certain amount of

trimming or easing may be required to facilitate this part of the
operation, but here again, teamwork between the spinnaker man
forward and the crew on the after-guy will make this a simple
job. We have used this "free-wheeling" method with great success for several years and find that it is far superior when jibing
from one reach to another reach. (Jibing from a run to a reach it
works better if the pole is hooked into the tack of the sail, i.e.,
into the swivel of the snap shackle, from the *bottom* rather than
from the top.)

   "Free-wheeling" jibes on a Lightning or an International One-
Design are one thing, but doing a "free-wheeler" on a 12-metre,
bouncing in an ocean swell off Newport, Rhode Island, was a

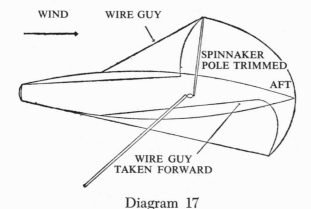

Diagram 17

different kettle of fish. We did it all right, by dint of good teamwork and much cussing and swearing (at times) and had things
actually pretty well under control. However, we were amazed at
the seeming ease with which *Vim* was able to jibe her kites, and
apparently we never got close enough for most of the season to
see what was being done. The third method described above (3)
utilizes a one-quarter-inch wire guy as well as a second rope guy,
the size of the latter depending on the strength of the wind. The
two rope guys, suitable in size for the strength of the prevailing
wind, are shackled into each clew with a swivel snap shackle and
into each of these guys is shackled a wire guy. In Diagrams 16,
17, 18, 19 and 20 you can see that the rope guys, which are led
way aft to blocks on the very stern, are used only as sheets—
alternately, obviously, depending on which jibe you are on. If

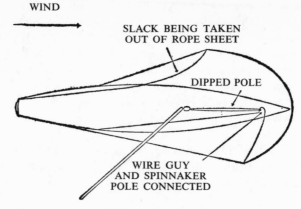

WIND

SLACK BEING TAKEN
OUT OF ROPE SHEET

DIPPED POLE

WIRE GUY
AND SPINNAKER
POLE CONNECTED

Diagram 18

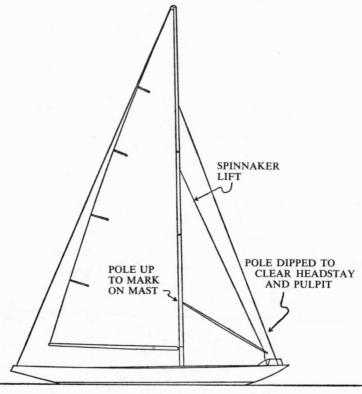

SPINNAKER
LIFT

POLE UP
TO MARK
ON MAST

POLE DIPPED TO
CLEAR HEADSTAY
AND PULPIT

Diagram 19

one is in use as a sheet, the other is slack and out of use for the moment because the wire guy on that side is in use as the after-guy, and vice versa. I might add that a fair complement of winches is necessary for this operation: two pedestal winches (or coffee-grinders) and two #6 winches on most boats. On *Weatherly*, at my suggestion I am happy to report, we had installed not two but three coffee-grinders and they were so nicely placed by young Phil "Bodie" Rhodes that they would take a proper lead from any genoa, spinnaker or main sheet. This third big winch, though it was heavy (250 pounds), more than paid its way, for we not only used it in this jibing operation, but we also put the

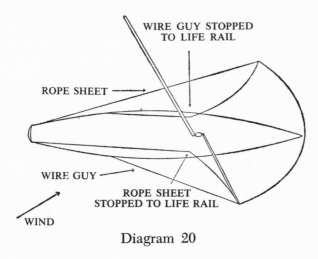

WIRE GUY STOPPED
TO LIFE RAIL

ROPE SHEET

WIRE GUY

ROPE SHEET
STOPPED TO LIFE RAIL

WIND

Diagram 20

main sheet on it when we were rounding the leeward mark to go to windward. I think it is of interest to note here that we very quickly found out that when we DID haul the mainsail in by this coffee-grinder, it was absolutely essential to have a relief grinder take over about halfway through the job. The first time we rounded a lee marker, Ed Raymond was delegated to "crank in" the main, and by the time he got the thing in, he was practically dead from exhaustion and completely out of breath—not from the strain of turning the crank, for the mainsail trimmed comparatively easily with this big winch—but from the hundreds of turns he was required to make to haul in practically 200 feet of mainsheet. (And ever after, we had a "spare" stand by to take over when the first man just "wore out.")

Great changes have been made in coffee-grinders since 1958—the design for those having been made by Sparkman & Stephens in 1937–38, with virtually no changes in twenty years. But 1958 saw other engineers enter the field—the basic design was altered and the horizontal chain (a very poor design from an engineer's point of view) was eliminated. Pedals and gears (for switching gears from a ratio of 3:1, 10:1 and 64:1) have been introduced over the ensuing years. Bases, pedestals, drums and gears have been made lighter. The Carter pedestal winch weighs only 35 pounds, compared with the 250-pounder we had on *Weatherly*. Rods and gears have replaced the chains I mentioned above. For example, *Barient* places two of their #35 drums somewhere aft the mast with two metal rods or drive-shafts connected in the middle (with a universal joint so that they can fit on any deck, no matter what the crown) to join these two drums. The trimmer has the lee deck all to himself to haul in on, with no winch-winders in his way to impede him. The winch-winders are up to weather (where they *should* be) with a double-handled handle to crank in with, as well as high- or low-speed gears (accomplished by merely reversing the direction of cranking). Barlow of Australia, Merriman Holbrook and others make similar but, of course, slightly different winches.

One wonderful thing has come out of all this new winch-design business: The winch makers have gotten together and agreed on a standard form of handle. In other words, unless you have a very ancient winch on your boat, winch handles are now interchangeable: the square lug on the end of any handle should fit any winch—a most marvelous and GREAT standardization of a simple tool. Matter of fact, you don't even HAVE to *buy* a handle now when you purchase a new winch, because you may have enough handles lying about. A small word of warning to crew members on a few points re winch handles:

NEVER, NEVER leave a winch handle in a winch when you are finished with it. Take it OUT, OUT, OUT!!

a. It may poke someone in the back, with obviously disastrous results.

b. It may inadvertently get knocked overboard, and *should* it, dear, clumsy bilge boy, it is your privilege, duty and "honor" to purchase a replacement for your Skipper. May I add that

the prices range from $75 to $150. ERGO, heed my warning.

c. This is as good a place to mention a small—but most important—detail, knocked into my thick head many years ago by
Rod Stephens, and which—with varying success—I've tried
to knock into other heads ever since. When you are asked
to trim a jib, put the handle in, grab the bight of the line
between the winch and the cleat and do your winching.
THEN, take the handle out, uncleat the sheet, snug up the
slack and re-cleat. WHY? you ask. Well, in the first place,
it's quicker—and time is of the essence—but secondly, it's
a safety maneuver; for if you slip when you are winching
in, ALL YOU LOSE IS WHAT YOU'VE TAKEN IN.
RIGHT? Get the picture? OK, DO it that way. May I add
that over the years it has been almost as hard to get guys to
use this method as it has been to get 'em to use that most
effective and useful rolling hitch (see page 369). Amen!!

At the command, "Stand by to jibe," one man snakes the bight
of the then unused lee wire guy up to the jibstay, the winch crew
on the other wire after-guy stand by to trim the pole fairly well
aft (if it isn't already aft), the inboard end of the pole is raised to
the top of the track (so that the pole will clear the inside of the
jibstay when it is swung across the boat), the man on the lift
stands by to trip the pull pin (by means of a line hanging down
from the pole) and release the spinnaker from the outer end of
the pole and then drop the spinnaker lift—and outer end of the
pole—to a pre-measured point marked with our precious Revlon
"Shocking Pink" nail polish.

At the command "Jibe," the main sheet is trimmed, the boom
jibed and the backstays released and/or set up, the man on the
fore-guy pulls the spinnaker pole foreward, the man forward
makes the connection between the pole and the slack wire guy
with no fuss or bother. He signals aft that he is set by pushing the
spinnaker pole out towards the new windward side, and the crew
aft winch back the new wire guy on a coffee-grinder. The old
rope sheet is taken off the coffee-grinder, dropped and forgotten
for the moment. The new rope sheet is put on this coffee-grinder
and trimmed as necessary. The trimmer of the former wire guy
has been adjusting as required, but now he can let go and forget
the wire for the line is in action and working. At about this point,

your author's polite and dulcet tones can be heard bellowing at the top of his lungs: "For Heaven's sake SOMEBODY take up the lift!"

The "double-guy" jibe does have many advantages, and the only disadvantage that we can see is the extra weight of the wire guy. But the only time that bothers you is in very light air, and if you are not going to be pressed for time, the wire guy can be unshackled until needed—though I'll be the first to admit that this operation can be a doggone nuisance and very unnerving to the man back at the wheel.

Another type of "double-guy free-wheeling" jibe was also dis-

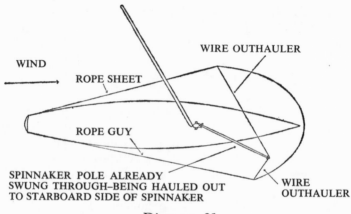

Diagram 21

cussed and tried out on *Weatherly*. This method involved the use of the second set of guys as messengers or outhaulers, in that they went from the two clews of the spinnaker to blocks on the outer end of the spinnaker pole, then along the pole to blocks at the inboard end of the pole and down to the deck through lead blocks to #6 winches. The normal rope guys, i.e. the "other" set, led to the normal blocks way out on the stern, thence forward to the coffee-grinders. In jibing, the sail was slacked off on one "out-hauler," the inboard end of the pole raised, the outboard end dropped and the pole pulled across the boat under the jibstay and then up to the sail by the other "outhauler." In the meantime, of course, a certain amount of jockeying was done with the two afterguys. The whole thing worked quite well, its advantages being about the same as the other "double-guy" method and the

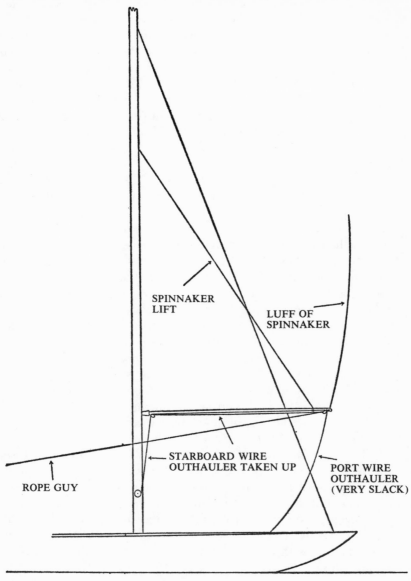

Diagram 22

same for the apparent disadvantages. For both methods, the outboard pole-end fittings could stand some redesigning and rework-
ing, but both ideas seem very practical and they certainly are an
improvement in large boats over the standard conventional
method of jibing and the original method of "free-wheeling" with
only single guys. See Diagrams 21 and 22. Now, in 1973, this
method is very often used, with much more sophisticated gear.

It might be interesting to note that in the 1937 America's Cup
Races the afterguard of *Ranger* worked out two methods of jibing her tremendous parachute spinnaker. One method involved
the use of one pole and a sort of modified "free-wheeling" (in the
sense that the spinnaker was not attached to any pole for a short
period of time). Double guys on either side were used in this
operation.

In the other method, two poles were used and the spinnaker
was attached or freed by means of messenger lines on the poles.
Unfortunately, (or fortunately, depending on your point of
view) the America's Cup Committee got wind of the goings-on
and requested a look-see. After a huddle it was decided that
neither maneuver was legal under the existing rules and *Ranger*
was prohibited from jibing its spinnaker.

The joker in the Rules was that the spinnaker must be attached
to a pole which must be attached to the mast at all times. And
while parachutes were jibed regularly on smaller boats at that
time without any question, the operation on *Ranger* took several
minutes to complete and there was either no pole or two poles in
use at some time during the jibe, strictly contrary to the existing
rules. Since no one, not even the British, had ever thought to try
and jibe these big kites (they always took them down and reset
another spinnaker on the other jibe), and since the Cup Committee did not wish us to be accused of unsportsmanlike or even
illegal conduct, jibing the parachute was *verboten* for that series.
However, as a direct result of this ruling, the Rules of the North
American Yacht Racing Union and its subsidiary organizations
were changed at the next Annual Meeting to permit any type of
spinnaker jibing desired or necessary.

TAKING IN THE SPINNAKER

While the time-honored method of taking in a spinnaker is to
let the tack fly and take the sail in to leeward by the sheet or clew
side, there is another method which seems to me to be safer and

quicker when sailing on a dead run or by the lee. This involves taking the sail in over the bow on the weather side. Many times there is a boat so close to leeward that you run the risk of hitting it with the spinnaker as you let the sail fly to leeward. Taking the sail in to windward eliminates this possibility. It also permits the spinnaker to be carried for a few moments longer, thus insuring a few extra feet which may result in a more favorable mark-rounding situation.

While this method is not feasible on a Class J yacht, it can be executed easily on a moderate-sized boat, or even on a larger one in light air. Before the jib is hoisted for the next leg, the sheet is detached from the clew of the spinnaker and taken in by the crew aft. Frequently the fore-guy may be unhooked too. The spinnaker trimmer, after unhooking the sheet, holds the clew of the sail in his hand ON THE WEATHER SIDE of the boat. At a given signal he releases the clew and takes the pole off the mast (the pole having been slacked forward at the same time). As the spinnaker trimmer CAREFULLY hands the pole into the cockpit, the lift is uncleated and slacked off. The spinnaker trimmer then unhooks the tack of the spinnaker from the pole and gathers it in, while at the same moment the crew aft unhooks the lift, lets it fly, and passes the pole CAREFULLY below. The spinnaker is lowered either on deck or into the cabin, whichever is easier, and the lift, (if it is not to be used again during the race) is quickly pulled *up* the mast by the crew in the cockpit. This particular maneuver is a great time-saver in split-second work and relieves the man forward of any worry or time-consuming effort in hooking up the lift. The lift can be easily hooked and brought down after the race with the messenger lines described in Chapter XVIII. The spinnaker halyard presents a problem that cannot be solved as easily and it must be hooked back on the mast. However, valuable time is saved on the lift, and the spinnaker trimmer (who generally has *only three hands anyhow*) can give his attention to something else more important.

Please note that the word CAREFULLY is capitalized twice in connection with handling the spinnaker pole. The pole must be *carefully* handed aft by the spinnaker trimmer or someone will lose an eye or get a helluva wallop on the skull. This can result in either a broken skull or a broken pole or both, and is to be avoided at all costs. While in the conventional method of taking the spinnaker in to leeward the pole is left on deck, with the after-guy still attached, when taking the sail in over the bow the pole must be handed into the cockpit in order to leave the man forward free to handle the sail. The sheet, in either case, is taken into the cockpit and, unless it is taken in immediately, care should be exercised to see that it is cleated somewhere, lest you suddenly see it disappear like a long snake over the stern—as I am afraid I must admit I have done on one or two occasions. Should there be any possibility of using the spinnaker again, guys should be rerigged, and the spinnaker restopped (however loosely or quickly) or restuffed in the turtle.

Another method of taking the spinnaker in has come into some use in recent years, letting go altogether on the after-guy so that it follows the spinnaker around the jibstay and comes in—with the sail—on the lee side. Of course, to accomplish this, you must have the guy itself (not the shackle or swivel) in the pole-end fitting. When you release the after-guy, the pole goes forward against the jibstay and the guy slips through the pole fitting and eventually runs all the way out and you take it all in on the lee side. This method does have one advantage, i.e., you don't have to have a man up on the bow. On the other hand, if the spinnaker whips about in a very strong breeze, the snapshackle has been known to open and you have lost one expensive piece of line overboard. Of course, if your guys are extra long, you can leave the bitter end on the weather side made fast and take the shackle end off the sail as it is lowered. The great advantage to this maneuver is that you can then shackle the two guys together and they are ready for another spinnaker set without having that man up on the bow to re-reeve the guys.

One major word of CAUTION on taking your spinnaker down —Boy, oh Boy! do I MEAN IT—NEVER, NEVER REMOVE THE SPINNAKER SHEET FROM THE SAIL UNTIL IT'S DOWN ON DECK and, preferably, down the hatch. We had a most wonderful chap on *Weatherly*, willing, eager and just a GREAT fellow. Out of respect and courtesy I shan't mention his name; but one day, in his excitement, he unshackled the sheet from the spinnaker. Somehow there were two groups—one on each luff. A puff filled the sail and they all let go, and that spin-naker blew out to leeward like a great big Trans-Atlantic, homeward-bound pennant. I hardly have to tell you that "ole eager-beaver" was in the proverbial Dog House the rest of that day, but he still is a great friend of mine, a great sailor and a great storyteller.

Actually, to finish that story on a happy note, we managed to get the sail down to "water level" very, very promptly by bearing way off quickly. The spinnaker dropped in behind the main and the boys grabbed it *tout de suite* and lowered away. I doubt if we lost ten seconds on the whole deal. HOWEVER, I REPEAT FOR EMPHASIS: Never, never take the sheet off the spinnaker until it's all the way down.

CAT'S CRADLE OR SPINNAKER NET

Shortly after the start of the 1948 Bermuda Race on Frank Bissell's lovely yawl *Burma*, a cold front hit, bringing a shift of wind from the southwest to the northwest, and a rough, confused, bobbly sea. A spinnaker was promptly set and all went well until the wind lightened and *Burma* started to bounce and roll in the cross seas. Suddenly the big spinnaker collapsed and took several rolls round the jibstay. Each succeeding roll of the boat served to roll the spinnaker tighter round the jibstay. A small, narrow spinnaker was set and Cap'n Bissell went up the stay in a bos'n's chair to do a splendid job of getting that doggoned spinnaker clear. Later, the small spinnaker did the same thing, but was not such a job to clear.

Upon our arrival in Bermuda, Rod Stephens laughed uproariously at our misfortune and brought forth a snapshot of a cat's cradle made of old useless lines. Two long lines, one from the foot of the jibstay and one from the base of the mast, were rigged at intervals with cross lines that were tied on the jibstay at their forward ends. The contraption, based on an idea originating on the West Coast, was hoisted on a spare jib halyard and so filled the foretriangle that the spinnaker could not possibly wrap around the stay. A mighty ingenious and yet simple device that would have saved us no end of time, confusion and trouble.

On *Weatherly* in 1958, we first had a rather complicated cat's cradle or spinnaker net, as it has come to be called, and it seemed to take hours to get it organized. A less involved one was devised, but even it took time. Then some of the "brains" in the foredeck —and they were picked for brains as well as brawn—developed a very simple and highly effective net of three different types of line. The one single main line was of $\frac{1}{4}$-inch filament Dacron, with a spliced loop in the head to take the jib halyard shackle, long enough to reach the deck and be fastened with a rolling hitch (see KNOTS, page 369) into a pad-eye on the covering board just aft of the mast. The first cross line of a lighter manila was permanently seized onto the main line down a few feet from the head and tied with a small bowline around the jibstay. The next line, some more feet down, was of linen, seized on the same way and tied again with a bowline to the jibstay. The last line of nylon was rigged just below the point of attachment of the spinnaker lift, and, likewise, was tied to the jibstay with a bowline. The different kinds of line made the darn thing easy to unravel and simple to rig and there was enough spring and elasticity in it to jibe without interfering with the spinnaker or spinnaker lift. And, what is even more important, it was "cool, man, cool," as the younger generation says. (See Diagram 23 page 167.)

Last Labor Day weekend, in the Vineyard Race, it was my pleasure and honor to be a Watch Officer aboard Bob Hubner's brand-new PJ-48, *Kate*, by S&S. We rounded the Texas Tower off Cuttyhunk some fifteen hours before that near-hurricane Carrie hit Nantucket. (It didn't bother us particularly, aside from giving us 20 to 25 knots of breeze from more or less dead astern.) However, the cross sea coming in from the Southeast made us roll quite some and broach frequently, with the ever-present possibility of a spinnaker-wrap. Being a very new yacht, there wasn't a net available, so I suggested making one out of odd lines (and, may I add, over the vociferous objections of a really salty and thoroughly sea-going member of the other watch who thought a net not only unnecessary but sissy-like). *Anyhoo*, I put a suitable net together in a few moments, quite similar to the one in Diagram 23, though the lower crossline *WAS*, I'm the first to admit, a bit low and fouled the spinnaker lift when we eventually jibed. However, an accurate and careful heave by Danny Sullivan, *Kate*'s able foredeck man, with a monkey fist on the end of a messenger line, made it very easy to pull the net back over to the proper side of the spinnaker pole and lift. I might add that we ran and reached roughly 130 miles in 15 hours, an average of over 8¾ knots. *Kate* just *flew* downwind—as did all the others. I'm sorry that I can't report that we won, but we did get a creditable fourth in Class. May I also add that a fine competitor behind us DID WRAP his "shpinnaacker" and "Butch" Lorentzen had one helluva time getting it de-wrapped. So maybe he should study the next few pages of the article on "de-wrapping spinnakers" by

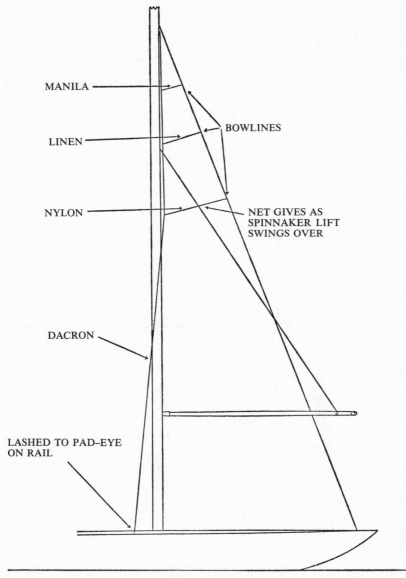

MANILA

LINEN

BOWLINES

NYLON

NET GIVES AS
SPINNAKER LIFT
SWINGS OVER

DACRON

LASHED TO PAD–EYE
ON RAIL

Diagram 23

Chris Moore. However, I must be fair and state that he beat us out for third place anyway.

I reprint it here with the express permission of C. L. Moore, Cap'n Paul Wolter, who devised the method, and Wm. W. Robinson, Editor of *Yachting* Magazine.

Chris Moore (a fellow Princetonian, but years apart in Classes), Cap'n Paul Wolter (that amusing, entertaining and able "Hamburger Yung"—that's a young sailor born in Hamburg, Germany, in case you didn't know), and I have sailed and raced many miles on *Palawan*, all of them pleasant, gay, laughing and happy moments, under the leadership of able Skipper Tom Watson, Junior.

Paul has often talked of writing the article below, but every time he saw some unfortunate competitor with a wrap, dropping further and further behind, Paul said: "Nein, I don't write that article. Let them find out for themselves." Finally, Chris conned Paul into letting HIM write the article, so here it is. May I say that in the 1960 Bermuda Race, the 74-foot yawl *Bolero*, then owned by Sven Salen of Sweden, had such a horrible wrap around the jibstay that they couldn't get it down at sea, and, eventually, had to take the whole headstay down to get the spinnaker off. And I'm not kidding; that's a true story. So, sometimes you *do* get a tough wrap.

The following article, originally entitled
CAP'N PAUL'S SURE-FIRE QUICKIE DE-WRAP METHOD
by C. L. (Chris) Moore
was printed in Yachting, *June 1971, page 65, under the title*
DE-WRAPPING THE SPINNAKER
by C. L. Moore

The treacherous spinnaker; after many happy months of benign usage, it can suddenly turn on you. And turn, and turn, and turn, until it finally swings to rest at last in a knotted five-story hourglass around the forestay. In a long race a boat loses time; in a short race a bad wrap can force withdrawal.

De-wrapping can be a messy business. After curses and vigorous leech-tugging have failed, an already overworked and confused foredeck crew will spring to the halyards to bring the thing down or send someone after it. In a skipper's nightmare, the last resort is The Knife.

A spinnaker net is a good defense against the wrap. Most spinnakers are fickle creatures at best, and will lose interest in wrapping when they encounter this kind of resistance. But even the finest of nets isn't foolproof. On one notable occasion, a very wily and determined spinnaker gobbled up the entire net on its way around the headstay. A stunned crew could only gape up at the seven monstrous bubbles with little bits of net peeping out between. The only sure defense against a wrap is a good-sized headsail set inside the spinnaker, but this cannot always be managed without interfering with the big sail's diet of free air.

We must face the fact that wraps will always be with us. The rare skipper who claims never to have seen one on his vessel is either a liar or hasn't lived long enough. Soon, this year perhaps, one of these slippery critters will strike *your* boat, and coil itself around *your* forestay, and defy you to get it off. Read on, and be prepared.

There is a way, a very simple way, without the halyards and without The Knife, to de-wrap your knotted spinnaker. All you need to do is utilize the same forces that wrapped it in the first place: wind and momentum. The procedure is very simple, and once it is in operation you can give your foredeck crew a rest.

Spinnaker wraps enjoy surprising you at night or in bad weather, and are usually accompanied by some confusion on the foredeck. The first thing a wise helmsman will do in this situation is send a crewman forward to stand at the shrouds where he can hold on securely, see the spinnaker, and call accurate steering instructions to the helm. *But first the crewman must determine which way the sail has twisted around the stay.*

Depending on which way the spinnaker has wrapped, steps must be taken to get the boat onto the right tack underneath it. To do this there is a handy rule-of-thumb: If the spinnaker is wrapped to the right—clockwise—then you should be on, or change to, the port tack.

If the spinnaker is wrapped to the left—counterclockwise— you should be on starboard tack.

Most often, the sail will wrap around to leeward, away from the pole. If this is the case, and it usually is, no jibe is necessary. Occasionally, however, a kite will be discovered flouting all natural law and slipping around the back way—to windward, toward the pole. This calls for a jibe.

Despite sloppy weather or darkness, this maneuver can be executed with a minimum of difficulty. The errant spinnaker itself has made things easier. Bottled up against the stay, it's unlikely that it will escape and overpower anyone handling the pole.

Once on the appropriate tack, the vessel should be well off the wind, with the pole carried wide and the mainsail out all the way to the shrouds. Any slack should be taken out of the spinnaker sheet and guy, and these should be kept manned in expectation of the de-wrap success. *A preventer should be rigged from the end of of the main boom to the stem.* This is most important, as the de-wrap success depends on the mainsail staying where it is even when the vessel is by-the-lee. The preventer should be made of nylon so that it will stretch.

Preparations complete, the de-wrap now rests with the helmsman. The deck crew need only stand by the sheets and guys and offer advice. It's a good idea to have one scout forward to report on the progress of the de-wrap, which should proceed as follows:

1. The boat is driven off sharply—a point or two by-the-lee. New air, backcurrents behind the mainsail, and momentum all combine to drive the spinnaker bubbles forward around the stay towards the pole.
2. Quickly but smoothly the boat is brought up again into the wind—a point or two above the original course. Momentum and air from windward combine to swing the bubbles back around inside the stay.
3. Each repetition of this pattern removes one turn from the wrap. How far up or down the boat must be steered depends upon wind and sea conditions and the tenaciousness of the wrap.

The helm must be handled firmly, and the man at the wheel must be aware of what's happening forward. He should not be afraid of steering by the lee. The main is secure, and the spinnaker, even bottled, will respond. A very few attempts will establish the effective limits of the swing, and after that, a sustained rhythm will accelerate the de-wrapping.

That's all there is to Cap'n Paul Wolters' sure-fire quickie de-wrap, and the technique has a number of advantages. It involves a minimum of finagling and a minimum of personnel, and although some distance is lost in veering on and off the course, boat speed is kept up—a must for passage races—and the sail is never off the boat. Remember that the same forces that wrapped the spinnaker to begin with are the very forces that can be used to de-wrap it successfully. The key lies in the understanding of these forces, and a firm hand on the helm.

CHAPTER VIII

The Boom-Jack

The boom-jack is an item whose great importance in connection with the tall, narrow, modern rig has not been sufficiently recognized. Known also as a kicking-strap, a boom-downhaul, and a boom-vang, the boom-jack has been more fully developed in recent years, but it is amazing to me that its advantages are not more fully known and utilized by builders, designers, and sailors. I mention designers and builders because surprisingly few boats are built and delivered with boom-jacks as standard equipment. They are generally added at some later date by an astute skipper, whose lead is later followed by the rest of his class. The short boom on the modern tall rig tends to lift on a reach or a run, with a consequent twisting aloft of the mainsail, and a most regrettable and inefficient consequence it is, too. The twisting of the upper area of the sail changes the shape of the sail, reduces its effective area, and as a result makes the boat go slower.

The boom-jack is a rope and wire tackle attached to the boom and the mast—or boom and deck—whose purpose is to prevent the boom from lifting on a reach or a run. Going to windward it is a detriment rather than a help and should be kept slack* or even taken off to get it out of the way—but running and reaching in any decent sort of breeze the boom-jack should be set up tight,

---

* Here, once again in 1960 I am happy to admit that I was wrong. In other words, I've found out that A BOOM-JACK CAN BE USED TO WINDWARD IN A HARD BREEZE AND VERY SUCCESSFULLY TOO! For emphasis and to prove my point I am leaving the original wording as set up, but right here I'll tell you again and again—and even repeat it in the later Chapter on Dinghies and Centerboarders—to be sure and set up your boom-jack *hard, very hard* in hard breezes. In light air DON'T use it to windward and set it up only mildly *off* the wind, because everything should be soft, flexible, resilient and gentle when the

the tighter the better. Experience proves that it can be used to advantage in light air, but care should be used in adjusting it, lest the mainsail become a flat board. However, in a breeze, set the boom-jack as tight as possible. On a dinghy or smallish boat, it is an easy matter to set up the thing properly just *before* you reach the weather mark, when the boom is sheeted in hard and is, therefore, about as low as it can get. The slightest easing of the main sheet, on the other hand, permits the boom to lift a bit, and the result will be that the boom-jack cannot possibly be set up to its optimum position, unless a winch is used.

On *Bumble Bee*, I finally had the good sense to install a winch on the cabin house to facilitate the job, and, believe me, when we cranked that winch, it brought that boom down. On a boat the size of an International One-Design, 33 feet overall, a #1 winch, with a base diameter of about three inches, is adequate. IT MUST BE EMPHASIZED THAT ON ALL BOATS DUE ATTENTION MUST BE GIVEN TO THE DESIGN AND STRENGTH OF THE GOOSENECK AND THE FASTENINGS THROUGH THE MAST, FOR A BOOM-JACK INCREASES THE STRAIN ON THE GOOSENECK FITTING, BOOM AND MAST TERRIFICALLY. NORMALLY, THERE IS NOT TOO MUCH STRAIN HERE, BUT THE ADDITION OF A BOOM-JACK WILL INCREASE THE THRUST OF THE BOOM AGAINST THE MAST TREMENDOUSLY, AND WHEN THE BOAT IS ON A DEAD RUN, WITH THE BOOM OUT WIDE, THE TWISTING MOMENT ON THE MAST IS A GREAT ONE.

"Skip" Etchells, 1951 World Champion of the Star Class, tells me that he broke a Star mast with a boom-jack. The Stars are not entirely suited to the proper installation of the normal boom-jack, for the boom is so low and so close to the deck at the mast that unusually extra heavy strains are set up. However, in the last few years, the Star boys have come up with a pretty efficient sort of boom-jack in the form of a semicircular track, facing forward to follow the arc that the boom takes as it swings from one side of the boat to the other.

---

breezes are light and variable. It took quite a few beatings by such experts in the Larchmont dinghies as Glen Foster in *Ordeal*, Jack Sutphen in *Rum Dum*, Dan Strohmeier in *Caprice* and others to convince me completely that I was wrong and they were right; but I finally became convinced that a tight boom-jack to windward in a good breeze is a practical and sensible idea. It has the general effect of flattening the mainsail ALL the way up, thus making the boat faster upwind.

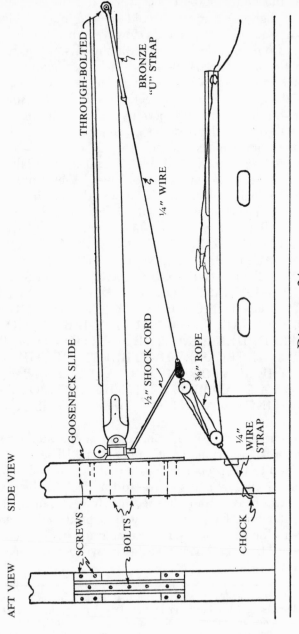

AFT VIEW   SIDE VIEW

THROUGH-BOLTED

BRONZE "U" STRAP

¼" WIRE

GOOSENECK SLIDE

½" SHOCK CORD

⅜" ROPE

¼" WIRE STRAP

SCREWS

BOLTS

CHOCK

Diagram 24
Boom-Jack

To be entirely efficient, the boom-jack should be in the plane made by the boom and the imaginary prolongation of the vertical gooseneck pin. In other words, the boom-jack should be attached at some point on the boom and at a point down on the mast— near the deck or the heel of the mast where the extension of the vertical pin in the gooseneck fitting would come. To put it another way, the boom-jack should swing with the same radius as the gooseneck fitting. This, of course, permits one adjustment to take care of every position of the boom on either tack, and it is most important, for who wants to adjust the gadget every time the main sheet is trimmed or eased? One adjustment at the start of a leeward leg is obviously time-saving and the only sensible way to handle this device. SO MAKE SURE WHEN INSTALL-ING A BOOM-JACK THAT THE POINT OF ATTACHMENT ON THE MAST, DECK OR MAST-STEP IS DIRECTLY BELOW THE RADIUS PIN OF THE GOOSENECK FITTING.

The greater the distance down the mast that this can be at-tached, the less strain there will be on the mast and gooseneck; therefore, get it as low as possible. Likewise, the farther out on the boom the better, for there will be less strain the farther out you can get your point of attachment. However, the greater the distance out, the more the boom will tend to bend and the whole thing will be a nuisance as it sweeps across the cockpit on each tack. So unless you wish to decapitate your crew once in a while —and a good crew is hard to come by and should be treated with greater regard than this—the distance out on the boom must be calculated with considerable thought given to the risks involved. In round figures the distance out on the boom on anything from a dinghy to an International One-Design should vary from about two to five feet respectively.

Construction of the Boom-Jack

The boom-jack should be designed and constructed for at least three-quarters of its length of wire, and the rest line. The reason? If the thing is all wire, there is no stretch or give, and conversely, if it is all line, there is too much stretch. On my Frostbite dinghy *Agony*, the wire, $\frac{3}{32}$-inch flexible, runs from the boom round a block bolted to the mast-step and thence to a two-part rope tackle which is fastened just forward of the centerboard trunk on the floor. The wire is possibly fifteen-sixteenths of the total length. The rope tackle, $\frac{3}{8}$-inch linen line, goes around a jam cleat and

is purposely heavy for ease in handling.* On a 110, the wire
should be about $\frac{3}{32}$-inch flexible with a single—or a two-part
tackle—$\frac{3}{8}$-inch line running for about one-quarter of the total
length. On the International One-Design *Bumble Bee*, the wire,
$\frac{1}{4}$-inch flexible, ran perhaps five-sixths of the total length with a
four-part tackle of $\frac{3}{8}$-inch manila at the lower forward end
running to a winch.

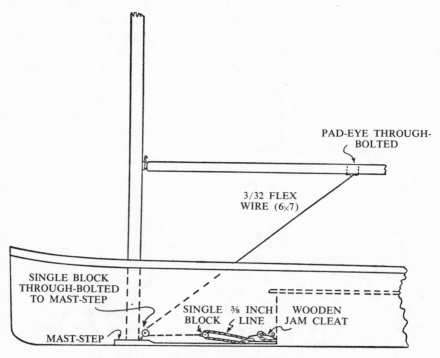

PAD-EYE THROUGH-
BOLTED

3/32 FLEX
WIRE (6×7)

SINGLE BLOCK
THROUGH-BOLTED
TO MAST-STEP

SINGLE $\frac{3}{8}$ INCH   WOODEN
BLOCK   LINE   JAM CLEAT

MAST-STEP

Diagram 25 Boom-Jack for Dinghy

Whenever possible, all fittings should be adequately through-
bolted, and if through-bolting is not practical, all screws should
be used so that there is a sheering strain rather than a pulling
strain. In other words, the pull should be sideways from the head
of the screw rather than directly down in line with the screw.
Through-bolting—or riveting—is far superior to screws for this
rig and is greatly preferable. (As a matter of general practice

* See diagram. The linen line here is *best*, for it is *less* slippery when wet!

anything on a boat—cruising, racing, or just plain day sailing—
that can be bolted down should be bolted rather than screwed
or—God forbid—nailed.)

The fittings on the boom to which the wire of the boom-jack is
fastened, vary on different boats; bronze bails, through-bolted on
the boom, Navy or Everdur bronze, or stainless steel straps fashioned to fit the boom and to lie in line with the boom-jack, or pad-
eyes—also through-bolted. At the lower end, pad-eyes may be
bolted to the deck or mast-step. On the International One-
designs, standard practice is to have around the mast a ¼-inch
flexible stainless steel strap fashioned with two eye splices which
are then shackled to the lower double-block of the four part
tackle. This strap, covered with rawhide, is fastened on the fore
side of the mast with a large chock or pad-eye, and each corner
of the rectangular mast is faced with a bent piece of light stainless-steel sheeting. The large pad-eye permits the rawhide to slip
around the mast as the boom changes position and the corners of
stainless steel prevent the strap from cutting through the mast.
This rig seems to work well and does not put the terrific twisting
force on the mast which a permanently fixed fitting would cause
when the boom is swung way out on either jibe.

Boom-Jacks on Ocean Racers

The problem of the boom-jack on a large cruising racer or
ocean racer is a bit more difficult to solve. The stresses and
strains are increased terrifically while the physical layout of
cabin houses, stowed dinghies, etc., increase the problems involved in successfully planning and installing the conventional
boom-jack. On the other hand, sail trimming and adjusting must,
by the very nature of their size, proceed at a more leisurely pace.
To put it another way, maneuvering must be planned further
ahead and with a longer time element. Therefore, there is more
time available to rig or unrig a boom-jack of some other type
which will be adequate for the job on any particular boat.

Shock-Cord

The type of boom-jack which seems to be the most practical
consists of a very heavy piece of shock-cord (say ¾-inch or 1-inch
in diameter) with a lanyard attached at one end to go round the
boom, and with a line attached at the other end which will go
through a snatch block hooked to one of several conveniently

located pad-eyes on deck, and thence to a free winch. Shock-cord, by way of explanation to those unfamiliar with it, is something given to the sailor by the aviation industry. It consists of a large number of rubber strands bound together by a braided cotton covering and resembles in appearance a piece of clothesline. Since the rubber shrinks as it stretches, the braided cotton covering is equal to the task of coming and going as the rubber stretches and takes up, and maintains its original shape and condition even with constant use. Captain "Des" Shipley, a Senior Pilot of American Airlines, who crewed on *Bumble Bee*, supplied us with a piece of it when we needed something to get the boom-jack out of the way. It proved invaluable for this purpose and also for another purpose described later on in this chapter.

Rod Stephens has experimented very successfully on his NYYC 32, *Mustang*, with shock-cord as a means of subduing backstays which, when slackened, whip about and cause undue chafe. He also has found it useful to take the bang and slap out of his topping lift by means of a small block fastened part way up his permanent backstay with a long, light piece of shock-cord running through it from the deck and to the topping lift. To mention one other practical use for shock-cord without digressing too far from our main theme, boom-jacks, Rod also used shock-cord to hold up a sort of *baby carriage* canvas spray hood that protected his companionway hatch in foul weather. The hood, which swings forward as someone goes below, is immediately swung back into position by an adjustable length of shock-cord. It is a great comfort, believe me, in disagreeable weather, for it keeps things dry below and yet allows plenty of ventilation, a most important detail on shipboard.

Shock-cord on a larger boat may be the answer to a workable and sensible boom-jack. For a racing boat in comparatively smooth waters, a positive, non-stretch, sturdy wire-and-rope boom-jack is fine, but on an ocean racer, which may dip her boom into a heavy sea without much notice, this type of tackle might cause an awful mess of trouble. Something would have to give and it would probably be either the boom or the gooseneck. Either one would be disastrous. And it would be almost impossible to design gear to take such a strain. As a matter of actual fact, I have seen very few boom-jacks, as such, on any sort of larger cruising, racing and ocean racing boats. Whether this is because they are afraid of breaking spars or gear, or because they are not aware of the advantages of the boom-jack, I do not know. And while many boats hold their booms forward with a fore-guy, comparatively few attempt to hold them down with a boom-jack. A heavy piece of shock-cord, suitably rigged for the particular boat, seems to me to be the answer. It will give sufficiently when required to, and yet will practically eliminate the *shock impact* which might cause a breakdown. The advantages of a shock-cord boom-jack for a larger boat would be the same as for the smaller racer and should not be dismissed lightly or as of no great value.

1973

Since writing these thoughts on boom-jacks and putting forth my ideas in print 22 years ago, it has been very interesting to watch and see the growing use of them in *all* types of boats, large and small. The boom-jack has become practically standard equipment on all racing boats, and a large majority of ocean racers that I have sailed on or seen, use them in one form or another. Now, all ocean racers—mostly with shorter booms and bigger foretriangles—use a wide traveller as well as a quickly adjustable three- or four-part tackle or vang (a "go-fast") to hold their booms down. Furthermore, the new aluminum rail—now installed on most new fiberglass yachts—has large holes about every four or five inches, to which sheet blocks, lead blocks, downhauls or vangs can be very easily attached at whatever absolutely ideal spot is best.

Much the same can be said of shock-cord. There is hardly a cruising boat that doesn't use shock-cord for one thing or another these days, either on deck or down below. For example, on *Weatherly*, an enterprising member of our crew rigged some ¼-inch stuff as a rack for our knives, forks and spoons. For years I have used ⅜-inch shock-cord on my dinghy, *Agony*, doubled and rigged across the stern about eight inches forward of the transom, with a three-inch lanyard tied to the tiller, to keep the tiller from swinging sharply across the boat when I tack in this "skegless" yacht. And it works beautifully, the tiller never swinging wildly across the boat and thereby putting it into a "tailspin."

However, it is my prime purpose here to point out again to designers, builders *and* owners that boom-jacks require redesigning and considerable strengthening of goosenecks, gooseneck slides, deck pad-eyes and other allied fittings. It is my feeling—

and I say this to you one and all in a constructive sense, certainly
not in a critical way—that in most modern boats I've seen or
been aboard, not enough thought and consideration has been
given to the terrific forces which are built up on a reach or a run
by a well-winched boom-jack. There are exceptions, of course,
but not too many. So, all I can say to you nice readers, be you
designers, builders or owners—take heed and do something
about it, *now*, before it's too late! And as the saying goes "It's
later than you *think!*"

For example, it is a comparatively simple matter to devise
some sort of tackle or suitable gear somewhere along the lee rail
which will hold your main boom down in the same manner as the
conventional boom-jack on a smaller racing boat. Many boats
DO use such an arrangement. However, DO NOT attempt to use
a genoa track as a lead for a tackle for a boom-jack or vang.
Genoa track is generally set down with screws, which are intended to have a strain "in shear" and not an upright pull in line
with the screws themselves. In cooperation with Phil Rhodes,
designer of *Weatherly,* we rigged up a very fine and substantial
boom-jack—held up by its shock-cord—but we also used
what we arbitrarily called a "go-fast," i.e., a four-part Dacron
tackle which went from a six-inch-wide heavy Dacron strap
around the boom down to a pad-eye, or one of several pad-eyes,
spaced strategically along the deck near the rail. These pad-eyes
were THROUGH-BOLTED with bolts, some of which were *fourteen inches* long—long enough, in other words, for at least two
bolts in each pad-eye to go through the shear clamp. The "go-fast"
was used to pull down the outer end of the boom when we were
reaching or to pull it down *and* forward when we were running,
and it supplemented or, you might say, relieved a part of the
strain on the standard boom-jack. The "go-fast" did require fairly
constant attention and adjustment whenever the mainsail was
eased or trimmed—while the standard boom-jack, rigged the
same way as *Bumble Bee*'s—See Diagram 24 on page 174—
complete with heavy shock-cord to help it "breathe"—plus a #6
winch instead of #1, required little or no adjustment, except for
changes in wind strength or velocity. A rather interesting feature
of the "go-fast," stated briefly above and repeated here for emphasis, was that, when running it pulled the boom down *and*
forward, via a through-bolted pad-eye *forward* of the main
shrouds. This simple rig, coupled with the light section of the

"tapered" main sheet, supplied us by Samson Cordage, practically eliminated the need for a cumbersome and awkward-to-rig forward boom-guy, and most certainly made it simpler to jibe in a hurry.

ADVANTAGES OF A BOOM-JACK

A properly adjusted boom-jack will increase the speed of your boat for a number of reasons:

First—It increases the projected area of your sail, i.e., it forces your mainsail to present its greatest area to the wind. With the tall, modern rig, there is a tendency the moment the sheet is eased for the boom to lift and for the upper area of the sail to fall away, thus reducing the area of the sail which will drive your boat along. The boom-jack prevents the boom from lifting, and therefore maintains the total area of your mainsail to push your boat along, and provides a larger "wind shadow." Obviously, the boat with the greater sail area will reach or run faster in anything but a whole gale.

Second—It forces the leech of the sail to maintain a more or less straight line or, perhaps, a fair curve. This, in turn, causes the whole sail to present to the wind a uniform optimum shape throughout the whole length of the luff. A cross section of sail at any point will look more or less the same as a cross section at any other point. Should the boom be permitted to lift on a reach or run, a cross section of the sail in the lower area would be considerably different from a cross section in the upper area. Furthermore, without a boom-jack (because the upper section of the sail falls away) the lower section must be *over-trimmed* to keep the upper part full. There can be only one conclusion: the boat on which the cross sections of the sail are more or less the same will go faster than the boat the cross sections of whose sails vary to any considerable degree.

Third—In a sloppy sea a boom-jack will prevent the boom from jumping up and down, which would cause a disturbance of the sail and a disturbance of the wind eddies across the sail.

Fourth—On a dead run in a strong breeze, a puff from off the end of the boom will strike the head of a sail, which is falling off to leeward on an improperly jacked-down boom, causing the boat to roll to windward. In a dinghy the results are fatal—a cold bath in icy water. In a bigger keel boat, there is incessant rolling which generally causes hard steering and over-steering with a resultant loss in speed. Many are the dinghies which have upset running dead before the wind because a puff by the lee—or off the end of the boom—rolled them over to windward in a twinkling of an eye, and all because they didn't set up properly and sufficiently on their boom-jacks. Watch a group of one-design boats running downwind in a hard breeze. The ones whose boom-jacks are well set up will be steady while the others will seem to want to roll their spars out. Put another way, a boom-jack is a definite safety factor, a safety factor which, in a Frostbite dinghy, is not to be sneezed at—for you may end up in the freezing cold drink.

To get the boom-jack out of the way for going to windward, on my daughter Corliss' 110, *Sosata*, a lanyard was rigged on the gooseneck so that the wire could be tied up, thus keeping it close to the boom and mast. Space in a 110 cockpit being somewhat limited, a boom-jack left hanging in its normal position would interfere considerably with the crew. In the Frostbite dinghies the crew is aft of the boom-jack at all times and does not get tangled up with it at all. On *Bumble Bee*, a piece of $\frac{5}{16}$-inch shock-cord was rigged to pull the boom-jack up snug to the boom when not in use, reducing windage somewhat, to boot. Though originally rigged for this object only, it was subsequently discovered than in light air this shock-cord served another very, very practical purpose. In a drift, instead of winching the boom-jack hard, we set it up rather gently, and it was amazing to see the shock-cord absorb the rise and fall of the boom, especially when there was any slop. The mainsail is soft and resilient, instead of being held like a board, for the boom reacts gently to each wave rather than banging hard. It *breathes*, you might say, as noted above.

As a further refinement of this idea in very light air, we often hook the spinnaker lift (when going to windward and the lift is free) on the weather side of the boom at the same point of attachment as the boom-jack and, take a slight strain on it to lift the boom slightly, thus relieving the mainsail of the boom's weight, and freeing the leech of the sail. Snugging the boom-jack ever so little brings the shock-cord into action and takes the bounce out of the boom. It is surprising how much better the mainsail will set and how much better it flows. On tacking, the lift must be unhooked and passed to the other side, something of a nuisance, but it's one of those little details that makes the boat go faster than the other fellow's, and helps win races. On larger boats a topping lift can be used for the same purpose, but on the smaller racing boats, topping lifts are excessive weight and windage and are seldom seen.

BOOM-JACK AND HEELING TO WINDWARD

Walter C. (Jack) Wood, the recently retired head of the sailing activities at M.I.T. in Cambridge, Massachusetts, pointed out in an article in *Yachting* Magazine some years ago that on a run a boat would go faster, and be easier on the tiller, if heeled to windward. His argument was that if heeled to windward somewhat—the exact amount to be determined by practice—the weather bow would dig into the water a bit and the lee bow, being a little higher, would make a hollow in the water. The general effect would be for the boat to develop a *lee* helm which would offset the *weather* helm effect of the wind on the mainsail. The net result would be that the boat would steer itself with very little help necessary from the rudder. And since every time you exert force on the rudder you tend to slow your boat by the amount of that force, it is obviously important to use as little rudder as possible at all times. Having tried out this idea in dinghies, International One-Designs, *Weatherly* and a 65-foot yawl on the New York Yacht Club Cruise, I have come to the conclusion that Jack Wood is a very smart sailor, for his idea works very well.

On *Bumble Bee* we piled all five of the crew on the weather rail; she heeled a bit to windward, got the boom higher in the air, so that it, too, benefited from the breeze higher off the water. I could hold the tiller with one finger and she really moved. While the results are not conclusive in a drift or very light air, in any sort of breeze, heeling to windward is good for a gain of five to ten boat lengths on a normal leeward leg. Steering is considerably easier and the rudder seems to flow after, or follow the boat, rather than to be pushing it. In a heavy following sea, the boat will surge ahead and seem almost to plane, with the rudder exerting no retarding drag. (See frontispiece.)

While I may seem to be digressing from the point, i.e., boom-jacks, it was very interesting to be able to try Jack Wood's ideas in a Star. The Stars being ideally suited, with their semiflat bottoms, to planing downwind in any kind of good breeze and a bit of a following sea, I tried to use as little of that big barndoor

Dennis Conners' Star #5669 showing boom-jack as well as the self-tacking jib.

rudder with a windward heel and yet get as much boom-jack effect by having my crew, Bob Smith of Noroton (whose Star I was racing) sit on the boom as near to the mast as possible while I sat way to windward. The general effect, though not perfect, was to heel the boat somewhat to windward and there was noticeably less pull on the tiller. Though the breeze was light in general, an occasional puff or wave would come along which would surge us ahead, and still *no appreciable* pull on the rudder. The point I wish to make is that with a practical and workable boom-jack, the crew on a boat of this type would be free to help heel the boat on a dead run—or keep it on its feet on a reach—and the boat would go faster. (These thoughts were written in 1960, before the introduction of the semicircular track now used on Stars for a boomjack, but I feel they are pertinent, so I'm leaving them in this new edition.)

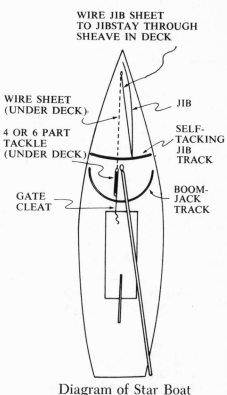

WIRE JIB SHEET
TO JIBSTAY THROUGH
SHEAVE IN DECK

WIRE SHEET
(UNDER DECK)

4 OR 6 PART
TACKLE
(UNDER DECK)

GATE
CLEAT

JIB

SELF-
TACKING
JIB
TRACK

BOOM-
JACK
TRACK

Diagram of Star Boat
With Self-Tacking Jib
and Semicircular Boom-Jack

Diagram 26

CHAPTER IX

Cleats, Winches and Jigs

Having put myself on record as favoring one-design sails and iron-clad, invulnerable hull construction rules for one-design classes, I am going to reverse my field, deviate, and admit that I am guilty of plain common tergiversation. (To save you the trouble of running for the dictionary as I had to do, tergiversation means fickleness or instability of conduct.) My position, I know, is more than slightly indefensible, and yet I feel that the planning and layout of cleats, winches, blocks, halyards, and deck gear in general, are a question of development or personal taste, and should not be militated against. Radical variations in hull construction which prove faster can render almost an entire class obsolete or out-built, while super-abnormal sails increase the already high cost of yacht racing; but the shifting or replacing of a cleat is only a small item of expense (either of time and effort or money) which may make life and racing somewhat pleasanter for the skipper and crew. I agree with you that having taken a definite position regarding one-design hulls and sails, I don't have a leg to stand on, so I will resort to what is known as woman's logic and say that I want to be able to settle on my own deck layout just "because."

There are very few designers that I know of who are able to turn out a boat, or a large yacht, on the deck of which certain changes in leads, winches or cleats are not almost immediately necessary. Imagine the myriad opinions that can and do arise from the fertile brains of a group of owners in a large one-design class. Actually very few classes do have rules against changes in deck and rigging hardware. The one class that I can think of which does prohibit such changes, is the one class which is rap-

idly building and pricing itself out of existence because of loopholes in its hull construction regulations.

Having delivered myself of the foregoing dissertation, I will go
on to say that the proper selection and location of various cleats,
winches, jigs, blocks and fairleads can do much toward making a
happy ship and a faster racing boat. Every skipper has his own
ideas about what sort of gear he wants and where he wants it. He
enjoys puttering round, figuring what should go where and
whether or not it will make work easier and quicker. He should
be allowed to fiddle and fuss to his heart's content. The chances
are against his coming up with anything too outstanding, though
occasionally he may. For example, when the late Arthur P. Davis
wanted to try an automatic steerer on his International One-
Design, *Patricia*, he requested permission from the rest of the
Class, and it was granted.

Arthur, an inventor and electrical wizard, had developed this
device which he felt might prove more sensitive to wind shifts
than the skipper. In general, it consisted of a fly fastened to the
jumper struts that directed a motor which steered the boat. The
angle of incidence of the fly to the course the boat sailed could be
adjusted, as the skipper felt necessary, to get the best speed out
of the boat. By another adjustment the electric steerer could also
be made to steer a set compass course. Arthur tried the thing out
rather successfully and apparently learned quite a lot from it, for
he subsequently (without it) won the Class Championship. The
only thing the gadget couldn't do was tell Arthur which way to
go round a mark, for one day, leading the fleet, *Patricia* rounded
the weather mark to port when it should have been left to starboard. Such a device is rather extreme and unusual. It is not
exactly the type of gear to which I refer or which the average
skipper would be interested in trying, but it did no one any harm,
yet taught Skipper Davis something and gave him some satisfac-
ion.

Cleats

Suitable cleats properly placed can make boat racing a pleasure and a joy forever; and, incidentally, make sail trimming and
handling a sure, quick proposition. Inadequate cleats, improperly
placed, can lead to torn sails, lost races and possibly even may-
hem. There are many different types of cleat for every possible
purpose imaginable: for instance, cam or gate cleats, wooden jam

cleats—with or without a base—metal jam cleats, "Jiffy" cleats (a patented type cam cleat), standard bronze or wooden cleats, and the rotating block and cam (all-in-one) cleat. (See diagrams.) They all serve a definite purpose in securing lines, and if properly selected for the special purposes required, conveniently placed, adequately fastened down, and properly serviced (in the case of mechanical cleats), they will save the crew many, many valuable seconds in situations which require split-second teamwork. Perhaps I seem to overemphasize the importance of an apparently minor detail such as a cleat, but I feel that, in its own small way, a cleat is just as important as a smooth bottom or a fine new mainsail. The right cleat in the right place, given the right kind of care and used in the right way, can be the little nail

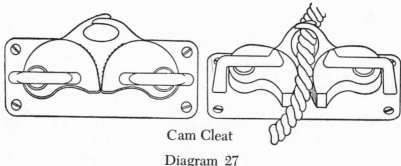

Cam Cleat

Diagram 27

in the horseshoe which can win or lose the kingdom. A cleat is one of the variables mentioned in the opening pages of this book, a variable which—if controlled, or made a constant, if I may put it that way—can be forgotten as far as being a factor in the results of the race. For instance, two cam cleats on the starboard side of *Bumble Bee's* hatch slide, right next to each other and well fastened down with 1½" screws, were used for the spinnaker lift and spinnaker foreguy. They were oiled regularly along with the rest of the mechanical cleats. For their designed and required purposes, I feel they were perfect. They were positive, easy to operate, accessible, and quick. In actual operation, they worked against each other, for as the lift comes in, the fore-guy goes out, and it is most convenient for them to be next to each other so that any crew member can operate them one in each hand. Minor details, you may say, but nevertheless quite important minor de-

tails, whose proper and prompt performance leave often busy
hands free for other necessary operations.

Many different types of these cams, or as they are sometimes
called, gate cleats, are available, in both metal and a hard fiber
material. At any good marine hardware store you can find something to fit your needs or pocketbook. And one small bit of incidental intelligence: the teeth on these cleats sometimes wear
down with time and constant use, with the result that your sheets
will not hold in them and frequently slip. It is quite a simple
matter to take the cams off and file the teeth to a sharp edge
again with a triangular file—and there is your cam cleat as good
as new. Check the springs, too, and get new ones if they look
shot. Or, with a bit of practice, and some spring wire (available
at certain hardware stores) you can wind yourself new springs.
Really not a hard job at all!

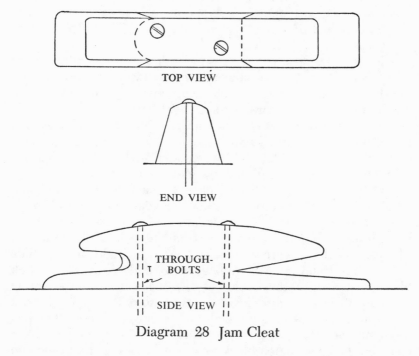

Diagram 28 Jam Cleat

The original design for our mahogany spinnaker-guy jam cleats
came to me from "Dick" Moeller, former 8-metre skipper turned
iceboat enthusiast. These cleats, which have rounded shoulders

for the guys to slip over at one end, and wedge-shaped openings at the other end to jam the guys into, are designed and made with a fairly long, high base which permits easy and quick cleating. Before fastening these cleats to the deck with bronze carriage bolts, due consideration was given to their placement and angling so that the one wrap-around turn could be done with a minimum of wasted motion and time. The wedge openings are deep enough and sharp enough to take any line from ⅜-inch diameter down to ⅛-inch reef line.

Bronze jam cleats come in various forms and patterns, some with wedges at both ends and some with wedges at only one end. Others are designed to have the line run through the center with two sheaves on either side as guides or fairleads, and may be cleated by jamming the line into a wedge at either end. While these various types are adequate, it is my feeling that the wooden jam cleat, with a base, is a lot more efficient and looks more shipshape and seagoing. While both wooden and metal jam cleats are a hazard to clothes and rain gear, the danger is definitely less with wooden cleats.

The "Jiffy" cleat, a patented type with a cam, operated either by a lever arm or a spring, depending on which is desired, is used mostly for smaller lines, ¼-inch or ⁵⁄₁₆-inch say. It consists of a quadrilaterally shaped bronze plate bent back on itself to form a curved channel which takes the line. The form of the cleat is held in position by the screws which fasten it down with spacer rings over them. My daughter's 110 was rigged with a "Jiffy" cleat for the main sheet and she tells me it worked quite satisfactorily.

The rotating block and cam cleat is the type most generally used in Star boats for trimming and cleating the mainsail. It is fastened to the "Barney" post in the center of the cockpit, the sheet leading directly down to it from the center of the boom. The cam cleat is securely fastened to a raised and angled plate that swings freely in a complete circle if desired. The snatch block, fastened to the center of the main part of the fitting (around which the cam cleat swings), also will turn freely in a complete circle and is equipped with a universal joint that further improves its lead position. Many Star boat skippers have changed the open snatch block to a closed block, so that the main sheet will not have any tendency to jump out of the block at any time. Others have pinned the block so that it turns in the same circle with the cam cleat plate. Either way you use it, it is a well designed fitting for a very special purpose and does its required job well. The Inter-Club dinghies were delivered with this type of rotating block and cleat, but after several definitely avoidable upsets in the wintery water, the dinghy boys decided that they had no use for cleated main sheets and removed the cam cleat section from the fitting.

Halyard Hooks

Halyard hooks are a device developed to relieve some of the compression strain on a mast. The normal single-part halyard, carrying a sail and cleated down on deck at some point, adds a compressing load on the mast that is equal to twice the downward pull or weight of the sail. It sounds somewhat complicated, but I think will become quite clear with this explanation. Suppose two men, each weighing 200 pounds, take hold of and hang on either end of the main halyard. They will remain in a state of suspension, neither one moving up or down. If one lets go, the other will fall to the deck. While they both hang on the halyard, there is a compression strain of 400 pounds on the mast—the total weight of the two. Now suppose you cleat one end of the halyard on deck and let one man hang on the other end. There will still be a compression strain of 400 pounds on the mast. But hang a line or halyard from the very top of the mast, letting the man hang on the end of it, and there will be a compression strain of only 200 pounds. In cases where rigs are very light and limber, halyard hooks will reduce compression (by half) and tend to make masts more stable and less whippy. All top-flight Star boats are equipped with halyard hooks on both jib and mainsail.

Ranger had a halyard hook on her mainsail, though not because her rig was light or limber. In *Ranger's* case, it was just plain good sense to relieve the mast of half the terrific downpull of her big mainsail. Her mainsail alone weighed a ton, and when you add the weight of the boom, plus the downhauling of the luff, plus the close-hauled sheeting forces, you really have quite a heavy load on the head of a mast. Why double it by running a taut halyard all the way down to the deck; why not hang the sail from the top?

Just this was done by means of a very clever but simple rig. A bail or loop to hang on the hook at the masthead was an integral component of the two-part, main-halyard-block assembly. The bail was held forward against the sail track by a spring as the mainsail was hoisted. Incidentally, all hands turned to when the mainsail went up, heaving it up by hand until it was almost all the way up, and then the halyard was transferred to the big 'midship pedestal winch. A painted mark on the wire halyard indicated when the bail had slid up over the hook at the top of the sail track. Slacking the halyard off a little let the bail seat itself on this hook. When it came time to lower the mainsail, the halyard was winched up until another painted mark, higher than the first, appeared, indicating that the bail had been hoisted far enough for a curved horn above the hook to bend the bail so far back that a ratchet slipped up and locked it in this bent-aft position. The sail could then be lowered without the bail catching on the hook.

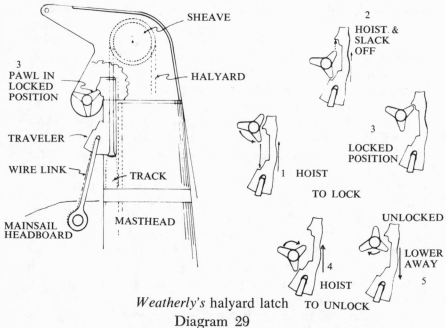

Weatherly's halyard latch
Diagram 29

At my urging, *Weatherly* had a halyard latch installed by A. E. (Billy) Luders, Jr., at Luders Marine Construction Company, in Stamford, Connecticut, in 1959. The general plans of this gadget were published in that fine column, "Gadgets and Gilhickies," edited by Ham deFontaine, in *Yachting*, November 1959, and are reproduced here courtesy of *Yachting*. Bill said that he originally got the idea from taking a gander at the trunk lock on a Ford car

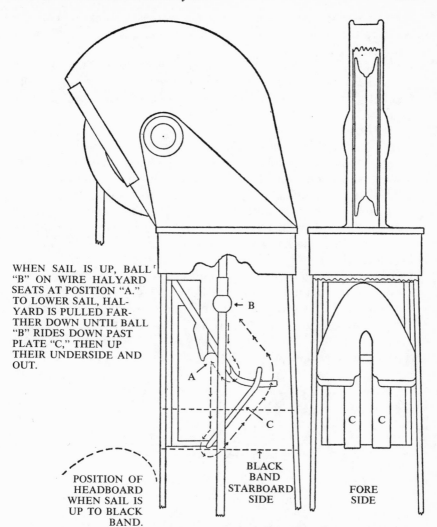

WHEN SAIL IS UP, BALL
"B" ON WIRE HALYARD
SEATS AT POSITION "A."
TO LOWER SAIL, HAL-
YARD IS PULLED FAR-
THER DOWN UNTIL BALL
"B" RIDES DOWN PAST
PLATE "C," THEN UP
THEIR UNDERSIDE AND
OUT.

B

A

C

BLACK
BAND
STARBOARD
SIDE

C   C

POSITION OF
HEADBOARD
WHEN SAIL IS
UP TO BLACK
BAND.

FORE
SIDE

FROM A PLAN OF *QUEST'S* MAST

REPRODUCED BY COURTESY OF
SPARKMAN & STEPHENS, INC., N.Y.

Diagram 30

some years ago, and used it on many 6-metres. It is sufficient to
say here that the thing worked very well and without a hitch all
summer. See Diagram 29.

Quest had a Sparkman & Stephens' version of their 6-metre
halyard latch—drawings of which appear here, courtesy of Olin
Stephens. It, too, worked very well and caused no problems or
trouble. (Diagram 30.)

Star boat halyard hooks are even simpler, consisting of a little
round ball soldered or swedged on the wire halyard a certain
distance from the shackle for the head of the jib or main. The
distance from the shackle depends, of course, on the particular
sail and the arrangement of the hook. The "hook" on the Star
boat rig is not a hook at all but a small plate fastened at an angle
near the head of the mast. Through a slot, shaped very much like
a keyhole, runs the halyard, the round-hole part of the slot being
forward. As the sail is hoisted up and reaches the top, the little
ball hits the slotted plate. By pulling the halyard forward, the
little ball is pulled through the hole end of the slot and then
worked aft, to be gripped and held there by the narrower slot.
The rig works quite well, but is a confounded nuisance when it
doesn't work, and therefore has no place on any boat that has a
substantial spar and proper staying. To go even further, it would

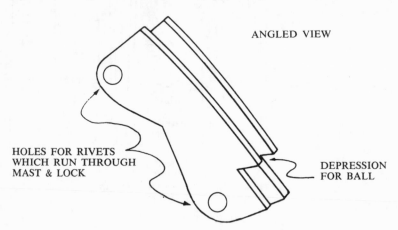

ANGLED VIEW

HOLES FOR RIVETS
WHICH RUN THROUGH
MAST & LOCK

DEPRESSION
FOR BALL

Diagram 31

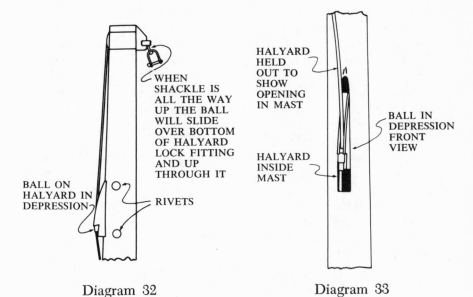

WHEN SHACKLE IS ALL THE WAY UP THE BALL WILL SLIDE OVER BOTTOM OF HALYARD LOCK FITTING AND UP THROUGH IT

BALL ON HALYARD IN DEPRESSION

RIVETS

HALYARD HELD OUT TO SHOW OPENING IN MAST

BALL IN DEPRESSION FRONT VIEW

HALYARD INSIDE MAST

Diagram 32

Diagram 33

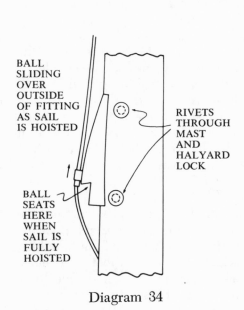

BALL SLIDING OVER OUTSIDE OF FITTING AS SAIL IS HOISTED

RIVETS THROUGH MAST AND HALYARD LOCK

BALL SEATS HERE WHEN SAIL IS FULLY HOISTED

Diagram 34

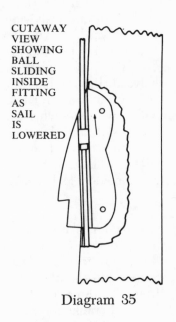

CUTAWAY VIEW SHOWING BALL SLIDING INSIDE FITTING AS SAIL IS LOWERED

Diagram 35

serve no useful purpose on a normally rigged and sparred boat, but Star-boat sailors have got themselves into such a (light) weight-minded state that their spars and rigging are much too weak to hold their sails up by conventional methods. They are to be complimented highly for their ingenuity and bravery in working out such light rigs, and likewise complimented for being able to keep them in their boats, but Heaven help the unhappy crew who doesn't get the weather backstay up quickly after a jibe. "Look! Daddy, No Mast!"

In the November 1972 issue of *Yachting*, my friend Dick Rose, Princeton '60, a former sailing student of mine who has gone on to be one helluva lot smarter than his teacher (and who hasn't?), describes what he terms "the lightest and most reliable halyard lock he has encountered." With his permission and that of *Yachting*'s editors, I shall describe it and include diagrams (see Diagrams 31–35), for it really is simplicity itself. Made of aircraft aluminum, it was designed and developed by Alan Holt and Dick Gates of Spar Tech, 4310 East Madison, Seattle, Washington, 98112, and priced at about seven bucks. Primarily for small boats, it consists of a U-channel with an "up"-angled cut at the bottom, just wide enough on the fore side to accept the wire halyard. As you hoist the halyard and guide the wire into this channel, the ball rides over the channel and eventually slips over the "up"-angled cut at the bottom. Slightly releasing the halyard slips the ball into this cut and you are locked. To release, you pull up a bit further, past the end of the fitting, and the ball will slip back—when the halyard is released—through a wider round slot, and down comes your sail. While I have not myself seen this halyard lock in action, I can see very easily that it WILL work, and besides, I take the word of Dick Rose on it. I recommend a look, again, at Page 34 of November *Yachting*.

WINCHES

Winches, like wenches, come in all shapes and sizes, from the big pedestal winches with two-foot drums on Class J yachts down to little 1½-inch snubbing winches used on dinghies, Snipes and the like. The big winches on J boats took their name from the three-foot-high pedestals equipped with double long-handled cranks for winding the drums. These drums were set off two or three feet from the pedestals to give the four men cranking, and the man "tailing" on the sheet, ample room in which to work. Sparkman & Stephens have developed a smaller, lighter-weight pedestal or coffee-grinder winch, for use on racing boats and cruisers in the 50-75-foot group. The J boat winches were geared with two speeds to give greater or less power, i.e., different mechanical advantages. The newer winches have not only a high and low speed (this change in power being accomplished by merely reversing the direction of cranking on the handles) but some special winches also have a device which permits a sheet to be "cranked out" as well as in, a real finger-saving invention if I ever saw one, for many's the digit that's been broken or bruised in attempting to "slip" a sheet out an inch or so around a winch drum.

Sparkman & Stephens designed for their boats in 1958, a new and better coffee-grinder, which, in effect, had more power in low speed and more speed in high. These also had an overriding drum, designed to make it easier for the trimmer to get his yards and yards of genoa sheet in faster. Unfortunately, these new winches were not available to the general public in '58, so Phil Rhodes had to design us his own version of the overriding drum and it worked very, very well. Furthermore, Phil designed the new drum a bit higher than the older flat-top type drum, the virtue of this being that the cleat was more or less "buried" down in the drum by the higher "lips" of the drum. This prevented, to a great degree, the sheet from catching in the cleat when the genoa was cast off in a tacking maneuver. We even gilded this lily by adding a gadget which had come from Jack Hedden's *Good News*, a light ($\frac{3}{16}$-inch) stainless bale, that could be flipped up to cover the ends of the cleat so that absolutely nothing could foul on the cleat. It was a simple little protective device and it solved the problem completely. And that WAS a problem, for if you ever snag a genoa sheet in a cleat in mid-tack, YOU HAVE HAD IT, FOR SURE! See Diagram 15.

Incidentally, *Weatherly* was the only Twelve to have three coffee-grinders, the others having two. It was an idea that I had promulgated and I believe that I can say for all our crew that they were happy with the extra one. It certainly worked well for many purposes, paid its way so to speak, and was invaluable in the "double-guy" method of jibing as outlined on page 155.

Some years back, two Californians, Jim Michael and Tim Moseley, well-known and able Skippers of *Baruna* and *Orient,* respectively, joined to found (and build up most successfully) a winch designing and manufacturing company, The Barient Company. Today there's hardly a yacht, racing or cruising, that doesn't have some type of Barient winch aboard—from bronze, titanium, stainless steel or aluminum pedestal winches (coffee-grinders to you), to halyard winches, plus backstay adjusters, insulators and sophisticated spinnaker-pole fittings. Barient's expertise and imagination has stirred up and shaken up all its competitors to such an extent that they, too, have "gotten on the stick" and improved their winches immeasurably.

Palawan has a splendid coffee-grinder designed by Graydon Smith, similar to ones aboard *Constellation* and *Intrepid*, two successful Defenders of The America's Cup. These winches had two speeds, a high and a low, which were operated by merely stepping on one side or the other of a double foot-pedal. In addition, the drums had a vernier adjustment, so that the genoa could be trimmed or eased a small amount without touching the main handles on the pedestal. Truly a helpful and efficient deal, for, as Olin Stephens puts it: "You can ease out or trim in without your competitor being aware of it, because you don't have to touch the cleat or drum."

Barlow, of Australia, has a line of winches similar to Barient's, while Merriman Holbrook, Carter, and Lewmar, of England (this last one comparing favorably with Barient) are other winch makers of note.

On the other end of the scale, the tiny snubbing winch used in little boats is a great blessing in its small way, helping the small boat sailor to trim or control his sheets with a minimum amount of backache. No handles are used, but power quickly applied serves just as effectively, and the turn on the winch will prevent any loss or slippage. It might be interesting and instructive to point out in connection with these little snubbing winches, that any winch can often be used in this manner at a great saving in time and trouble.

In light or moderate air, it is often a nuisance and a time-consuming operation to reach for a handle, fiddle about getting it in the slot and then pump. A quick jerk on the line will frequently solve the problem. Many sailors do not seem to realize this, but a person can apply a lot of power for a fraction of a second though he isn't really strong. Using a winch with this momentary surge of strength can accomplish quite a lot, with a minimum of time lost.

Fred English Photographs

Close-up of new Mark XII 2+2
3-speed Barient pedestal winch.

Close-up of Barient #32 winch. Winch
designers, for the most part, now
manufacture standard, interchangeable handles, thus making life simpler
for the winch-winders.

Fine installation of a Mark XII–3 2-speed Barient pedestal winch.
Note that by means of a foot pedal under pedestal either drum can be
activated.

As a case in point, at the end of the 1948 Newport-Annapolis race, *Burma* was approaching the finish line—maybe a mile away —with a true wind on the quarter of perhaps four or five knots, a light early morning zephyr. Now *Burma* has a terrific masthead foretriangle and, consequently a mammoth spinnaker, which we were carrying at the time with a balloon forestaysail set under it to fill up the lower section of the foretriangle. *Burma* was slipping through smooth water at possibly seven knots and, as a result, was drawing the true wind forward almost ninety degrees, the resulting apparent wind being well forward of the beam. Naturally all hands were on deck, keyed-up and in the anxious seat, for the leaders were not far ahead and we calculated our chances of doing very well were better than good. Chris Corkery, a 175-pound football tackle, who had been unhappy with mal de mer while offshore, was "tailing" on the spinnaker sheet. At one point the spinnaker showed dangerous signs of breaking badly, an occurrence which would have probably cost us valuable seconds, for our speed would have dropped immediately and course would have had to be changed to gather full way again. At a shout from the man forward, Chris, while the others were reaching for a handle, gave a gargantuan heave, the winch rumbled and the sheet came in enough to avoid a disastrous collapse. I have often thought about this particular incident with the happy feeling that young Chris really did himself proud that moment. It all goes to show that power properly applied in some cases can do the job faster even than a winch and winch handle.

Cam cleats, if situated and laid out so that you can get your back into the job, can be used in the same way. For example, on *Bumble Bee,* standard practice was to trim hand-over-hand quickly on the jib sheet as the jib went across the mast when tacking. The trimmer watched carefully as the jib started to fill and, with one final heave as the jib did fill, he put his back and shoulders into the job so effectively that he was able to release his grip on the sheet at just the right moment, the cam cleat grabbing the sheet and holding it just so. While the other end of the two-part sheet was equipped with a vernier worm-geared winch, it was very seldom that anything but a very minor adjustment was required, and the boat got away on her new tack with fully trimmed and balanced sails almost immediately. There is a knack to this deal, of course, but the cam cleats make it ever so much easier. Whether you use them or winches on your particular racing boat, training and practice will assist you in perfecting the operation and getting your boat off on her new tack with a minimum of delay and confusion.

BAVIER WORM-GEARED WINCHES

Various types of worm-geared winches have been developed on Long Island Sound over the years, for permitting vernier adjustments to sheets. These vary somewhat in design and construction, but in general consist of a drum on deck to which is attached a wire pennant that has a swivel to which is fastened the standing end of the sheet. In the International Class, three of these winches are used on the jib sheets and main sheet. The late Robert N. (Bob) Bavier, Sr., is responsible for a type of this winch developed by the Kretzer Brothers, Will and Clarence, of City Island, New York, that has proven very satisfactory and foolproof. The older type has open worm gears below deck that are operated by a handle or crank fastened to the coaming, the shaft for the handle being at right angles to the turning axis of the above-decks drum. The Bavier type winch has a cast-bronze, sealed casing which can be filled with heavy gear grease, thus insuring constant lubrication. Skipper Bavier's winch casing further prevents the gears from getting out of line (a failing of the other type) while his wheel, instead of a crank handle, makes the operation easier. Various types of special winches have been developed in aluminum for 6-metres, especially by Sparkman & Stephens, which permit rapid and efficient handling of genoa sheets and backstays. South Coast Co. and several Swedish outfits have designed and built other excellent types in general use.

WINCH CARE

All winches should be equipped with their own handles stowed in conveniently placed brackets. Nothing is as annoying or inefficient as having to hunt around a boat for a winch handle. After using, handles should ALWAYS be replaced in their own special brackets or locations. A minor point, you may say, but remember we are trying to arrange all these minor points so that they add up—to winning boat races. Bear in mind, as well, what I mentioned earlier in the book—namely, that the winch manufacturers have gotten together to standardize the lug on the ends of their handles in order to make them all interchangeable.

The double jib sheet lead discussed on page 45 with the standing end leading to a vernier winch illustrated in the next picture.

From top to bottom—a vernier jib sheet winch, a Bavier vernier winch for the main sheet, a wooden jam cleat, and the canted winch used for a direct lead of the spinnaker after-guy. See page 135.

It hardly seems necessary to remind you that winches occasionally need attention, oil and/or Lubriplate. I refer to you again to the chapter on Oil Cans and Grease.

Jigs

Winches are expensive items and not always readily available, especially in times of shortages. Adequate substitutes may be had for vernier jig winches in good old-fashioned, seagoing watch tackles or rope jigs. For example, a four-part rope tackle can be used on the standing end of a main sheet to get that last little bit of fine adjustment. Rigged with a small wooden jam cleat, this type of gear can be made fairly efficient and workable, though it naturally is not as easy to operate as a winch. However, when factors of expense, weight, and location are considered from all angles, jigs will frequently prove completely satisfactory. There is a new prefabricated jig available now on the market, four or six parts, which has its own little jam cleat built right into the shell of one block. Take my word for it: it's one helluva fine piece of gear—for many purposes.

As a matter of fact, as I go checking through the galley proofs of this book, I realize that Pat O'Gorman's PJ-43, *Wahini*, has a tallboy jib which is equipped with two of these adjustable self-cleating jigs, probably six feet each when extended. The net result is that you can, by relocating these jigs about the foredeck, set the tack of the tallboy anywhere in a myriad of places on the bow in relation to the spinnaker and/or pole, when reaching or running.

CHAPTER X

Dinghies and Centerboarders

M ost sailing experts will, if you give them half a chance, stand up and declaim at length on the many virtues of the centerboard boat as the ideal boat in which to learn to sail. They will point out that the centerboard will teach you to balance your boat, and the importance of balancing your boat. They will tell you that a centerboard boat is capsizable, that therefore you will learn to have the proper respect for your boat, especially after one or two dunkings. They will end up by saying that the centerboarder is safer for the beginner because in practically every case it will float, when capsized or overturned, while a keel boat is apt to sink. I agree with the experts entirely, but I wish to put further emphasis on the thought that centerboarders will teach you how to balance a boat so as to get the most out of it and how great a part this balance plays in successful boat racing.

In 1928, fresh from Princeton, fresh from winning the first "Big Three" Intercollegiate Sailing Championship, and fresh from a number of years of sailing keel boats (though my first boat was a centerboarder), I took a friend, Tom Childs, who knew very little about sailing, to Mystic, Connecticut to a little yard to rent a boat for a couple of hours. The owner of the yard put us aboard a twenty-foot centerboard catboat, upon our assurance that we knew all about sailing. We lowered the board, hoisted the gaff-rigged main and cast off, but nothing happened. Every time the mainsail filled the boat ran up into the wind and we couldn't get under way at all. We drifted off to leeward while all this was taking place, but no matter what I did, we just couldn't get that catboat to sail. Finally in desperation, I lowered the mainsail and paddled back upwind (fortunately it was light air). I told the owner what had happened and he offered to get us a ten-year-old boy who'd take us out. I thanked him and said something to the effect that I could sail well enough myself, but the boat wouldn't sail. It ended by his giving us our money back and us sheepishly making tracks away from there.

Do you know it was quite a long time before I realized what a donkey I had been? If I had only raised the centerboard a little, the balance of the boat would have changed and we'd have had a lovely sail. I had completely forgotten over my years of keel-boat sailing how really important a centerboard and its balance can be. I am sure the ten-year-old boy would have immediately recognized the problem and corrected it, but I was much too stuffy at that point to take any advice from a mere child. Forty-one years of winter dinghy racing have helped to replenish my knowledge of centerboarders and also (I hope) to reduce my stuffiness, for I have on occasion taken a word or two of advice from my current eleven-year-old dinghy crew, Ralph Petley— 1951–'52; Bill Kelly—1953; Joe Kelly—1954; Pete Kelly—1955 & '56; Bobbie Walden (my godson)—1957; Bruce Bradfute—1958 & '60; and (under duress) Wilma Bell, dinghy Ocean Race (across Long Island Sound)—1959; occasionally (Miss) Bernie Kelly and Steve Bell—1960; Barbara Kelly—1961; Judy Bradfute —1962; Steve Bell—1963–'65; Stuart Bell—1966–'70; John M. Daly—1971–'72; and last but not least, my own older Grandson, Ralph (Philip) Engle III, aged nine, on Monday January 1, 1973, in The Commodore's Race at the 42nd—just think of it: 42nd!— Annual Regatta of the Frostbite Yacht Club. I'm the only silly idiot who was there when that silly sport was started on January 2, 1932, who still is racing—if only semi–occasionally. Let me call your attention to the photo on page 334 of Steve Bell, who—at the tender age of four—raced with me in this same Commodore's Race on January 1, 1958.

In Chapter V on Sails, I pointed out the relationship between the center of lateral resistance of a boat and the center of effort of its sails. In dinghies and other centerboard boats, the problem in connection with moving these centers is reversed. In other words, in a centerboarder it is a simple matter to move the board forward or aft (which would be down or up respectively when the board is hung on a pin at its forward end) in order to move the center of lateral resistance and change its relationship to the center of effort. If you have a slight weather helm, moving the board aft or up will tend to compensate and correct the helm. If you have a lee helm, drop the board or move it forward. Even with dagger boards which are dropped down through an open center-board trunk, rather than permanently encased in the trunk and hung on a pin forward, there is generally enough clearance left at either end of the trunk to allow for this forward or aft adjust-ment.

Centerboarders in the natural order of things being smaller boats, the crew or live ballast comprises a greater percentage of total weight than in larger keel boats. It follows that it is even more important where this live ballast is placed in a small center-boarder. The same principles and rules should be followed in either case. All ballast, alive or dead, and all gear should be concentrated as nearly as possible amidships or near the center of balance of the boat. Keep it away from the ends of the boat for the same reasons mentioned on page 42. Place it where the boat balances best with the board in its most effective position.

It might be interesting to note that in Frostbite dinghies which have a minimum weight limit for the two in crew of 275 pounds, excessive weight in almost every range of wind velocity is a dis-tinct handicap. To put it another way, most of the dinghy sailors have found that it pays to race with a crew whose total weight is not over 300 pounds, somewhere between 275 and 290 being ideal. (This problem was "upped" a bit in December 1959 when the Larchmont Fleet of Inter-Club Dinghy Class sailors raised the weight limit—after 28 years—to 300 pounds.) An agile skip-per and crew can make up for their light weight in a hard breeze. It would seem to me that in such small centerboard boats as Snipes, Comets, Lightnings, and even Ravens, due regard should be given to the total weight of crew, though the percentage rela-tionship of crew to total displacement gets smaller as the size of the boat increases. Let it be thoroughly understood, however, that as the size of the boat increases, the total weight of the crew allowed assumes less importance. For example, on *Bumble Bee*, a keel boat with a displacement unloaded or approximately 7500 pounds, we always raced with five people (principally because I feel that five pairs of hands are extremely helpful at times), while at Marblehead, the International One-Designs seldom race with more than three (to keep the weight down, they say). A dinghy and its crew weigh in the neighborhood of 500 pounds. The addi-tion of a third person weighing 150 pounds would increase its weight by about 30%, while in an International One-Design the addition of another 150-pound person would only increase its total weight by less than 2%, almost an inconsequential amount.

Round-bottomed centerboarders seem to go to windward better in any sort of decent breeze if kept perfectly upright, or on their feet, so to speak. Whether their sailing lines are better when so sailed or whether their boards provide more efficient lateral resistance I am not prepared to say; but it has been my experience that they will sail faster this way. In light air, of course, like any other boat, they'll do a bit better if heeled slightly so that the sails will take some sort of shape. Boats with a chine (either keel or centerboard) do better to windward in either a breeze or light air if slightly heeled to leeward. They do a better job of knifing through the water this way, and eliminate that slap-slap of the waves on their almost flat bottoms. Reaching, both chine and round bottoms seem to do well if heeled to leeward somewhat, but running, *any* boat will do better if heeled to *windward* as described in Chapter VII—and—again—thank YOU, Jack Wood!

Heeling to windward on a dead run, particularly in a strong breeze, will really speed your boat up and make her move. It works in boats of all sizes, keel or centerboard, but care must be exercised not to have the crew so far forward in a centerboarder in a hard breeze that the bow buries too much. A hard puff may cause an upset, generally to windward, and the loss of the race. Usually, on a dead run, the centerboard can be pulled all the way up with no ill effects on the steering. Frequently, however, it will be found that lowering the board half or even three-quarters of the way will ease the steering, especially when it's blowing hard. It must be borne in mind that anything which will ease the steering will speed up the boat. The principal advantage of heeling to windward on a dead run arises from the fact that less rudder is required—the boat steers itself. Then it is sensible to use some centerboard if it will ease the pull on the rudder. A knife-like centerboard cutting through the water is certainly exerting less retarding force on your boat than a big barndoor rudder pulled across the boat.

Experiment with the two sometime when a competitor is close aboard. Try your board down (if you generally pull it all the way up). See if the steering effort required isn't less and see if you don't eventually pull away from your competitor. You won't do it right away, but time will tell. Any little thing which you are able to do to reduce the pull on your tiller will eventually find its way into the speed of your boat. To express a simple but important principle of Physics another way, every time you pull on your tiller you exert a small force which tends to slow your boat. The wind has given your boat a certain speed, but every ounce of energy you use to swing your rudder is transformed by the rudder into a force which will reduce the speed of your boat. These ounces of energy are multiplied by the length of your tiller. If you exert 12 ounces to push or pull your tiller which (let us say for the sake of argument) is four feet long, you have used a force of 48 ounces, or three foot-pounds, to retard the speed of your boat. If laid out in a parallelogram of forces the actual amount of retarding force would be less than three foot-pounds, but it would be enough, whatever the amount, to remove a certain bit of speed from your boat. I can only repeat in capital letters, USE YOUR RUDDER AS LITTLE AS POSSIBLE. Hold it lightly, hold it with one finger, and if you aren't able to, look around, check up, and find out what's wrong; find out what's out of balance, for something must be.

I suggested a few sentences back that care should be exercised not to have weight too far forward on a centerboarder when running in a hard breeze for fear of upsetting to windward. I refer you again to the chapter on Boom-Jacks, to emphasize the importance of a boom-jack in this respect. At the same time, a certain amount of board will help the situation too, preventing you from capsizing as well as easing the steering. Keep all four of these things in mind and their really great importance in avoiding "capsizals":

1. Boom-jack, to prevent a twisted mainsail leech which aids and abets capsizing to windward.
2. A little board to help ease the steering—maybe a half or even three-quarters.
3. A little board to add stability.
4. Weight a little farther aft in a hard breeze.

Believe me, my gentle readers, I know whereof I speak, for I have been frequently dunked in the chilled waters of Long Island Sound, not because I carelessly ignored my own suggested rules, but because I ignored one or two of them with a desire to sail faster. The race goes to the swift, the quick or the fleet. In dinghy racing it's the quick or the wet, and I wasn't quick enough.

The foregoing was written in 1952, and in 1960 I didn't change a word of it except (1) to emphasize the need for a proper and suitable boom-jack and (2) to add that: Use it to windward (as well as in reaching and running) in a hard breeze to help flatten the sail. And in 1973, I would only (3) stress the need for half, or even three-quarters, board in a hard breeze.

CHAPTER XI

Required and
Necessary Equipment

The U. S. Coast Guard demands that powerboats of all sizes, large and small, carry certain equipment such as life preservers, fog horns, proper running lights, Pilot Rules, etc. They very seldom board racing boats to check, but it seems to me that common sense dictates that the sensible racing man equip his boat with adequate protection in preparation for disaster of any sort. It is my aim in this chapter to give a list of the required gear, as well as the other items which will come in handy in making your boat sail faster. Obviously on some boats, because of their limited size or open cockpit arrangement, some of these articles will be superfluous, cumbersome or just plain in the way. In other larger cruising and racing yachts certain additional equipment will be in order, but I do not feel that it is necessary to go into such equipment here. For example, the extra canvas which you might carry on a 60-foot ocean racer for chafing gear would look pretty silly on a Snipe, as would dock lines and fenders; nevertheless, on larger boats they are standard equipment.

ANCHOR AND LINE

Anyone who goes sailing, much less racing, without adequate ground tackle is insane, or at least ought to have his head examined. You just can't tell when trouble will strike and when you want it, an anchor, of suitable size and weight, together with the proper line is an absolute essential. Cruising boats generally carry at least two anchors, one heavy and one light, and the efficiency of the light one can be improved by adding a length of chain between the anchor and the line. Danforth and plow-type anchors will hold with lots of scope, but they'll hold better if chain is added to keep the line down on the bottom. All anchors will hold better with ample scope on the anchor line. When you anchor, pick yourself a spot with plenty of swinging room, so that you won't whack your neighbor. Let your line run out so that the anchor gets a chance to grip the bottom properly and fully. Scope of six or seven times the depth of the water is considered a safe and adequate amount by old salts, so don't be stingy. Give her plenty, and you'll stay put.

In the matter of anchor or tow line, nylon seems to be about the best. It will last for years, is impervious to rot and worms, and is easy to handle. In addition, nylon will stretch, coming and going with the surge of the waves and the boat, thereby taking the jerk and strain off the anchor. This is one use for nylon on a boat that can't be matched by any other line that I know of. In towing, the same thing is true, for the stretch will make the job easier for both the tower and the towed. And while we are on the subject, the very same characteristics which make nylon a good anchor or tow line, also make it ideal for a permanent mooring line. Nylon can be easily coiled and dries out quickly leaving no little fragments or feathers to mess up your boat the way manila does.

A small kedge anchor is also a handy thing to have on boats bigger than 30-feet overall, together with a light nylon line of perhaps ¼-inch diameter. On smaller boats, the kedge would be in the way and a nuisance, while on boats over 30 feet, the regular anchor is generally so heavy that it is cumbersome and awkward to handle. The small kedge is light and easy to handle if you are caught in a foul tide during a race and can't make any headway. It is a simple matter to get it out of the bilge and slip it over the side. Incidentally, while you are getting it out and slipping it over the side, try and do it without advertising your maneuver to the rest of your competitors, a perfectly legal and smart trick if you can get away with it, and often good for several lengths. Many is the time that I have watched that wily and canny Corny Shields seemingly slip ahead of the rest of the fleet (and us) in an apparently flat calm. The passage of time and a pair of binoculars finally revealed that he had quietly slipped a kedge over the side when no one was looking. The light kedge has the additional advantage of being easier and quicker to pull up than the regular anchor. I recall the story of the enthusiastic and bustling guest on a big cruising boat caught in a foul tide near Plum Gut who wanted to anchor. Couldn't they toss the anchor over? "Ja!" answered the Swedish professional; "Ja!" But who vill pull it up?"

Lead Line

A lead line is a very convenient and handy thing to have aboard a racing boat, especially in the larger racing and cruising classes. On smaller boats there is less necessity and opportunity to use a lead line, but there may be times when you wish to work so close to shore to keep out of a foul tide that a lead line may be extremely helpful. Of course, a lead line will not detect a large "brick" on your course, but it will give you a fair idea of your situation at the moment.

Speaking of lead lines reminds me of the time-honored story of the sailor aboard the sailing vessel fishing out of Nantucket many years ago. It seems that he was such an expert with the lead line that he could tell by the taste of the bottom picked up by the tallow or grease in the cup on the bottom of the lead just where he was. On one trip from the fishing grounds, his fellow sailors surreptitiously dipped the lead in some dirt picked up for the purpose from a local farmyard. The leadsman on tasting, noting the character of the bottom picked up by his lead, bellowed to his fellow sailors, "My God, men! There's been a helluva storm and Nantucket's sunk. We're right over 'Marm' Hackett's chicken yard."

Other times, other customs, and *Weatherly* was fitted out with a very excellent Raytheon Recording Fathometer, although she had several lead lines; including one 300 feet long which Navigator Frank MacLear figured he might need sometime in the America's Cup Trials and (maybe) Cup Races. However, the Fathometer paid its way in quite a few races; one, from New London to Newport when we were skirting the beach off Fisher's Island in a successful effort to get out of a strong foul tide; and another during the Observation Races when we raced against *Columbia* and finished in a pea soup fog. Frank, by using his dead reckoning, Direction Finder *and* Fathometer, finally came up with the good word that the finish line was "just over there," and, by golly, we jibed over, ahead of *Columbia*, and won the race by a few seconds. Frank, from readings on the recorder was able to calculate his position quite precisely and accurately. Truly a Navigator's race to win or lose.

And now Raytheon has a very small, comparatively inexpensive Fathometer, which uses very little juice, that could be a great boon to the racing yachtsman many, many times over. Check with the marine hardware dealer. Or, get after Capt. Fred Lawton of *Columbia* fame and now with Raytheon.

Clint Bell's 34-foot fiber glass yawl, *Bumble Bee* (named at "Pop" Stanley's request after the original *Bumble Bee*, one of about a hundred such yawls built by "Dooley" Glander in Miami, Florida), was equipped with the "Seafarer" depth finder, a very fine and accurate instrument that had its own self-contained 9-volt battery. We used it without any problems of any kind for three years and I recommend it highly. There are a number of others equally good that are really more or less inexpensively priced when you consider their usefulness, accuracy and great help in many an emergency in fog, bad weather or just plain everyday navigation or coast piloting.

For more than 15 years Wilma Bell and I have raced in the Edgartown Regatta and Round-the-Island Race with the charming, affable and wonderful sailor Hugh Bullock, on his beautifully kept-up 41-foot Concordia yawl *Prettimarie*, usually successfully and always happily. For some time I have suggested and urged him to install some type of depth finder to help us beat up East Beach and through Muskegut Channel. With a foul tide it is absolutely essential to stay inshore, tacking along East Beach, and with any fog Muskegut Shoals are pretty nasty. Hugh's attractive and wonderful wife, Marie, gave him several Christmas checks toward this instrument over a period of several years, but he diverted them to other uses, until we finally "itched" him so much that he capitulated and installed a self-contained Fathometer that proved invaluable in the next year's Race around Martha's Vineyard, 'cause it sure was foggy, and a foul tide seemed to dog us all the way 'round, and there was very little wind to boot. I wish I could say we won because of the depth finder, but we didn't—and yet that fine instrument DID keep us off the bottom.

LIFE PRESERVERS

It hardly seems necessary to point out that life preservers are required by the racing rules, besides being a safeguard to the lives of you and your crew. And yet every day boats go out to race without any or without sufficient number for each member of the crew. Legal life preservers, i.e., those approved by the U. S. Coast Guard, are of such varied kinds that most any skipper can find the type he desires without any trouble and without great expense. But find them and have them aboard he must, else he will be disqualified for an infraction of the Rules, and justly so. Ocean racing boats are required to have on deck two service-able life rings to which must be attached suitable acetylene or electric flares, and a very sensible and splendid rule it is. So get yourself some cork life rings, kapok-filled cushions or vests, and store them some place in your boat where they won't be for-ever soaking wet; and have one for each person aboard. Frankly, I can't recall an instance when a life ring was needed, but there have been many times when it was reassuring to have them aboard.

On Tom Watson's 58-foot ocean-racing cutter, *Palawan*, there was installed on the after pulpit a bright yellow life preserver shaped like a horse collar, complete with water-light, dye-pack, shark repellent, whistle and "tall-boy" with flag attached. This horse collar preserver was encased in a box with a quick-opening latch that could be released by the helmsman merely by pulling a ring attached to a cable running aft along the life rail to the box holding said preserver. We tested this gadget often enough to know that it did work most successfully and quickly.

Foghorn

The foghorn or fish horn is another item on the *must* list. No racing boat is complete without one, either as a safety precaution or as a means of summoning your club launch. There are several types available in galvanized iron, brass, or chrome plate, but the good old galvanized type seems to be the toughest and cheapest. Bill Luders, prominent yacht designer, 6-metre skipper, and a champion in the International One-Design Class, has for years used an old-fashioned Klaxon on his various boats, and believe me when he cranks that Klaxon up he gets service from the launches. Some years ago the famous ocean racer *Dainty* came up from Bermuda with a ram's horn as part of her equipment. Blowing as long and hard as I was able, I could get no sound from it, while two Bermuda "gals" had no trouble in getting a rather melodious but loud toot from the thing.

I am sure most of you have seen the very noisy and raucous little Falcon CO_2 or freon horn which has been on the market for some years. It makes a terrific racket and is a very convenient thing to have aboard. But be sure and have spare cans of carbon dioxide aboard, because they have a habit of running out of "steam" just when you need 'em most. I had one constantly at hand in the cockpit of *Weatherly* during the Trial Races to push unconcerned power boaters off when they kicked up a continuous wake which bobbled us about furiously.

COMPASS

For years as a boy, I sailed a Star on Long Island Sound with no compass, until one day in a squall I found that the boat had been going more or less in a circle following the shifting wind. From that I learned the hard way that no boat should attempt to race without some sort of compass, even if it be a Boy Scout type. The liquid-filled compass is the only really satisfactory type and should be, if at all possible, permanently installed. Stars, 110s, and 210s, with their iron keels, present problems of installation, but I think that if a compass were fastened under the deck, either near the mast or near the rudderpost, with a suitable decklight or plastic window, it would perform satisfactorily.

Most International One-Designs and Atlantics have the compass installed under the cockpit floor with a decklight of glass as protection. On *Bumble Bee*, Egbert Moxham, her original owner, set up two compasses in the forward ends of the two cockpit seats with glass decklights over them. This rig works rather well, permitting the skipper to get a closer and easier view of the compass card, and we found it most satisfactory. Several boats have double compasses rigged under either coaming on brackets which can be swung out from under the deck when needed. This arrangement seems to be a good one and makes the compasses extremely easy to see, but there always is the chance of knocking into them with a resulting disalignment of the brackets.

TOOLS

Pliers, one or more screwdrivers, a sharp knife, a marlinespike, a sewing kit, a block of paraffin, and a can of oil are the tools of the successful racing man. Pliers and screwdrivers speak for themselves and need no explanation. However, it might be of interest to the fussy skipper to point out that recently some smart manufacturer brought out bronze tools for the yachtsman, pliers, screwdriver, and a wrench. They do seem like a good idea. A sharp stainless steel knife and a spike in a leather sheath is a very fine adjunct on any boat. Fasten the sheath in a convenient place and always keep the knife there, as well as the spike. Very often you will want one or the other in a hurry and if you must hunt round the boat for them, valuable time may be lost. The same is true of your pliers and screwdriver. Make a rack for them and keep them there always.

A sewing kit, such as is put out by Ratsey & Lapthorn of City Island, is a great help in keeping things shipshape. Lines need new whippings occasionally and ties come loose from the batten pockets. My sewing kit has been very helpful even in prolonging the life of my favorite Top-Sider moccasins when the stitching in the tops let go or the soles came loose. Containing all the usual tools of the sailmaker, such as palm, wax, thread, needles, bench hook, ruler, and knife, this little kit put out by those prominent sailmakers has really been a boon to sailors, racing and cruising alike. *Bumble Bee* received one of these Ratsey & Lapthorn sewing kits as a Christmas present one year from one of her crew, John B. Nichols, doughty Seabee and skipper of the dinghy *Misery*. Believe me that was one of the most useful Christmas presents a boat—or a sailor—could possibly receive. If you are puzzling over a suitable gift for a sailor, young or old, puzzle no longer; just put this sewing kit at the top of your list. But don't bother to give me one, thank you very much, for I STILL have the one from *Bumble Bee*, lo these years later, and it still has all its tools and appurtenances in it, in 1973.

LIMBER HOLE CLEANER

Keep a stiff piece of wire (a section of a wire coat hanger is excellent) or a piece of copper tubing aboard to use for cleaning limber holes. Limbers are easily blocked with dirt, making the pumping of your boat a problem. As suggested in the discussion elsewhere in this chapter on Pumps, try and keep your bilge clean. However, all dirt just can't be kept out, so have a bit of wire or tubing handy to help you. A limber chain is a convenient way to cope with this situation. It consists of a long piece of brass chain, similar to the type used on old-fashioned johns, run through all the limbers from bow to stern and fastened at each end to heavy brass springs. The limber chain can be grasped at any point and pulled back and forth, thus releasing any dirt in the holes. All well-designed cruising boats of any size are equipped with this chain nowadays, but frequently the limbers in racing boats are so small that the chain cannot be installed. Why good designers and builders permit boats to be built without adequate limbers I do not know, but sometime look over the boats in your fleet. You'll be able to count on one hand the boats with large limber holes.

CHAMOIS AND MOP

A good chamois is a great help if you want to keep your bright-work, deck and topsides in tip-top shape all season, especially around salt water. A good mop (with no metal parts) is a most helpful adjunct to the chamois, together with a bucket of fresh water. Salt left on your brightwork or enameled topsides on Gel-coated fiberglass will quickly remove the gloss and shine—as well as the paint and varnish. I venture to say that washing off your brightwork after each race will save you one or two coats of varnish each season, besides keeping up the general appearance of your boat. On *Bumble Bee* we used the remaining drinking water or the melted ice to mop down fore and aft, followed by a careful wiping with the chamois. The only times mutiny aboard *Bumble Bee* occurred were each afternoon after racing when the question of who would do the mopping came up. Bob Barker, spinnaker setter par excellence for several years, always felt it was the prerogative of the spinnaker man to do the mopping. His able successor, Stanley Bell, held the same view. The net result was that your author was generally the fellow who had to get down on his hands and knees with the chamois, though there was often a certain amount of discussion first.

Paraffin and the can of oil, heavy body oil, and Lubriplate are of such great importance that they have been given a separate Chapter (IV) and they are mentioned here again merely to emphasize their importance in the general scheme of things.

RACE CIRCULAR, CHART, PARALLEL RULES, AND DIVIDERS

If you are racing in an area where race circulars are provided, be sure and have *at least two* on hand. You can never tell when one will be lost overboard or mutilated in such a manner as to be useless. Aboard *Bumble Bee*, we always made it a point to jot down the letters of the course displayed by the Committee Boat under the selective course system. It is often helpful to know where the smaller boats (or larger boats, as the case may be) are going—they may be using one of your marks, or knowing where they are going may help you find your own marks—so jot down their courses as well. If your marks are written down on the circular, there is no chance of forgetting where you are going, or having a difference of opinion midway in the race as to your proper marks. So be alert, write down your course and those of other classes.

A large scale Hydrographic Office chart is another indispensable item on your required list. The charts on race circulars provided by most yacht clubs and associations do not provide detail enough in the way of soundings and landmarks. This is not intended as a criticism of the clubs or their committees. The circulars are just not big enough to carry the necessary information; so get yourself a large scale chart of your racing area from the nearest Hydrographic Office or ship chandler. Lay out the courses most frequently used and mark down the compass courses. It will save you time later. But most important of all—assuming you are not racing in mid-ocean—in penciling your courses with your parallel rules, let them run into the surrounding land. Isn't there a building, or a church steeple, or a bridge somewhere along one of these lines which you can use to steer that particular leg by? For example, there is a radio tower way over in Alpine, New Jersey which can be seen from the western end of Long Island Sound on a clear day. On a leg from Matinicock Point to Black Can C-1 off Delancey Point, this radio tower makes a wonderful landmark to steer by. From Matinicock to the Flashing Buoy off the southwesterly end of Hen and Chickens Reef, the Pershing Building in New Rochelle can be used to advantage. This method of finding marks of the course and steering the shortest possible distance is quicker and easier than using a compass. Parallel rules, pencils, and dividers are a necessary adjunct to the large scale chart. We used a rather large pair of brass parallels which got quite a kicking about at times, but seemed to stand up and proved eminently satisfactory.

SMOKES

Make sure you and/or crew are abundantly supplied with smokes of one sort or another. While I intend to endorse no special brand of cigarette, nor bore you with a discussion of my

personal smoking habits (I smoke pipes and cigars) I do heartily
endorse the use of smokes of one kind or another as a means of
determining the wind on a flat day. Time and again we have
literally smoked our way past other boats, puffing and checking
the wind for the least little cat's-paw. The masthead fly and telltales are wonderful when there is a breeze, but when it's flat,
Lady Nicotine will be more helpful.

In a recent dinghy race which took over an hour and twenty
minutes to cover the usual twenty-minute course, we always
seemed to be the first to jibe or tack as vagrant puffs came along.
Why? My trusty, beat-up, curved-stem pipe was going like an
open hearth furnace and giving forth great clouds of black smoke
which wafted, for the most part, straight UP, but occasionally
drifted off for a few moments in one direction or the other, calling for a quick jibe or tack as indicated. Some 49 years ago, in a
Junior Championship Series conducted by the Pequot Yacht
Club, the Bayside Yacht Club Crew composed of Rufus G.
Smith, the late Carl L. Weagant and myself, amazed the assem-
bled gallery by lighting and putting on the stern deck as a wind
indicator the uncovered bottom of a kerosene anchor light. We
had been in the habit of using this simple device to check the
breeze when there wasn't any, though at Southport, Connecticut,
it was new and surprising. But it hasn't been forgotten, for thirty-
odd years later, visiting the Pequot Yacht Club, I was reminded of
our youthful shrewdness by a friend who had witnessed the
Series.

Some years ago, we were presented with and tried out a type
of smoke bomb, which resembled in construction, though they
were considerably larger, the little breakable containers of spirits
of ammonia used by doctors to revive fainting patients. The
smoke bomb in a glass tube covered by a cloth bag was about the
size of a fountain pen. Hung in the rigging and broken with a
slight pressure on the glass, the bomb gave forth a white smoke
which lasted for ten or fifteen minutes. It worked rather well and
gave a good indication of the prevailing wind, if any, but it also
gave nearby competitors a pretty clear idea of the wind, a much
too generous and altruistic form of smoke. Being somewhat of a
nuisance to hang up, and as we are inclined to be selfish about
what little wind there is when it is flat, we decided to give up the
smoke bomb and stick to cigarettes, cigars and pipes. Any of
them seem to fill the bill, as long as the supply is ample.

PUMP

Most boats are equipped with some sort of pump, most boats, that is, except "dry-sailed" Stars. The skipper of a Star wouldn't be caught dead with a pump in his boat, much too much weight. He'd almost rather bail with his bare hands or his wife's new hat than add all the weight of a pump to his "crate." As a matter of fact, the average Star boat skipper will probably pooh-pooh this whole list of required equipment and end up with two child's-sized life preservers, a piece of Venetian blind draw-string for an anchor line, and the lightest aluminum anchor he can find (preferably one which will float). Be that as it may, a pump, and I mean a pump which really works, is an essential item on any fully found boat. Even in a Frostbite dinghy there are days when a pump, or even a rubber syringe, is a mighty handy instrument. When that water really gets cold and starts to form much ice in the bilge, it "ain't no time" to use a sponge, though under most conditions a DuPont synthetic sponge will do a fine job.

The "Step-On" pump, nothing more than the old-fashioned plumber's helper, with certain mechanical devices and valves added, came out several years ago and I used it very successfully in my dinghy, *Agony,* until it accidentally was dropped overboard. To operate the Step-On pump, you do just that. Put it in the bilge with the hose over the side and step on the metal top of the thing, releasing the pressure of your foot as the rubber hits bottom, so to speak. The round base, about six or seven inches in diameter, will fit between the frames of most boats and is so close to the bottom itself that it will suck out practically every bit of water in your bilge, providing, of course, that the limber holes between frames are clear. This Step-On pump, manufactured by Hunt-Miller Co., of Rochester, New York is not expensive as pumps go, and has few mechanical parts to get out of order.

The ordinary fiberglass bilge pump, in about the same price range as the Step-On, is equal to most all demands and has the advantage that it is made in various sizes suitable for larger or smaller boats. I speak of the type with only one hose, i.e., an outlet hose. The type with two hoses, the lower one of which is put down into the bilge, is, in my humble opinion, a nuisance and an abomination. The intake hose always jumps out of the water when you don't want it to, and it will not get all the water out because of its design and construction. There are rare instances when such a double-hosed portable pump is handy, such as in a very deep bilged boat, but in such a case a permanently installed pump would probably work anyhow. (See next paragraph.) In using any double-action *brass* pumps care should be taken not to wreck the strainer on the bottom. If the strainer has a hole in it, replace it, or cover the bottom with a piece of bronze mosquito netting to keep out particles of dirt, stones, etc. There is nothing which will render a pump useless quicker than a screw, cotter pin, or piece of thread or yarn sucked up into the valves. A spring overhaul for the pump is not out of order. The design and construction is quite simple and anyone can take a pump apart, grease it, check the packing, and put it together again without possessing a degree in Engineering. It is even advisable to grease the threaded barrel and end fittings so that they may be easily taken apart should trouble develop during the season. If these joints are set up only "hand-tight" without a wrench, you will make the job of taking the thing apart simpler. Waterproof pump grease on the packing will make the plunger work better and more efficiently.

Properly designed cruising boats are constructed with a built-in permanent pump which has a removable deck plate to cover it and keep out the dirt. These vary in design and may have a removable or permanently installed pump handle and plunger. The outlets run either into the self-bailing cockpit or out a permanent connection below the waterline, the latter, of course, being preferable. Since it is a nuisance and causes all kinds of confusion in the cockpit to lift the floor boards every time it is necessary to pump an International One-Design, when William H. ("Pop") Stanley bought *Bumble Bee* in 1944, we decided to install a permanent pump with the handle and outlet hose above the floor boards. Having seen another such installation I picked the Trident (Boston) Rotary pump and we used it successfully for eight years. The pump is bolted to the outside of the cabin bulkhead with a strengthening block inside. It takes 1¼-inch, inside diameter, hose, and standard 1¼-inch brass plumber's nipples. A right-angle sleeve takes the intake hose as it comes up through a hole cut in the floor, and the lower end of the intake hose is fitted with a standard brass check valve which is covered with several layers of bronze mosquito netting to keep out the dirt. It is amazing to see how much dirt collects around this intake covering—lint, pieces of thread and marline, paper match boxes, matches, cigarettes, and just plain "gurry." Though I try and keep the bilges and limbers clean, carefully and painstakingly hosing out the bilge during every haulout, it is still often necessary to lift up this intake hose and wipe it off so that the pump will work efficiently. The outlet hose is carefully coiled under the starboard seat where it is completely out of the way, and yet ready for instant use. In order to keep the system full of water and the pump primed, in conjunction with the check valve a thermos cork (available at any hardware or drug store) is kept in the outlet hose. This idea seems to work well, and though it is possible for some of the water to leak past the check valve, very rarely is it necessary to prime the pump. When priming is necessary, it generally indicates that the pump itself is in need of grease.

A permanent type of plunger pump known as the Navy pump has proven itself equally adaptable and workable, though a small section of floor board must be made removable so that the handle can be reached. (The shape, weight and design of the Navy pump preclude its installation above the floor.) Since weight in a racing boat is just as important as workability, care must be taken to get the pump low when a heavy one is used. Compared to the rotary pump described above, the Navy pump is heavy, so get it low. The same check valve and hose arrangement described above may be used and the same results accomplished. In either case, however, if you want constant and continuous action from the pump, don't be stingy with the waterproof grease, and keep your bilge clean. There may be times when a deep-bilged boat will go better with some water in it, but, by and large, your boat will be livelier and faster with a dry bilge, so keep your pump in good working order. Besides, under the Racing Rules, your bilge is supposed to be pumped DRY!

The old-fashioned galvanized iron pump with a broomstick handle and leather washers is a fine thing to use to get a tremendous quantity of water out of your boat quickly or to get the dirt out of your bilge. For the latter purpose, it is probably unbeatable, unless you have a screw plug in your boat which can be removed when you are hauled out. However, it takes up a lot of room, invariably rattles and bounces round your boat and is generally in the way, though it is probably the cheapest of all pumps. Unless you have a very leaky boat or make a habit of upsetting your boat with regularity, the galvanized pump is not the ideal one.

Weatherly had an excellent diaphragm pump manufactured by Edson, but quite heavy as it was made of bronze. *Columbia* later put one in similar to ours—and they really pumped water and required no priming—but were made of aluminum, considerably lighter.

The TAT Manufacturing Co., of West Haven, Connecticut, came out with a rotary pump which looks as if it might be the answer to a dinghy sailor's dream—no dishpan hands from freezing cold salt water. I bought one for *Agony* and installed it under the centerboard cap. This pump made of plastic and neoprene hose, unlike most pumps, WILL suck up small things like screws, nuts, bolts, cotters, etc., without damage to or clogging of the pump. The Handy Boy pump is another really workable pump and there are other similar types of pump which will do a bang-up job.

A ten- or twelve-quart plastic pail and a DuPont sponge will complete your bailing or pumping equipment. It seems hardly necessary to point out the many advantages of a pail aboard a boat, racing or cruising, but a check, I am sure, would show that less than fifty percent of the racers carry them. Why, I don't know, unless the racing fraternity, weight-conscious as they are, feel that the pail is the most dispensable item of all. The DuPont cellulose sponge is far superior to the natural sponge and is heartily endorsed.

PROTEST FLAG, CODE FLAG "B"

The Racing Rules of the North American Yacht Racing Union, under which practically all our races are run, demand the PROMPT hoisting of a protest flag, the square red code flag "B", when an alleged foul is committed. It is not enough to hoist it a half-hour later or even ten minutes later. The flag must be flown *promptly* in the main rigging after the infringement occurred or was first noticed, and must be kept flying until the finish. Most Committees will refuse to entertain or listen to a protest unless the protest flag was flown and *promptly* flown. Unless the Instructions specify otherwise, the flag does not have to be code flag "B"—anything red will do (except the ensign). To be on the safe side, however, it is advisable to have a red code flag "B" aboard stowed where it can be easily found and displayed in the rigging. While it seems to me that indiscriminate and frequent protests are to be avoided as poor sportsmanship, you should be prepared for an out-and-out foul and have your flag ready and handy.

On the question of protests may I point out that for 1973 the North American Yacht Racing Union at its annual meeting in November 1972 adopted a number of revised racing rules to go into effect April 1, 1973. Among them is a change in Rule 67 and I quote from the NAYRU/*News* of December 1972:

"Rule 67, Contact between Yachts Racing, provides that when there is contact between two yachts and neither of them retires or protests, both shall be disqualified. Under some circumstances, a third yacht may protest these two *without showing a protest flag* (ITALICS MINE), and also under some circumstances, the Race Committee may waive the Rule."

Quite frankly and honestly, I feel that this new Rule is a step in the right direction, for where there is contact between boats there just *has* to be a violation of the Rules and someone is at fault.

Reef Line and Spare Sheets

An extra hank of Dacron reef line (aside from any light weather spinnaker or jib sheets) is always a handy thing to have aboard. It has a thousand uses, weighs but little, and may be the very thing which will one day save the race and the day for you. A spare sheet which can be used either for the jib, spinnaker, or in a pinch for the mainsail, ranks high on my list of required gear. Sheets have a habit of popping at the most inopportune times, so have something aboard which can be used for a spare.

Odd Nuts, Bolts, Screws, Shackles and Cotter Pins

Ye Compleat Racing Skipper (and especially Cruising Skipper) will be well supplied with spare shackles, cotter pins, screws, and bolts. In the larger boats he will carry them on board, not enough to sink his boat, of course, but an adequate supply of assorted sizes. The weight-conscious Star skipper will scream about loading his boat down with junk, but woe betide him when something breaks down and he has nothing but his finger to put in the dyke to stem the flow. Things shouldn't break down, but no matter how careful you are something will eventually give way, and even a few odd bolts, screws or cotters may help to save the day. Even if you won't carry them aboard, have them somewhere nearby, in your boat locker or launch so that they can be picked up quickly.

Binoculars are expensive, fragile and delicate instruments. Their frames are comparatively easy to knock out of line, thus destroying their usefulness and efficiency. If you are fortunate enough to possess a pair, guard them well and carry them carefully. Keep them in their case at all times when not in use. Don't just toss them anywhere, but have a special place for them aboard ship and make a practice of putting them back there when you are finished using them. *Never leave them in the direct rays of the sun, for the heat will quickly ruin the lenses.* Salt spray will do nothing to improve glasses, so find a dry spot aboard to keep the case in and replace the binocs there immediately. Besides, if you want them in a hurry you'll know just where to look and won't have to hunt all over the boat.

Various types of field glasses and binoculars are available at all prices. For use aboard a boat, a 7×50 coated prismatic binocular seems to be the best. This combination of power and field will give the most efficient service, the 7-power giving sufficient strength and yet not too great magnification. Glasses of more than 7-power give too much enlargement to be used effectively on a jumping boat. A 10- or 12-power glass is fine ashore on a steady platform, but not at all satisfactory on the water. The 50-field provides a scope of view which seems adequate. The coated lens reduces glare from the sun and improves night vision, while the prismatic type of glass provides a smaller and lighter instrument.

Zeiss, Sard, and Bausch & Lomb coated prismatic binoculars are available at from $200 to $250, while there are cheaper foreign-made imitations of these excellent glasses available for as little as $50. Swift & Anderson, Inc., of Boston, Massachusetts are specialists in binoculars and allied gadgets. I have an outstandingly good pair of their "Commodore" 7×50s and I can find very little difference between these Japanese-made glasses and much more expensive German ones. Humphrey Swift insists that I send them back to them for cleaning, and they are always in good condition as a result. Pawn shops carry suitable glasses at, of course, reduced prices, but it is advisable to have someone who knows glasses help you select a pair. Though an item of considerable expense, binoculars are well worth their cost. For finding a mark, or wind-hunting they are of inestimable help and contribute tremendously toward the winning of boat races. Should they become dirty or the prisms or frames get out of line, there are many places specializing in nautical instruments that can clean and repair them at very reasonable prices.

Nowadays there are all kinds of Japanese, coated prismatic binocs to be had for as little as $45 or so. While they are not *quite* as good as a more expensive pair, they will do in a pinch, especially if you have a "flat" wallet.

STOPWATCHES

Stopwatches are in the same category as binoculars: expensive, fragile and delicate instruments. Take good care of them and they'll take good care of you. Abuse them and you will find yourself deserted and alone at the starting line. Keep watches of all types in protected dry places. Put in a few hooks to hang them on or keep them in waterproof drawers. On *Bumble Bee* it was standard practice for the crew to remove all watches immediately on stepping aboard and hang them on hooks in the cabin. It is easy to catch a watch strap on a cleat or projection and have it break with the result—one watch lost overboard. Put your stopwatches away safely right after the start, too.

Bumble Bee's three stopwatches were kept in a padded cigar box which was in turn carried about in a varnished wicker "lunch" basket about two feet long, 15 inches wide and 15 inches deep. This basket served also as a catchall for binoculars, lunch, racing rules, light clothes and bathing suits. "Look in the lunch basket," was the cry when anything couldn't be found readily. It served as a place for anything small, valuable or not, which we felt deserved special care and attention and which would be taken ashore every night after racing. Kept in its own regular dry spot aboard, woe betide the person who didn't handle it carefully, for we love and cherish our stopwatches and binocs.

Obviously, smaller boats cannot burden themselves down with all the nonsense suggested here, but some sensible arrangements can be worked out on any boat to keep watches safe and dry, be it hooks under the deck or some type of small waterproof drawer.

You will notice that I mentioned that *Bumble Bee* was equipped with three stopwatches. Bloated plutocrats, you may think to yourself, but believe me, it took me many years to accumulate that many watches which I am most happy to have. In line with our efforts to eliminate variables, it hardly seems necessary to point out that stopwatches are just about as variable and fickle as anything in this world of ours. No matter how much care and attention you lavish on a stopwatch, at some inopportune moment, it will let you down. If you are able to keep two watches going at all times you are indeed lucky, and the third is available when needed. If you only have one stopwatch, by all means use a wristwatch as a check, for you just can't tell when it will go out. There's nothing as frustrating as seeing the rest of the fleet whip across the starting line while you sit there with a silly expression on your face thinking there is still a minute or so to go. Eliminate the variables and start eliminating a very vital one by using more than one watch. Those three stopwatches are still with me, still working nicely (most of the time), still in their padded cigar box, still guarded "with my life," so as to speak, and still sent to Jules Racine & Co., Inc., for cleaning and adjustment.

To insure accuracy, check your watches occasionally against a chronometer known to be correct, or against one of the more reliable radio "time ticks," for example, Station WOR, New York, or shortwave Station WWV, operated by the National Bureau of Standards at Fort Collins, Colorado. Similar shortwave stations are operated by the Bureau in Hawaii and in Ottawa, Canada, by the Canadian Government. Have your watches checked, cleaned or adjusted during the winter. It'll pay off in the long run.

Many different types of stopwatch have been developed and can be procured through most any jeweler or good sporting goods store. Water-resistant stopwatches have finally made an appearance and seem to be ideal. (The Federal Government does not allow the term "waterproof" to be used any more.) Photographic timers used in film development are comparatively inexpensive. Resembling an old-fashioned wind-up alarm clock, they probably won't last more than one season, but they are so cheap it really doesn't make much difference.

A true yachting timer has a face with the figures on it in reverse order so that the time left can be quickly read without any calculations required, a feature not incorporated in the photographic timer. The time left is the important factor in making a start and therefore it is advisable for speed and accuracy to use watches so designed if the pocketbook will stand the strain. Of the many yachting timers on the market today, the one equipped with a repeating five-minute hand is by far the best in my opinion. Some watches have a 15-minute hand, but must be restarted at the end of the 15-minute period, for the hand doesn't swing back. Others have five little round holes in the dial through which a red-colored segment turns. At the end of five minutes this watch, too, must be restarted. These latter two watches are quite impractical and useless for the type of racing most of us do and I urge you to steer clear of them. Most starts are run on a five-minute interval basis, though some are run with only three minutes between each start. I have seen a regular stopwatch with conventional figures on the face which has the minute-hand dial laid out in three-minute intervals, but I confess that I haven't ever seen a real yachting timer of the type I prefer with anything but a five-minute-hand arrangement.

To that end, I am going to tell you about a watch that I think is far and away THE VERY BEST STOPWATCH YOU CAN BUY! Believe me, there is absolutely nothing to surpass it. I mean the GALLET YACHT TIMER of Swiss manufacture and sold in the United States by the above-mentioned Jules Racine & Co., which is run by the Smith brothers, Roger and Morgan. This watch is in a stainless-steel case, is water-resistant and, if properly cared for; is extremely accurate. I feel so strongly about this particular watch that I have included a picture of it! It also comes with lugs or fittings so that it can be worn as a wristwatch —albeit a rather large one. I am told that there are some sailors

The Gallet Yachting Timer— 5-minute-dial repeating watch with stainless steel case which is water-resistant.

in Finns, Tempests and Solings who wear this type of deal, not on their wrists, but on the thigh. Seems to me to be a bit tough on the watch—maybe even on the leg—but if it helps you win races, go ahead and God Bless You!! This may sound like advertising to you, but the Gallet is such a terrific timer that I feel I am doing you the greatest favor possible by bringing it to your attention.

And it isn't all that expensive. Yes, I do have two other Gallets, which, though not of the "water-resistant" variety, I keep in specially designed rubber cases with lanyards attached, and they work well too—again, when properly cared for. The water-resistant, stainless-case watch says on the back, "*Agony* 1950–51": twenty-two years old and still going strong. Do you *wonder* that I praise it to the heavens?

While it has nothing to do with stopwatches, I would like to go on record as saying that I don't like the three-minute starting interval used in some sections. There are, of course, things to be said on both sides of this question, but it has been my experience that when the three-minute starting interval is used, you generally end up racing either the class before you or the one after you. On Long Island Sound we have used the five-minute interval for as long as I can remember, without too many complaints from the late starters, the only ones who suffer from the longer interval between starts.

For many years it was my custom to read my own time before a start from a stopwatch around my neck on a line. The advent of Frostbite dinghy racing, with its system of blowing horns over a two minute period, fortunately broke me of this habit of looking at a watch, and trained me to avail myself of audible timing rather than visual. Looking down at a watch while trying to jockey on a crowded starting line is so distracting and confusing that I don't know how I ever could have done it successfully. Having someone call time leaves the skipper perfectly free to look round and concentrate on sailing his boat. Dinghy racing has been a wonderful trainer in this respect.

Your timer should be a person who does it regularly and who doesn't get excited or let his attention wander from the watch. Wilma Bell, "Pop" Stanley's daughter, was official timer on *Bumble Bee* and did a marvelous job of it, as well as her many other duties as a regular member of the crew. Cool as a cucumber, she riveted her attention on the Race Committee and their signals. Watches were fully wound and started on the first gun, then checked each five minutes. We always made an effort to be close to the Committee Boat, if it was at all possible, five minutes before our start so that Wilma could hear the man on the clock counting off the last ten seconds and be sure that her timers were right on the nose. Another variable is eliminated, for when such procedure is followed the skipper can approach the starting line secure in the knowledge that his watches are pretty sure to coincide with those of the Committee and all he has to worry about is hitting that line at the right moment.

ATTENTION ALL RACE COMMITTEES AND FOND PARENTS: Stopwatches or yachting timers of the water-resistant type make splendid prizes or Christmas gifts for the younger generation. Write or call the Smith Boys at Jules Racine & Co., Inc., 85 Executive Blvd., Elmsford, New York 10523.

Current Tables

Current Tables, published by the U.S. Geodetic Survey, and sold for about a buck, are much more helpful, I think, than the Tide Tables published by the same Government Agency. The Current Book gives you, after a certain amount of simple calculation, the time that the current changes in your particular area. The Tide Book gives you the time the tide changes. The two are different and are not to be confused. What you are interested in is the time the current begins to flow in another direction, not when its highest or lowest point is reached.

Many skippers prefer the Current Charts, also issued by the Department of Commerce. They are used in conjunction with the Current Tables and show, hour by hour, once the time of "Slack, Flood Begins" or "Slack, Ebb Begins," is ascertained from the Current Tables, the strength and direction of the current by means of arrows and figures. Personally I like to use the Current Tables alone, for they seem adequate for the type of racing I do, but for long-distance cruising or racing the Current Charts are vastly superior. Wind and weather will cause variations—and quite wide ones at times—in the current and tide predictions, so don't blame your Government if they happen to be out of line. This is one job your Government Agency seems to do very accurately and well. BE SURE AND ADD AN HOUR FOR DAYLIGHT SAVING TIME, if it is used in your area, for the tables are all printed in Standard Time. Incidentally, the Department of Commerce published a new set of tidal charts, in 1972, for Eastern Long Island Sound and Block Island Sound, updated and revised. I am told they plan to re-survey all their tidal charts over a period of time, and improve them.

Here is a very easy and a very inexpensive variable for you to take care of, one that you can control and control well, so be sure to have some method of tidal current prediction aboard.

Rule Book

A copy of the Racing Rules can be of great assistance at times. Although you can always check up on your Rules when you get ashore, there are times when you want to know what's what, so carry a copy aboard if you don't think the weight too great.

Housecleaning

Every once in a while it is a good idea to have a housecleaning aboard ship. Look over all your gear to see if there isn't something you can send ashore. As the season progresses you can collect a surprising amount of unnecessary junk. Get rid of it, if possible. Check your list of required items and then see what you can dispose of. While I feel that certain things are helpful and important, there is really no reason to load your boat down with a lot of gear which you'll never use. Weed it out and put it in your locker ashore. Keep all the required gear as near amidships as possible. Don't load the ends of your boat with life preservers, lines, etc. Keep the anchor low and in the middle of the boat. Keep the ends light so she won't "hobby-horse." The action or motion of the boat will be quicker and easier if the ends are kept free of weight and gear and the net result will be a faster boat. Quite naturally the gear should also be located so that the boat rides on an even keel. Even the weight up on either side, or you may find she sails better on one tack than the other. For example, in *Kate*, Bob Hubner's PJ-48, in the 1972 Vineyard Race, we stashed all the heavy headsails in the main cabin, just abaft the mast. Admittedly, it made walking about a bit difficult, but it kept the weight out of the ends of the boat.

CHAPTER XII
Tide, Wind and Weather

Tides and tidal currents seem to present an insurmountable problem to many sailors, especially those from lakes and places where there is no tide. Though we all use the term tide, currents, or tidal currents loosely and interchangeably, they are not the same, and the difference between tide and current should be made clear. Tide is the vertical rise and fall of water, while current is the actual flow of water from place to place which accomplishes it. Currents usually run for various periods of time after actual high or low water. The very thought of being obliged to cope with such things throws many a skipper into a tizzy and a blue funk. Forget it, for they are not hard to figure out.

Have you ever watched a stream as it runs along, or rainwater running down a gutter? Stop and study them sometime. Tidal currents run virtually the same way, except on a larger scale. Streams will seem to run faster where they are narrow and the depth is constant. At the same time they'll seem to run faster where the bottom shoals though the width remains constant. Have you ever noticed the back-eddies on the downstream side of boulders that are resting near the side of a stream? Same thing is true behind a point of land which runs out into a body of tidewater.

In their simplest form the following general rules may be stated regarding tidal currents:

1. The current runs strongest in the middle.
2. The current runs stronger around a point of land sticking out into the tidal waters, and at the same time there may be and usually are back-eddies behind the point.
3. The current turns or changes its direction first inshore, for

there the water is, on the whole, shallower, and the smaller mass of water is more easily influenced and its direction reversed sooner.

4. The current will tend to run straight in and out of a sound, river, bay or creek, but indentations, irregularities of the shoreline, or bays will influence its direction and strength.

5. Wind and weather conditions will exert a strong influence on the direction and strength of a current.

Current is the thing that the sailor is interested in, rather than tide. While it is nice to know when high tide occurs if you are going swimming off a beach, or if you are hauling your boat out, the thing that is of greater importance to the skipper is how and when the current is running. Current Tables, Current Charts and their advantages are discussed in Chapter XI.

The canny skipper takes every assistance that he can from a favorable current. Ascertain the time and direction of change in the current, and plan your race so that you take advantage of it. Other things being equal, take the tack which gives you a lee-bow tide, i.e., the current on your lee bow. This will be of two-fold benefit. In the first place, the lee-bowing current will have the general effect of moving your boat to windward over the bottom toward your mark. (By the same token a weather-bow current will push you away from the mark to leeward.) In the second place, the lee-bowing effect will increase your wind by a certain amount. Albeit this amount is small, it will be twice the amount of increased wind you will get on the other tack, for on the other tack the weather-bow current will have the net result of decreasing the wind.

Let me illustrate this with a splendid example, a typical summer southerly or "sea breeze" on Long Island Sound over one of the standard YRA courses. As shown in the chart below, the ebb tide runs from approximately west by south to east by north. With the starting line more or less in the middle of the Sound, the windward mark is usually Bell 23 off Prospect Point. From the starting line a boat on the port tack cannot quite lay west by south and hence gets the tide on his weather bow. However, a boat crossing on the starboard tack and sailing in toward Long Island for a certain distance will eventually get headed—the influence of the so-called shore breeze coming directly off the beach at practically a right angle. Getting into this "header" a

short way, you come about on the port tack and lay up to the
weather mark, assisted partially by the "lift" and partially by the
lee-bowing ebb tide, for your course has now become higher than
west by south, say about west-southwest.

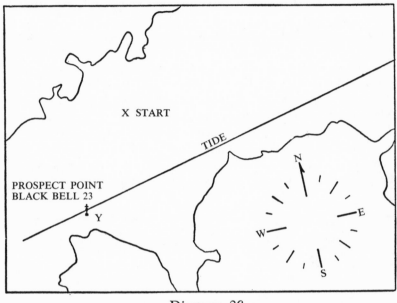

Diagram 36

Reaching or running in tidal currents where your racing area is
wholly or partially surrounded by land or landmarks, a very simple trick is to use ranges as a guide to any deviation from your
straight line course. Suppose you are reaching across a current to
a mark, but can't figure out how much of an allowance you
should make for it. You can hazard a guess, naturally, and maybe
you'll be right, or maybe you'll be wrong. If you are racing in a
really top-notch class, the difference of two or three lengths
which you may gain or lose may mean the difference between
winning or coming in way down the list. Find your next mark—
with your binoculars if necessary—and spot some object on shore
behind it. After a few moments check again and find out if the
object on shore has moved to the right or left of the buoy or
mark. If it has moved to the left of your next mark you are
steering a course too far to the left, and vice versa. Correct your

steering accordingly. This may seem like a very small matter, but it will gain you places in a boat race, believe me. Just an additional variable to watch.

Another method of doing this same job is by a parallelogram of forces. Suppose you wish to make good a course of east, and have a current in a southeasterly direction of about two knots, to make things simple.

What course shall you steer, assuming your speed will be about six knots? Lay off the line A-B, the course to the next mark (East— 90 degrees). Also lay off line A-C, the direction and estimated speed of the current (S.E.—135 degrees, two knots). Set dividers on C with opening C-D equal to estimated boat speed (six knots). Establish point D when dividers as set will fall on course line A-B. Then C-D (77 degrees) is course to steer. If estimates of current, speed and direction as well as boat's speed are accurate, as you leave point A, steering 77 degrees, you will progress directly along course line A-B at 7½ knots (made good).

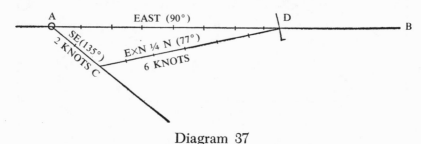

Diagram 37

Whatever you do, DON'T sail directly for a mark when you are reaching or running across a current as in the above diagram. Make some sort of allowance or you will sail a course somewhat similar to the one diagramed below, a circular one. You should know in which direction the current is running if you have the Current Tables. If you don't have them, check it as you round buoys, or look for lobster pots, oyster bed stakes, and the like. Check your ranges too. Steering straight to the next mark will result in your sailing a much greater distance, such as ADB. AC is the proper course, for the current whose direction and strength is indicated by the vector CB will set you down on the mark B just right.

I will never forget an instance of this sort which resulted in our doing extremely well in three races in a row many years ago (at the old Atlantic Yacht Club at Sea Gate on Gravesend Bay) in Star boats. I was sailing with Briggs Cunningham in the famous *Colleen*, owned by Fred Bedford of Southport, Connecticut. Briggs and I had not done very well in the first three-quarters of the race, for one reason or another. The last leg was a reach to the finish across a strong lee-bowing ebb tide. The leading boats held directly toward the finish line. We could see that they were sailing extremely high with the current pushing them up all the time, and believe me, the current really runs in Lower New York Bay. By sailing low of the finish line we were able to nip them all. The remarkable thing about this situation was that we were able to do it three days in a row with almost identical conditions against boats that sailed there all the time, while we were complete strangers. It ended, thank you, by our taking home one of Sir Thomas Lipton's Trophies for Star boats.

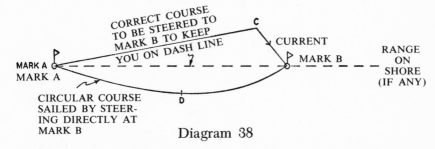

Diagram 38

When beating to windward against a head tide, and there is no chance to get a lee bow on either tack, make for the shore, boys, and get in the weaker tide there, other things (meaning favorable wind or slants of wind) being equal, of course. Since the current is always stronger in the middle make very effort to get where it's weaker, but always keep in mind wind factors. Perhaps by getting inshore you can get the first of the turn of the current, while the rest of your class is beating their brains out against the last of the old tide out in the middle. Take a few minutes out to figure the angles of your tide or current, but don't forget that where a point sticks out, the current may run faster.

As a case in point, let me mention the 1972 Vineyard Race aboard *Kate*. Some time before dawn, we were beating down Long Island Sound against a moderate breeze, somewhat north of east. The tide was agin' us (isn't it always?) and the question was, should we try and go through Fisher's Island Sound? The

tide turns OUT sooner there than it does in the Race. We sailed
on and, as dawn came, we were almost up on Race Rock. We
made our decision, took a short tack toward Fisher's and eventually went through Fisher's Island Sound without tacking until
almost the end—and a delightful sail it was, smooth water—and
the tide almost immediately started to go with us, as we could
see from the buoys and lobster pots. However, we also had
company—Irving Pratt's *Zest* was some two miles ahead and
stayed there until well past the Texas Tower on the way home
when we closed on him. Unfortunately, he outran us again and
finished first, second, third in our Class (B) to our fourth. We
were all reasonably sure that this maneuver through Fisher's
Island Sound helped with the rest of the Fleet, and yet it's only
the third or fourth time that I have (over a period of forty years)
been through that Sound on a Block Island or Vineyard Race—
the last time being so long ago I can't recall it.

WIND AND WEATHER

Wind and weather present problems in variables which are
almost impossible to control. You can cope with the rest of the
variables that we have discussed, generally arriving at a reasonable conclusion. But when you get to the question of wind and
weather most of us are stumped or up a tree. At times, certainly,
they will act according to "Hoyle," but other times they'll cross
you up and get you into the damndest mess you can think of.
"Local knowledge" is a term often used to describe the ability
certain skippers seem to possess which enables them to figure out
just what the winds are doing or going to do. It's a very apt
description too, for the fellow who has it invariably "guesses"
right in deciding or determining which tack to take to get the
most favorable slants of air. Actually there is not very much
guesswork involved. He generally can tell from long experience
what's going to happen. Not all the time, I'll admit, but quite
often. Occasionally he's wrong and takes a beating, but not too
frequently. If he's right from, say, 60 to 75 percent of the time, he
will win his share of races, or at least do reasonably well in
them.

The study of wind and weather, or Meteorology, is a long, hard
process, far beyond the scope of this book. Should you be interested in studying the whys and wherefores of our weather I refer
you to the METEOROLOGY WORKBOOK by Peter E. Kraght, published

by the Cornell Maritime Press. I shall confine myself to quotations from "Pete's" splendid book and my own observations, such as they (the latter) are.

By and large, winds and weather are caused by differences in atmospheric pressure, temperature, humidity, geography, and the rotation of our earth. Even sun spots, whatever they are, are blamed for changes and contrariness in atmospheric conditions. The sky above us is covered with a vast sea of air, turbulent, shifting and ever-moving in various directions. Just like great bodies of tidal waters with their many currents and cross currents, this air above us comes and goes in every direction. Differences in atmospheric pressure cause it to move from place to place, while differences in temperature and humidity cause it to move up and down and around in never-ending processions, both influenced to considerable degree by the rotation of the earth on its own axis and in its orbit about the sun. Is it any wonder that, with these vast forces at work, we sometimes have trouble in figuring out whether a wind is going to blow from the southwest or south-southwest, or whether it is going to blow five or 50 miles an hour?

By way of explaining weather phenomena, Mr. Kraght takes what he describes as an "Air Parcel" and tells what happens to it, defining parcels as follows: "It is both convenient and useful in (some) meteorological studies to make a mental division of the atmosphere into *parcels,* i.e., isolated portions, each of which may be of different size and shape from every other one. Parcels may be as small or as large as desired by the imagination of the reader or experimenter; they may be moved at will among other parcels or remain at rest. Whatever happens to a parcel's properties as it is moved or remains stationary is a clue to what happens in the atmosphere, because the atmosphere frequently assumes quasi-parcel characteristics and behaves as if these parcels, sometimes very large and sometimes extremely small, moved among each other." Parcels of air heated will rise, while other parcels cooled will fall or remain on the surface of the earth. Parcels of air will flow in from the cool sea over the hot land, causing what we know as a sea breeze in the summer time (or from a lake onto the hot surrounding land, a lake breeze). Wide differences in temperatures between land and sea cause these winds to blow and if we consider these individual parcels of air we can better visualize what makes our breezes flow.

Actually most of our winds are what are known as gradient winds, i.e., winds caused by a difference in atmospheric pressure. You are all familiar, or should be familiar, with the weather maps put out by the U.S. Government and published in many newspapers. These maps are covered with lines known as isobars or lines of equal atmospheric pressure, which show areas of high and low pressure. To quote again from Mr. Kraght's book, "Pressure is constant along an isobar; pressure varies along any line lying at an angle to an isobar, and the greatest variation is along a line placed at right angles to an isobar. The rate of change in pressure with distance along a line perpendicular to an isobar (or to an isobaric field on a pressure map) is known as the *pressure gradient*. . . .

"In general, the laws of wind direction in the Northern Hemisphere (Southern Hemisphere conditions are mirror images) are:

1. Winds must blow parallel to isobars.
2. Winds must blow counterclockwise about regions of minimum pressure, i.e., centers of low pressure.
3. Winds must blow clockwise about regions of maximum pressure, i.e., centers of high pressure.
4. Winds blow in such a manner that low pressure is toward the left and high pressure toward the right looking in the direction toward which the air is flowing . . ."

In these generalized rules, no allowance has been made for the effect of surface friction which will be dealt with later.

It must be borne in mind that parcels, large or small, with their different characteristics of varying temperatures and moisture content will exert an influence on gradient winds, and conversely gradient winds will effect the various parcels. Likewise, geographical variations such as mountains, valleys, rough terrain, extensive building and construction (as opposed to vast areas of trees, grass and fields), bays, indentations in the coastline and sounds will all have their effect on the wind.

Vertical currents of air are caused by the heating and cooling of various parcels of air. When mixed with the horizontal flow of a gradient wind they will cause a puffy and gusty wind such as our typical summer northwester. The diagram below taken from Peter Kraght's METEOROLOGY WORKBOOK shows such an effect.

On the East Coast, our summer northwest wind is a typical

example of this combination of vertical and horizontal currents. The nor'west gradient blowing over the land is influenced by vertical currents which pick up a lot of heat from the land, becoming very turbulent and gusty. At a considerable distance offshore, say ten to fifteen miles, the nor'wester becomes cooled, loses these vertical currents and becomes steadier.

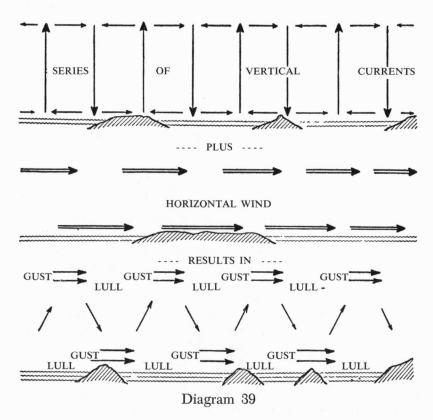

SERIES   OF   VERTICAL   CURRENTS

---- PLUS ----

HORIZONTAL WIND

---- RESULTS IN ----

GUST   LULL   GUST   LULL   GUST   LULL   GUST

GUST   LULL   GUST   LULL   GUST   LULL   LULL

Diagram 39

By the same token our sea breeze coming in off the ocean is flowing over water which is of a practically constant cool temperature and hence is not subject to vertical currents and is, therefore, less gusty and steadier. As it hits the heated land, there is, of course, an immediate heating effect exerted on it, and this may affect its steadiness to some extent.

Our east wind, rainy wind, is likewise less subject to vertical currents and hence, in general, is steadier than a nor'wester.

For years I have heard old-timers talk about the beautiful sum-

mer sou'westers we used to have on Long Island Sound—ALL
the time, they'll say. It can be shown that the sea breeze, as it hits
the land, is heated and that this has a tendency to lift it. At the
same time, a large elongated body of water such as Long Island
Sound is covered by a vertically stable bank of cooled air (cooled
by contact with the water). A theory has been advanced that the
breeze coming in off the ocean is heated so much by all the
buildings, roads, houses, (especially the wide ribbons of park-
ways with all the cars generating heat), etc., of Northern New
Jersey, New York, Brooklyn and Western Long Island that it lifts
considerably more than it did 40 years ago. Bear in mind that all
this area has been almost completely covered by construction of
one kind or another in that time, and there are very few trees and
open fields to absorb the heat of the sun which now heats up the
aforementioned construction. Farther down the Sound, say at
Southport, Connecticut, there will be a splendid sou'wester blowing, while we sit 'round Execution Light and Matinicock Point
with nary a zephyr. Along the south shore of Long Island, Rock-
away, Great South Bay, there'll be a slam-bang sea breeze, and
what do we have in Western Long Island Sound? The violent
wash of some speed-crazy jerk in a runabout, but not a breath of
air. I KNOW, for my friends from the South Shore delight in
telling me every Monday morning what beautiful sailing breezes
they've had all weekend and they're sorry we weren't able to
finish our races either Saturday or Sunday.

The heated sea breeze, actually more or less superheated you
might say, by all the construction, hits the cooled bank of air
over our end of the Sound and is lifted up over our heads, and
drops down again somewhere in the neighborhood of Mt. Kisco,
Bedford or New Canaan. The southerly eventually breaks
through when it has sufficient force and its temperature more
nearly equals that of the vertically stable air over the Sound
itself. This happens generally so late in the afternoon when the
sun has dropped that it's too late to get a good race.

It can be readily seen that there is considerable merit to this
theory, for building and removal of trees and grassy fields must
have a tremendous effect in increased heating of the surface of
Western Long Island.

Local winds, such as the sea breeze, as opposed to extensive or
gradient winds (caused by differences in sea-level atmospheric
pressure), are caused by differences in temperature. Lake

breezes, which are of the same general type as sea breezes, are caused by this difference in temperature between water and the surrounding land. Mountain and valley breezes fit in the same category.

How often have you heard some lake sailor tell of the terribly strong and gusty winds they get? Winds that come in such terrific blasts that they'll capsize almost any boat? This is because such winds, though in general mild, will get roaring down a valley, a fairly narrow passage between mountains and hills, or down a ravine, and pick up considerable force, more from the shape of the terrain, hitting the water and anything in their path with greatly accelerated speed and power.

Local winds will tend to occur almost anywhere that there is a difference in temperature between land and water. You have perhaps noticed that when there is practically no air at all, virtually a flat calm, there is more to be had close to shore or in under an island, and it pays to stay closer to shore. On the other hand, when there is a strong wind getting so close to shore, it usually results in less wind because of the blanketing effect of the shoreline. (And this seems to be true whether it's an onshore or offshore wind.)

Local winds will often occur in small bays off a large body of water—for example, in Manhasset Bay and Little Neck Bay off Long Island Sound—when there is little or no wind on the Sound itself. This has often occurred, and there has been good racing in these bays in the summertime, while we on the Sound have merely had a breeze from a passing steamer.

These local winds may be, and often are, quite different from the more or less general winds for the area. They may be, as the name implies, purely local and opposite to the general or predicted winds for the area. Weather reports with expected winds for an area must be by their very nature for a very large area, thousands of square miles, not for a small selected few square miles. The weatherman just isn't able to predict every little stray zephyr. He'll give the general picture, but he simply cannot tell you what MAY occur on Squeedunk Creek. There may be strictly local conditions which govern the breeze there, so don't curse him up and down if the wind is 90 or 180 degrees away from the prediction you read in a morning paper. Weather, like everything else, changes and the chances are that his prediction was made up maybe 6 hours before, possibly even 12 hours. For example, you often have seen clouds moving overhead in one direction, while you have a wind on the water in an entirely opposite direction. Possibly the overhead winds are what the weatherman predicted, while you have some purely local breeze, a thermal breeze, caused by differences in temperature.

Surface friction will bring about a reduction in wind strength and a 20- to 30-degree change in direction. Most predictions for wind strengths and direction are given with a certain height in mind. In other words, they are calculated for a given height above sea level, say 75 or 100 feet. Interference from shore lines, buildings, etc., will cause reductions in the wind's speed. Reductions also result from friction brought about by waves and contact with the surface of the land or water.

Have you ever noticed that the wind seems to be lighter in the immediate area of a tide rip? This is caused by two things, 1) friction with the waves themselves, and 2) colder water from below the surface coming into contact with the wind and causing a certain amount of vertical stability, and therefore, reduced wind.

In an elongated body of water, especially, though it is also true of any body of water surrounded by land, the wind tends to blow more directly at right angles to the shoreline, while in the middle the wind has a tendency to blow along the axis of the body of water. This point has been brought home time and again in our race weeks on Manhasset Bay in light to moderate breezes. Get near either shore and you seem to get slants off the beach regularly. On Long Island Sound, the experts always—or almost always—hit for the shore when they get a chance, in expectation of a favorable slant along the beach when they get around on the other tack. At the same time the breeze is frequently stronger nearer shore—and also gustier—though care must be taken not to get too close to a windward shore for fear of a blanketing effect. This strength and gustiness is frequently caused by the influence of vertically unstable air, i.e., parcels of heated and cooled air becoming turbulent and mixing with the horizontal wind.

It is interesting to note that the strength or speed of a wind will increase with height. In other words, 1,000 or 2,000 feet above sea level there will be a considerably stronger wind which increases even more at higher levels. Surface friction is responsible for part of this, but in general, it might be compared to well-known tidal currents. Tidal currents, it is well known, run stronger in the middle of a body of water, slower along the shore.

The winds at higher levels, two to three miles, tend to blow more or less regularly from west to east, though, of course, even these are influenced considerably by temperature and atmospheric pressure. On the West coast, this general westerly wind, combined with the normal summer sea breeze, brings in a moderate to strong nor'wester every day, just as people on Buzzards Bay almost set their watches by the summer sou'wester that blows in there with regularity every day about 11 A.M.

Winds blow counterclockwise about an area of low pressure and are known as cyclonic winds. It is from these areas of low pressure near the Equator that our Northern Hemisphere hurricanes originate. There is no limit to the speed of winds about a low-pressure system. On the other hand, because of the various forces involved, there are definite limits to the speed of wind about a high-pressure area, or anticyclonic system. The maximum limits to the wind are governed by the latitude of the system.

Peter Kraght's METEOROLOGY WORKBOOK has this to say about wind velocity: "The speed with which winds blow is directly related to the pressure gradient. Zero pressure gradient indicates calm and a large pressure gradient indicates large velocities. In determining wind velocity from pressure gradient, the gradient is usually measured by measuring the distance between isobars on the weather map. If the isobars are widely spaced, the indication is that the pressure change with distance is small, the pressure gradient likewise small and the wind light. If isobars are closely spaced, the indication is that the pressure change with distance is large, the pressure gradient large and the wind strong."

METEOROLOGY WORKBOOK gives the following rule of thumb formulae for calculating wind velocity in various zones North and South where V is the velocity and D the distance between 3-milibar isobars in miles:

1. 25-35 degrees North and South $V \times D = 5400$
2. 35-50 degrees North and South $V \times D = 3600$
3. 41 degrees (Long Island Sound) $V \times D = 3500$
4. 50-70 degrees North and South $V \times D = 3200$

These are, of course, uncorrected for surface friction, approximate, and it should be borne in mind that, if your calculations from a weather map show a wind velocity different from the actual velocity encountered, other factors may have entered the picture or weather system since the map was made up. Regularly checking a full and complete weather map, as published by the Government Weather Bureau, as well as your own barometer, will make a fairly successful weather prognosticator of you within certain reasonable limits—the reasonable limits being influenced to a considerable degree by the above-mentioned other factors entering the picture. Weather is never stable or static; it's ever-changing, just as the sea about us is never quiet but always on the move. Wind and weather are, if anything, more fickle and capricious even than that "old devil sea." You must be constantly alert, attentive and vigilant to grasp the opportunities presented to you by their vagaries and inconsistencies.

THUNDERSTORMS

Since most of you sail and race in areas where summer thunderstorms are more or less the rule rather than the exception, one or two hints which prove beneficial to your position in the racing results seem to be in order.

First of all, approach all thunderstorms (and/or cold fronts) with proper respect and due caution. Some of them can be downright nasty. Common sense should dictate your maneuvers and plan of action before a squall strikes. Don't be afraid of being called a sissy by your competitors, for conservative conduct, such as lowering all sail, may result in your eventual safe arrival at your home port, while some of the more reckless name-callers may have to swim for it. Have halyards and sheets carefully coiled and ready to let go on the run if necessary.

High-level thunderstorms are what the name implies, at high levels. There is generally a lot of rain in them, but the wind is so far up in the atmosphere that we don't feel it very much on the surface. In low-level thunderstorms, fronts or line squalls, the black, turbulent, rolling clouds are clearly visible and seem to make more or less of a line. High-level ones are generally obscured by a cloud formation below them and often thunder is the only indication of their presence. Nearly all thunderstorms in the East Coast area are low-level variety, so when you hear "thunderstorm" on a forecast, plan for a blow.

Secondly, if you are determined to continue the race, work

yourself over in the direction of the approaching storm. *Yes, that's right; get over to it, so that you get it first.* If you get it first, you'll have more wind than the rest of your fleet (and maybe more than you really want) for a short period of time which should benefit your position in relationship to theirs, and you'll also have a more favorable slant, which should also help you. If you are on a windward leg, take the tack which will put you nearest the squall and your next mark, for the eventual shift coming from the storm will turn your beat into a reach. Many is the time that I have watched Lou Pierson, who used to race with the Mosbacher boys when they were younger, pull such a trick and ALWAYS successfully. Now that Bobby and Bus have grown up and are on their own, they haven't forgotten Lou's clever teachings on thunderstorms (or on a lot of other good tactics for that matter), nor have I. After all, Lou only pulled the trick at least a dozen times before I caught on to what he was up to.

The morning of your race, before you go aboard your boat check the wind and weather. (The current you can check from your Current Tables aboard as you go out to the start.) Phone the Weather Bureau, examine the weather map printed in most newspapers, have a look at and tap your barometer to see if it's rising or falling, consult your Uncle Louie about the feeling in his rheumatic leg, or get some ideas from a local groundhog. Do it whatever way suits you best, but get some idea if it's humanly possible of what you may expect in the way of wind and weather.

Local knowledge, or long experience, may even tell you what you want to know without going to any or all of the above sources. Many experts I know can just look at the sky and give you a reasonably accurate idea of what wind you'll get for the next few hours. In the summer on Long Island Sound even I can prophesy, with some degree of success, when a nice whole-sail sou'wester is going to breeze up. There have been times, too, after a long afternoon of just sitting without a breath, when I have been able to actually *smell* that first faint breath of a new sea breeze (sou'wester on the Sound) and tell almost within 15 minutes when it will strike in. I don't mean to be boastful or immodest in making such statements, but they are really true. Such prophecies, I suppose, are the result of local knowledge gleaned over 59 years of sailing and racing in that area. For example, when the haze back in the hills of Lond Island gets heavier making the treetops in the background appear a lighter shade of green, you can almost bet your bottom dollar that a new breeze—a sea breeze—is trying to break through from the ocean. The same thing follows when the tall buildings in New York, the Chrysler, Empire State and the World Trade Center, fade from sight. If these buildings have been clearly visible during the early afternoon and then suddenly fade out, your sou'wester is on its way and will hit in eventually. Perhaps I should point out that in late Fall when it's cool and there isn't too much haze, these particular guides don't always work, and on occasion I have been caught out in left field when a nice southerly came sneaking in without warning; but in the real summertime, the haze will never fail you.

Conversely, when you can see the New York buildings, the George Washington Bridge and possibly the radio tower at Alpine, New Jersey, from western Long Island Sound on a hot summer's afternoon, there "just ain't goin' to be no southerly." Maybe a light northerly or a puffy nor'wester, but no sea breeze until the haze makes its appearance.

Another bit of local knowledge comes to mind in connection with this sou'wester on Long Island Sound. Many years ago, the late Butler Whiting of New Rochelle put forth this theory—and his daughter, Sarah Baylis, recently reminded me of it. "Butts" said that on a beat from the Westchester side to Long Island, in a sou'wester, IF the wind is south of southwest, take your first tack (and a long one at that) to the south. Conversely, if the wind is west of sou'west, take your first (long) tack to the west; and "YUH know what?" It very often works out that way.

Maybe that is why Teddy Weisberg in his great Shields class yacht, *Barbara,* did so well in the last race of Manhasset Bay Race Week last fall. If *that is* why, we didn't realize it at the time. Round the Red Gas Buoy, off the south end of Hen & Chickens (off Larchmont), we stayed in close to Huckleberry Island and Pea Island, because there were squalls, thunder and lightning over Pelham, Mount Vernon and New Rochelle—and YOU ALWAYS STAY NEAR OR TACK TOWARD A THUNDERSTORM (because you get it first if you do). However, the squalls never materialized, but we DID stay inshore, out of a foul tide, and eventually recovered a half-mile on the leaders and won the race (Teddy was properly happy and ecstatic). Maybe "Butts" Whiting's theory worked that day. I'll be honest; I'd forgotten it and just found it in my notes.

The United States Department of Commerce, by way of its National Oceanic and Atmospheric Administration, operates the National Weather Service. The National Weather Service operates and maintains roughly 60 VHF-FM Radio Stations which provide continuous weather information on a frequency of 162.55 megahertz or 162.40 megahertz, at coastal and many inland locations. The particular frequency of each of the stations depends on its own special location. The difference in frequencies is designed to prevent interference between two nearby stations, whose range is normally about 40 miles.

The National Weather Service recently announced a change in terminology for the traditional announcement to small-craft operators of marginally hazardous weather conditions. Instead of "Small Craft Warnings," these weather messages are to be called *"Small Craft Advisories,"* to reflect more accurately the true nature of their content. The change took effect for saltwater sailors on January 1, 1972. It was introduced to Great Lakes boaters in 1971.

The Weather Service—a component of the Commerce Department's National Oceanic and Atmospheric Administration—has an ascending series of alerting messages for mariners. These are keyed to increasingly hazardous weather. The lowest rung in the ladder has been the small-craft warning—for winds of about 18 to 33 knots and/or dangerous sea conditions. Next in urgency is the gale warning (for winds of 34 to 47 knots); then the storm warning (48 to 63 knots or more); and lastly, the hurricane warning (winds of 64 knots or more produced by a tropical cyclone).

All but the small-craft warning are based on well-defined meteorological conditions, and will remain the same. The small-craft warning is less precise, and varies in meaning from one locality to another. In response to objections from mariners about vagueness and variability, the Weather Service is switching to the word advisory, and informing mariners to decide for themselves whether the observed or forecast conditions constitute a real danger to them.

So: If you are a small-craft sailor and see the familiar red triangle fluttering in the breeze, the advice is: Tune in the latest marine weather forecast. Then you decide if you are experienced enough in boat-handling and if your boat is seaworthy enough to cope with the expected weather—or whether you had better stay in port.

A sample Small Craft Advisory is shown below, as it will be issued over the Weather Service's teletypewriter circuits:

DELAWARE BAY
SMALL CRAFT ADVISORY IN EFFECT
WINDS NORTHEAST 20 TO 30 KNOTS THIS AFTER-
NOON . . . SHIFTING TO NORTHWEST 20 TO 30
KNOTS TONIGHT AND 15 TO 25 KNOTS WEDNESDAY.
WEATHER . . . RAIN POSSIBLY HEAVY AT TIMES THIS
AFTERNOON ENDING TONIGHT . . . CLOUDY WED-
NESDAY. VISIBILITY . . . 1 TO 3 MILES IN RAIN AND
FOG . . . IMPROVING TO 5 MILES OR MORE TONIGHT.

Along with this change in terminology, marine weather fore-casters have begun to issue by radio a new warning that carries the label "Special Marine Warning Bulletin." No visual displays accompany the bulletin. It is issued whenever a severe local storm or strong wind of brief duration is imminent, and is not covered by existing warnings or advisories. Boaters will receive these special warnings if they keep tuned to a Weather Service VHF/FM or Coast Guard radio station, or to a commercial station that carries marine weather.

TONE-ALERT FEATURE ADDED TO NATIONAL WEATHER SERVICE VHF-FM CONTINUOUS RADIO TRANSMISSIONS

All National Weather Service Transmitters will have the ca-pacity to send a 1,050 cycles-per-second tone signal for 2 to 5 seconds preceding any announcement that:

    a. The broadcast area has been placed under a tornado or hurricane WATCH or WARNING.
    b. A flash flood WATCH or WARNING is issued which in-cludes any portion of the broadcast area.
    c. Weather constitutes an immediate threat to small craft safety.
    d. A WATCH or WARNING is issued for other major weather hazards which threaten life or property.

The purpose of this new feature is to allow users who have tone-alert receivers to leave their tone-alert receivers turned on in the "muted" mode but be assured that weather WATCH and WARNING announcements will be audible when transmitted.

With this system law enforcement and Civil Defense offices, schools, hospitals, industrial plants, and others interested can be informed immediately and positively of each weather WATCH and WARNING.

Compatible tone-alert receivers are available from a number of commercial sources. Equipment selected must be able to tune to *162.550 Mhz* and respond to a 1,050 cycles-per-second control signal to turn on the audio part of the monitor receiver. Good quality receivers and permanent outdoor antennas designed for the *162.550 Mhz* frequency will significantly enhance performance.

Tests of the tone alerting equipment when made are scheduled for Wednesdays between 1000 and 1300 EST. They are made only when no inclement weather is forecast for the general area. Tone alert signal activation for drills and tests is always accompanied by an explanatory statement.

IMPROVED RECEPTION OF VHF-FM
CONTINUOUS WEATHER BROADCASTS

For those of you who are having difficulty receiving our VHF-FM Radio Weather transmission, we offer the following information:

Frequencies 162.55 megahertz and 162.40 megahertz lie above commercial FM frequencies which end at 108 megahertz, therefore, Narrow Band FM receivers of ±5 kilohertz deviation and tuned to these frequencies are required. These receivers are available in a variety of types and prices. In general, the better the receiver and antenna combination the better the reception. The VHF-FM transmission can usually be received 35 to 40 and occasionally 60 miles from the antenna site. The effective range depends on terrain and the type of receiver used. Where transmitting antenna heights are on high ground, the range is some-what greater.

The following listening guide should be used when purchasing a receiver for reception of NOAA VHF-FM Radio Weather. The receiver of 20 microvolts sensitivity has a range of about 10 miles, 6 microvolts a range of 20 miles, 2.5 microvolts a range of 30 miles, 1.2 microvolts a range of 40 miles, .9 microvolts a range of 50 miles, and .6 microvolts a range of 60 miles.

These data are based on the following parameters: A standard 300 watt transmitting station with a transmitter antenna height of 300 feet; transmission over clear terrain, and receiver antenna height of 6 feet. Increased range may be obtained under difficult terrain situations by elevating a properly designed external antenna. A ¼ wave length ground plane antenna is recommended. For distances beyond the fringe reception area, a ½ wave length dipole antenna with a gain of not less than 4 to 6 dB should be used. This type is also available as a directional antenna which amplifies reception manifold. Use of low-loss coaxial cable to connect these antennas to the receiver is recommended.

We suggest that you consult your local electronic equipment supplier regarding these specifications prior to purchasing a specific antenna for any receiver.

I am indebted to John A. Mayer, Meteorologist in charge of the National Weather Service at 30 Rockefeller Plaza, in New York, for the above comments and information on weather broadcasts.

Here is a picture of the REALISTIC WEATHERADIO,® produced and sold nationally by RADIO SHACK of Fort Worth, Texas. I have had one of these little pre-tuned WEATHERA-DIOS® for more than five years. It works just GREAT—on one 9-volt transistor radio battery—and it has been a great help to me during these five years. I find it works very, very well if it is placed in the area of a TV-antenna lead-in wire or near any up-going BX house wiring. On a boat, it frequently gives better reception if you take it up on deck away from any interference

from wire rigging. Priced about sixteen bucks, the WEATHERADIO®
is now encased in a 3-inch-square
cube rosewood-finish plastic case,
with a neat telescoping antenna.
Natch, RADIO SHACK has available more sophisticated models—
at higher prices—but I have found
my model most satisfactory and
useful. However, perhaps I should
point out that this little inexpensive
set obviously does not have the
capacity nor the ability to be activated by nor receive the tone-alert
(the 1,050 cycles-per-second tone
signal) discussed above. This tone-
alert requires a much more expensive and sophisticated receiver.

Radio Shack

Realistic Weatheradio®, manufactured by Radio Shack of Fort Worth,
Texas.

CHAPTER XIII

Before the Start

Having reached some sort of a decision regarding the various possibilities of wind and weather, your next step is to settle on sails suitable for the kind of winds and weather you hope to have. If you own only one suit of sails, your problem is already solved, but if you have two or more suits, you must make up your mind which sails will do you the most good under the expected weather conditions, with the forecast at hand. (N.B. Let's not overlook the warning of the chapter on Sails.) Keep your new sails dry for a sunnier, lighter day. However, by all means take at least two suits of sails with you; even a third suit if you can't make up your mind what's going to happen to wind and weather. It is absolutely essential to keep unwanted and unnecessary gear off the boat, so don't load it down with junk you won't ever need; but it's a terrible feeling, I assure you, to get out to a starting line and discover that you've left your ideal suit of sails ashore, for what reasons it doesn't matter. You just don't have those sails, and it certainly can make you unhappy. There must be some powerboat at the starting line who will be willing to take on whatever extra sails you find you don't need.

The above paragraph was written in 1951 and concerned cotton sails. Should I take it out? No, I won't—because maybe you DO own a suit of Dacrons that are better in light air than a breeze. If so, save 'em for a better day.

Get an early start from your anchorage, making sure that you have all necessary gear aboard before you get too far from your mooring. It is a good idea to assign to each of your regular crew the responsibility for seeing to it that certain pieces of equipment get aboard your boat. Stuff left in a club launch or on the float won't do you much good in the race, so be sure it's all accounted for.

Whether or not you have a towboat or tender, get going early and get out to the starting line. It doesn't make any difference whether the line is just off your mooring or three miles or five miles away; get there with time to spare. Races are won from the starting line and not from the mooring. Get to that line early so that:

1. You are sure of being in the race.
2. You will have ample time to size up the weather.
3. You can look over your competitors' sail selections.
4. You will have time to change your own sails if necessary.
5. You can get semi-relaxed and, as a result, think straight.
6. You will be able to run the line, i.e., time it from Committee Boat to starting flag and determine the favored end.
7. You can select proper spinnaker guys, and give a last look at various fittings and gear.

It hardly seems necessary to point out that once you are in the starting area, STAY THERE and don't go sailing off any great distance. Stick around the Committee Boat, tacking back and forth in short hitches, or you may hear the distant boom of your starting gun as you sit becalmed a mile or so away. Elementary, you may murmur to yourself, but think back to the numerous times that someone in your class has been caught flat-footed and red-faced while the rest of the class go merrily on their way. Further, if you stay in the starting area, the odds are against the Committee making any last-minute changes in courses which will escape you. For years, I have driven my various crews almost wild because of my anxiety to be on our way before most of the rest of our class have even boarded their boats. However, we have missed mighty few starts as a result and our ship is a more or less relaxed one, comparatively speaking. ("Comparatively speaking," I add in self-defense, in case anyone might question the veracity of my statement.) There are, of course, times when inclement weather makes you look somewhat silly banging about a starting line hours before the start, but even so I maintain it is better to get out there early. Some latitude is obviously necessary under such conditions.

If you are racing in tidal waters, look up the times of current changes in your Current Book. Note down on your race circular when the current shifts as well as the direction. Since wind and weather will cause variations in the times of current changes, have a look at any available buoys or lobster pots if a predicted change is about to occur and thus provide yourself with a check. This isn't always possible and doesn't always work, but have a look anyhow.

Upon arriving at the Committee Boat, if various courses are used, note the course selected for your class and WRITE the course down on the circular. DON'T trust your memory, but get it down in writing. Maybe you are an elephant and never forget, but it can be quite embarrassing if the fleet is spread out as they approach two marks close together and you can't quite recall whether you are supposed to round "A" or "B." Racing as we do on Long Island Sound, with classes starting every five minutes for upwards of an hour, it is often quite helpful to note the courses to be sailed by other classes. Such information can be very helpful in locating marks when the weather or visibility is bad. In clear weather it can be used to determine the vagaries of the wind in the vicinity of the other classes, for you know what their supposed courses are and any variations in course will mean something. At some point in the race, several classes may use the same turning mark. If you know that, the convergence of two or more groups may aid you in picking up an otherwise indiscernible buoy. Standard practice on *Bumble Bee* was to have one man check the course signals as we crossed the starting line to be sure there were no last-minute changes. "Pop" Stanley, having no other special duties at the start—besides being a rather unexcitable fellow even when 20 Internationals are banging across a line—attended to this detail. Insignificant though it may seem there have been times when such changes have almost slipped by us.

While you are reaching back and forth before the start, look about you, noting the winds up under the shore, offshore, etc. Do boats sailing up under the beach seem to have more or less than you, and is the direction the same? Local knowledge will naturally benefit the skipper who has sailed time and again under those same conditions, but quite often it will be possible to spot some little difference in wind conditions which may be of advantage. At the same time, check and recheck the starting line to determine the best end. If the start is to be to leeward, is the leeward end favored enough so that if you start there, you will have a chance to "break through" the windward boats without too great a risk of being blanketed? If the start is to windward, is the line "square" to the wind, at right angles, or is one end favored? A quick luff dead into the wind with the boat on an even keel, will tell you which end is favored or if the line is truly square. Repeat this maneuver from time to time, noting the compass heading (if you have a compass) when you are right in the wind. Is the wind fairly steady or does the compass heading change appreciably?

Run the line from Committee Boat to starting buoy and back, noting the time required on your stopwatch. Since it is only sensible to start on the starboard tack on anything but the most horrible starting line, the elapsed time for a run from one end of the line to the other on the starboard tack is of paramount importance and interest. You may not want to run the line and start at the far end; you may want to start at the near end or even the middle, but it is still extremely helpful to know how long it will take you to run the whole line, so find it out. Once you have decided which end of the line you feel is the most advantageous to start at, stay away from it. "Confuse the enemy," so to speak, by giving them the impression that you think some other spot on the line is better. Maybe they'll decide that that is the better end, and when you finally whip around to start at your chosen spot, you'll have it all to yourself—you hope. Sometimes this idea will work, sometimes not, but it's still worth the try.

If you plan to start at the middle of the line for any reason (maybe you think you'll be free of the crush if you start near the middle rather than at either end), see if it's at all possible to line up some object outside the line which is actually ON the line made by the Committee Boat flag and starting buoy. To do this, sail your boat beyond either end of the line—but on the line—and sight past the other end of the line at some object which is lined up with them, maybe a flagpole, a tree, a yacht anchored, or a mooring, anything at all which is stationary. When you get back inside the starting line, the one end of the line and this object will provide a range which will make it quite simple for you to determine whether you are really up on the line when the starting gun goes. When you are near the middle of a starting line it is difficult if not impossible to gauge accurately your position with reference to the line, but the range will aid materially in solving this problem.

Start your stopwatches on the first signal possible. The first

gun will no doubt catch you unawares and your watches will be
some seconds off, but you'll have a general idea as to the time
and be ready for the next gun. Try to be near the Committee
Boat for your five-minute gun, so that you can actually hear the
time-keeper counting off the seconds. You'll get the rhythm as he
counts off the last ten seconds and really hit that button right on
the nose. Conditions, light air and such, may make it impossible
to be at the Committee Boat five minutes before your start. If so,
get the ten-minute gun and check your watches at the five-
minute gun by having a crew member look for the hoisting of the
signal or the smoke from the cannon as the timer keeps his eyes
glued to a watch.

Two suggestions might be in order here: First, the timer cannot do this checking job alone, for he cannot watch for the signal
or smoke and then look down at the timepiece without a minor
but possibly important time lapse. (Of course, the timer can re-
start the watches completely, but here again the chance for error
creeps in.) Secondly, it must be borne in mind that the visual
signals, hoist or smoke, are the truly accurate ones, not the aural
signals. Sound is so much slower than sight that there can be a
lag of two, three or four seconds. Whatever method you use,
make every effort to be sure it is positive and foolproof. Another
minor variable that can be eliminated with due care and attention.

There are only a very few places in the sailing world where
races start more or less regularly to leeward. The Edgartown
Yacht Club on Martha's Vineyard is one of them, because the
summer sou'wester strikes in there regularly—almost so regularly
that you can set your watch by it—and the geography of the area
is such that only a leeward start can be set up.

As I mentioned earlier, in connection with Fathometers, I've
sailed there many times over the past 15 years in the Edgartown
Regatta, with that most delightful and hospitable couple, Marie
and Hugh Bullock aboard their beautifully kept and equipped
Concordia-41, *Prettimarie*—truly a "yacht" in every sense of the
word, all spit-and-polish, with the mahogany trim varnished to
the Queen's taste, and maintained by her youthful and most enthusiastic amateur crew.

Obviously, with a leeward start and a downwind first leg in a
good southerly for six or seven miles, it's important—absolutely
essential—to "get away and running" quickly. I say this most

immodestly and boastfully, but nevertheless truthfully: with help of the *Vanderbilt Formula* (see below) and a number of practice starts, *Prettimarie* has been *Numero Uno* very often past that first big Gas Buoy, half a mile or so down the first leg or course. And any of you who have raced in that area know that your run on the Vanderbilt Formula has to be a relatively short one or you're on the Flats. The interesting thing here is that if you CAN get away—break fast, as they say in horseracing—even though you are not the biggest or fastest boat, the others pile up on each other and slow each other down; and the net result is that the leader literally takes off and keeps increasing her lead, to the extent that she's way ahead at the lee turning mark—and well on her way to victory.

VANDERBILT FORMULA

There are several methods of assuring a good start: sitting on the line, running the line and the Vanderbilt Formula. Sitting on the line is probably the least successful of the three, and under the present Rules of the North American Yacht Racing Union the most dangerous. In fact, the present Rules were designed in part to discourage this type of start. In small, light boats such as dinghies, sitting or parking on the line is quite common, for they can "get up and go" at the drop of a hat; but in heavier boats, that take longer to get moving, it is somewhat more difficult. In either case, a boat driving through to leeward with good headway can cause a lot of trouble for the sitters. It is always better, I have found, to keep a certain amount of headway, for your boat is under better control and will pick up complete headway considerably faster.

Running the line is probably the most frequently used system and the most successful, particularly if you have taken the trouble to find out ahead of time the exact number of seconds required to sail from one end of the line to the other, as suggested above. If you sail up on some sitter he may make a half-hearted attempt to luff you across the line. Occasionally he'll be successful, but more often you'll be by him, blanketing him in the process. Or you may elect to pass him to leeward, in which case you'll have the sitter over the proverbial barrel.

Mike Vanderbilt is my source for a system or formula for starting which is quite simple and has proven extremely successful, especially on leeward starts. It has minor drawbacks at times, in

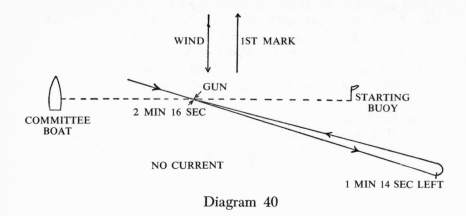

Diagram 40

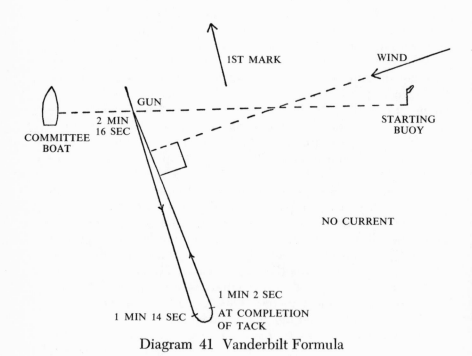

Diagram 41 Vanderbilt Formula

that currents or a luffer can cause you some trouble; you may
become blanketed by a mess of boats to windward, or you may
get "boxed" by other boats to windward and leeward, and are
therefore unable to make your turn at the proper second. However, these are predicaments which come up in any starting situation and must be met as they arise. In essence, the Vanderbilt
Formula is this: You cross the starting line from the wrong side
on a broad reach (90 degrees to the true wind) at the point on
the line at which you wish to start, noting the time LEFT to go,
and with your boat at its maximum or standard speed. You must
know the time it will take you under the existing wind conditions
to make a 180-degree turn, either a jibe or tack. You add this time
to complete a jibe or tack to the time left and then divide by two.
The dividend thus found is the time left on your watch, at which
time you commence to tack or jibe back toward the line. Theoretically, other things being equal, the formula should bring you
back to the exact point at which you wish to start just as the gun
goes. Currents, variable winds and blanketing boats will cause
obvious dislocations in the proper operation of the formula. A
certain amount of common sense must be exercised in its application and use, but more often than not it can be done successfully.
For example, a strong head tide as you reach away from the line
will bring you back too soon. Conversely, a current under you as
you reach away will bring you back too late. The main advantage
of the formula is that it permits you to hit the line with a good
turn of speed. Some boats may even be ahead of you, but your
extra speed may well carry you past them in a very short time.

   To give an example of the formula in operation, let us suppose
that you pass the point at which you wish to be when the gun
goes with 2 minutes and 16 seconds left. The wind is steady and
there is little or no current. The time for a 180-degree tack is 12
seconds (which you may have calculated beforehand or just
guessed). Add 12 seconds to 2 minutes and 16 seconds, or 136
seconds, giving you 148 seconds. Divide this by 2 and you arrive
at a figure of 74 seconds, or 1 minute and 14 seconds. When your
watch reads 1 minute and 14 seconds left before the gun you
commence your tack. If you do a normal tack—don't rush it or
slow it down—you will arrive back at the starting point desired
just as the gun fires. By way of further explanation to those skep-
tics who in the past have doubted my mathematics, if you subtract
1 minute and 14 seconds from the original figure of 2 minutes and

16 seconds you arrive at a figure of 1 minute and 2 seconds. If you then subtract the time for the turn, 12 seconds from 1 minute and 14 seconds you will come up with the same figure of 1 minute and 2 seconds. In other words, you sail away from the line for 1 minute and 2 seconds, take 12 seconds for the turn and sail back for 1 minute and 2 seconds. Should you desire to be early at the line you may add say five or ten seconds to the formula, but never subtract or you'll be late. See Diagrams 40 and 41 on the use of the formula for a reaching and a windward start.

The maximum or minimum amount of time which should be allowed for the most successful operation of the Vanderbilt Formula varies with the size of the boat. To start reaching a Class J yacht away from the line with 4½ minutes left would not be out of order, but to allow that much time on a 30-foot-overall racing boat would put it so far from the starting line that a minor drop in the strength of the wind might spell disaster. In other words the terrific inertia and weight of a J boat will carry her along despite a drop in the wind's velocity, while a small 30-footer would lose her speed almost immediately under the same circumstances. For the smaller craft a maximum time of somewhere between 1½ and 2 minutes seems to work well. If you go much under 1¼ minutes, by the time you have the formula figured out in your head, time has run out or you are in the middle of a mess of boats headed in the opposite direction to you and you aren't able to make your turn anyhow.

No matter what plan you use for starting, make every effort to hit the line with maximum speed. You may cross the starting line at the crack of the cannon, but if you are dead in the water at the time (in anything but a dinghy or a very light boat), a boat coming up from astern many seconds late, but with a good head of steam, will roar past you in short order. What I am trying to say is that the start itself is not important, but what is important is where you are in relation to the rest of the fleet about 15 seconds or one minute after the start. I don't care how you make your start as long as your boat is moving fast when it hits the line (and, of course, as long as you make it legally).

As a case in point: what seems like a very good trick, and a strictly legal one, was accomplished one afternoon on *Ranger* in a trial race in very light weather. Under the Rules all tows must be cast off and all engines turned off before the five-minute gun. (I mention the engines not because *Ranger* had one, but because we did the same thing on the 65-foot yawl *Good News*—which did have a power plant—and just as successfully on a NYYC Cruise port-to-port run.) The breeze was so light that we felt we might have trouble maintaining steerage way, so Skipper Mike had *Bystander, Ranger's* powerful tender, give us a line and tow us with all she had. With 5½ minutes to go to the start the towline was cast off. This is perhaps hard to believe, but with the additional help of her sails, *Ranger* held enough of the speed she had gathered under the tow to ghost across the starting line and out ahead of her competitors. (The results with *Good News* were the same, though I am unhappy to report that we weren't quite so successful at the finish line.)

Keep clear of the crowded areas of the starting line. Get to know your competitors' foibles and failings. If you race against them for any length of time, you'll get to know who are the "cowboys" in your fleet, who will run wild, and who will jam the best end of the line. Study the "enemy" and learn their starting tactics. When you've learned their plans of attack or starting, stay away from 'em, let 'em mess each other up and you pick for yourself a nice quiet, vacant spot on the line.

If you can get away and get away clear, you'll have a distinct advantage, even though you aren't at the most favored spot on the line. Maybe you only have to be a few feet down the line and to leeward (though ahead) of a bunch of boats who are all messing each other up. If you can get yourself a good flying start you'll be able quite soon to work up and backwind the whole of this group. You can't backwind them all, but you'll get one or maybe two and they'll take care of the rest.

Avoid setting new or additional sails during the period from just before the start until just after it, say for five minutes before the starting gun, until you are away with a clear wind. It is almost impossible to get a decent and successful start with a spinnaker set. Start with either a ballooner, genoa or working jib, so that you'll be able to maneuver considerably better. Maybe you'll even be able to luff any boats who make the mistake of having their spinnakers up. Get started and get a clear wind, then break out your spinnaker. A ballooner is all right to start with, provided you are not obliged to make frequent tacks, in which case it may get torn. Have your spinnaker and gear all set, even have it hoisted in stops if you like, but don't break it out till you're clear. A skipper attempting to start his boat with his crew jumping all over the boat, rigging guys and sheets, can't pay proper attention to his main job of starting. Such details should be organized beforehand, but if they can't be, have one person gingerly and quietly attend to them. Once away and free, all hands can turn to and have the spinnaker drawing in a jiffy, but get the start over with first.

While starting, one crew member other than the timer should advise the skipper of any unusual occurrences, though not too often nor unnecessarily, for he'll then only distract the skipper from his job. But, for example, if a boat to leeward suddenly luffs while the skipper is looking in another direction, let the skipper know. Keep him advised of boats overtaking to leeward, for as I have pointed out above, the skipper can't have eyes in the back of his head and see in every direction at once; but on the other hand, try not to distract nor confuse him by extraneous or (should I say) uncalled for advice. As a case in point, I was reminded, on reading Carleton Mitchell's complete and interesting account of the '58 season in the 12-metres, THE SUMMER OF THE TWELVES, of such an incident at the start of the New York Yacht Club Cruise Run from New London to Newport. The five 12-metres were there—*Weatherly, Columbia, Easterner, Vim* and *Nerius*. We were starting on a reach out to Race Rock and I was going away from the line on a Vanderbilt Formula start. Several of my cohorts in the cockpit started offering muttered (underbreath) comments that "the breeze was lighter, we were going to be late and there wasn't as much wind." Naturally, I could hear all this and take it in, and, foolishly, let myself talk myself or influence myself into tacking roughly 45 seconds before the formula had run out. Anyhow, we were early, had to luff, "S" turn the boat, and do everything but get out and pick the boat up, and as a result, when we hit that line, we were deader in the water than the proverbial duck. Now, mind you, I'm not blaming anyone. I did it myself—I had the wheel, and I turned the wheel, so I'm not blaming any of the boys. I did it myself with my own big fat hands, BUT—I did say at the conference in Newport after the race, when we gathered below to hash things out, "Boys, in the future, if I am going to louse up a start, please let me louse it up all by myself!" And we did louse up some starts after that, but we also got some pretty good ones, too!

Avoid tacking, if possible, during approximately the last minute before your start. Tacking (or jibing) so soon before the start

will retard your speed and make it difficult to avoid being overtaken by some other boat close aboard. On larger cruising and
racing boats (50–70 feet) this time for not tacking or jibing
should be even longer, say 1½–2 minutes. Experience in starting
both dinghies and International One-Designs over the years has
emphasized the importance of this to me. In a small fleet of five
to ten boats, the problem is not as great, but where there are
twenty or more boats attempting to get across the line, getting
set on your starting tack about 60 seconds before the gun, gives
all boats an opportunity to space themselves and get off with a
minimum number of protests and considerably less chatter, as
well as the aforementioned maximum speed. How often have you
seen some dreamy-eyed optimist come sailing along on the port
tack against the whole fleet 15 seconds before the start, hoping to
get a chance to tack and break through, while his harried competitors scream all sorts of impolite epithets at him?

Use your sails and rudder to control your speed. Slack your jib
off and maybe later your main if you are going too fast. Possibly
a couple of quick "S" turns by means of your rudder will be
advantageous, but try and not use any of these three tactics during the last 20 seconds before your start. You want all the speed
available when the gun goes, so don't kill her too shortly before
gunfire, or she may not—and probably won't—pick up in time to
stop an overtaking boat. In dinghies and light-displacement boats
you'll get away with it, but not in a heavier keel boat.

Generally speaking, where one end of a starting line is blanketed by headlands, buildings, trees or other classes of boats
(waiting to start), it is advisable to start nearer the other end.
(Even in open water, a mass of boats waiting for their start can
cause quite a blanketing effect or deflection of the wind; so avoid
them like the plague and get to the other end of the line.) Circumstances alter cases, but the smart skipper will consider this
problem along with all the others in working out his start.

Where your class is not the first group to go off, have a look at
the earlier starts, see where the so-called hot-shots get away, see
which end of the line they choose, and maybe even follow them
out for a short distance to determine whether or not they chose
well. You can learn a lot from watching how these other fellows
start their boats; you can see their mistakes, and help correct
your own errors.

Starting a boat in a race is not something which can be easily explained so that a novice skipper can jump aboard and make a perfect start. Starting requires experience and lots of it. One reason that I feel so strongly about Frostbite dinghy racing (as we know it) as a school for sailors is that it provides repeated and repeated experience at the same maneuvers, be they starting, mark-rounding or finishing, during one afternoon's racing. In fact, I feel so strongly about it that there is an entire chapter devoted to dinghy racing later in the book. Repetition and experience will tell you how to handle your boat under a given set of conditions. In weekend summer racing, a given set of conditions may not come up again for months, if at all. In dinghy racing, almost identical conditions occur every race. Experience of that sort has simply *got* to teach a sailor something.

Starting requires alertness, coordination and that knowledge of your boat which comes only through practice and doing. Knowing your boat will give you that ability and confidence to tool it through the narrowest of holes and to push it across that imaginary line at the crack of the cannon. With experience will come the elimination of the oft-mentioned variables. The variables discussed in this chapter must all be controlled to insure good, if not perfect, starts: stopwatches, correct sails, knowledge of the tide, weather, Race Committee, starting line, tactics of your opponents, and above all your boat. Know and control all these variables and maybe you'll get a good start. No one can get perfect starts every time, but if you get good average starts, you'll do well.

CHAPTER XIV

The Windward Leg

Boom! The race is on. All that has been said before is preliminary stuff, more of less cut and dried, but "wha hoppens" next? The variables discussed so far have been of a type which can be more or less controlled, but from here in, fellow sailors, the variables really become fickle, inconstant and changeable.

The start is over and passed, get her going and size up the situation. If you have a *clear* wind keep on the same tack and let nature take its course. If you feel the other tack is better for tactical reasons (better wind, better tide or whatnot) seize your first opportunity to get round on the other tack; BUT other things being equal, stay where you are and let the other fellow peel off first. Remember—make as few tacks as possible. I don't mean to drive yourself into some sort of hole because you want to avoid unnecessary tacks; however, THINK, and plan ahead. Weigh the advantages or disadvantages and THEN make your decision.

Tacking slows your boat down, especially in light air, and it should be avoided at all costs where possible. Every time you tack you lose the driving force of the wind for a few moments, and you use your rudder to turn, which exerts another force that tends to reduce your speed. Time and distance are consumed in gaining back your maximum speed, while the rest of your class are sailing merrily on their way. Weigh all the factors before you tack, making sure that you're not getting yourself into a position where you'll have to make almost immediately another tack which would be even more disastrous. Just remember this rule— *tack as seldom as possible.*

HOPELESS POSITION

In his excellent book, YACHT RACING, THE AERODYNAMICS OF

SAILING AND RACING TACTICS, Manfred Curry describes what he calls "The Hopeless Position or Berth," which has become the accepted term in yacht racing for this most unfortunate situation —if you happen to be the fellow who is in it. It is an area of disturbed wind and water surrounding a boat which is to leeward or ahead of another boat (or boats), quadrilaterally shaped, with

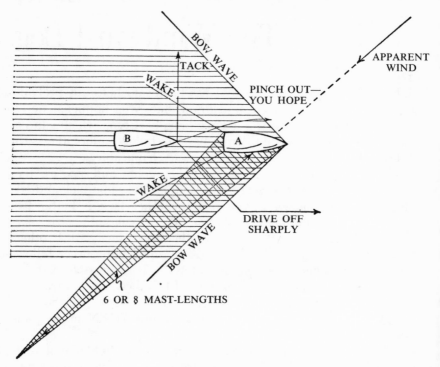

Diagram 42

the boat in question at the forward and leeward corner of the four-sided zone. Any boat in or entering this region of fluctuating and agitated wind or water will be impeded, hindered and held back by it. Opinions differ as to the effective distances and areas of these hindering influences, because different situations, together with varied wind and water conditions, will result in totally different consequences. For example, diagram 42 shows two boats, A & B, beating to windward, with B in the obviously hopeless position. On the other hand, when running dead before the wind, the hopeless position reverses itself and the leading boat A (diagram 43) is in a hopeless position for she is in the wind shadow of boat B, the only effective zone under these conditions. It is rather hard to say how far this blanketing zone extends. It depends largely on the strength of wind and the size of the boats; but as a rule, it can be said to extend for six or eight mast lengths of the boat which is in the hindering position. You'll know soon enough if you are in a blanketed area, for your boat will become sluggish and the telltales on the shrouds will become agitated and jump around, not staying in their more or less steady location. When beating to windward, the effect of the bow wave and wake will extend as much as four to five beams to windward, at an angle aft of somewhat less than 45 degrees. At the same time, the wind in a lesser section of this windward area is deflected and disturbed, reducing the effective power on the sails of any boat trying to work through it. It hardly seems necessary to point out that any boat astern and to leeward of the hindering boat is indeed in a bad spot for she is directly in the wind shadow of the weather boat. The hopeless position is truly a desperate and futile spot, so make every effort to get out of it with speed and dispatch.

Diagram 43

Note bow wave and wake which go out at an angle somewhat less than 45 degrees, but which will impede any boat in their path. Note triangular wind shadow which carries its effect possibly six or eight mast lengths aft, and in the direction of the wind.

If, for one reason or another, your start is bad, three courses are open; drive off to leeward to get a clear wind, continue on your present course, or tack when you get the chance. If you only have to drive off to leeward a short distance to get your wind free, maybe that's the best course to take, but bear in mind that by driving off you are losing to windward. In other words, is it better to sacrifice your windward position in order to get a clear wind? Experience has taught me that you can always go to leeward, *if you want to,* but you cannot always get to windward. I will go further and say that a majority of the times that I have driven off, sacrificing a certain amount of distance to windward, in order to clear my wind, I have later regretted it. Not always, but a majority of the times. (Maybe it's because I try to point my boat so high that I hate like the very devil to get off to leeward of anyone, for I just make it difficult for myself to get back up.) But there are times when it pays to drive off and get your wind free. If you continue your course, you may lose something from the backwind of leading boats, but they also may, in time, tack and allow you a clear wind. Think this over before you make any hasty decisions. If you elect to tack to port to get out of a bad start, you are probably taking the proper choice, though before you do so, you must make sure that you are going to be able to clear any boats approaching on your weather quarter. If you have to ease off and drive under the sterns of four or five starboard-tack boats, maybe you'd do better to stay where you are and await developments. Get out of a hole, if possible, but don't get yourself out on a limb by so doing. When I say don't get yourself out on a limb, I mean that, though your position at the moment may be poor, don't make it immediately much worse by driving off under a flock of boats, or by tacking into such a spot that you must ease sheets to go under a lot of starboard-tack boats.

There is one other way to get yourself way out on a limb—the classical way, it might be called. As soon as the race is on and the whole fleet is headed in what should be the chosen or ideal direction, you tack away from them, for any reason you can dream up, and go way off by yourself on a long hitch. You may win the race by a city block, but you also may end up last, and it will probably be the latter. This is a typical example of what is NOT *consistent* sailing, and it is generally indulged in by skippers who are not sure of themselves, who feel that they can't keep up with the leaders of their class, and who just want to take a long chance in a do-or-die manner. They'd do much better to stick with the fleet in order to learn WHY, HOW and WHERE the so-called experts get that way.

Quick Tack

Since there are exceptions to every rule, here's one to the rule about tacking as seldom as possible. Very, very often a quick tack or two will bail you out of a bad situation just after the start, especially if you have good headway when the gun fires. Let us suppose that you have your boat moving at comparable speed with the rest of the fleet, but you are being backwinded. If you

are able to execute a quick tack and can get clear of any weather-
quarter overtaking boats, the chances are you'll be able to clear
your wind. Stay on the second board if conditions warrant it, but
if the desired or chosen board is the first one, come back again
shortly. I have seen this maneuver executed with aplomb and
dispatch many times. On the face of it, it doesn't seem quite
sound and sensible; nevertheless it works and has been used successfully despite all rules against too frequent tacks.

The first few minutes after the starting gun are vitally important moments in a race, particularly if there is a large fleet of
boats racing. No doubt, before the start, you have decided what
course you wish to take, which tack is the ideal tack and what
your general strategy will be. If you get away with a free wind
on the desired tack you can continue with your planned strategy,
but if your start is fouled up for one reason or another, you will
have to make some quick decisions very shortly after the starting
gun and possibly revise your original strategy. If your start is
hopeless, maybe the best strategy is to split with the fleet and
tack off in the other direction. This often pays off, though it is
taking a chance and is not average sailing. It may be the best bet.
On the other hand, perhaps the sensible idea is to take your
licking for the moment, but stay with the fleet and await developments. If you are a believer in Harry Maxwell's ideas, you'll
hang on and wait for some fellows ahead to make their mistakes,
letting them fret themselves into a poor tack or some silly maneuver. Believe me, it's been done. Put another way, will you
attack or defend? If you decide to attack, drive off or tack in
order to clear your wind and get free. If you settle on defense,
stay where you are, waiting for an opportunity to present itself so
that you can attack.

During the '58 Cup Trials, we had aboard from time to time, a
most delightful sailor and pleasant friend, Capt. John H. Illingworth, R.N., Rtd., whom we called, by the by, "our British spy."
Captain John was here before *Sceptre* arrived and politely asked
if he might sail with us once or twice and promised not to reveal
anything he might overhear or see. He proved to be a wonderful
shipmate and was more than willing to lug his share of sails on
board or ashore. (In my book, anyone who is willing to pitch in
and help do the dirty work, must be an all-round good fellow and
a good sailing companion.) He taught us, too, the call or cry of
the parched or "unwatered" camel. I can't spell it here and can

hardly say it aloud either, but it served well at certain auspicious times.

Anyhow, Captain John went back to England and wrote a wonderful little book called WHERE SECONDS COUNT. I urge you to read it. For in it Captain John says more or less what I have just said above: "Attack or Defend?" He calls it "active or passive" sailing. Shall you *actively* go after your competitor or be content to sail along *passively* until a better opportunity to get past him appears? It makes sense and will help you win races. Matter of fact, just before the Queen's Cup Race on the New York Yacht Club in 1959 I'd just read WHERE SECONDS COUNT (and I hadn't read my own book in years and years). But anyhow we tried both active and passive sailing 'gainst *Easterner*, finally took her and won the Queen's Cup! (Author's note: We won TWO more Queen's Cups after that, plus a lot of other important silverware.) John, you did a good job!

WATCH CHIEF COMPETITORS

As soon as practicable, find out where your chief competition is or find out where the good boats in your class are headed. If you are in the group of front-runners in your class you'll want to know what the rest of them are doing. If you aren't in that group, you'll want to know where they are going, so that you can figure out why they are going that way. Whichever the case may be, have your crew locate the top-notch boats and let you know from time to time what they are doing. During a windward leg on *Bumble Bee* there was very little conversation amongst the five members of her crew and what little there was was generally confined to what our competitors were doing and how each was doing.* The astute skipper and crew keep a constant watch to locate and take advantage of any shifts which may be helpful, not only as indicated by other boats, racing or sailing, but also by their own independent observations.

KNOW CHIEF COMPETITION

Along the same line, after you have raced against the members of your class for a period of time, you will get to know their peculiarities and idiosyncrasies. Study them carefully so that you

---

* Avoid extraneous chatter. Leave things alone if the boat is "going." The Good Lord deliver me from the untaught, inexperienced eager-beaver who ALWAYS talks and ALWAYS wants to change things.

may plot and plan your race accordingly. For example, learn which skippers point or foot their boats, so that you may know whether you are strategically better off to tack respectively on their weather bow or lee bow in order to defend your position when ahead.

It won't take you long to learn which skippers know their racing rules and which don't, which skippers can get their boats moving quickest, which ones are sure of themselves at the helm, which are not, which ones execute an "Admiral's Sweep" around a mark, which ones will luff you (when overtaking them) miles out to windward of the rest of the fleet (and oh boy, can't they be stubborn?) and which ones are sporting in their mental approach to the spirit and letter of the rules. There are other things you should know about your competition, but this gets over the general idea. It is really worth studying and thinking about, for if you are alongside some "wild Indian" who would just as soon execute a quick English luff to tag you out, you must be unusually alert to protect yourself.

COMPASS

Don't neglect your compass. As soon as possible after the start, take a quick look and make a mental note of your course. Keep that course in mind and check frequently for possible changes which would indicate shifts in wind direction. If you tried the line before the start, how does the course you are now sailing compare with the course you could sail then? A minor detail, to be sure, but one that could prove very helpful. In boats which carry a crew of four or five, it will be a load off the skipper's mind if one of the crew is delegated to check the compass for him. Where the compass is mounted in a binnacle or in the cockpit floor, this poses no problem and it leaves the skipper freer to watch his other duties. When I was racing with George Esselborn in his International One-Design *Myth*, George took over this duty of checking our compass course and called out any appreciable shifts. It really was a splendid help and I strongly urge the use of this idea.

During our fifty-odd races a season in the International One-Design Class, we had occasion to use the same marks many times over. Knowing the compass directions to various marks, especially the "bird cages" (which are three marks, whose appearance resemble bird cages, put out each Spring by the YRA and hence are not ALWAYS in the same spots, requiring a new check each year), helps to make life simpler and racing easier. On clear days, we made notes as we sailed from mark to mark; then, when it was foggy or rainy, we had definite compass courses to sail which, with allowances for tide (current), would ease considerably the whole question of "Where's the next mark?"

As outlined under Required and Necessary Equipment, a large-scale chart is necessary and will simplify the whole deal. When beating, pick up some landmark as a guide. You'll be able to tell quickly when you get a header or a lift and take whatever action is called for.

WEIGHT OR BALLAST

Right after the start get your live ballast set and located as soon as possible. The question of crew placement is thoroughly covered in Chapter III, so there is no point in discussing it at length here, except to say that it's one detail which should be organized as soon as possible after the starting gun so that you can get everything out of your boat immediately. On larger boats, even before gunfire, it's sensible to have a few of the crew stretched along the weather rail if it's blowing hard. The others can climb out the minute they are finished adjusting sheets. Explain before the starting gun where you are going to want your weight and let your crew know how and when you want them to get there.

POINT OR FOOT?

The question of how one should steer a boat on a windward leg resolves itself into one of both personal preference and momentary necessity. It is said of a skipper who sails his boat very close to the wind that he points his boat high, while the skipper who sails his boat at a wider angle to the wind is said to foot. Which is correct? There isn't any really complete answer to that question, for both schools of thought have much proof that they are right and the other wrong. Both schools win their share of races, yet both can manage to get themselves into their share of trouble because of their respective desires to point or foot as the case may be. For my part, I love to point, working my boat up in the puffs and feeling her eat out to windward as she goes along. It has been beaten into my skull for so long that I can always get to leeward if I want to, that I think I always try to get as far to

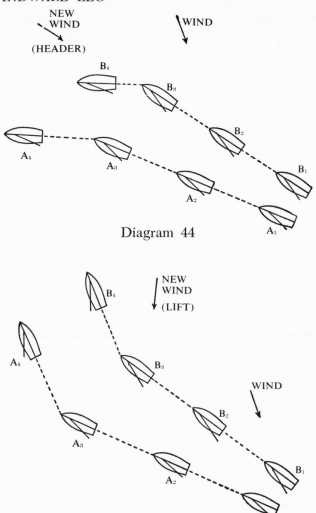

Diagram 44

Diagram 45

windward as possible when the opportunity presents itself. The problem of pointing high, I think, is one of knowing your boat, feeling her eat out or chop to windward and listening for a possible diminishing sound of the bow waves as you watch the slight luff in your sails. All these little details, silly as they may seem to the uninitiate, do help the helmsman to steer his boat and get the most out of her.

Don't misunderstand me, however; the fellow who makes his boat foot goes through the same motions, the same sensations, but tries to keep his boat at top speed by keeping his sails completely full at all times, as opposed to the pointer who sails his boat so close to the wind that they may luff and shake frequently. One sails a longer course faster, while the other sails a shorter course slower. The results depend on the fickleness of the wind. If two boats start off more or less together on a long hitch, one pointing and the other footing, if the wind heads them eventually, the footer will be leading. On the other hand, if the wind fairs or lets them up, the pointer will be in front, as in the accompanying diagrams.

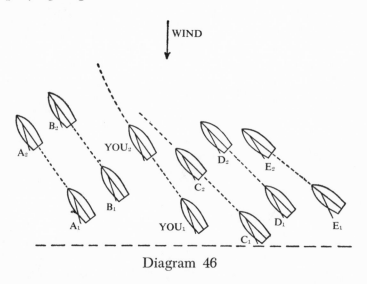

Diagram 46

Momentary necessity may determine whether you should foot or point and the alert skipper will be prepared to do either at the drop of a hat. At the start of a race you may find that you are being backwinded by some boat ahead. If you drive off, there are other boats below him to blanket you, too, and there are other boats on your weather quarter so you can't tack. What to do? Point high and try to work clear of the backwind of the boat ahead. Or maybe you are bucking a tide and by sailing your boat a bit high you can get it on your lee bow, so that it pushes you to windward. Isn't it worth pointing your boat even a bit too high to get the benefit of a lee-bowing tide? You're right, it is. You'll eat

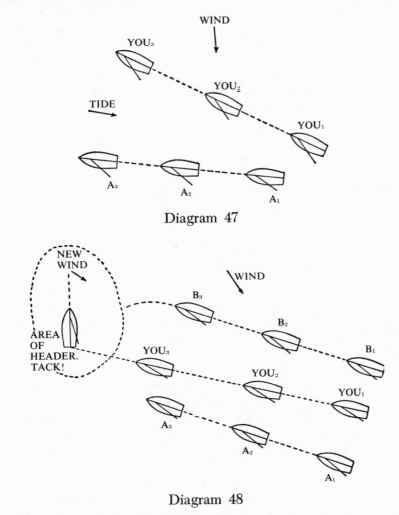

Diagram 47

Diagram 48

out rapidly on those who don't point so high—and keep footing
into the bargain. Maybe some time later you see a breeze on the
water ahead, or boats ahead which indicate that there is a definite header or wind shift which will drive you off in that area.
Foot your boat to get there first and be the first to take advantage
of the header (which will be a lift on the other tack).

I am indebted to Mike Vanderbilt for the following comment
on the Mathematics of Footing or Pointing:

"In a hard breeze you will point much closer to the actual

wind because the difference between it and the apparent wind in which you sail will be greatly reduced by the increased ratio of wind-speed to your speed. Consequently, if you can tack in seven points or less in a hard breeze, the perhaps ⅛-point difference between footing and pointing will not add nearly as much to the distance you must sail through the water to reach the windward mark, compared to what it would add if you were tacking in 8½ points in a light breeze."

Mike adds that "failure to appreciate the above probably cost *Weetamoe* the right to defend the America's Cup in 1930, and it cost Sopwith (*Endeavour II*) many boat lengths between Penikese Island and Vineyard Sound Light Ship in 1937." In the latter case, he refers to the Race from Mattapoisett round the Lightship to Edgartown, on the NYYC Cruise after the Cup Races that year. *Ranger* tacked in less that 5¾ points with a fair tide and a strong sou'wester under Penikese Island that day. She pointed high while *Endeavour II* drove (or footed). The net result was *Ranger* showed her real worth and power in a strong breeze in the open rough water between Penikese and the Lightship by picking up 4¼ minutes on *Endeavour II* in six miles, where *Ranger* had picked up only 4¼ minutes in the previous 13 miles from the starting line.

By the same token, in his book, ON THE WIND'S HIGHWAY, Mike points out what I have said above, that you should drive a bit in a heavy, confused sea to keep your boat moving. Don't let her get sluggish, for she'll slow down and probably develop a weather helm. Take advantage of the power in your sails and give her a rap full when the going is sloppy. Eat out to windward in the smooth spots.

As a general rule, it is better to foot in light air, in a strong wind with a heavy sea, or in a confused sea. By footing in light air, you not only keep your boat moving but you actually increase the strength of the apparent wind, albeit an extremely small amount. Even though it is a small amount, it will still be of considerable help to you, for you haven't got much wind to start with and any increase is bound to be beneficial.

When both wind and seas are heavy, it is best to give your boat as much power and push to get through as possible. To get as much power as needed you must drive your boat, or foot; don't try and point too high. If you do point high, your sails, not being completely full, will lack the drive to push the hull through the waves, and you just won't move through the water—except possibly sideways. Confused seas—which come from various causes: power boats, tide, or new winds—also demand that you foot rather than point, for they are generally quite heavy in comparison to the wind at the moment, requiring every bit of drive that your sails can provide in order to get through them and yet keep going.

TELLTALES AND MASTHEAD FLY

Just a reminder, lest you forget: Watch your telltales and occasionally the masthead fly. If I were able to describe to you the proper angle of incidence of either, I would cheerfully do so. It just can't be done. On the windward leg it varies with the strength of wind, and while reaching and running, the angle is again different. But once you've used them for a period of time and become accustomed to telltales and masthead fly you won't be able to do without 'em. If you are well-heeled enough to be able to afford that gorgeous and efficient battery of Brookes & Gatehouse navigational instruments, then count your blessings and keep BOTH eyes on all the instruments at all times—a rather difficult task, methinks, but continued use and practice will help you get more knots out of your boat.

SAFE LEEWARD POSITION

The "Safe Leeward Position," also described by Manfred Curry, is a corollary or complement of the Hopeless Position. It has likewise become one of the classic phrases of terminology in yacht racing. The Safe Leeward boat puts the boat astern, or astern and slightly to windward, in the hopeless position, whereas the fellow astern and to leeward is in the hopeless position because he's in the wind shadow of the leading weather boat. Safe leeward, a very apt and descriptive expression, has a broader meaning, in that it refers to any boat which is to leeward and ahead of another. The leader is "safe" in the sense that being ahead he can protect himself against a close following boat by his bow wave and wake as well as backwind, and if he is quite far ahead he can tack to cover or work up to cover when required. Being to leeward and ahead, he is an odds-on favorite to benefit from any headers if beating, while a lift may well let him up to his mark. To be sure, the latter is not always the case, but it does happen, and with a certain amount of unpleasant regularity—at least to me, when I am astern and to windward. The net on the whole safe leeward situation is that it can be made to work to advantage more than half the time, and any system that can be made to operate successfully more than 50 percent is certainly worthwhile when you are trying to beat the averages.

A terrific lift on a windward leg will naturally make it rather tough for the safe leeward fellow, but if he's far enough ahead and to leeward, he can always tack and get back some—if not all—of his lead or position. I am speaking, of course, in generalities, for you will agree, I am sure, that all sorts of holes can be picked in any of these arguments of mine. For several different types of safe leeward position, see the diagrams.

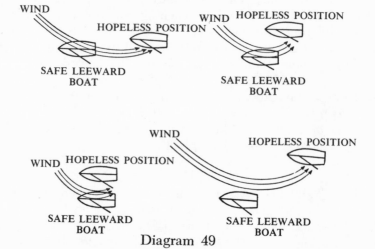

Diagram 49

The safe leeward position has definite and obvious advantages in certain special situations. A cardinal principle of racing strategy is ALWAYS TAKE THE TACK WHICH IS CLOSEST TO YOUR MARK. In other words where you must make a long hitch and a short hitch to get to a given mark, always make the long one first. Never take the short hitch first, unless you are in an awful hole or have no choice. During the period of time required to make the longer board, conditions (which never remain stable for long) may change. If you are let up, you may well lay your mark, and if headed, you will be in a more favorable spot to tack for it.

On long-distance races where you have a situation involving a

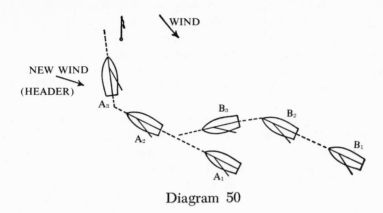

Diagram 50

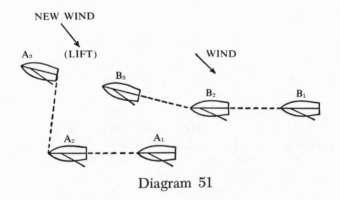

Diagram 51

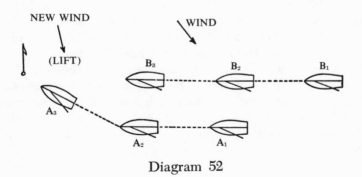

Diagram 52

long, more or less close-hauled course to sail, the safe leeward is an ideal place to be. Under these conditions, foot, don't point—the odds, because of time and distance, greatly favor some sort of change in wind direction which will greatly benefit you.

Safe leeward is a splendid location when you are racing under headlands or close to shore, for you'll get a better and truer breeze farther out. Safe leeward on one group of your class is a protection, as well as an assurance of consistent racing, when another group gets off by itself with a safe leeward position on you and your group. If your group and the other group get a bad header, the other group may be ahead of you, but at least you'll have your bunch. If you all get a lift, you may or may not be overtaken by your weather and astern boats, but you'll still be in front of the farther leeward group. You may not win but you'll be in the ball game at least. There are advantages to the safe leeward reaching and running which will be discussed in those chapters later.

To Attack or Defend?

The first few hectic moments of getting organized, after the start, are over. What will you do next? If you are ahead, "defend," but if you are behind or "boxed," i.e., caught or surrounded on all sides by your competitors, you must "attack."

If you have made the perfect start, have your wind clear and are in the lead, keep cool, calm and collected, for you are in the driver's seat. You have free, clear air, smoother water than the boats astern, and a choice of whichever tack you wish to take. So keep your wits about you, make no false moves (keeping in mind what Harry Maxwell said, to wit: It's the fellow who makes the fewest mistakes who wins the boat race), and wait to see what's going to transpire next. Let's assume that you are, or have put yourself, on the desired or optimum tack. As nobody's bothering your wind and you are sailing through less agitated water, you should pull out on the rest of your class. You have, in essence, licked a whole flock of variables, and you are in the best place to cope with any future variables. Be alert and keep your eyes open so that you can see 'em and deal with 'em as they come up. You are "defending," so plan your strategy to ward off any "attacks" by the most dangerous elements of the fleet behind. You must cover either:

Rosenfeld

"Skip" Etchells' *Shillalah*, #2125, has a fine safe leeward on the rest of his class. #2109 is already "sousing" his bow into *Shillalah's* quarter wave.

Rosenfeld

Etchells-22 Class starting to windward; #26 is in a good spot.

1. The closest boat or boats astern.
2. The boats who are closest to you in the series standings.
3. The boats who are sailing the most desirable or optimum choice of one or more courses.
4. The largest group of two or more split-up bunches of your competitors.
5. One boat which you are especially anxious to beat.
6. OR, a combination of the above.*

As you can plainly see, the covering possibilities and the implied reasons for each are rather broad, but very often there will be combinations of these six groups in the particular situation at hand and your problem will be somewhat simplified as a result. But cover you must, after deciding which group or combination will most satisfy you. If you keep your boat going and stay between them and the next mark, they just can't get by you—unless some catastrophe occurs.

In actual practice, covering at the start of a race must be of a general nature. Go with and stay on top of the group which takes what you feel to be the ideal or optimum tack. Except in rare instances, it is rather foolish to start covering individual boats right after the start. You'll get yourself so involved that the rest of the fleet will get miles ahead of you before you know it. It's far better to get off to a flying start, establish a substantial lead, if possible, and then start thinking about covering individuals. Covering means extra tacks, and they are to be avoided, as has been pointed out, unless absolutely necessary.

However, there is one situation that may justify two extra tacks. It can best be described as "keep your chickens all on the same tack." You are leading four boats on the same tack in, say, a six-boat race. The fifth boat on the opposite tack passes between them. Tack on his wind if your lead is sufficient to afford two tacks. When he tacks, stand on until he crosses your wake, then

---

* Several years ago, when your correspondent was Guest Skipper aboard *Palawan*, we had been leading a fleet of about fifteen boats in our class. It was a beat in a very light sou'easter from Bell 32A to the Black Bell off Lloyd's Point. We figured it was best to stay out in the tide, and so we let (or *I* let, 'cause I was steering) the majority of the fleet go inshore. You guessed it—they got a slant of air and beat us badly to the weather mark. Peter Cooper slipped below, got "The Gospel" out of its mahogany case and, in a *very* loud voice, read off the above six points. Needless to say, a hearty laugh was enjoyed by all hands at my expense. MORAL: *Always Cover*—or at least, almost always! P.S. I wish I could say we made it back, but we didn't.

tack. For the time being at least, you have your chickens all safely tucked away under your lee. Mike Vanderbilt did this in a five-boat race on *Ranger* and kindly provided me with the information.

Covering itself can be done in three ways. If your aim is to force your competitor into extra tacks or to force him onto a less desirable tack, tack ahead of him and to windward so that you cut his wind and he's in the hopeless position. On the other hand, if you wish merely to protect your position, stay between a certain boat and the next mark and hope he'll stay put; if you have sufficient lead to execute the maneuver, tack so that you'll be on his weather beam. Since his air will still be clear, he may be content to stay where he is rather than tack again, in which case you'll have him tucked away safely. Care must be exercised not to tack so close abeam of this leeward boat that you run the risk of getting yourself in the hopeless position by reason of being in his bow wave or area of disturbed wind.

In the event that you have a decent or substantial lead on some boat which you wish to cover, but he is on the opposite tack and splits tacks with you every time you go about, there is one more method which will work, except in the case of very violent shifts of wind. Where you have a lead of, say, five to ten boat lengths or more, and the other fellow keeps on tacking as you go around, tack as he crosses your wake, being sure to get your boat going as quickly as possible by slacking sheets a bit and giving her a good rap full. As your competitor again crosses your wake, go over again and, as before, get her going rapidly. This is known as "Open Cover." The advantage is on your side, for the other fellow is always sailing through your wind shadow. This sort of thing can go on for hours, until he gets tired and bored, or you do, but naturally some regard must be had for the rest of your class. Unless you simply HAVE to beat the other boat, there is little sense in continuing such maneuvers, because the other boats in your class will eventually creep up on you both and pass you. But where the results depend only on the outcome of the race between these two boats, tack him to death if necessary. (By the same token if you are the boat behind, tack as often as the leader does and don't give up. Maybe *he* will; you may get a shift and catch him.)

Where the situation calls for covering one or more groups of boats, as opposed to some individual boat, the decision (and possibly the control of the oft-discussed variables) on which group to cover must be made. A quick calculation of the odds involved—wind, weather, tide, other boats and other classes, etc. —must be made. Weigh all the factors and then cover the group which seems to have most of the advantages on its side. Avoid hasty moves, as you are in the driver's seat; and yet be prepared to alter and reverse any conclusions you have arrived at in the event that conditions change radically and quickly.

To "attack" when behind, as outlined earlier in the chapter, the first thing is to get yourself a clear wind at the earliest possible moment. Caution is the watchword, however, for it will avail you little to tack or even drive off hastily and get yourself further out on a limb. Look over the situation; maybe the fellow ahead giving you a good dose of backwind will get anxious and tack away (and maybe he won't, too). There may be a chance to pinch up without losing too much distance and clear your wind eventually, while at the same time, you will commence to put some overtaking boats in the hopeless position. If you can push the latter boats back somewhat, you may develop a good opportunity to tack away from your own bad position.

On the other hand, if you have carefully studied your competition, you may be aware that the skipper ahead is a pointer, and you may gain in the long run by driving off sharply through his wind shadow and get your clear wind that way. This is a particularly good maneuver when you are reasonably sure that the tack you are on is the better tack. There is considerable danger in this type of maneuver, however, for under the present Rules, there is nothing to prevent the weather leading boat from driving off with you if he likes. Frankly, I think that this rule is a grossly unfair one, and it is my great hope that the solons who make our racing rules will eventually see fit to reverse their position. The old rule which prohibited driving off on a leeward boat worked reasonably well, while the present one, in my humble opinion, gives much too great an advantage to the leading boat or boats.

To defend yourself in the last situation, if you are the weather leading boat, keep her going, full and by, don't pinch, as he tries to sneak through to leeward, but keep in mind, particularly in the early stages of your race, that there are other boats to beat. Don't neglect them right after the start to camp on one boat's wind.

To defend, when you are to leeward and ahead, with an overtaking boat driving down on you, pinch up or work up slowly so that you put the overtaking fellow in the hopeless position. To attack when you are underneath, though not blanketed by an overtaking windward boat, drive off with slightly eased sheets, so that you work a bit ahead of him. Then you can work up and establish your safe leeward. If you are the overtaking weather boat in this case, to attack you must seize your first opportunity to drive off on the leeward boat's wind before he gets the safe leeward on you.

To escape from a covering boat, feint a tack, letting your crew jump about as if you were going to tack and then fall back on the same tack. Occasionally you'll get away with it, but I must admit, very seldom, for an alert competitor will be watching you like a hawk. A generally more successful maneuver is to tack without any of your crew moving at the moment, when all those on your competitor's boat are looking the other way. Obviously, your own crew should be alerted for such a drastic maneuver; and it is almost impossible to get away with it successfully when a genoa is used. However, with a working jib, I have quite frequently been able to catch a covering boat napping and get far enough about, before they wake up, so that I was able to get a clear wind on the other tack. Your crew must be agile and quick in getting reorganized, or you are liable to lose one of them overboard, but it CAN be done.

Attacking or defending, as you sail round the course on any leg, be on the alert to improve your situation by keeping in mind the following general rules:

1. Watch the competition to see what they are doing and what wind they are getting.
2. Watch other classes ahead and behind for the same reasons.
3. Watch for puffs on the water and have your crew call your attention to them if necessary.
4. Watch smoke and flags ashore for wind indications, being careful not to be fooled by moving steamers and trains (a common failing of many careless sailors).
5. Watch lobster pots, buoys and oyster stakes as you sail by for helpful tips on the current.
6. In light air or no air, keep a sharp lookout all around the compass for any wind indications. Working your way first into a new breeze may mean the difference of many places to you at the finish.

Rosenfeld

Shields Class, shortly after start, showing #146, #83, #5 and #65 running in bad positions—whether to attack or defend? It looks as if it might be best to hang on a while and defend and see what the other guys do.

Rosenfeld

Three Shields approach weather mark on the starboard tack, very close together, with #88 in a fine inside position, obviously, with her spinnaker ready to be hoisted.

7. Keep your wind clear.
8. Avoid unnecessary tacks, but be prepared to tack at a moment's notice, if warranted.
9. Avoid oversteering and sawing on the tiller.
10. Avoid unnecessary motion on the part of your crew, keeping live ballast to leeward in light air, and move over the weather rail in a good breeze.
11. Watch telltales and masthead fly.
12. Take no chances on the port tack. It doesn't pay.
13. Watch for and tack into thunderstorms.
14. Avail yourself of a lee-bow tide where possible.
15. Tack on the headers in a shifty puffy wind.
16. Cover the fleet if ahead, or at least stay with them. Never split with the fleet when ahead or well up in the race.
17. If behind, give consideration to splitting with the fleet, but for average racing and average results, avoid getting yourself out on a limb by so doing.

Rounding the Weather Mark

A cardinal rule for racing your boat right is: APPROACH THE WEATHER MARK ON THE STARBOARD TACK. It hardly seems necessary to explain the advantages, and these advantages are multiplied as the size of the racing fleet increases. Plan your weather leg so that, if humanly possible, you arrive at the weather buoy on the starboard tack. It may mean the difference of a half a dozen places in the race and, despite all entreaties or rules to the contrary, it is often worth an extra tack or so to get yourself into this favored position.

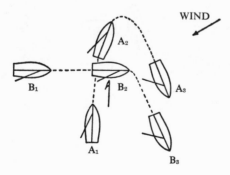

Diagram 53

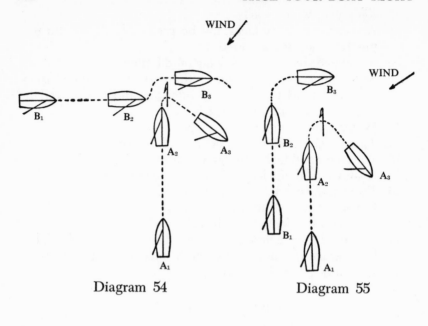

Diagram 54   Diagram 55

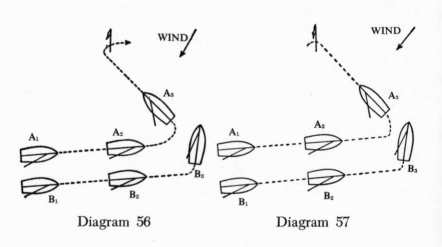

Diagram 56   Diagram 57

As a corollary to this most important maxim, keep in mind the direction and strength of the current. With a lee-bow tide you can afford to tack short of laying your mark, but with a head tide, allow sufficient room to compensate for the effect of the current. You can always drive off, but you'll look awfully silly if you can't make the mark and can't tack because of a boat on your weather quarter.

Study and know the turning circle of your boat, so that you don't jam it round the mark killing your headway in the process. Practice turning buoys so that you go close enough, but not so close that you risk hitting them. In light air with a smooth sea you can afford to cut closer to a mark than you can in a howling gale with a heavy sea. However, in either case, it's better to be safe rather than sorry. The penalty for hitting marks has been reduced by the solons of yachting from total disqualification to doing a complete 360-degree rounding on top of your normal rounding maneuver. I cannot say that I am in complete agreement with this new rule, although I will grant you that total disqualification is a bit rough. This privilege has been granted in Frostbite dinghy racing for many years, true; but with bigger boats, not so easily maneuverable, it is my feeling that it is a somewhat dangerous situation, especially when some wild "cowboy" at the helm is involved. Quite naturally, such a re-rounding yacht loses all rights of way.

Techniques for proper rounding of the weather mark are diagramed here. It is interesting to note that there is only one case, and a rather rare case at that, where the starboard tack boat does not come out ahead. That is the one (diagram 53) where an alert port tack boat is able to sneak between the stern of the starboard tack boat and the mark, thus preventing the latter from tacking.

CHAPTER XV

The Reach

BOOM-JACK

Whether you are going into a reach from a windward leg or from a start, ALWAYS HAVE YOUR BOOM-JACK IN MIND. If the wind is light, be gentle about tightening it, but if there is any kind of decent breeze at all, *snug it down well* before the windward leg or before the reaching start. This is particularly true on boats not equipped with winches for their boom-jacks, and I cannot put too much emphasis on it. We've discussed the boom-jack from all angles already; *just don't forget it.*

STARTING ON A REACH

Starting, too, has already been discussed, but for the benefit of those poor souls who must still start on a reach there are several

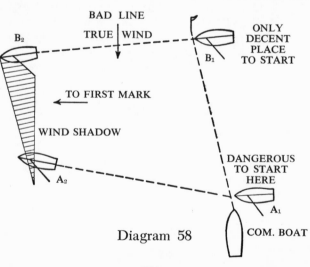

BAD LINE

TRUE WIND

B₂

ONLY DECENT PLACE TO START

B₁

TO FIRST MARK

WIND SHADOW

A₂

DANGEROUS TO START HERE

A₁

COM. BOAT

Diagram 58

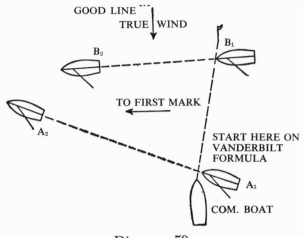

GOOD LINE
TRUE | WIND

B_2

B_1

TO FIRST MARK

A_2

START HERE ON
VANDERBILT
FORMULA

A_1

COM. BOAT

Diagram 59

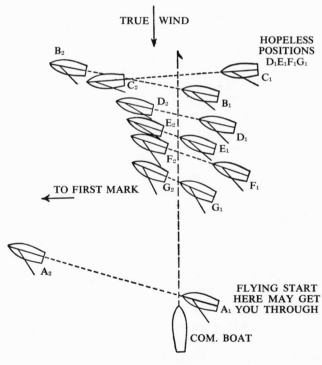

TRUE | WIND

HOPELESS
POSITIONS
$D_1E_1F_1G_1$

B_2

C_2

C_1

D_2

B_1

E_2

D_1

E_1

F_2

TO FIRST MARK

G_2

F_1

G_1

A_2

FLYING START
HERE MAY GET
A_1 YOU THROUGH

COM. BOAT

Diagram 60

diagrams which give a fairly complete picture of the problems involved. Diagram 58 shows a typical bad line—the weather end favored. There's only one place to start—if you can get through the mess of boats that will be there—the weather end. Starting at the leeward end is dangerous, for there'll always be one fellow who manages to get through at the other end and eventually he'll blanket the leeward boats.

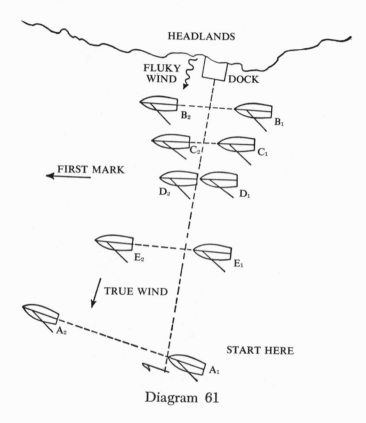

Diagram 61

Diagram 59 shows a good line for this type of start. If you can get away on the gun at the leeward end you'll break through the windward boats without too much trouble. The Vanderbilt Formula works extremely well under these circumstances.

Diagram 60 shows a line at right angles to the course with the wind right down the line. Since most of the boats will gang up at the weather end, interfering with each other and luffing each other out to windward after the gun, you may get away with a good flying start at the leeward end.

Diagram 61, with the line off the dock surrounded by head-lands, and consequently variable, fluky winds at the weather or dock end of the line, again means that there is only one place to start—the leeward end, for there you'll get a steadier, truer breeze.

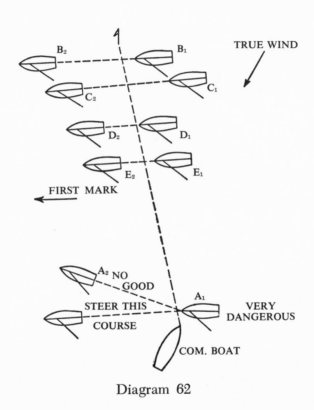

Diagram 62

In Diagrams 62, 63, 64, and 65, the wind is a bit further aft, and Diagram 64 shows a situation similar to 58, but in this case, the leeward boat is in an even worse spot. In 63, you can get away nicely to leeward and then sharpen up to cross the fleet and insure yourself a free wind. Bear in mind that the apparent wind will pull forward of the true winds shown in these diagrams. In Situation 64, you may get away with a start at the leeward end, if you stay to leeward and await an opportunity to sharpen up and

get a clear wind. In 59, you are probably still better off to start to
leeward because of the better breeze.

In all these starting situations, let me remind you again that it
is better to start without a spinnaker. Have it ready to hoist,

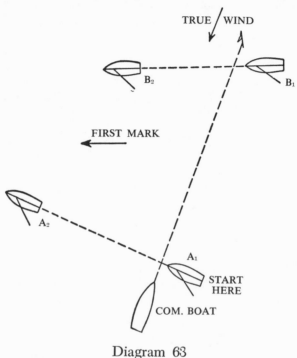

Diagram 63

certainly, but don't do it until you are clear and moving. A glance
at your masthead fly before you start, as you try the line and first
leg, will tell you if you can carry it.

SPINNAKER-REACHING

In view of the apparent difficulty that many novice crews find
in organizing the proper position of the spinnaker halyard with
reference to the jibstay, I am covering this matter (which has
already been discussed in the chapter on Spinnakers) once more,
in different words.

As you beat to windward, determine whether or not a spinnaker can be carried, and as you near the weather mark, make
the necessary preparations, being careful not to have all hands

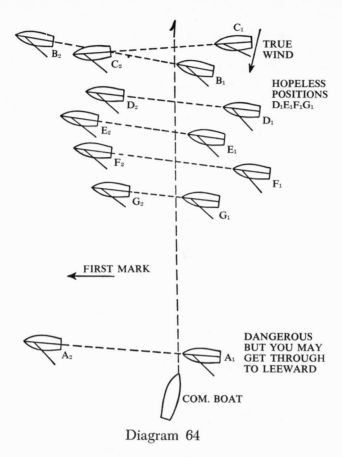

Diagram 64

jumping all over the boat at the same time. In this connection, it should be possible to decide before the start on which side the spinnaker is to be carried and the halyard rigged accordingly. With the modern jumper-stay rig and parachute spinnaker, the halyard block is rigged on the mast above the jibstay. Therefore, if the sail is to be hoisted to port, the halyard must come down on the port side of the jibstay. Many boats rig their halyards out on the bow before the start so that they have a quick and easy choice when hoisting their spinnakers. I have already *most definitely emphasized,* earlier in this book, that this causes excessive windage and is a *very, very bad* arrangement. In other words, I think it should be VERBOTEN!! It is impossible to set the halyard up so tight that it does not vibrate in the wind. Authorities tell me that this vibration causes it to occupy the space of several or more of its diameters, thus setting up considerable interference with the proper and direct flow of air past the luff of the jib. This may or may not be true—I am not prepared to say—but I will say that every time I have done it myself, the boat doesn't seem to do well. I may be exaggerating the situation, I admit, but on the other hand, if it does interfere one iota, it is not good, and therefore, I don't do it.

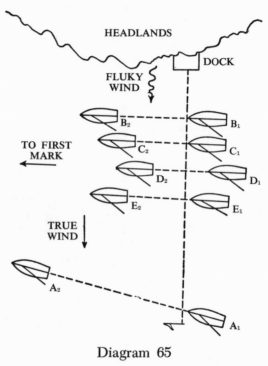

Diagram 65

It is easier and more practical to have the halyard forward, because it's a devil of a job to get the halyard forward from the mast (where it causes little or no wind resistance) around the lee side of the jib, if it happens to be on the wrong or lee side. It's a cinch, of course, to take it forward from the mast when the halyard is on the weather side of the jibstay. To make it easy for yourself, plan the problem so that as you approach the mark, preferably and usually on the starboard tack, your halyard will be on this weather side. I might add that even this does not always work out, for there may be times when you are forced by circumstances to approach the weather mark on the port tack, instead. If such is the case and it cannot be avoided, think ahead and lay your plans accordingly. Don't forget that, as described earlier, you can haul your spinnaker halyard to the proper side by means of the guys (which we will presume you have long since rigged and hooked together). It "ain't" always easy, so be sure and allow ample time.

It might be in order here to explain that to reduce windage from the halyards running up the mast, on *Bumble Bee* we always snapped our halyards across the spinnaker pole slide fitting on the mast, i.e., pulled the starboard halyards round to the port side of this slide, and the port halyards over them to the starboard side. This had the effect of holding the halyards close to the mast—in fact, made them almost blend into the mast, and reduced windage considerably. Due care must be exercised to uncross these halyards before the spinnaker is hoisted.

To determine whether you are going to be able to carry a spinnaker at all, two methods may be used. The first method is pure guesswork—the one I use most of the time and it seems to be satisfactory. Check the waves to windward—being sure not to be confused by your own bow wave—and determine the true wind. (You cannot use your telltales or masthead fly for this, because they indicate apparent wind.) Check your course from the weather mark to the next mark either by compass or by sighting. If the wind is abaft the beam, you may be able to carry a spinnaker, but if it isn't very far abaft the beam, you better hesitate a moment or so after rounding your weather mark to be sure the apparent wind isn't going to work forward of the beam, in which case no spinnaker, *unless* you have a Starcut.

The second method is by a vector diagram of wind, strength, course and speed, as the figures show. Diagram 66 represents a southwest wind of 8 knots, and an easterly course of 4 knots. An apparent wind of south by west ¼-west (195 degrees), is indicated, which is abaft the beam, so the spinnaker may be carried. In Diagram 67, we assume a southwest wind of 6 knots and an easterly course at 5 knots. The apparent wind in this case is south by east (168 degrees), which is forward of the beam; hence no spinnaker. There is a certain amount of guesswork in this second method, too, for you must be fairly accurate with all four factors —wind, strength, course and speed—to get a true picture. A bit of practice will help materially, of course, but my method of just "guessin" works well enough to suit me.

But suppose you own a Starcut spinnaker? Wouldn't Diagram 67 tell you it was time to set it? The answer is "Yes, most emphatically."

Often there is a question as to whether conditions are right to use a conventional spinnaker on a fairly close reach. Let's say it's occasionally doubtful if the apparent wind is far enough aft to make it draw well, i.e., barely abaft the beam, or maybe even a little forward of the beam. On *Bumble Bee*, unless it was blowing half a gale, we always set our spinnaker anyhow, secure in the knowledge that we could handle it better than a majority of our competitors, and yet keep our boat at top speed or even gain a

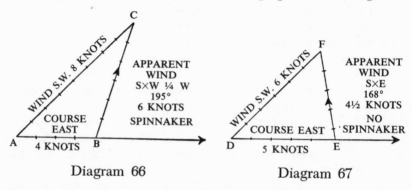

Diagram 66   Diagram 67

little speed. We knew, too, that a number of the rest of the fleet would follow our lead and hoist their spinnakers. Maybe it was "dirty pool," but we always managed to gain a few places with this maneuver, for some of them couldn't seem to control their kites and we'd pick up distance on them without too much trouble.

After rounding the weather mark, hold your course a bit high of the next mark, if you plan to carry the spinnaker, until it is broken out, thus keeping up your maximum speed, until the kite can pull its load.

Ease off your backstays or permanent to straighten your mast and give the rig some spring.

Get Set

As soon as possible get your boat and crew organized and

quieted down. There is always a certain amount of excitement in
rounding marks and setting a spinnaker and very often a distinct
increase in blood pressures. Cool off and calm down, so that you
can concentrate on the job at hand, i.e., getting the most out of
your boat and spinnaker. Check the trim of your mainsail. In
anything but a gale, steering should be easy, two fingers. If you
have to haul and pull on the tiller, the trim of your sails or the
weight distribution is wrong. Investigate. Pump the boat if required. Keep weight to windward and low if it's blowing, and
make 'em lie on the rail, not sit up, so that windage is reduced. In
light air, keep some weight to leeward so she heels a bit. Check
the spinnaker halyard and head of the sail. If the head is cutting
on the jumpers, slack off enough so that it doesn't.

Regarding this situation in extremely light air, Bob Barker, one
of my able and talented spinnaker men, and I have had considerable difference of opinion. Reaching in a drift where there are
only little cats-paws of wind, he has always wanted to slack off
the halyard to such an extent—which is necessary to get the limp
rag off the jumpers—that the skirt of the sail drags in the water.
I, on the other hand, have always felt it better to get the sail up
in the air, not only to take advantage of what little air there is
above the water, but to get the dead air out of the sail. Naturally,
this makes a mess of the head of the sail. The result is a continuous hoisting and lowering of the spinnaker halyard as one or the
other gets the ear—or the eye—of the person nearest the cleated
line. I still don't know which of us is right, but since I am writing
this and Bob isn't, I'll say I am. You can decide what to do for
yourself.

Keep alert and keep your wind clear. Watch the boats around
you to see how they are doing and what they are doing. You don't
have to keep turning around to look at the boats close astern. If
they are gaining, you'll soon know it by the sound of their bow
waves. Yes, that's right, the bow waves. Keep your ears open as
well as your eyes. You can hear them if they are closing the gap,
for the waves will sound differently. You don't need any stadim-
eter, that pessimistic instrument which tells you whether you are
gaining or losing on another boat, to find out what's going on. In
watching these other boats, *keep your wind clear at all costs*,
EXCEPT at the price of being luffed way out to windward of the
rest of your class by some wild cowboy. Certainly, go up with
him a little way, but if you know your man—and if you've sailed

Lawrence Marx, Jr.

The results of too short a first leg with a more or less windward-leeward course. Two International One-Designs tangled masts near the weather mark with the results shown in the following three pictures.

Bumble Bee (dark hull) owned by William H. Stanley and sailed by your Author was on the starboard tack going upwind approaching the weather mark. *Annie* (white hull) owned and sailed by B. Glenn McNary of Manhasset, had rounded the weather mark in first place and was running downwind on the port jibe. In attempting to pass *Bumble Bee* to leeward and to windward of a third boat, *Annie* was too close and the top of the mast of *Bumble Bee* (heeled over by a sudden puff) hooked into the rigging of *Annie*. *Annie*'s mast already broken in two places, is being held up by *Bumble Bee*'s mast. Note the bubbles in the water in the foreground, showing *Bumble Bee*'s wake as she was pulled in a circle around *Annie*. *Bumble Bee* is heeled to windward, her mainsail is about to jibe and she shipped considerable water.

In the second picture *Bumble Bee*'s mast is collapsing, the starboard lower spreader has collapsed, and the hull is straightening up. The tops of the masts are still hooked together by *Annie*'s rigging.

The third picture shows both rigs down with *Bumble Bee* completing a full circle about *Annie*. The hulls never touched and no one was hurt.

Lawrence Marx, Jr., on another International, hearing the crash, grabbed his camera and made these shots in about twenty seconds.

against him for any length of time you should—don't be a sucker and let him take you way out above the others. It's better in the long run (or if you want, long reach) to let him go.

There may be times, of course, when you'll want to go up with a luffer; for instance, if you see a new or better breeze to windward, or if he happens to be some boat you must beat with no regard to the finishing positions of the others. But in most other cases, especially if he's a bigger boat than you, it's much more sensible for average and consistent racing to let him go.

Aboard *Palawan* in situations like these two, Cap'n Paul Wolter would say in a very loud voice, FLY NOW, PAY LATER! The helmsman and the rest of the crew generally got the message.

TIDES AND COMPASS

Make allowances for possible current and keep your eye on the compass. If it's a clear day and you can see the next mark, fine, but take a reading anyhow, and, if you haven't already done so, make a note of it for future use. In bigger boats it is often impossible to see the next mark and steering by compass is a necessity. However, it has been my experience in boats 35 feet and under that you can steer a straighter, better course, and at the same time get a clearer picture of the whole panorama of the boats in your group, if you can use your next mark or some landmark in back of it as a guide rather than the compass. Put another way, it seems to me to be easier to maintain your proper relationship and position with the other boats racing about you, if you can see your next buoy. So pick it up quickly on rounding your weather mark and at the same time line up your bearing behind it for indications of the amount you may be set by the current.

TRIM

Watch the trim of your sails carefully and keep after them. Keep an eye on your masthead fly for large fluctuations of the apparent wind. With the tall, narrow mainsails used today the most efficient angle of trim, or most efficient angle of incidence of wind to sails, is a very broad one. With the old, low, wide sails, improper trim immediately resulted in a loss of speed, but this is not as true with modern boats. Therefore, it is often better, if your boat is going and you are gaining or passing other boats, to leave things alone and not disturb the sails by monkeying with them. The spinnaker, on the other hand, should be kept "on edge" and demands constant attention. A collapsed kite is good for the loss of a length or more, so keep after that spinnaker trimmer to be on his toes. And remember the fundamental principles of spinnaker trimming:

1. Let the sheet or clew rise and fall as it will, adjusting the tack or pole-end as required, so that the foot is parallel to the water or horizon.
2. Adjust the inner end of the pole to keep it at right angles to the mast.
3. Adjust the after-guy so that the pole is square to the apparent wind as shown by the masthead fly. Never have it more than square, but err, if necessary, on the forward side.
4. KEEP THAT FELLOW ON THE SHEET AWAKE.

Centerboarders

A discussion of centerboarders may be found in Chapter X. It is sufficient to say here that some board will help the steering in a hard breeze with a spinnaker and prevent "crabbing," i.e., moving ahead with the centerline off its axis. In a hard breeze, some board and the weight further aft will reduce "tripping" with a spinnaker set.

Look Ahead

Many races lost on the windward leg can be won back on the leeward leg if you play your cards right. If you've done all the things outlined above and keep after them, you'll probably have your boat going nicely and you should begin to pick up on boats ahead, or pull away from those behind. Just remember that your spinnaker can really pull you along when it's properly set and trimmed. It's a big sail which can deliver power to your boat. Please, *please* don't neglect any little detail of its ideal adjustment.

Look ahead and plan ahead just as you did on the windward leg. Think out the problems which will arise as you sail down the reach. For instance, ahead there's a known slow boat who has a weakness for luffing. Don't overtake him dead astern and then try to pass him. Chances are he won't let you without luffing you. Work up to windward of him while still well astern. You may have closed up so much before he realizes that you are gaining that he'll be unable to luff you and hold you off. Then you're by him.

Can you see far enough ahead to know where you'll be with regard to boats around you when you get to the mark? Will you be able to get an inside berth when you turn in? Tactically, it's often sound policy to let some fellow get a good overlap to windward when you have to jibe round the next buoy. He'll be on the outside then and be more or less out of your hair; but be sure you can hold him off until you get to the mark.

By the same token, if rounding the next mark is a tack rather than a jibe, try to get to windward so you'll be on the inside at the turn. It may even pay you to work a bit to windward of your whole group to accomplish this, but watch boats way off to lee- ward; they may be able to harden up a bit, increase their speed and round ahead of you.

While under most conditions the straight line (with proper allowances for current) is the shortest distance between two marks, if the wind is inclined to be puffy, drive off somewhat during a hard gust and then sharpen up when it gets light again. This is especially true when you are sailing on a broad reach. On a close reach under spinnaker you can't really increase your speed much by this maneuver, for you are already getting the maximum drive from your spinnaker.

Catching a "Tow"

Since larger boats are by nature faster than smaller ones, it is often possible for a slightly smaller boat to get a "tow" from a bigger one. It is quite difficult to accomplish and hold this tow, I will admit, but it can be done. Nothing illegal about it either if you are successful. On a broad reach in *Bumble Bee,* we have on a number of occasions towed 110s, whose water-line length is not too different from ours. (Actually, on a broad reach in a moder- ately smooth sea, 110s will slide along *almost* as fast as an Inter- national One-Design.) The tow is "hooked" by getting in the stern wave of the larger boat and staying there as best you can, but it can't be held in anything but a broad reach as I have said. There is too much backwind on a close reach. The stern wave, assisted by your sails, will hold you there as long as you can stay in it. Cross waves, a lightening of the wind, or blanketing will break up the tow. I have heard some experts say that they felt such a tow impeded the tower. This I cannot subscribe to nor believe. There is no physical connection between the leading boat and the stern wave or towed boat; therefore, there can be no retarding action on the tower. The theory is the same in the case of a dinghy towed behind a powerboat. Adjust the painter of the dink so that she rides on the forward side of one of the waves in the wake of the powerboat, and the dink seems to slide downhill with almost no strain on the painter.

Relief Helmsman

On *Bumble Bee*, it was often our practice to have a relief helmsman during the reaches and runs, something I will freely admit to having copied from Mike Vanderbilt on *Ranger*, who always turned the wheel over to Olin Stephens after the windward leg. Frankly, I do it for two reasons: the first being to get a chance to relax a little from the constant tension of steering (though anyone who has ever sailed with me will tell you that's a gross canard—I never relax) and the second, so that the steering job will get its proper attention. This attention is often lacking when it is necessary for the skipper to look in sixteen different directions at once to see what's going on about him. Wilma Bell, "Pop" Stanley's daughter, did our relief steering with aplomb and dispatch and was alert at all times to the skipper's orders of "head up," or "head off a bit." While this idea would seem ridiculous on a boat with a crew of two or even three, it does work well on larger ones and I strongly recommend it.

Safe Leeward on a Reach

The safe leeward position is a fairly good spot to be on a reach when ahead, especially if you can keep your closest competitor in your bow or stern waves, for they'll serve to impede and delay him if he should get any stray puffs which you don't. Furthermore, it gives you the opportunity to trim sails and sharpen up to increase your speed if you are broad-reaching, thus protecting your position. Maintain your safe leeward, but just don't let him get too far out to windward on you, or he'll be out of the hopeless position and in a spot where he'll have clear wind and no backwash; in other words he'll be a threat.

Have you ever noticed how a leading boat always seems to draw ahead, especially when he is followed at some distance by a closely grouped bunch of boats? This is because he has free air and comparatively undisturbed water to sail in. He may or may not be in the safe leeward position, but the net results are the same. Of the bunch aft, some are in the safe leeward with respect to each other, while the rest are in the hopeless position. Those in their own particular safe leeward spot will pull out on the others, IF they keep their wind clear. (I may seem to lay too frequent emphasis on this question of keeping your wind clear, but believe me, it *cannot* be over-emphasized.)

IF BEHIND

When behind, keep your eyes open so that you may profit by the mistakes of those ahead. When you're behind on a reach you have a much better chance to avoid mistakes than the fellow ahead; in fact, the odds are almost two to one in your favor. He has already been through the water—and therefore the conditions that you are about to experience. If he sails, for example, into a soft spot or vacuum, you can profit by it and maybe sail around him. With a bearing on the next mark—or even on the last mark—you can tell at a glance whether he's sailing too high or too low, and make money thereby.

If you are a lone boat, not too far behind a group of boats ahead, don't give up hope, for they'll interfere with each other all the way down the leg, while you sail merrily along with unobstructed wind and water. If they luff each other all over the lot, don't go up with them; stay on your chosen course and you'll close with 'em. Very often a leeward course chosen by one boat of a group will be highly beneficial, putting him well ahead of the others by the time they arrive at the next turn, because they are so apt to luff each other out to windward in their efforts to pass one another. It might be advisable (particularly in larger boats), when say six lengths ahead, to keep to leeward in a light breeze and cash in only when approaching the mark, or when the. wind is about to freshen.

As you approach your mark, don't forget to change the spinnaker guys BEFORE you round, as discussed in the spinnaker chapter. (This is assuming, of course, that your guy leads to a winch or fairlead amidships, while the sheet is all the way out on the stern.) Make the necessary changes before the rounding, not after, so that your boat will pick up and get moving without any delay. She should be moving well as you approach the mark, but will slow down during the rounding maneuver. Help the boat take off quickly again, by making required gear alterations ahead of time. Make sure at the same time that all your crew are thoroughly aware of what maneuvers you plan to make, so that they can execute them with maximum teamwork. Jibing from a close reach to another reach or run, the "free-wheeling" described on page 154 works to perfection if properly carried out. And when you execute your actual jibe and turn, do it moderately slowly, wide on your near side, close on the far side, so that you are to windward of any overtaking or following boats. There may be times when a jibe is not necessary. You may decide just to square away on your present tack and keep going for a distance before jibing. Do this maneuver slowly, too, so that you don't kill your boat with the rudder, and at the same time keep your sails full.

In rounding a leeward mark to go to windward, use the same technique. Round the mark wide on the near side and close on the far side (you cannot spin a boat about a mark in the first place, and you'll only kill its speed if you try it in the second place) so that you'll have the weather gauge on any following boats. You may even, by rounding a mark smartly, give yourself a good start toward getting out of the backwind or hopeless berth of some boat ahead which has made a poor turn. But beware of making a wide turn when a boat is close astern and to windward. You may tempt her to intervene between you and the mark, though legally she probably has no right to do so.

Just remember in this last case that under the present rules of the North American Yacht Racing Union you may not tack around such a leeward mark, if the next leg is to windward, without due regard for a close following boat.

CHAPTER XVI

The Run

HEEL TO WINDWARD

Lest you forget, let me again refer you to Chapter VII and Chapter X, for a discussion of the importance of heeling your boat to windward on a run. It works and I have proven it to my complete satisfaction time and time again. In light air or when drifting, it doesn't make much difference one way or the other as far as the boat's speed or the effect on the steering is concerned. It does make a limp spinnaker look a trifle better and there are those who think it gets the mainsail higher in the air, though I doubt that you get the main up far enough to do any practical good, even in a flat calm, and it certainly wouldn't make any difference in a breeze. However, in any sort of decent breeze, heeling to windward on the runs really reduces the pull on your tiller and, as a consequence, makes your boat fairly fly downhill.

On *Bumble Bee*, in a hard breeze, we piled all five of the crew on the weather rail including the skipper and spinnaker trimmer (he was obliged to sit as far out as he was able to and still trim his sail efficiently). Even in my Inter-Club Frostbite dinghy, we heel her to windward, though not as much, for considerably more caution is necessary in that type of boat. Just remember to heel her to windward, and if you wish more detailed information I refer you again to Jack Wood's article on the subject in *Yachting* some years ago.

NEXT MARK

As on the reach, pick up your next mark as soon as possible, so that you may know *exactly* where you are going and can plan ahead accordingly, and can calculate your drift because of current, and make whatever corrections to your steering that are required.

Masthead Fly

Again—glance aloft frequently at the masthead fly and check it against the trim of your spinnaker pole. Use the masthead fly to tell you if you are on a competitor's wind, or if he is on yours. It's a perfect indication on a run for it shows the apparent wind and is in a convenient spot to see for both the above-mentioned purposes.

Spinnaker

On a run, puffs and vacuums will influence the clew of the spinnaker almost more than on a reach. Have your spinnaker trimmer keep an eagle eye on the base of your spinnaker, i.e., the tack and clew, so that he may call for the adjustment of the lift and foreguy when needed. Where a radical adjustment of the lift is indicated, the spinnaker trimmer must be alert to slide the pole up or down the mast so as to keep it at right angles to the mast.

Don't neglect light sheets in light air.

If your boat develops a terrific tendency to roll when running dead before the wind on a very windy day, easing the spinnaker pole somewhat forward of its normally squarely trimmed position will help the situation without materially affecting your speed. Chances are you are traveling at almost better than maximum speed anyhow, and excessive rolling increases the odds on breaking gear.

Keep Wind Clear

Running presents a wonderful opportunity to blanket the competition, especially since the base of your wind shadow, and therefore the whole shadow, is substantially increased by the addition of a spinnaker. Blanketing is great if you happen to be the fellow who's doing it, but it can be an awful headache when it's done to you—even if it is all part of the game. Make every attempt to blanket the enemy, but by the same token, make every effort to avoid being blanketed. Luff out, if you must, a discreet distance, but it's almost suicidal on a run to get involved with some eager-beaver who wants to luff. As on reaches it is generally better to let him go by. Actually on a run you have a better chance to get free of overtaking, luffing-minded skippers than

you do on a reach for you can always drive way off to leeward
without too much loss, and if you can eventually get your wind
clear you'll have an excellent opportunity to gain back all the
distance lost.

On a run, staying to leeward is a better than average bet,
paying off more than not by the time you've gotten to the mark.
True, it requires patience and intestinal fortitude, for there is
that ever-present impulse and desire to squeeze up to windward
with the rest of the boys. Stifle the impulse if you can, for you
may very well work through the whole group that have gone
away out there to windward. Tactically speaking, a run is a
tough leg to sail for the wind shadows are broad, long and difficult to escape. Check the masthead fly or fluctuating telltales on
the shrouds for indications that you're being blanketed and then
do SOMETHING, no matter what, to get clear. Sharpen up,
drive off, or even jibe. (The best way I can think of to avoid these
nasty wind shadows is to work out a big enough lead on the
windward leg so that they can't touch you! Many's the time I've
wished I'd been able to do just that.)

TACKING DOWNWIND

Tacking downwind is something which can be done more successfully by schooners than yawls, sloops and cutters. Schooners,
with their large spreads of canvas but small spinnakers, can utilize them to greater advantage by reaching or tacking downwind
instead of trying to make a dead run of it. It is my opinion that
tacking downwind in small boats is greatly overrated, though
there are infrequent times when the air is extremely light that it
can be helpful. I am sure there are those who will argue that
tacking downwind can be most beneficial IF you know how to do
it. Maybe so; but my own experience in most cases has been that
I have made my boat move faster through the water, sailed a
longer distance and then come out in approximately the same
position as when I started the maneuver. During World War II
when the International One-Design Class raced without spinnakers, Arthur Davis in *Patricia* was generally successful in light
air whenever he tried it. Maybe his mechanical steerer had provided him with the proper tips on how to do it; I don't know, but
I have not been as successful as he.

The theory behind tacking downwind is that by sharpening up
and pulling the apparent wind around, instead of sailing dead

before the wind, you will increase the strength of the apparent wind, which increases your speed, which, in turn, increases the apparent wind some more. In other words, as you get a better apparent wind, your speed picks up and this makes your apparent wind even stronger. Theoretically, it would seem that there would be no limit to the amount you could increase your speed, but as we all know you can go only so fast in a boat. This is not necessarily true of catamarans (see Chapter XXI).

Below is a diagram with an imaginary set of figures to give you a general idea of how tacking downwind should work. The data used are pure supposition and I do not mean to suggest that it would or could work out exactly as shown, but you'll get the theory involved. Let us assume that you are sailing a leeward leg from A to Mark K, 10 nautical miles in a northeasterly direction with a southwest wind of maybe four knots. The wind is indicated in direction and strength by the vector AG. Let us assume that your speed dead before a four-knot wind would be two knots, vector AB. If you alter your course and steer higher, say east by north, you will draw the apparent wind forward, almost abeam, and increase your speed to, let us say, three knots. At the end of two hours you will have reached point E and sailed six miles, while another boat sailing dead before the wind will have reached point G and sailed only four miles. If you jibe at point E and head for Mark K, course north by east, you will have the

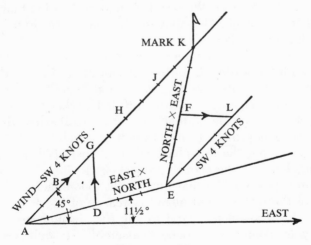

Diagram 68

apparent wind FL almost abeam again and should reach Mark K
at the end of another two hours, while your competitor sailing
dead before it will only have arrived at Point J, still two miles
from the mark. You will have worked out a lead of two miles,
which, as they say "ain't hay." Purely figures out of thin air, mind
you, but they give you a fairly clear picture of the theory behind
tacking downwind. Maybe you wouldn't gain as much as two
miles, but even if you gain only a dozen boat lengths or a half-
mile, it seems worth it, doesn't it?

WATCH PUFFS

As on reaches, but to a greater degree, when the wind is puffy
and variable, you can profit by driving off to leeward in the
strong gusts and then sharpening up to move faster in the light
spots. This really works well under such conditions, but when the
breeze is steady, stick to the straight and shortest distance to the
next mark. It might be in order to remind you again not to over-
steer or "saw" on the tiller. Again, minor points, minor variables,
but they'll add up to win or lose your boat race.

BOOM-JACK

Here we are back to the boom-jack again. Running in light air,
ease it off somewhat so that your mainsail isn't too rigid and tense
like the skin of a base drum. Let the boom "breathe" up and
down a bit with your shock-cord control. It doesn't take much
imagination to see what the results would be in a light air if your
mainsail is set up like the above-mentioned base drum. Give it
some spring and resiliency.

In this connection, slacking off the outhaul and downhaul will
have an additional effect in softening your main. In a hard breeze
the latter can be done too, but the actual benefits to be gained
then are somewhat vague and doubtful. In other words, my experience in slacking the outhaul and downhaul when there is a
good breeze has provided no outstanding conclusion either way.
Actually, slacking the downhaul when a boom-jack is used will
do no good unless the sliding gooseneck is pinned in its somewhat raised position, for the pull of the boom-jack will stretch
the luff of the mainsail out again by reason of the transfer of its
stresses. May I again point out to you the absolute necessity for
having your complete gooseneck assembly strongly reinforced

when a boom-jack is added. The increased strains and forces caused by the boom-jack are simply terrific.

CHECK COURSE AND SPEED

Check your course and speed with the other boats about you. Because boats get so spread out on a dead run it is often impossible to tell how you are actually doing—whether you are gaining or losing in relation to their various positions. But keep alert and watch them, trying to judge just what you are doing and if it's apt to get you to the mark ahead of them. Plan your strategy and think ahead, visualizing the general picture as you'll approach the next turn, and make an effort to get yourself on the inside. If, for example, by continuing your present course and speed, you'll be in the middle or outside of a large group of boats as you get to the mark, slow your boat down or alter your course so that you let them get ahead of you. Let them get into a mess at the mark and you follow round behind them, BUT on the inside. On the other hand, rather than sacrifice distance at this particular stage of the game, you may be able to alter your course slightly to windward (almost tack downwind), pick up your speed and out-distance your immediate group.

CREW PLACEMENT AND MOVEMENT

Arrange your crew placement in a fore-and-aft manner to get the most out of your boat. Experience and practice will tell you where to put them. If you are a novice in your particular class, look about you and note where the experts place their crews. (In fact in all details, if you are just starting out in a class, check the "hotshots" and see what they do. If they won't tell you, you can learn it anyhow by watching them.) Fore-and-aft placement is just as vital and important as heeling your boat to windward. Experiment, if you aren't going well, and find out for yourself by trial and error. Train your crew not to jump about the boat all at once. If you need something or a sheet needs adjusting, let ONE person do the job. Don't have everybody leap for the sheet at the same moment.

CURRENT

Take a frequent check on the current as it relates to your position. Lobster pots, buoys and oyster stakes will give you a fine indication if there happen to be any in your area. We've been over this too, before, but don't forget to watch your bearing on the next or last mark. Either one can be used to great advantage.

New Winds and Thunderstorms

When the breeze is light and fluky, keep an eye peeled for a possible new wind from another direction. Many a race can be won if you can be the first one to pick it. If you see one coming, work over toward it. Having spotted a new breeze, DON'T POINT. It is bad manners to point at anything except French pastry, so there is absolutely no reason why you should advertise to the rest of the fleet that you've found something new and different. The same thing is true of a mark that is difficult to find. There's no reason to point at it, either. I suppose that good sportsmanship dictates that, if you are asked where a certain mark is, if you know you should say so. However, other things being equal, you cannot be criticized if you don't scream about it from the masthead. Some skippers I know of make it a habit, having found the mark in question, to have their crew keep looking in another spot for it. Pax vobiscum. Enough said!

When you see thunderheads over the horizon, as previously suggested, watch them carefully. They may come on or they may stay put. When they do progress, work over toward them, for sure as you are a foot high, the wind's going to come from that direction eventually. Be in a position to get it first.

Anchoring

Don't forget your anchor or kedge if you can't make headway against the current in a drifting match. We have discussed this too, but *remember to slip it over the side UNSEEN, if possible.* Also remember that at anchor you are an obstruction and cannot be legally run into.

Hold Spinnaker

With a well-trained crew, you should be able to hold your spinnaker until the last minute and thereby get every ounce of push out of it. I strongly recommend taking the spinnaker in over the weather side on a dead run which will permit you to carry it even longer. For details see page 162. However, Heaven help you if you don't get the kite down as planned. I can't think of anything as useless for going to windward as a spinnaker halfway down. That will hinder you much more than the help you'll get from holding it a few seconds too long.

WHISKER POLES

One hint I should like to give to boats using whisker poles on their jibs instead of carrying spinnakers. Most such poles are the right length for running before the wind or with the wind slightly off the weather quarter. However, if you get absolutely dead before the wind or slightly by the lee, and for one reason or another don't wish to jibe, the jib often goes aback and becomes useless. By sliding the pole up or down the mast a couple of feet, you'll shorten the distance from the mast to the clew of the jib sufficiently so that the jib will draw again. In actual practice, it is better to slide it up the mast, for that has a tendency to tighten or harden the leech, while lowering the pole has the effect of lifting the clew and making the leech so loose that, again, it will not draw properly. This maneuver is simple if you have jaws on your whisker pole, but if you use a hook and pad-eye there is a solution—another pad-eye further up the mast.

DISCONCERTING THE COMPETITION

If you are overtaking a competitor who is inclined to be nervous and fidgety (and don't forget—you are supposed to study and know your competition and their good points or failings), rattle a winch or make a racket when he isn't looking. You'd be surprised at how much this will disconcert him, especially near the finish line in light going. I know of another fellow who talks or gets one of his crew to talk to a competitor as he sails alongside. It's always good for a length or so of gain, and awfully disconcerting. Wilma Bell and I won the Arms Trophy in Star boats doing just this in 1945. We beat our competitor across the finish in light air by one foot.

CHAPTER XVII

The Finish

"Church Ain't Out 'Til the Singin'."

As you approach the finish line just remember that "Church ain't out 'til the singin'." I cannot repeat it too many times, for many a race has been won (and lost) a few yards, and even feet, from that imaginary tape. Don't give up until you know you are over it and know you are licked—or have won.

There are so many different things that can happen before you actually cross the line that I couldn't begin to describe them all. As an example, however, several years ago we were racing on the Sound in a Saturday Series. Came 6:15 p.m. and a thunderstorm. We had only one suit of sails aboard (I've already pointed this particular day out as a reason for carrying two suits of sails) and still had three miles to go. We calculated that we probably wouldn't make the 7 p.m. time limit so we accepted a tow. Bill Luders sailed on, finished at 6:58, won the race AND the Series. In another race against the same Bill, we had maybe 25 yards to go to the finish and a lead of a similar distance over him. I tacked to cover Bill, banged into two head seas, stopped dead in the very light air and A. E. Luders, Jr., sailed gaily around us to cop first place. (This might also be cited as an example of an unnecessary extra tack.) The net on the whole deal is to keep in there plugging until you cross that finish line.

If behind the leader, confuse him by making extra tacks (my suggestions to the contrary just above notwithstanding) although you must have due regard for any boats close astern. There is hardly any point in getting into a tacking duel with the leader and letting one or more other boats in ahead of you and/or him.

If you are the leader and your closest competitor does try to start short-tacking, cover him as best you can, staying either between him and the finish or on what you feel is the best side of him, i.e., the side where you have the greatest advantage, the right of way.

If you are the leader on a reach or run to the finish and the nearest boat starts to luff out, you'll have to go with him, but here again, you must have due regard for the other boats astern. If they don't count in the series, you may want to stay with him, especially if he is up in the standings. But if they DO count, don't let him take you too far. Remember that after all you are still in the lead and therefore are closer to the finish. You may be forced, if you have to beat him, to carry him out far enough so that you can jibe over and come into the finish line from that other angle. Teamwork, with appropriate and quiet signals to your crew, will help you stay on top. Watch him carefully and be ready for any maneuver, as he'll try and be prepared for any maneuver you may make. In the end teamwork will count, so make sure your crew understands thoroughly what you plan to do.

When you are working up to a finish line in a closely grouped bunch of boats, crossing at the short or near end of the line may benefit you by one or more positions in the results column. But it is often extremely difficult to tell which is the short end of the line. Distances are deceiving under these circumstances and the various-sized finish buoys and flags only serve to complicate the problem. When such a situation arose on *Bumble Bee,* we evolved the system of each person taking a look to size up the line, forming his opinion, but keeping it to himself until everyone had a chance to do the same. We then settled on the majority opinion, right or wrong and stuck to it. Generally, I might add, it was right.

Many years ago I heard the late W. W. (Bill) Swan, that Long Island Sound veteran skipper, give a talk on racing tactics. Among other things that he said, one stuck in my mind: If you have a choice, always finish as close to the Committee Boat as you are able, for the Committee will see you first and can see you better. If there is to be a close decision you'll get it by being closer. By the same token if you are away off at the far end of the line, your sail and number may well be obscured by the nearer boats with the result that in a mess of boats you'll get left.

CHAPTER XVIII

After the Race

Sailing home after the race, slack off the outhaul and lower the main halyard (sufficiently so that the boom rests freely on the bottom of the gooseneck slide and there are puckers in the sail) so that the mainsail gets a chance to "wring" back into shape, to take up on all that you've stretched it during the race. The bolt rope will spring back a bit toward normal position and the material itself will also shrink a little along the luff and foot.

Slack off the backstays or permanent and let the boat also "relax" somewhat, if you care to put it that way. If you set the permanent or backstays up the way we did on *Bumble Bee* for a thrash to windward, your boat is bound to be pulled up at the ends. It can't help but be. Give it an opportunity to spring back, and the chances are it won't start to leak as soon over the years.

If you want to keep your brightwork in good shape without running up a big yard bill for varnishing and painting, wash your topsides, deck and varnish off with fresh water and chamois them down afterwards. If you carry drinking water aboard, or a pail of ice to cool it with, the water or the remains of the ice will be sufficient to do a fine job. Hand somebody the mop and someone else the chamois and let 'em go to work.

Take ALL sails ashore and store them in a dry place if you do not plan to race the next day. Leaving sails aboard in an open cockpit overnight is strictly *verboten,* and they should only be left on board a cabin boat if you expect to race the next day. Actual practice leads me to believe that it's even somewhat silly to leave 'em in the latter case, for invariably the weather next day is entirely different and you need other sails anyhow, and must lug one set out while the other goes ashore. It means the same amount of work no matter how you look at it. I might add, as a further reason for leaving no sails aboard, that the time consumed taking sails ashore in the morning is time that you might have spent getting out to the starting line.

Take all sails wet with salt water ashore and wash them out with fresh, as already discussed in the chapter on Sails. If you have sails wet in rain water, leave them aboard if you like, in the expectation of fair weather the next day, but DON'T leave them in bags; just spread them about the boat and get up early the next morning to dry them, *with the battens in place.*

All halyards, wire and rope, were sent aloft on messenger lines (⅛-inch reef-line) when *Bumble Bee* was on her mooring. This not only saves the rope tails on the wire halyards—as well as half the rope halyards—which are stowed in the cabin, but the lighter reef-line aloft eliminates a lot of chafe and wear on the paint job on the mast. In this connection, we use a piece of shock-cord as a gil-guy on the halyards and lash it to the jibstay, thus pulling all lines away from the mast itself, but allowing them to shrink or stretch a certain amount without becoming too slack, or too tight.

One last word, if you are on a permanent mooring. Your permanent mooring is probably a mushroom with chain, a rope pennant whose length depends on the depth of water and a buoy attached by a lighter rope pennant. The eye splice on the main pennant fits over some type of cleat on the bow. ALWAYS take a couple of turns of the buoy pennant around this cleat too, just to be sure the main pennant doesn't jump off. It used to be that I found nothing as good as manila line, dipped in Cuprinol to prevent marine growth, for a mooring pennant. Other skippers preferred nylon, and I have now come to the opinion that nylon really is by far the best, even though it is more expensive than manila. I am of the opinion that no manila line should be used more than one year—Cuprinoled or not—but nylon can be. Due care must be given, however, to the possibility of chafe at the bow chock. I wouldn't have a stainless-steel pennant if you gave it to me, for I have seen nothing but trouble come from their use. How they can get twisted into the messes they do, or break the way they do, I do not know, but I do know I DON'T like 'em.

CHAPTER XIX

Team Racing

TEAMWORK

Team racing is a variation of boat racing which can be quite exciting and interesting if:

1. The teams are more or less evenly matched.
2. Each team truly acts as a team and not as individuals.
3. The race itself is a good, evenly sailed one, not fluky and not an obstacle race.
4. The boats are one-design and have fairly even sail equipment.
5. There are at least four boats on a team and not more than two teams racing.
6. There are windward starts only.

Experience over the years in various team races leads me to believe that if they are held and conducted under the above-listed conditions, the racing can be fun, but otherwise it's almost a waste of time.

As to point #1, if the teams are not more or less evenly matched, the race, team tactics or no, will end up quite soon in an uninteresting parade. The superior ability of either team will soon serve to put them out in front and the race, to all intents and purpose, ends right there.

Skippers must give up their desires to be individualistic and to go out and win the race for their own boat. The points that are made by the fellow who comes in next to last are just as important, even if not as large, as those of the winner. That extra quarter-point given to the first place boat is not to be sneezed at, but in your desire to acquire it, don't forget that you are expected to do your bit as a member of the team, and not let the rest of the boys carry the ball while you romp away out in the lead. There are times when this is advisable, but not often. As an example, let me describe a situation which excuses a skipper from helping his teammates and, at the same time, proves the basic necessity of having one-design boats and fairly even sail equipment (point #4). After a number of quite even races in a match between Long Island Sound and Rochester in 14-foot dinghies, it was decided by our team that the skipper getting a certain boat should avoid all team tactics and get out ahead and stay there. This particular boat had done well—extremely well—in the previous races, so it was felt that to win the Series, it should be used to garner that extra quarter-point, letting the rest of the boys take care of themselves and the other team as best they could. The plan worked to perfection, and with good team tactics on the part of the other three on our team, Long Island Sound won the final race and the Trophy.

As for point #3, it seems to me that both teams and Race Committee should agree beforehand to start no races except in a reasonably decent wind. Goodness knows, breezes can get light and fluky after the start, without deliberately starting a race during such conditions. Someone may say that races should be held and started whatever the wind (or even weather conditions), that the real sailor should be able to cope with any sort of wind. True, but won't the racing be more interesting and give a truer picture of the team's abilities if the wind is steady at the start? How can you engage in any sort of team tactics when there's hardly wind enough to keep steerage way, or so fluky that one boat's rail is down, while a boat 30 feet away has nothing. Local knowledge and sheer dumb luck become the important factors in such a team race, not sailing ability.

Local knowledge is a great help to the home team in the matter of marks, too. A properly run team race includes adequately sized and capably manned marker boats to stand by or lead the way to turning buoys. If such are not supplied or do not do their job, the visiting team will be obliged to spend half their time mark-hunting. It doesn't take much of an error or divergence from the right course to cause a shake-up in the positions in the race. Local knowledge can be of benefit in other ways too. In a recent Bermuda versus Long Island Sound Team Race in International One-Designs, a thunderstorm came up, wrecking the comfortable team score the Bermudians had managed to work up in that particular race. Local boats, seeing the storm, sailed themselves into position to get it first and sailed around several Bermudians. The next leg, a reach, had to be sailed by compass, for the rain obliterated all trace of the buoy and the large marker boat. Accustomed to sailing this particular leg, the local boys picked up the mark on the nose and turned the race into a rout before it was over. Such circumstances are rare, to be sure, but they do occur. This one happens to illustrate two points: (a) the importance of local knowledge (not only in team racing but in all kinds of racing) and (b) the importance of starting and holding team races in a decent breeze.

Point #5 says four boats on a team and not more than two teams. You can have more than four boats on a team if you wish, but never less. Two-boat team races are a complete waste of time and the three-boat proposition is not very much better, for there isn't enough chance for any real team tactics or teamwork. If you can't dig up a "fourth," as for bridge, you'd do better to have individual racing rather than team. It just isn't worthwhile. Three teams in a race is equally bad. One team gets out ahead and the other two battle each other almost "unto the death" while the first team goes freely on its way. The Long Island Sound, Marblehead and Bermuda three-way series in 1951 brought this out only too clearly to me and I strongly advise against it in the future.

Windward starts, of which I have made such an issue in Suggestions to Race Committees, are absolutely essential in team racing. In fact, I don't think I can ever recall a team race with anything but a beat on the first leg. It takes little imagination to see the mess which a leeward start could cause in and to such racing.

Get Your Start First

Tactics are naturally quite different in team racing than in other types of racing. Each member of your team is expected to do his part in assuring a team victory, but not necessarily a personal victory. As already stated, this is often the rub, and some over-anxious teammate will see an opportunity to win the race (he hopes) by taking a short tack or even a long one alone. He tacks away, leaving the opponent he was covering; a shift unexpectedly occurs, and his opponent takes advantage of it to either nip him or another of his teammates. The important thing is always to keep in mind that you are racing as part of a team and that you must be guided in your tactics entirely by that thought.

A major point in these tactics is to get your start. Experts on team racing have from time to time suggested all kinds of different starting maneuvers which are splendid, simply splendid, in theory. They read well and sound fine, but just try and put them into actual practice. Almost impossible. I won't say they are impossible beyond question, but so often some small detail will go awry, upsetting the whole plan and messing up your own start to such an extent that you are behind the eight ball almost before the smoke of the starting gun has dissipated.

My own theory has always been that you are smarter in the long run to try and get as good a start as possible and THEN commence your teamwork or team tactics. It is advisable to arrange beforehand with your teammates to distribute yourselves along the starting line in such a manner that you won't interfere with each other's starts or put one another in a hopeless position. Obviously, if your team is all bunched at one end of the line, you'll mess each other up badly, while at the same time you'll be giving your opponents the lion's share of the line to maneuver and start in. If you have the opportunity to push an opponent across the line before gunfire and hold him there, do so by all means, but don't ruin your own start to do so—unless perhaps you can also mess up the starts of all or nearly all of the opposing team while your own teammates get away unmolested. In this latter case, of course, it's a good thought and a fine maneuver, and your sacrifice will benefit your own team greatly. Naturally, your opponents will rarely get caught in such a spot, but be ready for it if such a combination of circumstances should occur. However, by and large, it has been my personal experience that your whole team will be exercising the best strategy if you all get your starts and then look about for a chance to tack on or cover the opposition. Getting a good start is a tough job, requiring every bit of the skipper's skill and attention, and if his brain is filled with all sorts of theoretical tactics and dreams of glory which involve the defeat of the enemy practically before the race · has begun, the average helmsman is very apt to botch up the whole deal instead. At least, such has been my belief and also experience, and I think I am an average skipper. Sure, be alert, and seize whatever opportunity is given you, but get away with the gun to a flying start. Chances are much more favorable then that you'll be ahead and in a position immediately to begin covering tactics. Ball up your own start and the enemy will pounce on you instead.

Scoring And Scoring Possibilities

It might be well to digress for a moment before discussing weather-leg tactics to consider the scoring possibilities. In a team race with four boats to each of the teams, the winner receives 8¼ points, the extra quarter point for first place breaking the many mathematically possible ties. Second boat gets 7 points, third 6 points and so on with last place receiving 1 point. With all points for both teams totaling 36¼, it is readily seen that the closest combination is 18¼ to 18. There are, of course, mathematically speaking, many different winning and losing combinations. For purposes of simplification, if your team can each beat a boat of the other team you'll win, 20¼ to 16; or if your team can get first and second, all you need is seventh and eighth to have the higher score of 18¼ to 18. Below is a table which gives a general idea of possible winning scores and combinations.

To Win

If your team is	You have Points	& You need (or better)	Points	To get Total Points
1 & 2	(15¼)	7 & 8	(3)	18¼
1 & 3	(14¼)	6 & 8	(4)	18¼
1 & 4	(13¼)	5 & 8	(5)	18¼
		or 6 & 7	(5)	18¼
2 & 3	(13)	4 & 8	(6)	19
		or 5 & 7	(6)	19
2 & 4	(12)	5 & 6	(7)	19

Each of your team should be supplied with the above scoring combinations so that you can all tell at a glance just where your team stands. If you have a winning group of figures, stick with 'em; if you haven't, plan to attack. It is worthwhile to bear in mind that any change in positions in a team race causes a two-point change in the scores, for if you move up one position your opponents move down one; in other words, you add a point to your score while they subtract one from theirs.

Scoring

Scoring can be calculated on separate races or total points. If separate races are used, the first team to win either three out of five races or four out of seven wins the match. If total points are used, generally four races are sailed and the team with the highest point score takes the trophy. It seems to me that the separate race method is the preferable one, with the four races out of seven determining the winner. Total points generally results in a relaxing or forgetfulness of team tactics and the resultant increase in individualism on the part of each team. When each particular race counts as an integral part of the final score, teamwork counts and remains the paramount issue, as it should.

Windward-Leg Tactics

The team that gets the jump at the start makes every effort to cover the other team as soon as practicable, while the latter does its best to get free and get a clear wind so as to attack. If a quick calculation after a look-see reveals that you have the winning combination, some of your team may be obliged to tack, others to pinch up and put an opponent in the hopeless position, or others to drive off to cover. But cover and pair off you must if you wish to maintain your lead in the point score. If your team can pair off, as pointed out above, in such a way as to cover each of the opposing team, and you can maintain those positions, you have won the match for that race, with a score of $20\frac{1}{4}$ to 16. In such a situation it is probably better to pair off and cover in such a way that your opponents are covered but not blanketed. In other words, keep ahead of the other fellow or between him and the mark, but do not make too much effort to blanket him, for, if blanketed he may try to short-tack you to get clear. Give him enough clear air so that he'll keep going on that tack and then concentrate on working out on him. If, however, you know that you are up against a fast boat, faster possibly than you, then you must cover to blanket him or to push him back so that he cannot sneak away from you.

When paired off, caution must be exercised to prevent an opponent in another pair-off with the right of way from pushing you back or forcing you to tack away from your man. Often a swap of opponents will solve such a problem as in Diagram 70.

In the event that your team is behind after the start, make

every possible attempt and effort to get yourself clear so that you
have a free wind. Drive off or make short tacks, but do something so that you can get away somehow. Possibly you are more
adept at tacking than your opponent, or perhaps he'll get tired
and let you go your own way. No matter how you do it, you must
get away from him. It may be that a right-of-way situation similar in some respects to the one diagramed in 69 will come up
and allow you to escape; but escape you must, or a teammate
may be able to come to your rescue and tack on your opponent,
thus giving you the opportunity to clear your wind and work
out.

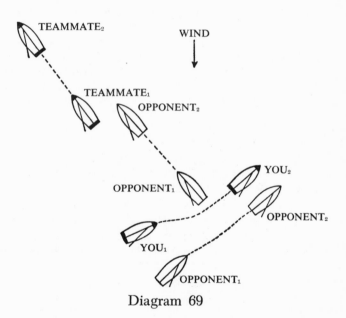

Diagram 69

On the other hand, by sacrificing yourself you may be able to
coax an opponent away from a teammate, thus leaving the teammate free to sail off on a more desirable course, or slant of air.
For example, suppose a teammate and an opponent are having a
tussle close by and you are uncovered. By tacking away you may
draw the opponent off on you (as the easiest one to cover), leaving your teammate free to sail on with a better slant of air or
toward a better slant.

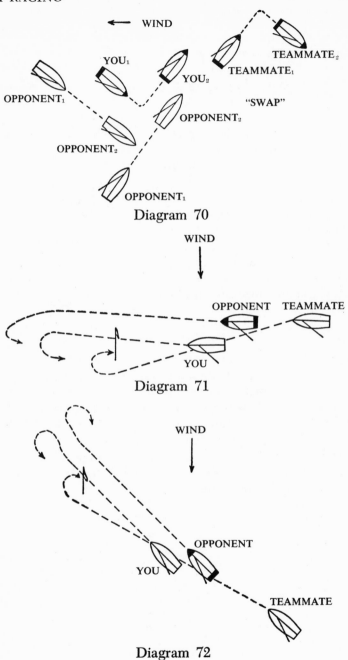

Diagram 70

Diagram 71

Diagram 72

AT MARKS

Suppose you are leading an overlapped opponent to a mark with a teammate close behind. It is possible and sensible to carry the opponent past the mark on the wrong side, thus letting your own man through ahead of you both, and then get back to the mark ahead of the opponent. (Diagram 73.)

Your opponent's obvious answer to such a maneuver is to luff up and drive off under you if he possibly can, as in the following Diagram 74. In which case, you must, if you are able, luff with him to prevent it.

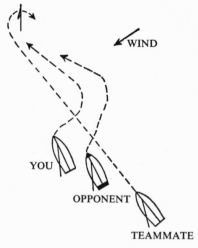

Diagram 73

AT FINISH

At the finish the same maneuver can be tried, i.e., luffing a competitor to allow a teammate to go through. This I have seen tried by boats which lingered (when way ahead) near the finish line in an attempt to put a teammate over first. It must be executed with quite accurate timing and considerable dispatch, for the overtaking opponent, generally traveling at a greater speed, and therefore with much greater maneuverability, has a choice of passing either to windward or leeward of the leading opponent which is trying to hinder him.

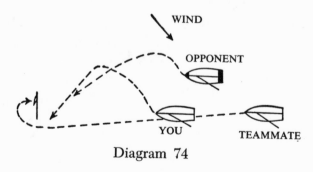

Diagram 74

CHAPTER XX

Frostbite Dinghy Racing –
A School for Sailing

On January 1, 1952, Frostbite dinghy racing as we know it today came of age, with the Twenty-First Annual Regatta held by the Frostbite Yacht Club under the auspices of the Manhasset Bay Yacht Club. The Frostbite Yacht Club, an organization unique in the annals of yachting history, in that it has "no dues, no assets, no nothing," has prospered and grown to the extent that 1952 saw it run its first truly formal Regatta, a Championship YRA Race in September. This date was chosen late in the summer season to be as close to the Frostbiting season as possible. Surely no club in the country is better equipped from a manpower point of view to run a successful Regatta, for it is able to organize a Race Committe composed of the outstanding Committeemen of most of the various clubs in the New York and Connecticut area. Its own officers for the past forty-one years make up a reasonably fair picture of the outstanding small boat skippers of the eastern seaboard.

January 1, 1958, saw the 27th Annual Regatta of the Frostbite Yacht Club held on Manhasset Bay, with 112 boats in 4 One-Design Classes. The overall length remains the same—11½ feet —though there ARE many other small classes. And the sail area on these 11½-footers is still (theoretically) 72 square feet. In the Annual Commodore's Race (for past Commodores of the Frostbite Yacht Club) I had as my crew, Stephen Ward Bell, aged 4, whose father crewed with me in 1940 and '41, a second generation crew!

And January 1, 1973, saw the 42nd Annual Regatta of the Frostbite Yacht Club. My crew in *Agony* in the Commodore's Race that day was none other than my own grandson, Ralph P. Engle, III, aged 9. It was blowing like stink, we didn't win, but

Harvey Weber

Dinghy picture taken before the start of the "Commodore's Race" of the Frostbite Yacht Club on January 1, 1958. Stephen W. Bell, age four, at the helm with your Author as crew. As my father often said: "Catch 'em young, treat 'em rough and tell 'em nothing!" I am trying to start Steve off on the right track at the earliest possible age. (Now, 1973, Steve is 6-foot-2, a Sophomore at Dartmouth and the Junior "Champ" in tennis at the Larchmont Yacht Club.)

we didn't upset either, and Grandpa was inordinately proud of young Philip.

Starting more or less as a joke in the "bathtub gin" era of the thirties, winter dinghy racing quickly became nicknamed "Frost-biting," and the name has stuck and become synonymous with the sport. It has been my pleasure and good fortune to have been constantly engaged in dinghy racing on Long Island Sound and elsewhere since that wet, cold and snowy day after New Year's Day of 1932 when the first winter Regatta was held and the Frostbite Yacht Club was founded, and may I say—possibly im-modestly, nevertheless proudly—that in 1973 I am the only one left of that original band who raced on the first day who is still more or less *actively* racing. And IT IS STILL FUN FOR ME!

It is my opinion that anyone who Frostbites regularly is at-tending one of the finest schools in boat-handling ever organized, and that includes boats of all sizes, not just 11½-foot cockle-shells. In most cases your ardent Frostbiter doesn't realize he is attending school. He is out for fun and fresh air, to try his skill against the next fellow, to experiment with a new gadget or new idea, for the thrill of feeling a lively and tricky boat under him in a fresh breeze, and occasionally, for a dunking in very cold and very wet water. But, whether the sailor realizes it or not, every time he starts a race he is learning.

Let's consider two questions which are always asked by the uninitiate: "Isn't dinghy racing cold? Don't you freeze out there in those little boats?" Sure it's cold, but you don't freeze. Ice-boating is cold; so is skiing, skating or any other outdoor winter sport. If properly clothed with several pairs of wool socks under galoshes (no shoes inside) or thermal socks, Dacron underwear, wool trousers and shirt, sweater and some kind of nylon wind-breaker or slicker, one needn't be cold. The water is cold if one goes overboard, naturally, but there are other boats sailing nearby, as well as a crash boat. It is absolutely mandatory that anyone in the neighborhood of an overturned boat go to her assistance, so no one is ever in the water for long, and the swamped boats will support you. To my knowledge, no one has ever got pneumonia and there are few colds resulting from a dunking.

By way of background, let us consider the evolution of the present Frostbite dinghy. At the first Regatta of the Frostbite Yacht Club there was an odd assortment of dinks and other

Ellsworth (Lank) Ford

The Moment of Truth—This 40-year-old photograph captures that exciting and much-to-be-avoided split-second in time when a boat is about to capsize. The date is March 5, 1933, during the first Frostbite Regatta ever held in Essex, Connecticut. The unfortunate sailors, Allan Clark and Sheridan Fahnestock, sailing dinghy A 6—*Feather*—tipped over while running downwind and were picked up by *Sideboard Annie* (A 155), sailed by your Author and Bill Dodge.

boats, all small, of course. The dinks were for the most part 11½ feet long, most of them prams with a long overhang forward.

The late George Ratsey had imported a number of prams from England, and William J. H. (Bill) Dyer, of Providence, had built several from his own design. The rigs were of the lug or sliding-gunter types with approximately 72 square feet of sail. As interest increased in this new sport, designers, builders and sailors vied with themselves and each other to produce a faster dink. About the only measurements now remaining of the original designs are the overall length, 11½ feet, and the sail area, 72 square feet, and the sail has even changed shape considerably. There is a class of 10-footers designed and built by Dyer—almost a thousand of them—which have proved so efficient and handy as sailing tenders for larger boats that they are primarily used for this purpose, though also for racing. Classes of 8-footers and 9-footers by Dyer have also made their appearance.

Interest at first centered in the so-called open classes in which boats of various but limited dimensions raced together, all of course, with the 72-foot sail area. This proved expensive, and after several years most people turned to the one-design classes in the interests of economy and fairer racing. The Alden X one-design, the Potter B one-design (more popularly known as the BO's), the Rhodes Penguins and in 1946, the newer Sparkman & Stephens molded plywood Inter-Clubs resulted, with roughly 80 skins having been molded of three plies of "cooked" mahogany veneer, before the limited demand ran out. (Finally, the mold fell apart some years later, precluding the building of any more wood boats.) Our molded wooden boats are in remarkably fine shape after 27 years, many of them in "mint" condition with finishes like a piano, mainly because of the efforts of John B. Nichols of Nichols Yacht Yard, and Apley N. Austin, Jr., of the Austin Boat Shop, Route 61, Morris, Connecticut, who have made what look like brand-new boats out of almost complete wrecks.

Subsequently, George O'Day arranged with Sparkman & Stephens to build our splendid Inter-Clubs in fiberglass, which O'Day Yachts has manufactured by the hundreds and sold throughout the country and abroad, to individuals, Clubs and colleges. The "bathtub" bow, very broad as it ascends from the waterline, has made these craft much less susceptible to upsetting downwind, because their bows do not bury in a hard puff the way the narrow-bowed B-One Designs did, and, therefore, there is less tendency to trip and go over to windward. Manhasset Bay Yacht Club dinghy sailors, as well as Knickerbocker, have formed a very fine fleet of these fiberglass O'Days, and for the first time in many moons, they have done just as well—if not better than—the wooden I-Cs from Larchmont. The shape and measurements of the sails of these four classes are practically identical, with a tall, narrow rig, loose-footed, with the luff rope in a grooved mast. The hulls are different and each class has its special advantages; but the important thing is that each class gives snappy and exciting racing.

The valuable "school" angle of Frostbiting comes from the great number of races held in one day. There may be four, five, or ten, the weather and the Race Committee determining the exact number. The Race Committee also decides whether the day is suitable for racing at all, and calls the whole thing off if it is blowing too hard for safe sailing. This is as it should be, since there are always one or two die-hards who want to race whether conditions are proper or not. Racing is supposed to be for fun and not an endurance test, and, thanks to conservative and considerate Race Committees, in forty-one years of racing there have been no drownings.

Under the system evolved over the years, racing generally commences at 1:30 P.M. and continues until 4:00 P.M., weather permitting. During the late morning, boats are trailed down from the garages or wherever they are stored. (At Riverside Yacht Club, they are kept in slips which are part of a special float built for the purpose. By means of a well-thought-out gadget, each dink may be lifted clear of the water in its own special slip.) Other places, light dollies or two-wheeled trailers are used and each boat generally has its own. They are carried down to the float by a paid crew of young men, who also lug them up after the racing and wash each boat out with fresh water. Owners rig and unrig their own boats. Courses of about one-half to three-quarters of a mile are laid out by the Committee, with the help of the crash boat, and starts are practically always to windward.

At Manhasset, a converted landing barge with a house built on it, known as the *Worry Wart*, is generally used, or I should say generally *was*, for Manhasset now has a new Committee Boat (or raft) called *Kraus' Kastle*, after Howard Kraus, perennial Chairman of winter sailing at Manhasset. Its house—or kastle—is not

The Author's *Four Deuces*, BO 22, and Corny Shields' *Softy*, BO 68. The weight in #68 is more centered and a bit further forward—note position of the two bows—which may account for its being in the lead!

B. V. D. Harrison's *Blubber*, BO 48, with weight well placed to keep boat on an even keel, the ideal position for these dinks in a moderate breeze working to windward. Ben Harrison is famed for calling out to the crash boat after he had upset: "Never mind my daughter, save my watch!"

as resplendent and solidly built as ours at Larchmont, for a couple of years ago Kraus' Kastle blew off in a half-gale into Manhasset Bay. But, but, it does have a "head," something we lacked at Larchmont until last year. At Larchmont, a pontoon float with a house built on it, and known as *The Little Scorpions' Club*, takes care of the Committee. On each of these "tubs," a small potbellied stove insures a certain amount of warmth for the long-suffering Committeemen.

"The Little Scorpions' Club" is nothing more than a float, built with four pontoons in the corners, used in the summer (without the house) as a dinghy float, and towed about Larchmont Harbor each race day so that a windward start may be set

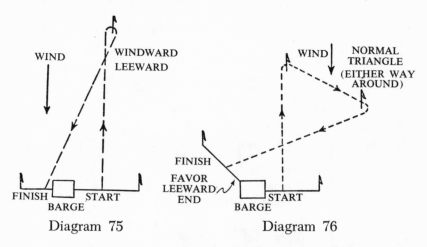

Diagram 75   Diagram 76

up. The name was borrowed from that well known cartoon series originated by Fontaine Fox—"The Toonerville Trolley"—and came about because the house and stove pipe made it look like the drawings of the kids' "Little Scorpions' Club" in the comics. The name has stuck and Life Membership cards are presented to those who annually supply the Committee with that liquid refreshment which keeps them (the Committee) from catching cold and/or freezing to death. The Club has its own flag, a rectangular blue flag with a red scorpion on it, holding a highball glass in one claw. This flies on the float from a staff opposite the burgee of the Larchmont Yacht Club every race day.

Courses may be either windward-and-leeward or triangular, depending on conditions—triangular, with long flat reaches

being safest when it is blowing over 12 to 15 knots. Windward-
and-leeward are fine in moderate air, but when it blows up, dinks
have a disagreeable habit of turning over to windward on a dead
run, especially when the boys pull their boards up all the way in an
effort to make them go faster or plane. When fleets of 30 to 35 boats
are racing, windward-leeward courses also cause confusion and
crack-ups when rounding the weather mark, and are to be
avoided. A second mark providing a short reach—although it is
virtually a windward-leeward course—will eliminate this last
problem, see Diagram 77. For heavy breezes on what you might
call border-line racing days, a no-jibe course, a refinement of the
above-mentioned triangular course with long flat reaches, has
been developed. (See Diagram 78.) This course has an extra
mark placed a short distance to windward of the second mark of

the course. The starting mark and
first mark are left to starboard;
then the second mark is left to port;
and the third mark, directly to
windward, is left to port; thence
to the finish. This eliminates jibing,
a very dangerous mane·iver in a
dink on a breezy day. This course
should be laid out, if possible, so
that the first two marks are left to
starboard, and therefore the third
mark will be more logically ap-
proached on the starboard tack
with its short beat to windward.
This will tend to eliminate, or at
least decrease, crack-ups which
might occur were the course laid
out in the other direction.

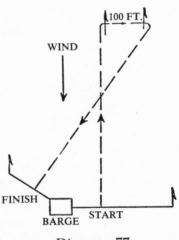

Diagram 77

Courses are announced verbally and may be changed the same
way if conditions warrant. Signals for the start are given by four
powerful horns hooked up to a storage battery, so no watches
need be carried. (At Indian Harbor Yacht Club, Greenwich,
Connecticut, races are started from a second-floor, glassed-in
porch and George Lauder, the presiding genius, cleverly rigged
up a phonograph record which calls the time for the start
over a loudspeaker.) In either case the skipper merely listens or
has his crew listen and count. A series of short blasts signifies an

impending start, followed by two long blasts for two minutes to go, one long and one short for a minute and a half, one long for one minute, three short for thirty seconds, two short for twenty, and the last ten seconds are short blasts followed by a long blast for the start. A megaphone suffices to call back any premature starters, but if so many are over ahead of the gun that the Committee can't see them all, the whole race is called back and restarted by signal again.

As soon as all contestants have crossed the finish line, another race is started, though time is given in case anyone wishes to change sails or make minor repairs. This is where "school" starts. The second race is generally a repetition of the first. Conditions are usually identical. The same is often true of the third and

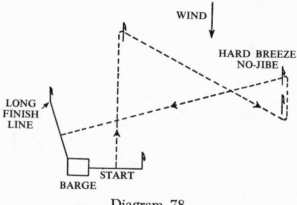

Diagram 78

fourth race, sometimes even of the ninth or tenth. Possibly a novice skipper was way back of the starting line in the first start. Each succeeding race he has the opportunity to correct this mistake. He may be unfamiliar with the length of time it takes for his boat to pick up and get away, or he may be afraid to get up in close quarters with the other boats, but each race he sails makes him better acquainted with his boat and encourages him to take her into closer quarters.

The same is true of working up the windward leg. Possibly you find after the first race that you have tacked too soon for the weather mark and fallen short of it. The next race you have the opportunity to gauge things better and you go on a little farther before tacking. Maybe you can line up a winter-stick or mooring by which you can judge the proper time to go around for the mark. Possibly you have come up to the weather mark on the port tack and have been forced about by one or more starboard-tack boats. "Aha!" you say to yourself. "Next time I won't get caught like that!" So you think ahead and get yourself in a position to be on the starboard tack at the weather mark. If you're on the alert you may notice that your weight is not quite in the same place as that in some of the "hotshot" boats, so next race you try your weight in a different spot. Maybe you go better, maybe not, but all the time you are becoming increasingly familiar with your boat and learning to do things instinctively and quickly without thinking them out step by step.

By the end of the afternoon, you may still be in last place, but it is probably a lot closer last place than in the first race. By the end of the season, you may be giving the so-called experts a run for their money. And I will guarantee that you'll do considerably better in your summer racing than you did the previous season. I could name you example after example of this sort of thing happening with regularity as a result of participation in Frostbite racing.

The so-called expert is never so smart that he can't learn a few new tricks from his competitors or get enough practice to keep his tiller hand in. The same is true of crews. The crews in many cases are youngsters just learning to sail, youngsters who will soon come along and beat the oldsters, and they, too, can learn by keeping their eyes open. Remember: "Be Observant!" The Boy Scout standby is a fine maxim for crew as well as skipper. A crew can win a race, or even save a dunking, by watching puffs on the water and hiking out at the proper moment; by watching for other right-of-way boats; and in any number of other ways.

Tight situations come up many times during the sailing of even one race, when 20 or 30 boats are competing. If you are unfamiliar with the racing rules, you'll learn them backwards and forwards in short order with even the slightest effort or attention. Dinghy sailors at Larchmont and Manhasset were two of the guinea pigs for the first Vanderbilt Rules years ago, and several changes were adopted by Mr. Vanderbilt as a result of those trials.

The system of using horns for the start is a splendid way of training skippers for their summer racing. As already discussed under Stopwatches, it is much better to have someone call time to you when starting a larger boat in summer racing, than to have to take your eyes off the general situation to look down at a watch. For keeping your ears alert for an aural signal, what better training than the many daily starts in a dinghy regatta? It may seem minor, but it's another variable which you can tuck under your wing, so to speak.

If you can handle an 11½-foot sailing dinghy, you can handle a 30-foot racing machine, a 60-foot cruising boat, and are well on your way toward taking the helm of an America's Cup Yacht. The larger the boat, the heavier the gear and the slower her maneuvers, but the same basic knowledge and the same basic adeptness at handling are used in any boat, be she a dinghy, a 12-metre or a Class J cutter. In addition, the main thing you get from Frostbiting regularly (outside of the well-known sailor's delight, wet pants) is the ability to handle a tricky small boat in close quarters—quarters so close at times that an extra coat of varnish might be scratched—without consciously thinking about it; doing the job instinctively while lighting a cigarette, bailing or reaching out to pull some unfortunate competitor from the icy water.

Many of the Sound's successful summer champions have come up through the dinghy-racing school. Men and women who five years ago could barely keep a dinghy "on its feet" are now the champion and expert skippers of their various summer cruising or racing classes. Truly, Frostbiting is a good school, albeit at times a cold one, and it is one worthy of consideration by many of our clubs and their members, for it lengthens, in most cases, a four- or five-month season to a twelve-month one and increases the interest and ability of the individual member. Need I mention the additional revenue which accrues to the club itself because of refreshments and meals served to the dinghy sailors and gallery? Almost every yacht club in the United States, whose harbor is free of ice part of the winter, can race dinghies, and every such club would do well to consider the possibilities of developing its skippers and crews in this fine Frostbite school.

CHAPTER XXI

Catamarans

For many moons, Clinton M. Bell (Chairman of the Larchmont Winter Dinghy Committee for the past 30 years) dreamed of transporting his "Frostbitten" Winter sailors to warmer climes and having a three- or four-day Regatta during the coldest part of the Winter in Florida. It had been done once many years ago, about 1935 or '36, by the Class X dinghy sailors who had a fleet in Miami. It was called the Sunshine Regatta and was a huge success.

Finally in 1970, through Skip Allen, a transplanted Northerner who now lives on Sunset Isle #2, Miami Beach, arrangements were made to get 12 to 15 of the 14-foot Hobie Cats together in the middle of February and to race off the Miami Yacht Club which abuts on the MacArthur Causeway. It was a lovely and completely suitable body of water for neophytes in Cats. The officers of the Miami Yacht Club were most hospitable, turned over the facilities of their Club to us (for each of the four years we've been down), gave us everything we needed or desired—including some delightful and appropriate prizes—and made us feel entirely at home. A fine bar was open and the food served by the delightful husband and wife team, Pat and Joe, who ran the Club practically alone, was just out of this world. And, I might add, four years later, it's just as good. Joanne and Skip Allen have continued their interest in our Ice-Breaker Regatta and are largely responsible for arranging for boats, etc. Two days were consumed in putting eleven Cats together, and four days of fine racing were enjoyed by all hands—men, wives and children. Clint took his own Committee down, ran the racing Winter-Frostbite style—three, four or five races each of the four days. The Series was won by Bob Coulson, that former Marblehead expert, with his boys as crew.

Rosenfeld

A successful port-tack start by Dick Fraser in Big Hobie Cat #2051 crossing ahead of #2314 (on the starboard tack), at the flag end of the line, on the gun.

Rosenfeld

Your Author, pipe in mouth, in #2314, emerges from behind Dick Fraser, and is off and running, leading the fleet.

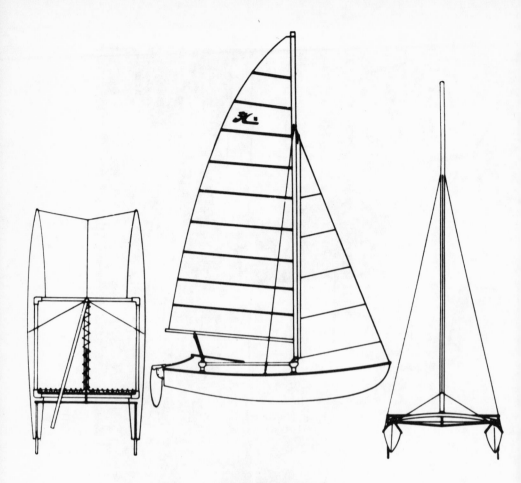

SPECIFICATIONS

Length O.A.	...16'7"	**Beam**	........7'11"
Draft	.... 10"	**Weight**	.....315 lbs.
Mast Height	.. 26'	**Racing Crew**	2 persons

Construction

Molded fiberglass with vacuum foam sandwich

SAIL AREA (with spars):

Main & Jib	..218 sq.ft.	Jib	...... 55 sq.ft.
Main only	..163 sq.ft.	Main reefed	. 128 sq.ft.

Diagram of and specifications for the Hobie Cat.

The following year, 1971, the racing was held again at about the same time, but this time in Aqua Cats, courtesy Bill Levy, the President of the American Fibre Glass Company. Jack Sutphen and his wife Jean were the winners.

Last year, we again traveled down to the Miami Yacht Club and held a third Series, this time in the Big Hobie, the 16-foot Cat with a jib. Dick Fraser took first-place honors, while Jack Sutphen and his wife were second, and your correspondent, with Wilma Bell, wife of the Chairman, was third.

This past Winter, February 1973, the Larchmont Dinghy Fleet, or at least 12 crews, went again to Florida and enjoyed the hospitality of the Miami Yacht Club for the fourth time. While we were hopeful that we'd get the big Hobie-16s, we ended up—because of transportation difficulties—with the 14s. Over four days, Clint Bell's Committee (consisting of Don King, George Wilson and "Boots" LeBoutilier—some of his stalwart Winter Dinghy Committee here at Larchmont), ran 16 races in three days (one day was blown out). Jack and Jean Sutphen (with little Georgie Allen as a substitute crew on a light day) won. Jonathan Ford with the cook, Holly Evarts, of the SORC sloop *Froya*, on which they were racing this Winter in the Southern Circuit, copped second place. Bill Baxter and his wife Pat took third; and your author—after a lousy beginning—took fourth place, with Wilma Bell as crew, and only ONE little point behind. The Hobie 14s and 16s are GREAT boats to sail, but if you get in irons in the 14s, you've had it—and your author managed to do just that frequently. I caught hell from my crew for "bouncing" around too much, and, y'know, she was right. When I settled down, moved about gently, and tacked the Cat slowly, then held the rudders firmly in one position on a tack, I had no problems. But my 210 pounds don't lend themselves to the gyrations of a ballet dancer. On the other hand, if you follow Hobie Alter's rules to the letter, as laid down in his little booklet on the Hobie Cats, you really don't have any great problems. They are great racing boats and lots of fun to sail. As a result of these four years of "catamaraning," I have become an "expert" and feel able to speak out with authority on Cats.

In the first place, we veteran Frostbite dinghy sailors all started out even, on an equitable basis, for none of us had ever sailed or raced a Cat before. We spent the better part of a couple of days uncrating the hulls and gear and putting 'em together.

After the first one, the rest were comparatively easy and all went together easily. All the parts were there, and if you followed the directions in each of the three designs, there was no problem. In other words, all the bits and pieces were in each carton and it was just a question of putting 'em together as the directions ordered. For that, I congratulate the designers and builders. Renamed the ICE-BREAKER REGATTA, these four annual events were well-run and provided excellent racing with fine competition.

All right—but how does that make me an "expert?" The fact is, as stated above, none of us knew a thing about Cats, but we learned fast. When you have sailed for years against the type of dinghy-sailor we have at Larchmont, against the caliber of the competition—40-odd guys and gals racing six and seven races a day for some 20 days a winter—you learn awfully fast or drop by the wayside. I venture to say that the sailing competition in the Larchmont dinghy fleet is as tough as you can find anywhere— and the group in Miami was composed of the toughest and most gung-ho of the whole lot.

STARTING— A few practice runs up and down the starting line gave each of us a little bit of the "feel" of the Cats. They would, we found out very quickly, accelerate amazingly fast—provided, of course, there was a good breeze—and for the most part we did have good breezes. We discovered that the Cats would jibe much quicker than you could tack 'em; and we also found out very quickly that in tacking, you had to hold the rudder bar or tiller very, very firmly, and not change the angle of the rudders the least bit or you were dead in the water. In other words, you moved the tiller over a bit, maybe 10 or 15 degrees, and held it there until you had completed your tack—alter it during this tacking maneuver and you stop dead. In the 16-footers, with their jibs, tacking was no great problem, no more of a problem than a conventional monohull, 'cause you hold the jib sheeted in until your Cat has gone through the eye of the wind. Almost let the jib pull your bow off on the new tack, and then, AND NOT UNTIL THEN, quickly tack the jib itself. But the Lord help you if you don't tack the Hobie 14 or the Aqua Cat in a sort of long circle—you just cannot jam them around, for they'll stop stone-cold-dead in the water, and while you are fussing around trying to get 'em moving again, the rest of your fleet is well on its way to the next mark. So, for safety, I have found that before the start, it is better to jibe rather than tack. You'll get yourself in less trouble and be much more maneuverable. Jibing, of course, requires that you get yourself into a position, sort of to windward, where you CAN jibe, where you have the room to jibe without interfering with some competitor coming up astern of you, or coming at you from ahead (before your jibe). Obviously, you must regard the starting rights of others, and keep your eyes peeled and alert for just where the competition is.

In starting dinghies and Cats, I like to get myself (and my boat) all set on the line, with about one minute to go—and I am assuming that the standard two-minute dinghy starting time is being used: i.e., two long horns for 2 minutes; a long and a short for a minute and a half; one long for a minute; three short for thirty seconds; two for twenty and, starting at ten seconds, ten short blasts, with one long blast for the start itself.

Getting yourself (in a fleet of 11–15 boats as we had) "set" on the line on the starboard tack, with approximately a minute to the start, gives you a chance to size up the situation, see where your competition is and plan where you are going in the next 60 seconds. Obviously, you can't be too far down the line or you'll sail over the end of it before gunfire. And you should have sized up the line beforehand and decided just which is the favored end of the line—which end, if you start at it, will put you further up toward your weather mark (I'm assuming here that you ARE starting to windward. Who starts on a reach or a run these days? Not many, although, yes, some do!!) after the starting gun.

Depending on the strength of the prevailing wind I like to move sort of slowly, or even stall if possible, down the starting line by easing the jib and main way out. Care must be taken at all times to have your boat, your Cat, under complete control—you have to be ready to trim in and take off if some guy roars down the line behind you and luffs you, or tries to luff you. After all, before the start, he can overtake you to leeward *and* luff—and if you can't respond, you are in deep trouble. You can luff head-to-wind, provided you have the necessary speed and control, but suppose you are head-to-wind and can't get your boat off and sailing? Again, you are in trouble—and Cats won't always respond that quickly. In the 16s, your crew can back the jib and get your head off, but in the 14s and Aquas, you don't have this help, so beware. Therefore, if humanly possible, I like to sort of laze along the line, take it slow and easy, look about me, listen to the starting horns and be ready, at maybe ten or five seconds to the starting gun, to sheet in and take off. Sounds simple, doesn't it? Well, it "ain't" always that simple, and you've got to do it all by trial and error, and by rehearsing. And the other guy is trying and rehearsing too, and don't forget it. But the fascinating thing about Cats is the amazing way that they will pick up and accelerate, from an almost dead stop to top speed, in a comparatively few seconds. Earlier on, I outlined the Vanderbilt Formula for starting, but in Cats—or in dinghies for that matter—Mike's Formula isn't practical. Sure, if you hit it just right, you can sail away from the line for a distance and then tack or jibe back; but with aural starting signals, it really doesn't work too well. Besides which, Dinghy Committees have a habit of cheating a bit on their time signals: i.e., they've been known to "rush" the last ten seconds if they feel the whole fleet may be over. Natch, they deny this, but nevertheless they do it, so you can't depend too much on the Formula.

In Cats, you are sitting on your fanny and must move about, either by sliding or rolling over, though sometimes you are on your knees and can move fairly quickly about the trampoline with ease. I mention this because there are times, when a puff hits, that you must (1) either move out to windward fast, or (2) move aft quickly, to prevent the lee hull from burying. Should the lee bow bury too deeply, brother, you are in deep trouble, and if it goes underwater, you are in immediate danger of "tripping" or "pitch-poling"—in other words, you'll go over and land in the drink. Therefore, watch the placement of your weight and be prepared to take positive action, either aft or out to windward.

Since we raced our Cats with two in crew, weight in the 14s and Aqua Cats was a most important factor, a factor which most of us were not aware of in the beginning, but which soon became quite obvious, especially when the wind went light. Going to windward in a strong breeze, no problem. We were able to hold the boat down—and in this case I'm speaking of a total weight, crew and skipper, of maybe 320 to 340 pounds, compared to a total of 225 pounds where a father and young son were aboard. (And I am not pointing the finger at anyone nor being overly critical, because—unlike our home dinghy fleet—there was no minimum-weight limit in our quite informal type of racing.) However, when you got on a reach or run, that extra ninety or one hundred pounds just killed you; the boats were sluggish, while the lighter crews took off and flew.

In the larger Big Hobie, the 16-footer, weighing 315 pounds, total weight was definitely not such a factor. The 14s, weighing 215 pounds, are generally raced single-handed. We chose to race with two just because that was our custom at Larchmont, but it is fairly apparent that if you add 330 pounds to a 215-pound Cat, it will have more of a deleterious effect on that boat than the same weight on a 315-pound model.

Since this was a sort of family-type deal, with mostly wives and/or children as crew, by mutual agreement trapezes were not allowed on the 16s; and yet, in the area we were sailing and with the strength of wind that blew, the trapeze did not seem necessary. And I feel the racing for our group was more equitable. A quick, agile and able crew is, of course, a great help and an important factor, but the gals in our group who made up our crews for the most part, proved able and up to the job, moving about with alacrity. Matter of fact, they learned to move quickly, for none of 'em wanted to go swimming, even in Florida—at least, not off the Miami Yacht Club.

Now, mind you, the observations here are mine, gleaned from my own experience in the four sessions in Miami, Florida, over four years, in three different types of Cats. They are not necessarily those of Hobie Alter, who provided the 14s and 16s (the Big Hobie), nor of Bill Levy who loaned us the Aqua Cats. (Actually, Bill Levy has disposed of his interest in the Aquas and is no longer connected with them.) Hobie Alter and his able cohorts have worked up a remarkably complete set of directions, suggestions, instructions and racing rules for his two classes of Cats. He has covered every detail, as far as I can see, and has done a fine job of keeping his boats as "one-design" as possible, prohibiting any radical changes or alterations which would give any one boat an advantage over another. Truly one-design boats, with no extra gimmicks or gadgets, make for much fairer and finer racing—a true test of the skipper—and Hobie has made every effort to keep it this way. I say: "More power to him—and don't let any "Sneaky Petes" slip any rule-beating in!!" But I urge you to read his instruction booklets thoroughly and follow them.

AFTER THE START— It is more or less self-evident that you should get moving and get your wind clear as quickly as possible.

As one of the first rules I would advance, *tack as infrequently as possible*, would be one of the most important. I think in a Cat, I'd rather give away a bit of time and/or distance to a competitor than make a whole lot of tacks. Your boat dies during a tacking maneuver and the other guys are still "flying," leaving you five to ten lengths behind. Of course, when THEY tack, you are going to gain on 'em, but I still feel it advisable to tack as few times as possible. You may be obliged to drive off to go through someone's lee, or you may have to "pinch up" to clear your wind, but I say: Look ahead, plan ahead and attempt to figure out just where you'll end up if you do.

Hobie Alter suggests not pinching, but driving your Cat a bit and keeping her footing. I won't argue with him, 'cause he's a National Champ in the Cats; but on the other hand, I did find that in smooth water, I could "feather" the boat up and work out to windward. Hobie Cats have asymmetrical hulls, i.e., the outside of each hull is practically flat, while the inside is curved somewhat. The flat on the outside acts as your centerboard and keeps you from sliding off to leeward—and believe me, this is one of the things that amazes me about these Cats: "Look, Ma, no centerboard!!" And yet they work to windward very well. But again, we did "pinch up" and work out on our Big Hobie and gained by doing so. It depended, natch, on the strength of wind and the condition of the water, but it did work. Furthermore, contrary to directions in "The Book," we trimmed our jib in quite hard and flat—harder than the instructions tell you—yet we ate out and did well. Trimming the main is practically the same as in a monohull—trim and look up the leech, allowing the leech to have a nice, gentle curve to it up near the top, up near the second batten. This has been my criterion for years and years in all types of boats from dinghies to 12-metres and it works in Cats, too. Obviously, you'll trim a sail, main or jib, harder in a good breeze than in light air—and if a strong puff lets go, you must ease your sheets. By the same token, in a Cat, you must pull down harder on your luff and out further on your outhaul when the wind is strong, and ease 'em off when it lightens.

As a case in point on this business of pinching up, I recall last year's races on one particular day, when we were beating up on the last leg from near the Causeway to the finish line at the dock of the Miami Yacht Club. From the last mark, you could almost lay the finish, but apparently not quite. We would be maybe fifth or sixth around that mark. Some of the boats would go a bit inshore and we'd tack at the mark. But sort of pinching and working up, yet keeping going reasonably well, we eventually got let up and laid the finish, picking up three or four boats in the process each time. A lucky break you say?? Yeah, but it worked! And if it worked once, maybe it would work again and again— and it did.

Keeping the Cat flat going to windward we found very important, as the instructions say, so we did it, ever alert to move aft and to windward should a sudden strong puff come along. Moving about, which shakes or vibrates the boat in the water, is to be avoided. While you are obliged to move quickly, you should move with, shall we say (no pun intended), catlike grace. In any boat, any motion should be attempted in an easy and gentle manner, so as not to shake the sails and/or the hull. The Cat, being so very light, is no exception.

Contrary to the instructions, I DID cleat the main in the cam or gate cleat, being very careful to have the sheet lying over my leg or close at hand for a quick release. And the jib was cleated too, even harder than the instructions suggested, as I've already stated above. When a hard puff hit, I wouldn't necessarily have to ease the main, but could luff up a bit and absorb the real strength of that puff without easing sheets. We got caught once by a real "whizzer," lifted up on one hull and almost reached the point of no return, but eventually she fell back on two hulls and we were OK.

Reaching legs were really fun and in the Big Hobie, Wilma Bell and I did rather well. In fact, in the four-day series, we ended up three points out of second and five points out of first in 14 boats. We had had to drop out of three races in the approximately 21 races sailed by reason of my being careless, stupid and/or too greedy—or by a combination of all three. The Big Cat is a wide boat, something I guess I am unaccustomed to, for in close quarters I got myself in a bind on three successive occasions and had to withdraw, losing at least 30 points, I would imagine. But the afore-mentioned reaching was where we shone (if you'll forgive my lack of modesty), and we just sort of happened on the secret. As always, we put telltales on the shrouds, but the yarns halfway up the main did the trick. On a reach, when a puff hit, we would drive off to leeward, easing the main and watching the curling or vagaries of the two yarns on the main, both windward and leeward. This maneuver would drive us well off to the lee of our nearest competitor, going just as fast. When the puff let up (as they ALWAYS did) we would sharpen up, have a better sailing angle and fetch the next mark some five or six lengths ahead of that closest Cat. It was amazing how well and how often this worked—and it was likewise amazing that most of our competition never caught on.

Tacking downwind on a run was quite successful, too, though I must admit that Bill Baxter was better at it than we. Cats just die dead before the wind and you can afford to sail a greater distance if you can make 'em go a reasonably bit faster. The problem in Miami was that the breeze on the dead downwind leg had a bad habit of coming in near the leeward mark from the wrong direction.

We also found—courtesy of Ed Raymond who did it first—that lifting up the weather rudder on a leeward leg (unlocking it and pulling it up) decreased our resistance and made us a bit faster. However, I'm somewhat "agin" this practice when it's blowing hard—more of a question of safety and ability to handle your Cat properly than anything else.

Now comes the question of the traveller—on the wind in a good breeze, it seemed best to allow the traveller to swing 4 to 5 inches on either side of center. In very light air, I kept mine directly amidships so as to allow the upper leech of the sail a bit more freedom. Contrarily, in a breeze it seemed best to have that upper leech a bit harder or tighter; but again, as I mentioned above, I like to look up the leech itself and see a bit of a curve (to leeward) in the area near the second batten. On a close reach, we would ease the traveller off, maybe another foot or foot-and-a-half, and on a broad reach or run, ease it all the way out. While the traveller itself is aluminum, with a nylon fitting inside it for the mainsheet block attachment, and while it SHOULD slide easily, I always had a tube of white Lubriplate handy and gave the track a good dose to make the traveller car move more easily. It made things a bit dirty and gummy, but it sure made the car move better.

The jib leads I found worked better, or rather, made the boat go better, when they were set almost all the way inboard—maybe an inch or so from the inside end of the track.

Since our particular group of Cats was not equipped with boom-vangs, we were not permitted to rig any; but it is my very definite feeling that the boats would have sailed better and faster, and would have been under better control downwind in a hard breeze with a vang. A boom-vang prevents the upper part of the sail from twisting to leeward and therefore makes the boat more stable when running.

All Cats should be equipped with righting lines. The first day out, my erstwhile dinghy crew, Stuart Bell, essayed to skipper one of the boats and managed most unceremoniously to upset it. He and his crew Pete Wojtul, Executive Vice President of Continental Can (and himself the owner of a Hobie-14, on Candlewood Lake), had one helluva time righting the Big Hobie, mainly because there were NO righting lines. The next day all boats were more properly equipped.

The Big Hobies are comparatively easy to get out of IRONS, for you have a jib, and the crew can jump up, hold the jib out, and with the rudders backed on the same side as the jib, the boat will back down. With the jib retrimmed on the proper side, the main trimmed in—slowly—you are off and running again. The 14s and the Aqua Cats are a different kettle of fish, for you must push the main boom out on the (shall we say) preferred side and push the rudders to the opposite side (from the main). The boat will then back down and you can, hopefully, take off again. However, believe me, it can be a slow maneuver—and while you are doing it, your competition is well on its way to the next mark, if not further.

During the times we sailed the three different types of Cats, I made every effort to keep both hulls in the water. We did not "fly" the weather hull—as they phrase it—i.e., I did not allow the weather hull to come up out of the water for more than a brief second, for I immediately headed up somewhat into the wind (not all the way, obviously, for we WERE racing and trying our damnedest), but I would luff up a bit and drop the "flying" hull back into the water.

Only one other point about the Hobie Cats that I'd like to mention—and I did write a note to Hobie himself on the matter, with my apologies. After poking my crew in the face several times with the hiking stick, I took a hacksaw and cut off about nine inches from the end. It was still more than ample in length for me to sit way up in the forward end of the trampoline and hold it easily. Matter of fact, I did the same thing for a number of my competitors and then we taped most of the stick with adhesive tape to prevent our hands from sliding off the slippery aluminum. Other than that minor detail, it is my opinion, as well as that of the other Larchmont Frostbite dinghy sailors, that these Cats are all beautifully designed and engineered. Every part fits where it should and in the manner it should—no problems putting the boats together, assuming you can read English and can handle a screwdriver and pliers or wrench. They steer nicely, balance nicely and sail beautifully. A really *great* boat and I hope to sail more of 'em.

For those who would like to delve into Catamarans more deeply, I would like to recommend a book on really big Cats, ocean-going Cats, that I have just read with much pleasure and even more amazement, for these multihulls have done some great things and made some remarkable ocean passages. I refer to Rudy Choy's CATAMARANS OFFSHORE. Rudy has been in on Cats almost since before their inception in these recent years. He writes well and lovingly of Cats. I'm sure you'll enjoy his book.

CHAPTER XXII

Ocean Racing

Although I am neither notorious nor famous as an offshore ocean-racing man, I have done my share over the years since 1928—nay, even since 1921, when I was bilge boy at age 14 on J. Henry Esser's *Sakana*, out of Larchmont, the winner of the very first Bayside–Block Island auxiliary race, where we were given 25 gallons of gas and could use it, or sail, as we saw fit.

Since 1928 I've made probably 12 to 14 Bermuda Races, never actually winning, but taking several seconds or thirds in Class or Fleet, on such well-known yachts as *Dorade, Jane Dore, Burma, Mustang* and *Palawan*. And there have been similar races in the Southern Circuit, or Annapolis–Newport aboard *Finisterre, Sea Lion, Sagola, Golliwog* and others. Trans-Atlantic? "Nuthin' doin'"—that's too long to be cooped up with the same guys and no blondes around, but I have raced Cowes Race Week and The Fastnet aboard the 74-footer *Capricia*, Einar Hansen's great S&S yawl. Sometimes on these "buckets" I've been a deckhand, sometimes a watch officer, but I've always had a great time, enjoyed the racing, blow high or low, and been seasick only once. This qualifies me as an EXPERT and I have a few minor hints to add to the thousands of words which have been written by many authors on the subject of Ocean Racing.

1. Two minor but important suggestions I have to make are prunes and plenty of sleep. Sure, go ahead and laugh—people always do when you say prunes—and they've laughed at me many times when I arrive aboard with several boxes of dried prunes and prune juice. But when the chips are down (a morning or two later, and at sea) the chaps who had a couple of prunes or juice are laugh-

ing at the guys who are constipated and unhappy. Believe
me, this is Gospel truth and it works—as well as the
prunes. On the question of sleep, I am a firm believer of
getting all you can. When you are off watch get below
or, if you insist, stay on deck, but get what sleep you
can. Don't fool around. You may not think you are tired,
but if you don't keep up on your sleep you'll be doggone
tired when that "jerque" from the other watch shakes
your shoulder (and very roughly too) and says: "C'mon,
it's time to rise and shine!!!" Being overtired is one great
cause of seasickness, and the combination of the two will
take all the pleasure out of the race for you, and will
reduce your efficiency to practically zero. A man who is
dead-tired cannot make good decisions, can't think straight
and is no help to his ship.

Furthermore, in some yachts I've raced on, the other
watch has frequently been a bit "porky," a bit jealous,
a bit disagreeable even, about anybody from your watch
staying on deck and/or putting his two cents in. So unless you are in stifling hot weather, take your body below
decks and sleep. Leave them alone—they'll foul up the
deal anyhoo—and if you are in your bunk sleeping soundly
you won't get blamed.

As a corollary to this business of getting enough sleep,
I also urge and plead with you to get aboard your yacht
the night before the start WITHOUT being loaded. A
splendid hangover is nothing to take to sea—and it'll take
you a couple of extra days to get rid of that hangover
just 'cause you are at sea. Of course, may I add that it is
only in very, very recent years that I have come up with
this intelligent advice. When I was young and agile, I
am quite sure that I never would have heeded any such
suggestion, but maybe I'm getting smarter—or is it just
older??

2. Speaking of the other watch brings to mind the so-called
   Swedish watch system for offshore racing, and to my
   way of thinking it is a fine method. You can start it at any
   hour of the day you wish, depending, of course, on when
   your race starts. Aboard *Palawan*, in the three Bermuda
   Races I sailed on that fast vessel, starting at 1 P.M., there
   was a six-hour watch until 7 P.M., when a four-hour

Palawan, Cowes Race Week, 1969: Note perfect adjustment of pole as to tack and clew of spinnaker, well set up vang on main boom; and most of the crew lined along weather rail to ease the steering. *Palawan*, during her five years of racing with Tom Watson as Owner-Skipper, participated in 29 races. She took first, second or third in 20 races and won 8 Class firsts and 8 Fleet firsts. With René Coudert, Spenny Leech, Peter Cooper, Warren Brown of Bermuda, Ed Scheu, airline pilot Captain William MacDougall, Eric Goetz, Paul Wolter, Chris Moore, Arthur K. Watson, Skipper Tom Watson, and your correspondent, as the nucleus—as well as many others from time to time —*Palawan* always had a happy, eager, willing and able crew.

The 1972 Newport-Bermuda Race, Class "D" Yachts. Commodore Arthur J. Wullschleger's *Elske*, #1823, off to a good start at the leeward end of the line, right alongside Brenton's Reef Light Tower.

watch commenced. At 11 P.M., the other watch came on until 3 A.M., with a last four-hour watch till 7 A.M. when a six-hour tour rounded out the 24-hour period to 1 P.M. The effect of this was to have two long watches in the daylight hours, shorter watches at night, and the total of five watches in 24 hours "dogged" the watches, thereby making life happier for all hands. It's a great idea and I thoroughly recommend it.

3. Pump the ship every day—whether it needs it or not— or whether you THINK it needs it or not. Water has a nasty habit of sneaking in when you least expect it, as we unhappily found out aboard *Elske* in the 1972 Bermuda Race. She's a tight and sound boat, but in the horrible weather of the '72 Race, she did take water through some spots we didn't think about, and while it was most certainly not dangerous nor disastrous, that surplus water did make some things "kinda" damp.

4. Safety belts—These are a *MUST*, a most definite MUST, on all ocean racers. You should always wear them at night, and most certainly during the daylight hours if the weather is at all threatening. All hands should have their own belts, adjusted to their particular shape and size, and kept where they are very, very handy. Hook 'em on before you start moving around and be most careful. That's one helluva big ocean out there and you, big as you are, will be very hard to find if you fall overboard. On *Elske*, in the past Bermuda Race, when at times it blew a steady 40 knots with puffs of 55, we rigged a ¾-inch Dacron line from the mast up to the bow so that a safety belt could be hooked on for anyone going forward. It worked well and I recommend it. Even a line from the mast back to the cockpit would be good, for it would leave both hands free: one for the ship and one for you, as the saying goes.

5. On any decently sailed and handled ocean racer, you'll be assigned drawers and lockers, as well as a spot to hang your slickers. Put your gear away, put your slickers away, put your boots away. Keep the ship neat—and while you are at it, neaten up your bunk and put your own sheet and/or pillow away, so that your bunkmate can climb into that bunk in a hurry.

6. Wire Spinnaker Guys—With the great big foretriangles

on modern yachts, wire spinnaker guys are another MUST. You simply cannot close-reach a spinnaker with a rope guy, or two double-rope guys—even if they are made of Samson cord. The rope is too stretchy—even though it may very well be strong enough—and you are going to be in trouble, so get wire guys.

7. On a reach, with the spinnaker up, in a very hard breeze or sea, cock your spinnaker pole up and lower the inboard end a bit so that the spinnaker pole is in the same plane as the after-guy. Your spinnaker pole will take it in compression if the pole and guy are, shall we say, lined up or in the same plane. But if the pole is in its normal position, perpendicular to the mast (see Chapter on Spinnakers), there will be undue strain on the lift—which could break —and the pole itself will be in a bending moment, a rather bad situation in any kind of strong breeze at sea. Just forget all your previous training and rules about having the pole perpendicular, and set it in the plane of the after-guy.

8. In this day of high-aspect mainsails, by all means put a stout vang on your main boom when reaching or running, to prevent the boom from rising and falling on each successive wave. This will not only steady your boat and make it considerably easier to steer but it will also reduce chafe of your gorgeous new mainsail on the shrouds and spreaders. I must be fair and honest about this thought, and will point out to you that it was given me this last Fall by Chris Scanes and Bryan Axford who manage Hood Sails in Lymington, England, when we were trying out sails on Tom Watson's new *Palawan*, prior to her departure for Portugal. It was fairly easy to see where the main would chafe on the upper shrouds and rigging were it not properly vanged.

9. Do not leave any headsails lying on the bow when not in use—or else stop them down very, very securely. In the last Bermuda Race on *Elske*, we lowered a #1 jib topsail and replaced it with a #3. We thought the #1 was well tied down and stopped, but several hours later discovered the sail ripped and even torn off the luff wire by the teriffic forces of the wind and waves. The moral:

NEVER LEAVE A HEADSAIL ON THE BOW IN HEAVY WEATHER.

10. And one last thought or suggestion, for which there is no positive guarantee. For forty-four years, on and off, though not every Race, I've been to Bermuda, and almost every year—though not positively every Race—it has been prudent and wise to get west of the rhumb line before entering the Gulf Stream. One decided exception occurred in 1972, for *Robon* came out from the West Coast and showed the East Coast boys how to get to Bermuda "fustest"—she sagged off, went like hell, got way east of the rhumb line, tacked at the right time and came home first boat across the Finish, with my old sailing buddy, Ben Mitchell, as navigator. *Noryema IV*, one of the several British entries and the first foreign boat ever to win the Bermuda Race, had that 64-year-old veteran Ted Hicks as Skipper, also went east and took home all the silver. But just keep it in mind, old buddy, it "ain't" always that way—ninety percent of the time, get west of the rhumb line before the Stream.

CHAPTER XXIII

Conclusion

A Successful Summer's Campaign

Having discussed at length the various problems, details and situations which confront the skipper in making his boat go fast, it would seem fitting to lay down some rules or generalizations for the successful campaigning of a racing boat, together with some ideas which may help you to control and take advantage of the variables which are the theme and backbone of this book.

1. Plan to race in as many scheduled regattas as possible. Not to race is to give away to your competitors a potential first. There are, of course, days when weather conditions are so atrocious or so light, variable and indefinite that it's no fun to race, in which case maybe you are smart to play golf or go to the movies; but on all other days get out and do your best.

2. Be consistent. This has been discussed from all angles. Just don't be first one day and last the next. Settle for a second, third or even sixth. In a fleet of twenty boats, an average over the season of third or possibly fourth will win the Championship for you.

3. Be alert and be prepared. Think ahead and be ready when situations present themselves. Make certain that all details have been attended to, even down to the last cotter pin. Inspect your boat and its gear frequently, so that a breakdown will not occur.

4. Have the same crew, if possible, so that you have maximum teamwork.

5. Take care of and know your sails. Bear in mind that one

good suit of sails, properly washed, dried and cared for, may often be equal to or better than five suits of mediocre sails, especially when, in the latter case, you have the wrong suit aboard. It can be said when you own only one good suit of sails, that you are not burdened by one of the problems which beset the skipper with several suits, "Which suit to use?"

6. Avoid possible fouls or situations where you may be protested. On the other hand, if deliberately fouled by a competitor, carry through on your protest.

7. Avail yourself of "local knowledge." Know your racing area, tides and weather.

8. Take advantage of haul-outs permitted under your class rules and keep your boat's bottom in A1 condition. Don't forget liquid Lux!

9. Keep your stopwatches and such gear in perfect running condition.

10. Know your various race committees. All have their own peculiarities and idiosyncrasies, mostly good, but make sure you know what they are and how to cope with them.

11. The same for your competitors. They all behave in a certain pattern; just find out what it is, and you'll be able to cope with them too.

Appendices

Knots

There are six knots which I think are the most useful and the handiest aboard a boat. If you can tie these six readily you have all you need to know to do a complete job. There are others, certainly, hundreds of them, but if you can tie a square knot, a figure of eight, a bowline, a clove hitch, two half hitches and a rolling hitch you really don't need any more. They all have their own special uses and it doesn't seem necessary to go into details on any except the rolling hitch. The latter seems to be a comparatively unknown knot among most sailors of my acquaintance, but those who have ever used it quickly become very fond of it and find many varied uses for it. It is invaluable as a semipositive and easily adjustable knot. I say semipositive because it can be slipped, though it rarely does unless you want it to. But since it is so readily adjustable it fits extremely well into many categories and usages that cannot be supplied by other knots. Diagrams follow, through the courtesy of W. H. DeFontaine and *Yachting*.

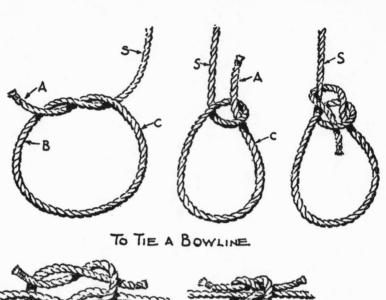

To Tie a Bowline

Reef Knot or Square Knot

Rolling Hitch

Figure of Eight Knot

A Round Turn
and Two
Half Hitches

Clove Hitch

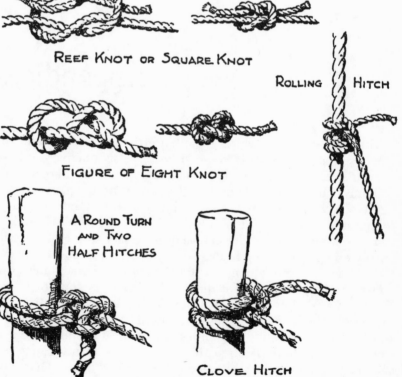

Diagram 79

Suggestions for Race Committees

Fifty-eight years of boat racing, man and boy, have brought me
into contact with many, many Race Committees, the great majority of them excellent groups of hard-working, interested men who
have tried week in and week out to provide good racing for large
groups of (generally) unappreciative racing men, women and
children. They have laid out fine courses with splendid windward
legs only to have the gods of wind and weather turn fickle. In the
words of the song of that famous Race Committee Chairman,
the late Alec Gest, (sung to the tune of "From the Halls of Monte-
zuma") "Oh! We don't make the Weather, Boys, so you know
what you can do!"

At the same time, I should like to offer a few suggestions which
are intended for what they are and nothing more, constructive
suggestions. There is no thought of criticizing Race Committees
in any way, shape, manner or form, for I have long since learned,
the hard way, that it pays to keep on the good side of your pals
who run your races. There isn't any point, brother, in antagoniz-
ing the men who so willingly go out there in fair weather and
foul to start your races. Some day they may get their fill and tell
us all where to head in. Actually, why some men continue so long
I don't know. The late Bob Fraser guided the destinies of the
Frostbite Yacht Club dinghy racing for countless years from its
inception 42 years ago. Clint Bell has run the dinghy racing at
Larchmont for over 30 years, while Alec Gest had been on
so many Race Committees that sometimes I wonder that he even
remembered how to sail himself. The late Ed Lang and the late
George Cormack were Chairman and Secretary, respectively, of
the New York Yacht Club Race Committee for so many years
that I am sure there are few who can recall when they first took

office. There are countless others, too numerous for me to mention, but to all of them this book is dedicated with many, many thanks for their untiring and sporting efforts. May I now offer a few suggestions that might be welcomed as representing a sailor's point of view.

STARTING LINES

It is my firm belief that all races should be started to windward, i.e., with a windward start. This means that the starting line must be situated so that the first leg is a beat. Starting lines off club docks are fine for the spectators and are agreeable to the racing fraternity if they can get away to windward. Nine times out of ten this type of set-up means a reaching or running start, and while the rocking-chair fleet gets a perfectly lovely view, most of the racing fleet gets off to a completely blanketed start. Put another way, it means that a majority of the fleet starts the race with two strikes against them. Sure, one or two boats get free, and get away, but most of the boys are left in the lurch, blanketing each other so badly that no one ever has a chance to catch up. The same is true, but perhaps to a lesser degree, when starts are made to leeward from a Committee Boat in open water. Where there is open water surrounding a Committee Boat there is at least a chance to luff up and maybe get clear. The one or two leading boats are still able to get away and be completely free of the mess.

The principal feature of a windward start is that it allows every boat (on a properly laid-out line of sufficient length) to get away with a clear wind. Every boat has an equal chance in a good clean start to get its share of wind. Starting to leeward is a mad scramble for the first few minutes to assure oneself of an unobstructed shot of air. A greater proportion of races are won at the starting line where the first leg is to leeward than when the first leg is a beat. Get yourself "boxed" at the start with a long reach to the leeward mark, and a third or more of the race is over before you can get free to try to catch up on the distant leaders. If you are covered or blanketed when the start is a beat, a few judicious tacks will eventually give you a clear wind, before any of the leaders are too far ahead to be caught.

Years ago, the Frostbite dinghy sailors, unhampered by custom or tradition and realizing the essential importance and innate fairness of windward starts, saw to it that where possible their race committees were provided with adequate and reasonably comfortable boats or barges from which to start them. The original "Little Scorpions' Club," at Larchmont, was a barge about 25 feet long and 14 feet wide, with a six-foot-square house equipped with a small pot-bellied stove, providing a stable and warm place for our hard-working committeemen to operate. Unfortunately a hurricane wrecked the original barge. The successor, a float of about the same dimensions equipped with pontoons, has an identical house and stove, is somewhat less stable, but serves its purpose well. Clint Bell and his various committee members over the years have always seen to it that their "ugly tub" is situated in Larchmont Harbor so that a windward start can be provided with a minimum of wind interference by the surrounding land. They've done a magnificent job for years to provide what I think is the finest dinghy racing in the country. I'd be willing to bet my last dollar that they'd jump into Long Island Sound before they would attempt to give us a leeward start.

The Yacht Racing Association of Long Island Sound has in recent years come round to the same point of view as the dinghy sailors, and two standard central starting areas have been laid out, one west of Rye and the other about three miles east of Rye. Depending on the location of each member club, one of these two general starting areas is used. Wind direction determines exactly where the Committee Boat will be anchored to give the best windward legs. In past years each club started its races at some point nearest its anchorage, necessitating leeward starts in most cases. The new system eliminates these entirely and has improved the caliber of the racing beyond words. I sincerely trust that we shall never have to return to the old plan.

Over the past two years a modified Gold Cup course has been developed by the YRA of Long Island Sound for its various classes. With the starting line more or less in the middle of the Sound, off Larchmont and/or Rye, it is comparatively easy—IF the wind holds up, and *THAT* is one helluva big IF—to lay out a windward leg to the first mark. While there are many bird cages, (i.e., marks put out by the YRA themselves to fill in the holes where there are no Government marks), in general the first mark IS a Government mark, in its proper place and easy to find. The next course is normally a reach, either a port or starboard reach, depending on the wind and the whims of the particular Race Committee. The third leg is a broad reach and/or a run, with the fourth leg a beat back all the way to the first weather mark—truly a really good test of windward work and ability, which is what we all are striving for, isn't it? Then—if the wind has held its direction—there is a dead run to a mark perhaps a half-mile to leeward of the Committee Boat, with a short beat up to the finish. (See Diagram 81.)

Frankly, when this system was proposed two years ago, I had quite a few reservations. BUT it has worked out well and from talking to the sailors themselves, I have found that they like it. ERGO, I'm wrong and apologize and pull in my horns.

To be sure, every once in a while, some dissident voice is raised demanding leeward starts, on the theory that we are raising a generation of boat sailors who won't know how to make a leeward getaway properly. Suppose, they say, our younger sailors go afield to participate in racing elsewhere, they'll be lost. There is something to be said for this point of view, and yet in most championship or important racing anywhere in the country, an effort is made to provide starts to windward. On the other hand, in most places where I have seen leeward starts used, the line is so badly laid out that the start is a proverbial rat-race and it really wouldn't do anyone any good to know how to start properly. No matter how you try to start on such a line you'll end up behind the 8 ball, so what difference does it make? Racing ceases to be a question of skill and becomes one of just plain luck, generally bad at that. There are enough informal races held by various clubs for their junior sailing classes to give the youngsters an idea of what leeward starts are and can be, so let's stay away from that type of start for the more formal racing.

Many long-distance cruising races must obviously be started with reaches and runs, but here different factors are involved. The race is long and the boats are of different sizes. (Though God knows, if you are a small boat and have got a good start, it is an awful, a discouraging, and a horrible sensation to have some great big tub come roaring by in a few minutes to leave you sitting there blanketed and frustrated.) But even so, if the line isn't properly angled, the start can be discouraging to say the least. I think I have made myself quite clear on the question of starting lines. I don't like leeward starts, for they are grossly unfair to all concerned.

If nothing else will do, however, please, please favor the leeward end of a leeward starting line. Don't make the line perpen-

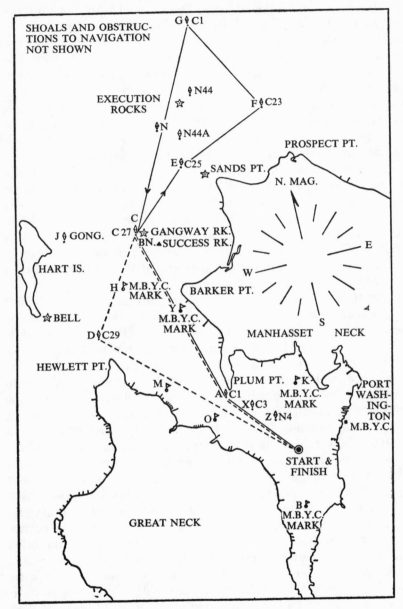

Diagram 80

dicular or square to the first leg. Swing the lee end toward the first mark anywhere from 20 to 30 or 35 degrees, for this will give the fellow who has the courage and guts to start underneath the rest of the fleet a chance to get free and get his wind clear. The boat starting at the weather end of the line has a definite advantage, i.e., he has his wind clear. Give the chap at the other end of the line a chance to make up for this handicap; give him a few yards toward the first mark. If the latter is a clever skipper he may get a good start at the lee end and be able to break through the blanket formed by the windward boats. Experience will give the Committee an idea as to the correct amount to favor the leeward end. It is better under the present Racing Rules to favor the leeward end too much (rather than too little) in the interests of safety and good seamanship. In other words, there will be fewer crack-ups and protests under existing rules, for the leeward boat has the whip hand before the starting gun and can cause no end of trouble if a number of boats crowd the weather end of a line which favors this weather end.

The Race Week conducted by the Manhasset Bay Yacht Club is an example of unavoidable leeward starts. From a glance at the accompanying diagram of courses on their Race Circular, it is quite evident that it is necessary to get as many of the fleet of over 300 boats out of the restricted waters of the inner bay as soon as possible. Since the prevailing wind is sou'west, a start to leeward is the only possible one if various classes are not to be inextricably mixed up with each other. This type of Bay racing, I might add, is quite different from racing in more or less open waters, and is lots of fun in its own peculiar manner, for the shifts of wind and the pitfalls resulting therefrom are many. I have had the pleasure of racing in many of the past years of Manhasset Race Week, for the most part with the afore-mentioned Bob Fraser as the guiding hand of the Race Committee. Bob's leeward starting lines have been in general so good that often two boats, one starting at the weather end of the line and the other starting at the leeward end, will reach Plum Point Buoy, about a mile away, nip and tuck. I don't know how one could ask for anything much fairer than this. Your author and others have, upon occasion, seen fit to offer suggestions to Bob about his starting lines. Upon occasion, Bob has seen fit to adopt such suggestions, but upon other occasions he has seen fit to invite us politely but firmly to "get the hell off the starting line" so he can lay it out. Such is the life of a Race Committee Chairman, for, as Jimmie Durante says, "Everybody's always trying to get into the act."

PROPER LAYOUT FOR WINDWARD STARTS

One of the first rules for a Committee in laying out a starting line—whether it be a windward or a leeward one—is to get to the starting area in ample time. I am happy to say that in all the years I have sailed on Long Island Sound and other places, too, the Race Committee late in arriving has been definitely the exception. Whether you always think so or not, skippers, Race Committees are conscientious men, completely aware of their responsibilities—if you care to term them that—to you. When Committee Boats are late, bad weather or motor failure are practically always the cause. However, Committees, give yourselves ample time to anchor, to get yourselves organized and to establish a starting line.

Some Committees first determine what courses will be raced, then drop their starting buoy and establish their line by maneuvering the Committee Boat and then dropping anchor. Others anchor their Committee Boat first, then set courses and finally establish the starting line by means of a launch. Either way is equally satisfactory and will provide good lines. If the first method is used, it is advisable to allow ample scope on the Committee Boat anchor line so that minor adjustments may be made as indicated. If the second method is followed, it seems to me that it would be a splendid idea to attach a pick-up or trip-line and a small buoy to the anchor of the starting marker. Standard procedure at present is to have a Committee launch pick up the marker or anchor and move it as required by some authority on the Committee Boat. If the marker itself is picked up—which is obviously quicker and easier than pulling up the whole anchor line and anchor—and taken tideward or to windward, when it is finally dropped, the anchor may not have even moved and the buoy will eventually drift back to its original position. If the whole rig is picked up and moved, it is somewhat difficult to tell where the mark will end up when the anchor is dropped. A pick-up or trip-line can be very neatly used to move an anchor tideward or to windward, guaranteeing that the mark itself will be in the desired spot. Moving a mark downwind, or with the tide, presents no such problems and can be easily accomplished. It is

YRA OF LONG ISLAND SOUND
COURSE I   LONGEST

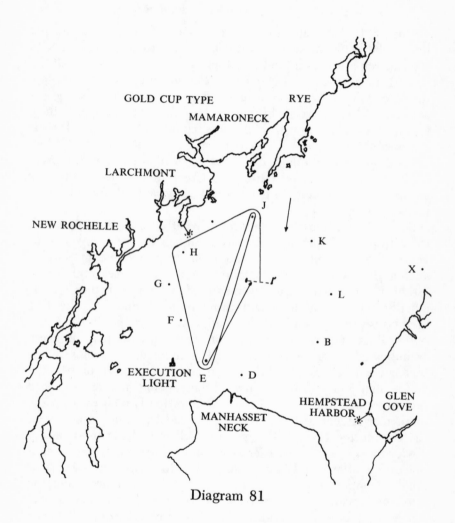

Diagram 81

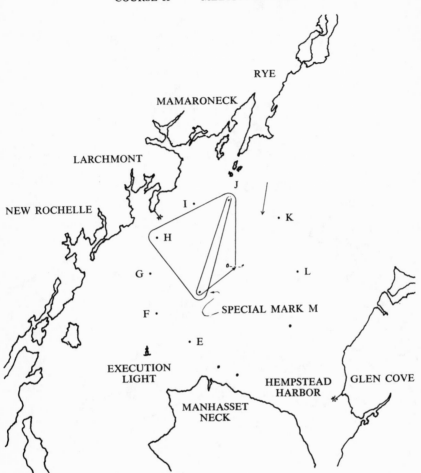

YRA OF LONG ISLAND SOUND
COURSE II   MEDIUM LENGTH

Diagram 82

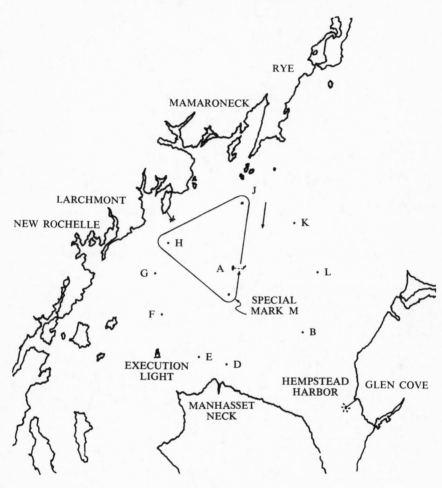

Diagram 83

plainly evident that the less scope permitted on a marker the better, for the marker will wander less and the chances of getting the anchor line fouled in someone's keel or rudder will be reduced. This is one of the disadvantages of the trip-line; someone may get it fouled in his keel or rudder. However, the trip-line can be lashed to the main marker after final adjustments are completed.

It is amazing to me that so many Committees fail to realize that the men in their launch cannot hear them above the noise of the motor and waves, even though they use bullhorns or loud speakers. They bellow and scream, but the poor souls in the launch just cannot hear. A very simple set of visual signals for guiding the mover of a mark can be set up. The large megaphone with which most Committees are equipped—or should be—can be pointed in whatever direction it is desired to move the mark. It is held pointing in the desired direction until the location is reached. A back and forth motion in a wide arc indicates it is time to drop the anchor or mark. The well-organized Committee launch will keep its eyes on the Committee Boat at all times.

The Committee's problems in laying out a good windward starting line depend on a number of factors. The size of the class or fleet, the direction of the wind and tide, the idiosyncrasies of certain classes or skippers, as well as possible changes or variations in any or all of the foregoing, all must be taken into consideration. Is the line long enough to accommodate the largest class racing, either numerically or by size? What effect will the tide have on the starters, or on the starters' decisions? Is the wind shifty or steady and what effect will that have on the starters' decisions? How do certain classes react to different wind and tide conditions; certain skippers, too?

If I were to lay down a general rule for windward starting lines, I would say they should be square to the wind. The position of the weather mark DOES NOT enter the picture at all. Many Committees I have seen have attempted to place their starting line so that it is at right angles to the course to the first mark. This is absolutely wrong and should not even be considered. The weather mark is to windward, of course, but not necessarily dead to windward of the starting line. Select the weather mark and then forget it. The line wants to be at right angles to the wind, so that two boats starting on opposite tacks at either end of the line on the gun would meet bow to bow a certain distance from the line. That to my mind would be a perfect starting line.

However, the question raised above must be considered, tide, wind direction, etc. What will various reactions to these be? Will they cause boats to jam one end of the line or the other in order to gain advantage of certain conditions? Yes, they will, and the experienced Committee will be thoroughly aware of the various possibilities and their results, and will make minor changes in the angle of the line to compensate. The Committee's main objective should be to get a class started with the whole group spread as evenly as possible along the line. Then everyone has an equal chance with a clear wind.

Theoretically, the line square to the wind will do this, but in actual practice skippers will gang up at one end or another of such a line, for there will be special advantages in being at that end later on. Moving the line a bit one way or another will offset these supposed advantages and spread the boats out more evenly. For example, in a medium to strong easterly on Long Island Sound, starting at the Larchmont Mooring Can for a beat to Parsonage Point, astute skippers generally try to start at the right hand end (as you face the weather mark) or the offshore end of the starting line and immediately go over on the port tack, for they have learned that they get headed on this tack as they go out and will be correspondingly lifted on the starboard tack when they finally can lay Parsonage. Committees, long accustomed to this ganging-up at the offshore end of the line, drop this end of the line back so that boats will be tempted to start farther down the line. Occasionally, though not often in a large group of boats, someone will even get away with a port tack start.

As another example, on Long Island Sound with a typical summer sou'wester, it is definitely advantageous to get to the southward as soon as possible to pick up a possible header on the starboard tack which will provide a nice lift on the port tack. Boats running the line on the starboard tack seek to be at the far or left end (as you face the weather mark) when the gun goes. Wise Committees will seek to avoid a jam at that end of line by dropping it back some. Boats seeing an advantage in the right hand end of the line will try to avoid the jam by holding back, and starting farther back on the line.

The actual physical job of laying out a line square to the wind should not be too difficult in anything but a very shifty, puffy wind. I am frank to say that there are some who make it difficult for themselves, for they insist on using some guide which is not a true indication of the wind. Anyone can look up at a flag and measure a ninety-degree angle with reasonable accuracy, but these men invariably pick some misleading flag to go by which is subject to some distorting influence. A high masthead Committee flag, or a racing boat luffing head to wind on an even keel directly to windward of the person sighting the line, are excellent for giving a true and accurate gauge of wind direction; but some little flag down low is invariably influenced by cabin houses or the boat itself. Using the latter flag to judge by will result in a horrible starting line.

Government Marks

The use of Government marks as turning marks in foggy and rainy weather when visibility is poor is something I should like to urge to Race Committees. Government buoys are generally large and easy to pick up and furthermore they are generally in the spot shown on your chart. Temporary racing marks can be most anywhere except where they are supposed to be. Boat racing is not an obstacle race. It is supposedly a test of skill and there isn't any skill in locating a mark which was misplaced in the first place or has drifted. That's just luck. When sailing by compass this can be important.

While discussing Government marks, it might be worthwhile to take up the question of passing them on the channel side. Most racing instructions for local triangular races demand that they be duly regarded and passed on the channel side, while most cruising racing and overnight racing instructions state that they may be disregarded (with possible minor and detailed exceptions). It seems to me that there is proper merit on both sides of these apparently conflicting regulations. If allowed in local triangular races, some would take undue chances to gain a few yards. On the other hand, in long-distance overnight racing, it is often impossible to tell whether you are on the channel side of a given buoy, though you can take adequate precautions to prevent running aground.

Organization of Committee

Since the Chairman of a Race Committee is usually either an experienced racing man or experienced in his Committee work, it is up to him to assign and fully explain each particular job to the various members of his Committee. Each job is vitally important. The man on the clock must have a sense of timing and rhythm, for if he doesn't have it, he will only confuse the men on the gun and the hoist. The man on the hoist, the signals, executes a particularly serious duty. Racing Rules state that the hoisted signal determines the start of a race, that the gun or horn merely calls attention to it. Stopwatches are set when the signal is hoisted, not when the gun goes. The gun and signal hoisting should, of course, occur simultaneously, but if the gun doesn't fire, the race is still on when the signal goes up. The signal hoister must be on the ball and alert at all times. Herb Clarke of the Larchmont Race Committee is my idea of an able signal hoister. When he yanked that cylinder up it went up fast and no fooling. In fact, he was so energetic that Captain Charlie "Seagull" Simpson, owner of *Ilse,* former perennial Committee Boat of the YRA of Long Island Sound, had to replace and strengthen the signal hoists more than once. The point is that signals should and must be displayed quickly and on time.

The man on the gun or horn must be equally on his toes. Guns misfire frequently and no one is to blame, so most Committees equip themselves with two cannons, just in case. Of course, it is advisable to inspect cannons to be sure live shells are being used. I recall, without mentioning any names, one red-faced Committee who discovered, when neither of their cannons would fire, that spent shells from the previous Regatta had not been replaced.

Obviously, it is essential that the Committee clock be accurate. Many Committees have chronometers at their disposal. If a Committee doesn't own a chronometer, hack watch, or reliable timer with a large, easily readable dial, beg, borrow or steal one. All the crack skippers have accurate stopwatches, maybe two or three, so don't get caught with your watches down. Make sure that your timer gives 300 accurate seconds to a five-minute period. Make sure also that your Committee understands that there is one standard clock aboard by which all starts will be made. One harassed Committee Chairman, after a number of fouled-up and confused starts, discovered that the man on the gun had a stopwatch of his own which he was using instead of listening for the count of the man on the clock. Everything would have been

fine except for the fact that the stopwatch ran three seconds fast
in every five-minute period.

These may seem to be minor problems, hardly worth talking
about. To the serious-minded skipper, intent on making a good
start and equally intent on eliminating variables which may
cause trouble, they are vital and important questions. If skippers
are sure of the Committee running a particular race, they are
sure of having a good race without any worries about decent
starting lines and proper starts. Believe me, Committees, the boys
and girls out there racing have you all well catalogued and figured out, just as you probably have a pretty good line on them.
Please, if you are starting out with a green Committee, invite
some more experienced fellows to join you for a race or two until
you get the hang of the details. Bus Mosbacher, a Champion of
the International One-Design Class, doing his stint on the Race
Committee of the Beach Point Club, and running his first YRA
Races, invited several members of an experienced Race Committee to show him how things should go. Beach Point ran some fine
Races and Bus's Committee did themselves proud.

POSTPONEMENTS

When in doubt—postpone! There is no Rule or thought which
a Committee should give more attention to. If conditions are not
right—if there is little or no wind, if the course is not right, if the
line is not right, if the fleet is not able to get to the starting area,
if all the various necessary details are not arranged—POST-
PONE! Boat racing is not a problem of railroad timetable accuracy. If everything is not set and organized, have the courage of
your convictions and delay the start. I am quite sure that I speak
for all the racing fraternity when I say that we would prefer to
wait in order to get a better race. Many Committees seem to feel
that if a race is scheduled to start at a certain time, it MUST start
then, no matter what. Such is not the case and blessed is the
Committee which delays things when they deem it necessary or
desirable.

There's a bad apple in every barrel, and, of course, there's a
jerque in every racing fleet who'll bellow "LET'S GO!" When it's
obvious that there isn't enough wind to get around the course.
But he'll yell just the same, and occasionally the timid Committee will let themselves be rushed. If the line isn't right, or a wind

shift makes a mess of it, let go with a horn, a bellow and a postponement signal. The fleet will be grateful and appreciative. If the signals are just starting, begin all over again. If you are in the middle of a long series of starts, reset the signal of the last class that started and go on from there. The boys and girls will catch on, for they are not stupid. But do everything in your power to provide a good race, not an obstacle race or a rat-race.

It is my firm opinion that the right of postponement is one prerogative of a Race Committee that is not as widely nor wisely used as it might be. Postponement for proper cause is just as important to good racing as, for example, a good starting line or a good windward leg. Don't start a race blindly, just because your race circular says it should start at that particular moment. Make sure all factors contributing to good racing are organized first. We'll all understand and duly appreciate your efforts.

It is customary to dedicate a book to someone who has been kind or helpful, who has done some little thing for the author, or to whom the author is indebted for one reason or another. In hunting round for a suitable dedication, it suddenly dawned on me that to my knowledge no one has ever dedicated a boat racing book to Race Committees. My Dedication is a modest effort to draw attention to those hard-working fellows who with the patience of Job run our races for us and say to them "Thank You."

It is my feeling that every skipper should put in some time as a member of a Race Committee. He will learn a lot about the problems of running races as well as the failings and foibles of his fellow skippers. Two winters as the Chairman of the Dinghy Committee of the Larchmont Yacht Club, when physical infirmities kept me from racing, helped me in a measure to understand the difficulties which beset Race Committees, as well as to show me what "jerques" we racing skippers can be at times. So, Carry On, Committees, You've Done Well.

Index